TELLING IT OUR WAY
Essays in Gender History

In memory of Hilda Tweedy (1911–2005)

friend, feminist and inspirational link in the
unbroken chain of the Irish women's movement

Mary Cullen

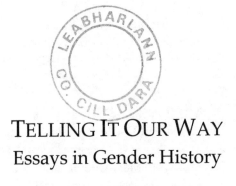

TELLING IT OUR WAY
Essays in Gender History

Foreword by Maria Luddy

ARLEN
HOUSE

Telling It Our Way

is published in 2013 by
ARLEN HOUSE
42 Grange Abbey Road
Baldoyle, Dublin 13
Ireland
Phone/Fax: 00 353 86 8207617
Email: arlenhouse@gmail.com
arlenhouse.blogspot.com

Distributed Internationally by
SYRACUSE UNIVERSITY PRESS
621 Skytop Road, Suite 110
Syracuse, NY 13244–5290, USA
Phone: 315–443–5534/Fax: 315–443–5545
Email: supress@syr.edu

978–0–905223–87–2, *paperback*
978–1–85132–040–0, *hardback*

Typesetting: Arlen House
Printing: Brunswick Press
Cover Art by Barry Castle: 'Three Women Fishing for the
Salmon of Knowledge' is reproduced courtesy of her estate

CONTENTS

ACKNOWLEDGEMENTS

I want to thank Alan Hayes for suggesting this collection, and for introducing me to the art of Barry Castle, whose evocative painting is reproduced on the cover. I am both grateful and deeply indebted to Maria Luddy for writing such a generous Foreword. Looking again at these essays brings home to me the social nature of historical work. I have learned from, and drawn on, the work of so many in Ireland and elsewhere; first the pioneering second-wave feminists who opened my eyes to seeing individual situations in their social and political context, and then to so many working in and contributing to the development of women's history and gender history in Ireland. My debts to them are evident throughout. I have also learned a lot in discussions with students at NUI Maynooth and the Centre for Gender and Women's Studies at Trinity College, Dublin, and with community groups. The Women's History Association of Ireland has always provided a collegial and supportive environment for the exchange of ideas to everyone interested in women's history. Finally, I owe a major debt to The Ireland Institute's commitment to the study of republican thinking, particularly in its journal *The Republic*.

The publisher wishes to acknowledge the original editors and publishers of these essays. We also wish to thank Margaret Mac Curtain, Maria Luddy, Mary McAuliffe and the Women's History Association of Ireland for their support.

FOREWORD

Maria Luddy

Jane Austen, through the words of the female protagonist in *Northanger Abbey*, passed a celebrated judgement on history texts:

> History, real solemn history, I cannot be interested in ... I read it a little as a duty but it tells me nothing that does not either vex or weary me. The quarrels of popes and kings, with wars or pestilences, in every page; the men all so good for nothing and hardly any women at all – it is very tiresome.[1]

Irish women's history is now much better served by its historians. It was in the nineteen seventies that the first modern treatments of Irish women came to be written. The landmark was the broadcast on radio, between October and December 1975, of a Thomas Davis lecture series on the position of women in Irish society. This series was published in 1978 as *Women in Irish Society: The Historical Dimension* edited by Margaret Mac Curtain and Donncha Ó Corráin.[2] The end of the 1980s boasted three edited collections and three monographs directly concerned with women in Ireland in the nineteenth century. By the end of the 1990s there were in the region of 60 articles and about 43 books dealing either with, or at least containing substantial information on, women in

Ireland in this period. The number of articles and books that relate directly to Irish women's history now numbers in the hundreds. One of the pioneering figures in creating the history of women and gender in Ireland is Mary Cullen.

In this volume we have a collection of over thirty years of Cullen's writings published between 1980 and 2013. While arranged in chronological order of publication, these essays show the range of her historical interests and her concerns with understanding the origins and meanings of concepts, such as 'feminism', and the experience of historical lives as revealed in individual biographies or the analysis of key events.

Women's history was 'created' primarily in the 1970s[3] within the context of the rise of 'second-wave feminism' and under the impact of the 'new' social history. During the 1970s, especially in the United States and in Britain, women historians began to question the exclusion of women from historical studies and argued, with justification, that the dominant narratives of political and economic history saw history as a male phenomenon. At the same time the 'new social history', in its insistence that historians seriously consider the poor, workers and the marginalized in history, further challenged the ways in which history had been written. Historians also broadened the range of sources that could be utilized for historical purposes, moving away from a reliance on those state documents and papers that elite men had left behind. They now sought out prison records, the records of institutions, poor law records, and other material, which documented the experiences of marginalized groups, in which women were as evident as men.

Women's history thus emerged as a major research field, though it was not without its problems and obstacles. For many years women's history endured a lack of academic status. This history was most often written by women who were not necessarily working in academic history departments. 'Women's history' as an academic subject was often marginalized and left as a 'special study'. Even social historians often relegated women to a chapter in a book rather than integrating their story into the fabric of a monograph, or women's history became subsumed into 'family history' where it was thought, erroneously, to have a natural place. Much of the early writing on women's history was concerned with locating women in the past; it often saw women as victims of patriarchy and feminist historians of the 1970s emphasised the 'separate spheres' theory, where men's history was primarily located in the public sphere of politics and work, and women's history was associated within the sphere of the home, the domestic world. Here women's work was primarily reproductive, nurturing and care taking.

However, by the end of the 1970s the writing of women's history began to move beyond the descriptive recovery of women's lives and new theoretical visions emerged which sought to move beyond the limits of recovery. Feminist theory was a rapidly developing and evolving field and historians such as Joan Scott began to argue for a more theoretical view of history that would remove 'women's history' from the margins and transform male-centred history by creating a new paradigm. In 1986 Scott published her much-cited article 'Gender: A Useful Category of Historical Analysis'[4] where she argued that 'gender', the social and cultural construction of sexual difference, must become the central category of historical analysis. For Scott the ways in which different societies and cultures interpret and understand male and female sexual difference signifies how 'power' lies in the ability to name, define and categorise. She argued that in the effort to deconstruct 'absolute categories of gender differences' historians would be able to 'attack normative rules ... linked to gender and the power attached to gender discourse'. Gender history thus advocated that both men and women needed to be studied together, as the history of one group could not be understood without the history of the other. Ideas around masculinity, for instance, could not be understood fully unless there was an equal understanding of the construction of femininity.

Gender history has of course evolved since the 1980s and been further influenced by postmodernism and the linguistic turn. Here there was an emphasis on the ways in which language determines what we experience and how we experience it. Some historians, of the postmodern bent, argued that our understanding of ourselves and our societies comes to us through language and that our understanding, determined as it is by language, is in constant flux. Gender identity, for instance, can only be understood through an analysis of discourse, that is attention to the structured systems of language by which human beliefs and perceptions are expressed and constrained.

The evolution of women's history, and gender history, has been explored in Mary Cullen's work and she has been instrumental in bringing these ideas to the fore in Irish historical writing. From her early writings, reprinted here, there is a steady exploration of feminism, and the meanings of feminism in its earliest manifestations in the suffrage campaign in Ireland in the nineteenth and twentieth centuries. She is concerned too with exploring how feminist theory deconstructs patriarchy and how it questions the very nature of society and what is means to be human. 'Until something is named and defined', she writes, 'it is impossible to think about it in an ordered way, still less to discuss it'. Her concern with understanding the significance of feminism, its fight against the discrimination of women, and its central tenets of equality and humanity for all women remain relevant today in a society where feminism and its necessity is often ridiculed or denied.

Moving beyond the study of feminism, Cullen has contributed to our understanding of Irish social and political history in a number of ways. Her original study of women's place in the family in rural Ireland, analysed through the reports of the 1830s Poor Law Commission, offered the first detailed examination of women's roles as breadwinners within the family household. While there are still very few articles on women workers in the pre-famine era and our knowledge of general working practices for women is hazy, Cullen has made it clear that a woman's domestic contribution was not confined to cooking, cleaning and child-rearing alone, they also made a vital contribution to the family economy by working alongside men. She has estimated, through a meticulous analysis of budgets presented to the Poor Law Commission, that labourers' wives' earnings from pigs, poultry, spinning and occasional labour, and when times were really difficult, begging, accounted for at least fifteen per cent of the families' income and this percentage could rise to thirty-five per cent at times. Cullen's work on Anna Haslam offered the first detailed analysis of a pre-eminent feminist activist who spanned and engaged in all the major feminist campaigns of the later nineteenth and early twentieth centuries. Exploring Haslam's life is also a way of examining feminist activism in these centuries. Among the campaigns in which Haslam was active was that organised to repeal the Contagious Diseases Acts, which were introduced in the 1860s. By 1871 three branches of the Ladies' National Association for the Repeal of the Contagious Diseases

Act were formed in Ireland at Belfast, Cork and Dublin. Although the Association was small, it marked a new departure for Irish women. For the first time they were willing to discuss openly matters pertaining to sexual morality and to initiate a public campaign to question and attempt to alter the sexual double standard that existed.

The demand for suffrage was the principal means whereby women fought for political involvement on the same terms as men in the late nineteenth and early twentieth centuries. While Isabella Tod established the first suffrage society in the north of Ireland in 1872, Haslam, a friend of Tod's, organised a similar society in Dublin in 1876. By the end of the nineteenth century, through vigorous campaigning, mainly by women involved in the suffrage campaign, success in ensuring their places as poor law guardians was guaranteed with the passage of the Irish Women Guardians Act in 1896. Haslam remains a significant figure in the history of Irish feminist activism.

Cullen's engagement with how we understand history, what is left out of Irish history, how we are blinkered by gender blindness in fully understanding the ways in which women and men have contributed to history, is evident in her work on the rebellion of 1798. 1998 marked the bi-centenary of that event and saw a considerable range of publications and public engagement with the meanings of 1798. Many of the events organized around commemorating 1798 were substantially funded by the Irish government. Her article on the women of '98 is incisive and clear in detailing how an understanding of women's roles in that event, whether as political thinkers, or rebels, enriches our understanding of the entire episode across class and gender divides.

Cullen has had an abiding interest in not just how modern feminism as a philosophy and ideology has developed, but also a keen interest in how modern republicanism has evolved. Tracing the growth and meanings of modern republicanism and feminism from the eighteenth century she argues that these concepts are 'about combining individual freedom with social responsibility'. The importance of individuals questioning received opinion, of understanding how concepts have evolved, of the impact of gender relations in the shaping of the world are key elements in Cullen's thought and her mission, as one might justifiably term it, is to encourage people to think deeply about such issues because they are too important to be ignored or left unevaluated in our society. Her work encourages debate and engagement with the viewpoints of others. Nothing is accepted at face value and there are no ideologies, including feminism, that are left unquestioned. She constantly stresses the need for dialogue and debate as a way of enriching society, and as a means of reaching goals that are beneficial to all members of society.

Mary Cullen is one of the few Irish historians who embrace both theory and empirical research. Her work allows us to see that ideas are also about people, as much as they are about concepts of social and political organisation. This collection of essays reveals both the worlds of ideas and the material and social worlds of Irishmen and women in the nineteenth and twentieth centuries. These essays show a historian totally engaged with major issues, such as feminism and republicanism, which have, in many ways, shaped Irish society over the last forty-odd years. What she encourages us to do is to continue to question how feminism can remain relevant in our society, how it can stay a vital part of the ways in which we understand society and gender relations within it. Dialogue, discussion and debate are what keep societies vibrant. This is where Mary Cullen's legacy is most important, in encouraging us to engage in that dialogue, maintaining an ability to disagree, and from this dissent and dialogue to help shape new ways of being in the world.

NOTES

1 Jane Austen, *Northanger Abbey* (Harmondsworth, Penguin, 1972), pp 123–4.

2 Margaret Mac Curtain and Donncha Ó Corráin (eds), *Women in Irish Society: The Historical Dimension* (Dublin, Arlen House: The Women's Press, 1978).

3 Between 1900 and 1930 there had been a number of works published on women's history, again within the context of the increasing militancy of the suffrage movement. Ivy Pinchbeck's work on women workers and Mary Beard's earlier work on women are prime examples. Many of these works were 'rediscovered' in the 1970s.

4 Joan W. Scott, 'Gender: A Useful Category of Historical Analysis' in Joan Wallach Scott, *Gender and the Politics of History* (New York, 1988). Scott first delivered a paper on this subject in 1985 and a version was published in the *American Historical Review*, 91, 5 (1986).

Introduction

Looking back at the essays in this book, I am struck by how the themes relate to my location at a particular time and place in history. The first focus is on the relation between history and the self-identity of individuals and groups. It then moves to the history of feminism and feminist thinking. The later essays focus on gender analysis as a tool for historical research in what is seen as mainstream history.

The generation of women I belong to grew to adulthood in Ireland before the advent of the second wave of the international women's movement in the 1960s. Few, if any, of us knew that there had been a first wave of the movement in many countries, including Ireland. We did not read about it in history books, learn about it from teachers, or hear about it from family or friends. Many lived their entire lives without ever acquiring that knowledge.

In the story books we read as children, the usual pattern was that boys and men enjoyed a wide range of activity, were leaders and deciders, while girls and women had a more limited range and were more often followers than leaders. From about age ten I was aware that how I saw myself fitted the male rather than the female pattern. Yet it never crossed my mind that books could be wrong. I thought I was among a minority of odd ones out. I did not discuss this with family or friends. None of my friends spoke to me about it, though other girls must have felt the same way. In the novels we read as we grew older, the female role was even more restricted. The ultimate achievement of the heroine's life was usually romance leading to marriage. The time-honoured ending, 'lived happily ever afterwards', suggested that marriage marked the end of growth and change in women's lives.

Some of the more privileged among us went to university, and there some studied history, still without ever learning that there had been and still were feminists in Ireland. The shaping of societies, their administration, the ideas and philosophy, the discoveries made, the music, art, literature, science, not to mention war, were all masculine achievements. Women were seldom mentioned except for a few individuals who were there because they performed some role that was usually a male preserve, for example as queen regnant or warrior. The absence of women was not referred to, commented on or explained. Again, I was aware of the differences, and now conscious of an uneasy feeling of paradox. I saw myself as sharing in the history of western civilisation, and yet at the same time as being an outsider. Again, I did not question the accuracy of the books, did not speak about my unease to anyone and none of my friends voiced unease to me.

The same paradigm of gender relations permeated Irish society. We knew from history books and novels that women had not always done many of the things we could do, such as attend universities, enter the 'higher' professions, vote at parliamentary elections, and sit in elected parliaments. The unspoken explanation was that we could do these things as a result of a general benign progress in society. Few young women felt much pressure or expectation from family or society to do them. The marriage bar operating in the public service was an added disincentive. Most middle-class families saw marriage as the desirable life objective for their daughters. In my secondary fee-paying girls' school, the large majority left after the Intermediate Certificate examination with only a handful staying to do the Leaving Certificate, and fewer still going on to university.

I eventually confronted the paradigm in the mid-1960s when I was married and the mother of young children. All Irish society appeared to expect of mothers was that they looked after the interests of their immediate family circle, with no pressure for further self-development or for sharing responsibility for the organisation of society. As a model this increasingly appeared to fall short of what a human being should aim to be. It was good to care for one's family, but not good to limit one's responsibility to that. Nor should it be a question of choosing one or the other but of combining responsibilities. Again, I did not discuss this with anyone, saw it as a personal problem and looked for a personal solution.

At this stage American and English writings of the second-wave women's movement began to come on the scene. They showed that many other women felt the same way. The difference was that these women had made a pioneering breakthrough and had identified the problem as the accepted gender roles themselves. Betty Friedan gave a name, the 'feminine mystique', to the model of femininity that I was struggling with. In a comprehensively researched study Friedan showed that in the 1950s and 1960s this model was widely and explicitly accepted throughout American society, from the scientific elite of psychoanalysts and psychiatrists to the general public. At the same time it was a recognised phenomenon that significant numbers of married women were reporting symptoms of depression and dissatisfaction with their lives without anyone, including the women themselves, knowing why. Friedan challenged the general diagnosis that these women were somehow maladjusted to the correct female role. She pointed to the difference between the prescriptions prescribed by the experts for the development of the adult male and the adult female human being. The mystique ignored woman's 'basic need to grow and fulfil her potentialities as a human being ...'. The 'problem that has no name' was essentially 'a problem of identity – a stunting or evasion of growth that is perpetuated by the feminine mystique'.[1] For women the challenge was not to find individual ways of circumventing the accepted roles but to change them. I became a feminist.

As second-wave feminism developed, it sparked off a wave of research and publication in women's history that continues today. Not surprisingly, the first questions feminists asked concerned identity. Had the lives of women in the past been as passive and unchanging as their absence from the history books suggested? It emerged that this was far from being the case. Women had a history of continuity and change and over the years since research continues to add to our knowledge. One discovery was that feminism itself was not a new creation; it had a history and Ireland had its own feminist history. In the nineteenth and twentieth centuries groups of Irish women had come together to campaign to change laws, regulations and attitudes, and to gain for women personal autonomy, opportunity to develop potential, economic independence, better education, admission to the universities and the professions, the right to vote and take an active role in political life and decision-making. They had won many of the freedoms we took for granted. Furthermore, it emerged that, even as second-wave feminists thought we were creating something new, an earlier generation of feminists was still active in Ireland and successfully pressurising the government to set up the first Commission on the Status of Women in 1970.

The discovery, first that women in fact had a past of action and change, and then that the impetus behind the emergence of organised groups campaigning for women's rights in the mid-nineteenth century was their rejection of the limits imposed to women's development of their full human potential, had particular significance for my generation. And, as the holistic view of a fully human life that underlay pioneering feminist activism and arguments emerged, feminist thinking took its place in the history of western political thought. It addressed questions of what it meant to be a human being and a citizen, how society was and should be organised, relations of power and authority, the purpose and aim of political structures. It drew on the body of ideas and ideologies in circulation, focused on those that appeared relevant to its most pressing questions, adapted and developed them, and then itself added new ideas to the body.

Second-wave feminists realised the extent to which they themselves had been socialised by the dominant paradigm of gender relations, and identified this as a key area for action. Consciousness-raising was a strategy devised to enable groups of women to discuss their own individual situations among themselves, question whether they had conformed to patterns of thinking and behaviour they now realised to be oppressive, and, if they had, consider what changes they thought necessary.

As women's history expanded it developed the concept of gender analysis as a tool of historical investigation. From an early stage the new wave of feminist historians realised that a basic problem in the current writing of history was the tendency to attribute all differences in the position of women and men in all societies at all periods to an all-embracing biological determinism. As the mounting evidence made such a reductionist explanation increasingly problematic, they used the word 'gender' to denote the complex of political, social and economic relationships existing between the sexes in any given society at any period in time. The concept has been developing over the years since. Gender analysis allows for both biologically-determined differences and human constructions. It takes account of the interaction of physiological sex with other factors, such as geographical location, race, colour, religion, social class, age, education and many more. Gender relations can change over time, and they can differ from place to place. They include differences between women, for example between women of different social and economic classes, as well as differences between women and men, and allow for situations where women oppress men as well as vice versa.

Looked at through the lens of gender, the widespread, usually tacit, acceptance by historians and society that the position of men in a society is 'natural', the human norm, in need of neither analysis nor explanation, is no longer tenable. It becomes clear that gender history is as important for men's historical identity as it is for women's, and its absence is as detrimental to men's self-knowledge as it is to women's. This might appear paradoxical in the light of feminist criticism that historians have focused their attention on the doings of men. However, few historians have examined men from a gender perspective or questioned the relations between the sexes from the point of view of their implications for male identity. While the position of women in a society may be analysed in relation to that of men, the reverse seldom happens. The headings 'women', or 'the position of women', or even 'feminism' can appear in indexes, but seldom the corresponding headings 'men', or 'the position of men'.

The absence of gender analysis in the writing of history deprives men and boys, as well as women and girls, of an important part of their group and individual memory. The political, social and economic implications of being born a male rather than a female at a time and place in history are not examined. Differences between the sexes in terms of legal authority in the family, civil and political rights, education, access to wealth, property and the higher professions, participation in public political life and in passing laws affecting all members of society, tend to be taken for granted rather than analysed and included in assessments of significant patterns of continuity and change. The same applies to the power of prevailing stereotypes of masculine and feminine human 'nature' and attributes, and of expectations, support and encouragement from family and society.

This points again to the significance of historians' own location in history. Boys and men are less likely to see gender roles as restricting their personal development, or to experience the sense of absence and exclusion that girls and women can, and hence the same personal drive to ask questions about gender relations. Two of the best-known nineteenth-century male supporters of women's rights bear witness to this. The *Appeal of One Half of the Human Race, Women, against the Pretensions of the other Half, Men, to retain them in Political, and thence in Civil and Domestic, Slavery*, was published in

1825 and *The Subjection of Women* in 1862. Both show an understanding of the detrimental impact of discrimination against women not only on women themselves but on society as a whole. Both men whose names appear as the sole authors of the books, William Thompson, the Cork socialist theoretician and leading thinker in the Cooperative movement, and John Stuart Mill, the English philosopher, explicitly stated that many or most of the ideas came from their women collaborators, Anna Doyle Wheeler and Harriet Taylor Mill respectively. In his 'Introductory letter to Mrs Wheeler', Thompson wrote that he aimed to express the 'feelings, sentiments, and reasonings, which have emanated from your mind ...' As a man he could 'not feel like you ...' and '[t]hough long accustomed to reflect upon this subject, to you I am indebted for those bolder and more comprehensive views ...' He had hoped she would write the book herself, regretted that she had written only a few of the pages, and saw himself as 'your interpreter and the scribe of your sentiments'.[2] Mill wrote that, while he had long supported the case for the equality of the sexes as an abstract principle, it was through his friend and future wife that he came to understand 'the vast practical bearings of women's disabilities', and how the 'consequences of the inferior position of women intertwined themselves with all the evils of existing society and with all the difficulties of human improvement'.[3]

Women's history is not the only hitherto unexplored area of human experience opened up to historical research by pioneers motivated by rejection of the existing relationships of power and authority and distribution of resources in their society. Labour history and Marxist history are other examples. With such driving forces there is of course a danger that the historian will, consciously or unconsciously, look for evidence that supports the preferred outcome and overlook evidence that does not. However, historians who believe themselves to be value-free may be in danger of unintentional bias if they are satisfied with the prevailing relationships of authority and power, and the prevailing ideas of what is significant or important in history. There are no easy answers and the best approximation to an accurate reconstruction of the past is likely to come if as many different perspectives as possible are brought to bear on the choice of questions asked, the search for historical evidence, and its interpretation, followed by constructive debate and argument as to their respective merits.

As the body of women's history continues to grow, the incorporation of some of its findings into mainstream surveys has already begun. As this incorporation develops it has the potential to broaden definitions of what comprises political history. It challenges the existence of rigid boundaries between 'public' and 'private' spheres, and so between political and social history. The inclusion of gender analysis in particular can push historical enquiry and analysis towards assessing societies in terms of the quality of life they offered all individuals, women and men, across all social and economic classes. The challenge to us all is to actively encourage and engage in the development of a more wide-reaching, inclusive and genuinely human history.

Starting from awareness of the exclusion of women's experience from 'mainstream' history, the search for it contributes to the self-knowledge and location in historical context of both women and men, and is liberating for the development of human potential for both. And, of course, women's history and gender history, important as they are, are themselves in relatively early stages of development and are two contributions among many to the process of discovery and recovery of the past. They interact and engage with other tellings of history to their mutual development and enrichment. In the case of women's history itself, it has so far been for the most part researched and written by middle-class women and men, who are those more likely to have access to sources and means of publication. Others in Ireland, working-class women and Traveller women for example, have so far had less opportunity to ask their questions, search for answers and publish their findings. And many other groups have yet to pose their questions to the historical record, and write history from their perceptions of what is significant. When they do, their tellings will also engage and interact with the existing tellings, will lead to revisions and modifications of present assessments of the significant, and no doubt have unexpected consequences for the self-knowledge of many groups. And so the 'unending dialogue between the present and the past',[4] as E.H. Carr described history, will continue.

NOTES

1   Betty Friedan, *The Feminine Mystique* (London, Penguin, 1992, first published 1963), p. 68.
2   William Thompson, *Appeal of One Half of the Human Race, Women, against the Pretensions of the Other Half, Men, to retain them in Political, and thence in Civil and Domestic, Slavery* (London, Virago Press, 1983), pp xxi–xxiii.
3   John Stuart Mill, *Autobiography* (Boston, Houghton Mifflin, 1969), p. 147, fn.
4   E.H. Carr, *What is History?* (Penguin, Harmondsworth, 1967), p. 30.

WOMEN, HISTORY AND IDENTITY

Throughout the 1970s the influence of the women's movement was felt everywhere in Ireland. During International Women's Year of 1975 Trinity College New Library in Dublin hosted an exhibition, 'Votes for Women: Irish Women's Struggle for the Vote'. The accompanying booklet Votes for Women *contained an essay, 'How We Won the Vote' by Rosemary Cullen Owens, and the hitherto unpublished 'Reminiscences of an Irish Suffragette', written in 1941 by Hanna Sheehy Skeffington, a leading figure in the Irish campaign for women's suffrage. In the same year Radio Éireann broadcast a series of Thomas Davis lectures organised by Margaret Mac Curtain, and these were published in 1978 by Arlen House, the pioneering Irish feminist press.* Women in Irish Society: The Historical Dimension, *edited by Mac Curtain and Donncha Ó Corráin, contained contributions by ten established scholars, six women and four men, covering a wide range of disciplines and periods. The book broke new ground, and the fact that Margaret Mac Curtain was an established historian, teacher and mentor to many, as well as an eminent figure in the women's movement, added to its impact. In the 'Introduction' she wrote: 'Many Irish women find it difficult to learn about their historical identity, or their role in the life of the country because they have neither the information readily available, nor the skills of evaluation at their disposal'. The question of identity, and the lack of knowledge of what in fact women actually did in the past, and whether what they did supported today's sex-role stereotypes, was a major one facing women who challenged the accepted conventional views of women's 'nature' and proper role in society. It was a central driving force behind the international upsurge of research and writing on women in history. This essay appeared in the* Maynooth Review *in 1980.*

Belief in a link between historical awareness on the one hand and adulthood and maturity on the other has been with us for a long time. It was not new over two thousand years ago when Cicero wrote: 'Not to know what took place before you were born is to remain forever a child', and historians are still saying the same thing. It is

> only through knowledge of its history that a society can have knowledge of itself. As a man without memory and self-knowledge is a man adrift, so a society without memory (or more correctly, without recollection) and self-knowledge would be a society adrift.[1]

Individual men and women come equipped with personal memories. The society or group has to rely on its historians. Growing concern among women with the question of historical awareness has led to the recent upsurge in exploration of their past. This concern itself originates in the search for identity which is at the core of the current wave of the women's movement. Identity became the key issue as more and more women became convinced that the stereotype of femininity to which they were expected to conform was positively damaging to human development.

The process of conformity to the stereotype was given a name in 1963 when Betty Friedan published *The Feminine Mystique*. Symptoms of depression and frustration were being presented by American housewives in sufficient numbers to gain recognition as an identifiable syndrome. Betty Friedan diagnosed the problem as essentially one of personal identity, a schizophrenia caused by conformity to the accepted model of femininity. This model insisted that the true fulfilment of every 'feminine' woman was to be found in a total and exclusive commitment to marriage, motherhood and home, with no serious commitment to the development of other talents or to any other contribution to society. The content of this role had been increasingly eroded by the take-over by public services of functions previously seen as belonging to the family, and, more particularly, to the mother, in such areas as education, health care, social and psychological services. Friedan argued that the automatic allocation of this limited career to every woman created a conflict of alienation and lack of purpose. Growing up as a human being involved working through an identity crisis and resolving it by making personal decisions as to who one was and what one was going to become. This could be traumatic but was essential to growing to adulthood. The feminine mystique cut women off from this growth process by telling them that their identity and way to fulfilment was determined by their biology, the fulfilment of the passive, nurturing woman who devoted all her energy to helping her husband and children to develop their talents and felt no duty to develop her own. In the light of this analysis she did not find it surprising that so many women who accepted and tried to conform to the stereotype became depressed without being aware of any adequate cause. The response her book evoked, not only in the United States but around the world, confirmed that she had articulated feelings that many women had experienced in their own lives.

From dissatisfaction with the stereotype it is a short step to history and 'knowledge of what took place before you were born'. Women who rejected the feminine mystique because it seemed incompatible with the drives and feelings they were aware of still faced the question whether they were odd women out. To a large extent public opinion still sees them as an untypical minority. Freudian-based psychoanalysis, a powerful influence on western culture for many decades of this century, supported the view that women who rejected the generally accepted definition of femininity were simply maladjusted, and that any feelings of frustration resulted from their failure to accept the one role that could have led them to fulfilment. The fault did not lie in the stereotype but in the individuals who rejected it. For women who find themselves out of line with the majority view it becomes important to know more about women in the past. How traditional is the 'traditional' woman's role? Have women always been exclusively wives, mothers and housekeepers, subordinate to men and dependent on them for economic support, non-participants in the higher levels of artistic and intellectual creativity and in the organisation of society's affairs? And if they have, why? Have they been coerced by force, conditioned by socialisation, or is it simply a matter of biologically-determined differences?

Once the questions were asked the answers came in profusion. It is not intended in this article to attempt anything as ambitious as an overall critique but to discuss the implications of some of the work that is being done. However, a few preliminary points may be made. The first is that women found that they had been virtually written out of the history books. If historians were to be taken at their own valuation as selectors, recorders and interpreters of what was significant and what had contributed to change in human history, then the phenomenon of the invisible women seemed to bear witness that women had indeed been insignificant, unchanging and non-contributors – all hallmarks of the feminine mystique woman – throughout human history. The feminist movement of the nineteenth century had sparked off a considerable output of women's history but by the mid-twentieth century this had largely dropped out of sight. Even that highly organised movement itself received little or no attention in the books in general use.[2] Next, it was discovered that there had been persistent efforts to coerce and condition women to conform to a subordinate and passive role. An example of each of these taken from the second half of the eighteenth century, the age of Reason and Enlightenment and a period relevant to points to be made later, can illustrate this aspect.

Under the English common law husband and wife became one legal entity, and that person was the husband. The wife could not sue without his permission or be herself sued without his being involved as defendant. Her personal property was absolutely vested in him and he could sell or dispose of it at his pleasure, while he was entitled to the rents and profits of her real estate. Any money she earned belonged to him. The children were his property, and after his death their guardianship passed to his nearest male relative. She was incapable of bequeathing lands, or of bequeathing chattels without his licence. He had a legal right to chastise her and to restrain her liberty. Divorce was almost impossible for a woman to attain, and if she left him she forfeited all rights to maintenance, while anyone who harboured or aided her could be sued by the husband. Sir William Blackstone, whose *Commentaries on the Laws of England* (1765) was the standard source of information on the content of the common law, earned particular opprobrium in the eyes of feminists for his remark that these disabilities were, 'for the most part', for the 'protection and benefit' of the wife, 'so great a favourite is the female sex of the laws of England'.

From the same period probably the best known example of a male definition of women's proper role in society came from Jean-Jacques Rousseau, and it has rivalled Blackstone's comment in its power to infuriate women. The first chapter of *The Social Contract* opened with the declamation: 'Man was born free but is everywhere in chains', but elsewhere Rousseau made it clear that where freedom was concerned man did not include woman. In *Émile* (1762) he outlined his view of women's proper contribution to society:

> The education of the woman should be relative to that of the man. To be pleasing in his sight, to win his respect and love, to train him in childhood, to tend him in manhood, to counsel and console, to make his life pleasant and happy, these are the duties of woman for all time, and this is what she should be taught while she is young.[3]

Yet historians hailed Rousseau as a prophet of liberty while neglecting to mention his advocacy of perpetual subordination for half the human race. They praised the common law as the protector of individual rights and ignored its treatment of women. Accumulating evidence of overt exclusion of women from civil and political rights and of propaganda to the effect that women's 'nature' deprived them of entitlement to such rights made the invisibility of women in the history books take on the complexion of a conspiracy. The very fact that so much energy appeared to have been expended to make women conform to a feminine mystique stereotype suggested that the foundation of the stereotype was shaky.

And so it turned out to be. The historical records contained evidence that women had not always been economically dependent on men and confined to an exclusively domestic role. Throughout history the vast majority of women had worked beside men in primary production to support themselves and their families. In spite of laws, customs and conditioning the sources were full of creative, dominant females. In many societies at many periods they had exercised political and economic power, had ruled countries and led armies, and many had performed respectably in virtually every area of the arts, humanities and sciences. It appeared even that women had invented agriculture and some of the first manufacturing techniques. Female voices had consistently been raised against oppression, and the nineteenth century had seen the emergence of an organised feminist movement demanding civil and political rights. The titles of many of the first pioneering classics of the current wave of women's movement reflect the first shock of anger at the discovery of the extent of women's past oppression and of women's reaction to it: *Sexual Politics* (Kate Millett, 1969), *The Female Eunuch* (Germaine Greer, 1970), *Not in God's Image* (O'Faoláin and Martines, 1972), *The Dialectic of Sex* (Shulamith Firestone, 1972), *Women, Resistance and Revolution* and *Hidden from History* (Sheila Rowbotham, 1972 and 1973).

Already it could be shown that in the search for historical identity quite a lot had been achieved. It was evident that history did not support a definition of women that limited in any absolute way the range of their abilities and attainment. The feminine mystique stereotype had been found to have no universal validity. But there were problems with the new identity that seemed to be emerging. Naturally enough, the attention of the researchers concentrated in the first place on the oppression of women, their resistance to that oppression, and their achievements in spite of it in areas of human activity and creativity usually associated with men. This resulted in a tendency to continue to define women in relation to men, to emphasise their oppression and to evaluate women by comparing their attainment with that of men. While it was encouraging to find that women had fought back with some success, and that so many more than had been realised had asserted themselves and made their mark in many different ways, yet the identity of a perpetual victim, however brave and resilient, was not in itself very attractive or liberating. It hardly did justice to the creative, assertive women who kept emerging from the sources. While it was reassuring to find that women had contributed to the arts, humanities and sciences it did not seem convincing to evaluate the achievements of women as a sex by the size and quality of that contribution. For one thing, this would be to pit what women had done against what men had done in areas where men started with advantages in opportunity, encouragement and self-image that might be obvious but were not easy to quantify. The phenomenon of the invisible women suggested that there might be other, more subtle difficulties in the way of any attempt to evaluate women's achievements. Any head count of big names would always put men in the lead. Even if sophisticated scales were devised to compensate women for restriction of opportunity and lack of recognition, for most people the ultimate test would remain how many Leonardos or Einsteins each sex had produced. More important, any method of defining women that took male achievement and male values as the norm was going to be irrelevant to the lives of the vast majority of women. Did they not count or were they failures in some way because they had not openly rebelled against oppression or transcended it and achieved recognition in some 'male' area of activity?

A consensus is emerging that, while it is both valid and necessary to investigate the historical oppression of women and the achievements of 'great' women, these two areas do not by themselves constitute the whole history of the female sex, and can indeed only be understood in the context of a social history of women. Historians are devising questions which will relate directly to the experience of all women at a particular time and link that experience into the contemporary structures, values and attitudes of the particular society. One model of the new type of framework being used is that put forward by Juliet Mitchell, whose own approach aims at reconciling a radical feminist and a Marxist viewpoint. She lists four 'key structures'[4] of women's situation applicable to any period: Production, Reproduction, Sexuality and the Socialization of Children. Women's position in relation to each of these separate but inter-related areas can vary from one period to another, but when the respective states are put together they make up the 'complex unity' of the situation at a given time. Frameworks of this type are now widely used and have proved their value for the endeavour to reach the actual experience of women. However, interpretations of the material discovered by this or any other method vary, depending on the viewpoint and values of the individual historian. Different ideological approaches, which each see some one factor, such as economic conditions, male oppression or biological differences, as the ultimate determining agent, will suggest different explanations of the data, with consequently varying implications for women's historical identity. In this context it is relevant to note that a feminist approach to history has been defined by one historian as a 'view of women as a distinct sociological group for which there are established patterns of behaviour, special legal and legislative restrictions and customarily defined roles'.[5] Other historians are coming to believe that attempts to fit all women and their experience into a limited number of categories is not possible and that to regard them as in some way a homogeneous group or sub-group is too limiting.

The experience of women during the period of industrialisation and urbanisation of western culture which began around 1750 seems particularly relevant to women's identity today. This is a huge area where vigorous research is underway and a great deal has yet to be discovered. But a brief comparison of two different ways of looking at some of the findings can illustrate the different hypotheses possible. Patricia Branca[6] looked at western European women, using evidence drawn mainly from England and France, while Sheila Rowbotham[7] examined the position of women in England.

In pre-industrial Europe[8] the majority of women lived and worked in agriculture within a family situation. The family functioned as an economic unit. Marriage was the goal for all women who could achieve it because it was the ticket to survival and security. The duties of a wife were to produce children, manage the house and share in production work, in that order of importance. Women were generally responsible for dairy management and for the care of poultry and animals. On a sizable farm the wife was a working manager of a 'small multi-purpose factory' which turned out nearly everything the family consumed, soap, candles, butter, cheese, beer, salted and smoked meat, cloth and clothing. Women worked in the fields and could be employed as day labourers, though most single women worked in households similar to the one they came from. In the towns the wife of the artisan or shopkeeper was involved in his work, often in an informal partnership, and some women were in business on their own. From the middle of the eighteenth century the spread of domestic manufacture, particularly spinning, gave supplementary wage-earning employment to large numbers of women. Women's work was an essential part of the work of the family unit, which aimed at providing for all its members, and demanded the contribution of all, but their work was seen as supplementary to that of men and women themselves as subordinate.

The speeding up of the industrial revolution and the transition to urban life had a deep impact on women's lives. It separated the workplace from the home and so broke up the old family economic unit. The traditional way of thinking of the family persisted but the reality of independent wages received by individual members gradually undermined it. Married women brought their work tradition with them, continued domestic manufacture as far as they could, and some went to work in factories. But the separation of work and home made the former integration of roles difficult, and, since there was general agreement that a woman's first duty was to the home, most of them stayed there and tried as best they could to continue to combine functions. Single women went mainly into domestic service and the textile factories, both of which reflected the type of work they had been used to. Marriage remained the ambition for women, and their new individual earning power made it more easily attainable and allowed a greater element of choice of partner. Towards the end of the nineteenth century there came the start of a huge expansion in new and more attractive areas of 'white blouse' work as shop assistants and office workers. The work was cleaner and easier, and the opportunity of social contacts better, including the possibility of meeting eligible males from a wider variety of backgrounds.

While work opportunities for single working-class women were expanding, those for middle-class women were contracting. This was the continuation of a long-term process and was contributed to by developing ideas of what was or was not suitable work for women of the growing wealthy bourgeoisie, and by increasing professionalisation, which was used to exclude women. The only available jobs which were considered suitable, those of governess and companion, were of increasingly low status and badly paid. From the ranks of the middle class women came the leaders of the first feminist movement.[9] Their first demands were for access to professions for single women, and control over their property for married women. Later came demands for the education and training required for entry to the professions, for reform of some of the social manifestations of the double sexual standard in areas such as prostitution, and finally for the vote to allow easier access to law-making and changing. By the end of the nineteenth century they had achieved a considerable measure of their original aims, and women professionals were beginning to appear. Some became doctors and lawyers, but the professions which women entered in large numbers were teaching and nursing. The choice seems to have been determined to a large extent by the priority given by most women and their families to marriage as the ultimate career for a woman. The more stringent requirements of professions like medicine in terms of career commitment and financial resources put them beyond the range of ambition or possibility for most women.

Meanwhile within the middle-class family a revolution in the role of the wife and mother was taking place. Changes already underway in the recognition and treatment of childhood[10] as a unique and special stage of an individual's life, and in the growth of deeper mutual emotional bonds[11] between family members, continued in an altered environment, where the father was absent from home for most of every day and the mother was increasingly free to devote time and attention to her children. Improving standards of nutrition led to higher fertility. More children were born, and survived birth and infancy. Increased use of birth control followed and limited the number. The emphasis moved from motherhood as child production to motherhood as child rearing and socialization. Developing medical science was called in to help make pregnancy and child-birth less painful and dangerous and to advise on the care of the infant and the young child. Not only the physical but the educational and emotional needs of the child received increasing attention. The concept of childhood itself expanded to include adolescence, and with it the responsibility of the mother for the successful development of her children into early adulthood. For middle-class women a new kind of motherhood together with full responsibility for running the home and managing the family budget emerged as a full-time career. Legal changes reflected the new status. The position of the wife and mother under the English common law, which was pretty typical of her status in other European countries, changed steadily in the direction of replacing the rights of the father by the rights of the mother-child relationship, until the situation was reached in the twentieth century when marriage breakdown almost automatically meant that custody of the children went to the mother. Yet, at the same time other changes were underway. While women seem to have been the active agents in the early stages of the involvement of medical science in motherhood and childcare, yet during the late nineteenth century, and increasingly in the twentieth century, science tended to take over the role of authority, and the mother was gradually relegated to a subordinate role, taking instruction from the child pyschologists and other professionals. What had been regarded as a 'natural' function in every woman became something controlled by the 'experts', who were, of course, usually men. In the housekeeping dimension, cooking, cleaning and managing the balancing of the family budget took the place of the productive household management of pre-industrial society. The extension of state responsibility for the provision of such services as health, education and social welfare removed, diminished or down-graded the mother's contribution in those vital areas which had formed the basis for the original up-grading of the concept of motherhood. Marriage, motherhood and housekeeping had been elevated to the status of a full-time career, which society represented to women as all important and totally fulfilling, yet the content of house-keeping was increasingly limited and the autonomy of the all-important mother was increasingly diminished. Because the role seemed to be a natural continuation of women's primary duties in the old economic family unit few questioned the total economic dependence of the new wife and mother. Finally, it may be noted that married women from the middle classes played a leading role in the foundation of feminist movements.

Any attempt to analyse twentieth-century developments is particularly difficult for many reasons, not the least of these being the present rapidly-changing activities and consciousness of women. A few areas that seem to be of particular relevance to women's historical identity can be picked out. The percentage of European women marrying has continued to rise and so has the percentage divorce rate, while changes in the perceived function of marriage and motherhood have continued with the emergence of the 'intensely self-centred, inwardly turned, emotionally bonded, sexually liberated, child-orientated family type'[12] we know today. To put it another way, the demands for sexual and emotional satisfaction placed by both partners on marriage have increased, and so has the perceived responsibility of the mother for the proper physical and psychological development of her children. Secondly, the life-span of the marriage in which so much is invested has lengthened because people are living longer and marrying earlier, so that a couple who enter marriage with such increased expectations can have something in the region of fifty years together, as compared with perhaps twenty-five in pre-industrial society and thirty-five during the nineteenth century. Thirdly, the new perceptions of marriage and motherhood have spread to some extent from the middle class to the working class. Fourthly, the age of women at marriage has generally fallen, in this instance the middle class following the working class pattern, while for all classes the number of children per family has fallen. Fifthly, both the number and the percentage of married women working outside the home have increased dramatically. Today's typical woman worker in Europe is 'older, married and a mother'.[13] Sixthly, while more women are entering the professions, the majority of women still work in the service area in jobs well below management level. Finally, the new wave of the feminist movement appeared in the 1960s and its major concern has been women's consciousness and self-awareness, while its radical wing has attacked the family as the basic institution in the perpetuation of the economic and social exploitation of women.

Sheila Rowbotham's interpretation of these developments is based on the premise that the emancipation of women can only come with the overthrow of the capitalist system, and she tends either to pay little attention to any activity by women that was not directed to this end or to see it as the product of the continued conditioning and exploitation of women. She sees the role of women in work outside the home as the vital area. Capitalism both used and undermined the pre-industrial family economic unit. In the long run it undermined it by the wage labour system which enabled individuals to rebel against the family, but it also used women's subordinate and supplementary role to exploit them in the workforce as cheap and largely un-unionised labour, and in the home as unpaid producers of the next generation of workers and unpaid servicers of their equally exploited menfolk. The new areas of employment as shop assistants and office workers simply continued the traditional subordinate, service aspect of women's work while removing the productive element, and still left women open to sexual and economic exploitation. When lack of employment made it convenient to keep women at home the status of motherhood was elevated, and women's conditioning to see it and marriage as their real vocation was used to keep them from unionising to demand better pay and working conditions. On the other hand, capitalism's need for new reserves of labour began to draw married women increasingly into the labour market since the second world war. As for middle-class women, during the nineteenth century they were cut off from production and made economically dependent on men, and Rowbotham sees an ambiguity in the attacks of the feminists on male domination of women while they did not see the need to overthrow the whole system of private ownership of capital and wage labour. There was, she thinks, a brief period during the early twentieth century when feminism did have a vision of a real revolution in sex roles linked to a world socialist revolution, but it passed and only today does she again see the possibility of a new socialist feminism. Otherwise the emphasis has been on individual reforms which cannot achieve emancipation and can even hinder and delay it by confusing the issues.

Patricia Branca, looking at the same developments, does not deny that women were exploited, but insists that they were also active contributors to the emergence of the feminine mystique. She transfers the focus of attention from women at work outside the home to women in the family. She argues that the family was the stepping stone to female emancipation and that women were the 'primary agents in the development of the modern family'.[14] She sees married middle-class women taking the initiative in the further growth of inter-personal relations and the increased affection and care for the children. The fact that there were limits to women's freedom of action, whether imposed by economic conditions, patriarchy or whatever, did not necessarily mean that they could exercise no control or choice. Nor does today's judgment that total commitment to an exclusive wife-mother- housekeeper role did not turn out to be the best possible choice for women – and their children – prove that there was no value in their increased attention to these areas. From where nineteenth-century women stood the new type of marriage and motherhood could seem a big step forward for women and children. She argues that a positive side can be seen to the general reluctance of women to commit themselves fully to any outside career, and suggests that it may be worth considering whether the male pattern of self-identification by job may also be conducive to something less than optimum personal development.

From this point of view, European women of the nineteenth century might be seen as adapting to new circumstances and, within those limits, experimenting with new methods of self-expression, trying out new identities, and, when they tried something and found it wanting, being ready to modify or reject it. Branca points out that, even while the new total wife-and-mother identity was being created, some married and single women of the middle class were making it clear, through their involvement in the feminist movement, that their need for self-expression went beyond the confines of a dependent identity to seek economic independence as the essential basis for personal freedom. They went on to demand access to political power and law making. During the twentieth century, while the feminine mystique was spreading to some extent to the working class, married women, even while they expressed lip service – and perhaps more – to the mystique, were also expressing their anxiety and rejecting its extreme forms by further limitation of family size, by rising divorce rates, by working outside the home, and, as Betty Friedan pointed out, by turning up in the psychiatrist's consulting room. In Patricia Branca's interpretation these developments can be seen, not solely as a response to the demands of capitalism, but also as a further stage in the search for identity, with all the accompanying confusion and conflict that are inevitable to such an endeavour.

In this connection the relation between feminists and other women is interesting. The majority of their contemporaries rejected the first feminists and their demands with some hostility, and especially the demand for the vote. This could fit into a woman-as-victim analysis as suggesting that the conditioning of women to see themselves as inferior led them to refuse civil and political rights. Patricia Branca argues that it is more plausible to see not a polarity but a dialogue between the feminists and the women who criticised or felt threatened by them. The feminists, more aware, more articulate and more radical, led the way in trying to express and come to terms with the tensions that went with women's changing roles and the attempts to create new lifestyles. Given time to assimilate and come to terms with what the feminists were saying, the majority of women eventually accepted it and followed their lead. It is then no coincidence that the current wave of the feminist movement has concerned itself so much with the relation between the modern family and women's drive for self-fulfilment.

Differing interpretations such as those of Sheila Rowbotham and Patricia Branca raise the question whether women, individually and collectively, may have exercised a greater degree of control over the direction of their lives than would seem to be allowed by an approach that identifies any single factor as the determining one. Can women then be seen as having been active agents of historical change, reacting to and interacting with political, social and economic developments, and in the process participating in the development of new lifestyles and cultural values? But historians have tended to look for the sources of the important changes, those in the 'frame-work of society' and in the 'pattern of culture', in the places 'where the power to make change is'. The places in question were usually occupied exclusively by men, and, as J.J. Hexter pointed out,

> through no conspiracy of the historians the College of Cardinals, the Consistory of Geneva, the Parliament of England, the Faculty of the Sorbonne, the Directorate of the Bank of England and the expeditions of Columbus, Vasco da Gama and Drake have been pretty much stag affairs.[15]

This line of reasoning raises two other questions relevant to women's historical identity. Why have all the societies of which we have definite knowledge been patriarchies and what is the implication of this fact for women? Does it mean that women can never have had any influence on change in the framework of society or the pattern of culture as Hexter suggests, and that the most we can hope to establish is that they managed their own lives as best they could within male-determined structures and cultures without any possibility of contributing to change in either?

Various explanations of the origins of patriarchy have been put forward but none has yet found general acceptance. Engel's theory in *The Origin of the Family, Private Property and the State* (1884) was that it appeared with private property and private control of the means of production. One feminist view sees it as partly biological and partly cultural in origin.[16] This theory argues that, because of the disadvantages and disability of child-bearing, women were completely dependent on men for survival and so completely subordinate until the widespread availability of effective contraceptive methods created the means of liberation. A third theory is a simple biological one, that hormonal differences between the sexes make patriarchy and male dominance always and everywhere inevitable.[17] As far as the historical identity of women is concerned the immediate question is not whether any of these theories is correct, but how the actuality of patriarchy relates to change in society. If Hexter's argument is accepted a syllogism follows: Change in human society is made by people in dominant positions; People in dominant positions are males; Therefore change in human society is made by males. It should be noted that this reasoning excludes the vast majority of men as well as virtually all women. However, if for the sake of argument the syllogism is accepted then it can be asked whether the decision-makers actually make their decisions in total freedom from all outside influences, and, if not, whether some of those outside influences could be women. The stereotype of the dominant woman manipulating the man in the position of power is a familiar one. It may be worth asking who makes the decisions at these stag affairs. More to the point, it can be asked, and of course is already being asked, whether changes in culture and society come about so simply from the decisions of privileged groups. This pushes the inquiry into the area of historic causation, re-evaluation of sources, and the relation and interaction between political, economic and social change, ruling elites, and groups excluded from formal positions of power. The question is being asked whether 'decentralized, collective forms of decision-making and behaviour are ultimately the main source of fundamental forms of social change'.[18]

It seems that the search for women's historical identity leads us beyond seeing women as a separate group or caste, and raises fundamental questions about the history of the human race. As far as women's identity itself is concerned the search seems to be only beginning. The feminine mystique stereotype as a definition that limits women's potential has been left far behind, but the real identity of women remains elusive. Progress is being made in formulating new methods of inquiry to recover more and more of the historical experience of women. New possibilities and potentials keep appearing but so do new problems. Some historians are beginning to question the validity of any concept of 'women's history' because it seems impossible to find any basis on which to postulate a shared historical experience except in mutual oppression by men. The diversity of the experience of women, their presence among oppressors as well as oppressed, their separation from each other by differing and often opposed interests of class, race, creed and ideology make the concept of a shared history increasingly difficult to accept. Yet at the same time it would seem to be premature and a mistake to discard the concept before it has been fully worked through to extract its full potential. The reality that women as a sex did have a history of exclusion, however hard to reconcile with the other reality of the diversity of experience of individuals or groups, must be of basic significance to human history. If there is an identity problem for women in their oppression there must be one for men in their role as oppressor. What is the significance for men of their history of denying women the civil and political rights they claimed for themselves, and of the steady stream of male theorising about the inferiority of women? This is only one of the challenges to the conventional ways of looking at men's history that are raised by the investigation of women's history. One suggestion for a possible way forward is that 'women's history' may turn out to be the history of a separate women's culture, and that the comparative study of the historical experience of women and of men at given periods might lead the way to a synthesis and eventually to the possibility of a universal history.[19]

Women's exploration of their past may not yet have solved their identity problem, but in the process they have made a contribution to historical understanding which unquestionably satisfies the criteria for creativity posited by one historian:

> Progress in human affairs, whether in science or in history or in society, has come mainly through the bold readiness of human beings not to confine themselves to seeking piece-meal improvements in the way things are done, but to present fundamental challenges in the name of reason to the current way of doing things and to the avowed or hidden assumptions on which it rests.[20]

From The Maynooth Review, May 1980, Vol. 6, No. 1, pp 65–79.

NOTES

1   Arthur Marwick, *The Nature of History* (London, Macmillan, 1970), p. 3.

2   In the Irish context see F.S.L. Lyons, *Ireland Since the Famine* (London, Weidenfeld & Nicolson, 1971). In over 300 pages devoted to the period from 1867 to 1922, the only reference to

the feminist movement comes in a phrase describing Constance Markievicz: 'interested above all in women's rights – it was the suffrage question that first caught her interest …', p. 284.

3   *Émile* (London, Dent, 1974), p. 328.

4   *Woman's Estate* (Harmondsworth, Penguin, 1971), p. 101.

5   Hilda Smith, 'Feminism and Methodology in Women's History', in B.A. Carroll (ed.), *Liberating Women's History* (University of Illinois Press, 1976), p. 370.

6   Patricia Branca, *Women in Europe Since 1750* (London, Croom Helm, 1978).

7   Sheila Rowbotham, *Woman's Consciousness, Man's World* (Penguin, 1973); *Hidden from History* (London, Pluto Press, 1977, 3rd edition).

8   Ivy Pinchbeck, *Women Workers and the Industrial Revolution 1750–1850* (London, 1930); Richard T. Vann, 'Women in Preindustrial Capitalism', in Bridenthal and Koonz (eds), *Becoming Visible: Women in European History* (Boston, Houghton Mifflin, 1977), pp 194–216.

9   Richard J. Evans, *The Feminists: Women's Emancipation Movements in Europe, America and Australasia 1840–1920* (London, Croom Helm, 1977).

10   Philippe Ariès, *Centuries of Childhood* (Harmondsworth, Penguin, 1979 [1960]).

11   Lawrence Stone, *The Family, Sex and Marriage in England 1500–1800* (Harmondsworth, Penguin, 1979, abridged edition).

12   Stone, *op. cit.*, p. 425.

13   Branca, *op. cit.*, p. 206.

14   *Ibid*, p. 85.

15   *New York Times Book Review*, 7 March 1946, quoted in *Liberating Women's History*, p. 40.

16   Shulamith Firestone, *The Dialectic of Sex* (London, Paladin, 1972).

17   Steven Goldberg, *The Inevitability of Patriarchy* (London, Temple Smith, 1977).

18   Sheila Ryan Johansson, '"Herstory" as History', in *Liberating Women's History*, p. 417.

19   Gerda Lerner, 'Placing Women in History' in *Liberating Women's History*, p. 365.

20   E.H. Carr, *What is History* (Harmondsworth, Penguin, 1967), p. 155.

INVISIBLE WOMEN AND THEIR CONTRIBUTION
TO HISTORICAL STUDIES

This essay originated as a talk at a History Teachers' Association conference and was published in their journal Stair *in 1982. Teachers who were interested in the developments in women's history, and wanted to find out more, both for themselves and their pupils, were faced by the scarcity of published material. Like so many others, they were frustrated by the invisibility of women in the history books in general use. Yet, while we waited for the volume of research and publication to develop, there was much to be learned from examining that invisibility itself. Why did some areas of human experience, that, once our attention is drawn to them, have obvious significance for patterns of continuity and change in the history of human societies, such as labour history or black history as well as women's history, go unexamined by professional historians for so long, while the politics of elites were given so much attention? Why have the pioneers who first recognised and named these invisibilities, and who, by doing so, opened them to historical enquiry, often been activists rather than academics? Looking for answers raises further questions relevant to all history writing and reading: what question is the historian posing; where does he or she go to look for answers; how do both the original question and the historian's choice of sources relate to the historian's own location in history, and his or her perception of what is significant. E.H. Carr summed up the issues in* What is History *(1961) where he advised the student thinking of attending Professor X's lectures, to first find out what bee that particular historian had in his bonnet.*

If the feminist scholars had not already started to research women's history and to exploit its potential for raising questions that open up new historical perspectives and avenues of approach, we might be forgiven for speculating that history teachers must have done the job themselves. Certainly they would, once they realised how valuable it would prove to be as a teaching aid. As it is, they need only be grateful to the feminist pioneers and seize the opportunity for bringing their pupils and themselves face to face with historical questioning and argument in a context to which every girl and boy can personally relate from her or his own experience.

The aim of this article is to indicate some of the ways in which an interest in the historical experience of women can contribute to and extend historical understanding and to suggest that raising some of these questions may encourage students to do their own thinking on the subject.

The Case of the Invisible Woman

This seems as good a starting point as any. If we look at the history books in use in our schools it may well seem that if we are looking for 'women's history' we are looking for something that does not exist. The books mention very few individual women and group action seems to be interpreted as action by men. The named individuals who are seen as leadership figures, for the most part rulers, statesmen, politicians, military leaders, perhaps revolutionaries, seem to be at least 90% men. Their followers, the membership of political parties, of armies and trade unions and so on, seem also to be almost all men.

What are we to conclude from this as to the role of women in human history? Does the relative invisibility of women relative to men mean that the important actions and decisions which have shaped human societies today and in the past, and also the value-systems and beliefs underlying these, have been pretty well exclusively the work of men? Have women throughout history filled what is basically a service role, tending to and supporting the male as he got on with the creative thinking, the deciding and doing? Have women simply accepted and followed the ideas and leadership of men? Does history tell us that women as a group have been passive and non-contributors to change in society? The answer to this depends on what we mean by 'history', and what we mean when we say 'history' tells us something.

What do we mean by 'History'?

Arthur Marwick[1] identifies three meanings which the word can carry. It can mean the entire past of the human race; or it can mean attempts by human beings to record events, interpretations or explanations of that past; or it can mean history as it is taught as a discipline in universities. Obviously the implications of saying 'history tells us' something are different depending on which meaning of the word we actually intend. It could be a rewarding exercise for students to ask what they themselves mean when they speak of 'history'; do they always mean the same thing; and do they think people can switch from one meaning to another without being aware of the change. If people can switch like that, how important is it?

To return then to our invisible women. If it is the entire past of the human race that tells us women have done nothing that is significant historically, the case seems hopeless indeed. But, as Arthur Marwick says, in fact we are dealing with books written by human beings, so we may perhaps be more optimistic. It seems possible that we may be able to argue the matter further.

Historians do of course aim to select the significant and important, that is the events, ideas, actions and movements that have contributed to change and development in human societies. So far this aim seems to have led them most often into the arenas of politics and war, which is a problem we will return to later. One contributing factor here is the relative availability of written evidence which is the basic raw material of the historian. However, since it seems to be established that throughout the history of the human race far fewer women than men have taken a leading role – any role – in either politics or war this immediately reduces the chances of their figuring often in the material available to historians. If these are indeed the key areas it is going to be difficult to argue for women's contribution. The case against them has been made by some historians and most tellingly by J.H. Hexter who said that it was

> through no conspiracy of the historians that the college of Cardinals, the Consistory of Geneva, the Parliament of England, the Faculty of the Sorbonne, the Directorate of the Bank of England and the expeditions of Columbus, Vasco da Gama and Drake have been pretty much stag affairs.[2]

If we accept for the sake of argument that Hexter correctly identifies the areas of major decisiveness in human history, we encounter a new kind of invisibility – the invisibility of the political woman, who should surely be noted by the historian as she battled to gain access to these privileged male reserves. But such is not the case. From about 1840 to about 1920 a vigorous and widespread women's emancipation movement developed, ranging across Europe from Ireland to Russia and flourishing also in the United States, Canada, Australia and New Zealand. It had high public visibility. It attracted copious newspaper coverage and the attention of public figures, politicians, churchmen and intellectuals as well as of the general public. It was successful in achieving a substantial amount of its radical aims, including control of their own property for married women, more or less equal access for girls and women to second and third level education, entry to most of the professions, the right to vote, to sit in parliament and to take government office.[3] The methods of the suffrage campaign included petitions, lobbying, large-scale public meetings, obstruction, heckling and harassing of public figures and destruction of public property. They led to imprisonment, hunger strike and forcible feeding. Public reaction ranged from applause to outrage and horror. It was in short a very public, very political movement aiming at radical change in society and achieving a respectable instalment of that change. Yet this movement gets no mention at all in most of the history books in use in our schools. We must ask why.

An instructive Irish example is F.S.L. Lyons' *Ireland Since the Famine*.[4] This is a particularly useful example because here we are discussing a highly regarded book by a very distinguished author, and a book which shows an unusually wide range of sympathetic interest and understanding. Over 300 pages are devoted to the period from the mid 1860s to 1923. Detailed consideration is given to many of the powerful political, cultural and intellectual movements moulding Irish society during these sixty odd years, including the Gaelic renaissance, the Fenians, Home Rule, Sinn Féin, the rise of the labour movement. How does it deal with the women's emancipation movement? It does not appear in the index and the only mention it gets is on page 284. Here Constance Markievicz is introduced in the context of her relationship to the Citizen Army: 'Interested above all in women's rights – it was the suffrage question that first caught her interest …'.

The implications of this are worth thinking about. Professor Lyons is obviously aware of the women's emancipation movement. His attitude to it seems neither unsympathetic nor disparaging. But, by what he does and does not say, by mentioning it in passing, seeming to assume readers will know to what he refers, but saying nothing more about it, he, consciously or unconsciously, conveys a clear though unspoken message. This is that the movement, while known to the historian, does not concern him or her *as a historian*, and hence, by definition, is not a significant or important historical event. The implicit judgment is that it has not contributed to the 'real' history of the human race, and is in some unexplained way 'outside' that history. This is a serious situation, because we are talking about a book that has achieved definitive status and is likely to remain the standard reference work for its period for a considerable time to come. And its message, doubly powerful because unspoken, is that women's political and intellectual movements do not concern the historian of Ireland during this period, and hence do not concern human history.

Varieties of Visibility

By now we may be beginning to wonder if there is something more behind the invisibility of women in the history books than a simple non-participation by women in the kinds of activity that rightly attract the attention of the historian. Has it also something to do with the way historians and societies regard and have regarded women? Another example from *Ireland Since the Famine* is interesting and enlightening on this point. Also it has the dual attraction of being something students can try out themselves and something that will probably make them laugh. Both are useful in stimulating thought.

The subject at this time is Maud Gonne. Most people will have heard her name, but will probably be hazy as to who she was and what she did. So we go to the index and find eight page references to her. This looks promising so we proceed to look at them in turn. On page 232 we are told that W.B. Yeats 'met and fell in love with Maud Gonne in 1889' and was influenced by her republican extremism. On page 237 there is mention of Yeats' *Cathleen Ní Houlihan*, 'the play he wrote for Maud Gonne'. On page 239 Conor Cruise O'Brien's view that Yeats was involved with republicanism *before* he fell in love with Maud Gonne is discussed. Page 241 finds W.B. downcast by 'the loss of Maud Gonne by her marriage to a man he was unable to respect ...'. On page 251 we find Maud Gonne herself actually doing something – she becomes an honorary secretary to the National Council set up in 1903 to organise protests against the visit of Edward VII to Ireland. On page 284 there is reference to Constance Markievicz working for 'Maud Gonne's organisation Inghinidhe na hÉireann'. (This is also interesting because it is the only reference in the book to Inghinidhe na hÉireann). On page 317 the reference concerns Major John MacBride who, 'by marrying Maud Gonne' had incurred Yeats' hostility. By now we are prepared for the final reference on page 553: Maud Gonne 'who had enslaved W.B. Yeats in the early years of the century'.

No-one could say that Maud Gonne is invisible here. On the contrary she has high visibility of a sort, and yet anyone who had hoped to find out who she was and what she did is little the wiser. We have learned that W.B. Yeats loved her, so that basically we now know something that *he* did, but not what she thought or said or did. A new conundrum seems to have emerged: 'When can a woman be visible or invisible at the same time?' Our question now concerns what goes on in the minds of historians rather than simply the material available to them. This brings us face to face with what students often find disconcerting, the fact that history books do not consist of infallible revelations, but are written by individual human beings who may be male or female, tall or short, conservative or liberal, in fact people like the rest of us who may have eccentric personal ideas or who may accurately reflect the accepted majority consensus values of their society. This is something that historians, reflecting on their craft, have long recognised.

What is a Historian?

E.H. Carr in *What is History*[5] calls the historian 'a social phenomenon, both the product and the conscious or unconscious spokesman of the society to which he belongs'. If a society and its historians expect to find only men when they look for political or other activists, it seems possible they may pass over as unimportant the evidence of women's activity. Carr provides a colourful metaphor to illustrate the selectivity of the historian dealing with historical facts:

> The facts are really not at all like fish on the fishmonger's slab. They are like fish swimming about in a vast and sometimes inaccessible ocean; and what the historian catches will depend, partly on chance, but mainly on what part of the ocean he chooses to fish in and what tackle he chooses to use – these two factors being, of course, determined by the kind of fish he wants to catch. By and large, the historian will get the kind of facts he wants.

So, while our simple faith in the infallibility of historians may be somewhat shaken by all this, we have at least found grounds for a more optimistic approach to the quest for active women in history. If historians can see and yet not really see a woman's political movement, and if historians may be missing evidence because they are not looking in the right place or not asking the right question, perhaps they have missed other evidence of female activity and contribution. This indeed has proved to be the case. Feminist historians, men as well as women, have already explored and recovered some of the historical experience of women, and have found a much wider and significant contribution to the arts, sciences and humanities than most of them anticipated. One interesting example of this is Mary Wollstonecraft and Enlightenment thinking.

The Invisible Rationalist

In 1792 Mary Wollstonecraft published *A Vindication of the Rights of Woman*. This was a response to Enlightenment thinking generally and in particular to two works by Jean Jacques Rousseau, *The Social Contract* and *Émile*. Rousseau opened the former with the famous declamation: 'Man was born free, but is everywhere in chains', and went on to argue the right of every man to self determination and participation in public affairs. When feminists complain of discrimination against women the counter-argument often is that 'man' and 'he' include 'woman' and 'she'. Rousseau however made it clear that he did not include women in 'man'. In *Émile* he outlined his ideas – very attractive and stimulating ideas – about the proper education which would allow a boy to grow to full and autonomous adulthood. But when he turned to the education of women, he went into reverse gear. Women should not form independent judgements but should take all their opinions, including religious and political, from the male authority figures in their lives, first father and then husband. This was because women's purpose in life was to serve men:

> The education of the woman should relate to that of the man. To be pleasing in his sight, to win his respect and love, to train him in childhood, to tend him in manhood, to counsel and console, to make his life pleasant and happy, these are the duties of woman for all time, and this is what she should be taught while she is young.

Mary Wollstonecraft responded enthusiastically to Rousseau's ideas about liberty but with equal vigour disputed his attitude to women. Women were rational human beings as well as men, but, when they were educated as Rousseau and others advocated, they could not develop into responsible adults, but could only become irresponsible, frivolous and lacking in moral sense. In fact they became a moral danger to all over whom they had influence or control, including husbands, children and servants. The *Vindication* was a pioneering book which claimed the rationalism of the Enlightenment as the birthright of women as well as men. It was a contemporary *cause célèbre*, read, discussed, and often denounced. Daniel O'Connell, as a young law student in London, busily reading all the current intellectual offerings, read it as well as Paine, Godwin and the rest. But the *Vindication* is mentioned in few if any of the standard histories of the Enlightenment, though a few years back the historian E.P. Thompson, in a review in *The Listener,* claimed for it recognition as a serious contribution to Enlightenment thought.

Visible Women

Mary Wollstonecraft seems to be another case of a woman's contribution being visible and invisible at the same time. But not all female activity has been treated in this way. There are a few famous women in the history books whose names we are all familiar with and whose achievements are discussed and analysed like those of men. Elizabeth I of England, Catherine the Great of

Russia, Maria Theresa of Austria spring to mind. So do Joan of Arc, Teresa of Avila and Catherine of Siena. Why have these women not become invisible to historians? Can we ask if the reason has anything to do with the fact that they all operated within the male-dominated establishment and did not either challenge its existence or by-pass it? The queens, even Catherine the Great, came to rule by virtue of their relationship to a particular man. They did not appear as unknown contenders for power and their tenure of it did not shake or challenge long-term male claims to precedence. The three saintly women may have challenged individual men but they did not claim, or lead movements that claimed, equal rights for women within the male-controlled political or church structure. Is this why they are more easily seen by historians? This is an area where further research, theorising and theory-testing could be valuable.

Whatever the reasons for it, the visibility of such women to historians has been a valuable starting point and encouragement to feminist historical enquiry. Their place in the history books has demonstrated that women, once they got the opportunity by whatever means, could rule, and think and teach, could display leadership and charisma as well as any man.

Causation in History

At this stage it is time to return to the quotation from J.H. Hexter. Seldom has the point of view it expresses been put so clearly and so unambiguously. His argument is that all the really important decisions that actually affect human history are made by people in the sorts of position he defines. This raises one of the most basic questions in historical thinking and one that has special relevance to discussion of women in history. If we agree with Hexter the implications would seem to be that we believe that a very tiny, indeed infinitesimal, minority of individuals have been responsible for the major developments in human societies, for changing patterns of culture, and changing value-systems and beliefs. The logical conclusion would be the automatic exclusion of the over-whelming majority of individuals who have ever lived, men as well as women, from even the possibility of direct contribution to such change. Here we have two basic questions concerning causation in history. Do we accept that decisions made by people in public leadership positions in political, military and economic life have been the main causative factors in history? And, if we are reluctant to give unqualified assent to this proposition, what other or alternative driving forces do we think operated?

Prejudice a Good Thing?

It has to be admitted that behind the discussion so far there has been an undeniable bias or prejudice, and it is time I declared my interest. In fact the driving force behind feminist historical inquiry can be defined as a bias. The best way I can define this bias, and this definition might or might not be accepted by other feminists, is to relate it to the identity problem faced by many women today. As more women became aware that their experience of themselves and their abilities, potentials and ambitions did not fit the current definitions of womanhood and woman's 'role', they were increasingly driven to history to find if it supported or contradicted the general belief in the eternal passive role. This is to admit a vested interest. History would justify rejection of the view of women's role as purely domestic and supportive if it showed women as at least not always happily acquiescent and at best contradicting it in word and deed. If E.H. Carr's argument that the historian 'will get the kind of facts he wants ...' is true, it is still applicable when the historian is a feminist, and we can hardly argue that feminists are immune from blind spots and wishful thinking.

It has then to be conceded that there is a danger that the wish to find that something is so will help us to find that it is so. But two other points are also worth making. The first comes from Carr again, who also advises the student to study 'the historian before you begin to study the facts', and ask 'what bees he has in his bonnet'. If there are none the historian 'is a dull dog'. So bias, or, less invidiously, enthusiasm for a particular point of view, is seen to have a value of its own, though to benefit from it the reader must be at pains to be aware of it. The second point is to suggest that it is all important for the historian to be aware of his or her bias. A recognised bias can stimulate new lines of thought and approach and also sensitivity to evidence which disputes as well as that which supports the favoured hypothesis. Unrecognised prejudice seems far more dangerous. Unconscious acceptance of certain values and ways of seeing things must be much more powerful in its ability to distort in the first place the judgment of the historian. Then, because the material is presented to the reader without any indication of the underlying assumptions, the reader is also more likely to accept and internalise these unquestioningly. So perhaps it can be agreed that, while both historians and readers need to be alert to the prejudices of themselves and each other, a bias in favour of a new hypothesis can push us to challenge accepted ways of thinking – which must be a good thing – in ways that probably could not be achieved without this sort of stimulus. The aims of this article have been to suggest that this is so and to indicate some of the challenges made by feminist inquiry.

Some Further Challenges

There are a few more challenges which cannot be ignored. We have been discussing some of the ways in which women have been invisible to historians even though they were acting in ways which by definition should have demanded attention, and we have considered some of the implications of this invisibility. But women have also been strangely invisible in some areas where they were not active but where they should have been seen by historians. The reality of discrimination against women has gone largely unrecorded until very recently, and it is still untouched on in most of the history books in general use. This in turn means that a whole dimension of men's history as well as women's history has been lost to sight. Once we advert to this omission it becomes one of the most startling invisibilities of all. Two examples of this will suffice here.

Historians have continued happily over the years in their praise of the English common law as the foundation of the liberty of the subject. The position of married women under the common law is seldom adverted to as an example of its failure to protect the liberty of one large section of the population. As expounded in Sir William Blackstone's *Commentaries on the Laws of England* (1765) the position of women within marriage derived from the legal duty of husbands to support their wives. But the condition to which this reduced women in the eyes of the law is best appreciated if 'white man' or 'master' is substituted for 'husband' and 'black man' or 'servant' for 'wife'. The legal concept was that husband and wife become one legal entity, with the husband the active agent. She could not sue without his permission and if she was sued he was involved as defendant. He had absolute rights over her personal property and could sell or dispose of it as he decided. He was also entitled to income derived from her real estate. If she earned money it legally belonged to him. He had absolute rights over their children, and it was his male heir and not his wife who was their legal guardian if he died. He was legally allowed to chastise her and control her freedom of action. If she tried to leave him, divorce was almost impossible. She forfeited rights to maintenance by him and he could sue anyone who helped her.

The second example is Rousseau's view of women's proper role and education already cited, but now looked at from the different angle of philosophical thought. What are we to deduce from the silence of historians who praise Rousseau as a champion of human liberty and do not put in the balance his denial of liberty to half the human race?

Our inquiry at this stage is moving its original focus on women and female identity to take in men and male identity also. Feminist history, by looking at historical evidence from a new point of view, and by seeing what had remained unseen, is now bringing attention to bear on a new area of invisibility, the oppression of women by men, both by restrictions on their actual freedom and autonomy, and by obstructions in the way of their personal growth to autonomy. This area of inquiry can only be indicated here, but we can end with three final questions. How unbalanced and misleading has the writing of human history been if there have been so many areas of invisibility and one-sided judgments? How drastic will reassessment and revision of accepted historical interpretation have to be to correct these omissions and distortions? And, if women have turned to history to help in their search for identity, will men now have to turn to look at *their* identity as they face the challenge of feminist historians?

from Elma Collins (ed.), *Stair* (1982), pp 2–6.

NOTES

1   Arthur Marwick, *The Nature of History* (London, Macmillan, 1970).

2   J.H. Hexter, *New York Times Book Review*, 7 March 1946, quoted in B. Carroll (ed.), *Liberating Women's History* (University of Illinois Press, 1976) p. 40.

3   See Richard J. Evans, *The Feminists: Women's Emancipation Movements in Europe, America and Australasia, 1840–1920* (London, Croom Helm 1977).

4   F.S.L. Lyons, *Ireland Since the Famine* (London, Weidenfeld and Nicolson, 1971).

5   E.H. Carr, *What is History?* (Harmondsworth, Penguin, 1961).

HOW RADICAL WAS IRISH FEMINISM
BETWEEN 1860 AND 1920?

The sixteenth biennial Irish Conference of Historians was held at St Patrick's College, Maynooth (today NUI Maynooth) in 1983 and the conference papers were published in Radicals, Rebels *and* Establishments *in 1985. As the editor Patrick Corish explained in his 'Introduction', the conference theme was chosen as being 'central to what have been appearing to scholars over the last generation or so to represent the real complexities of Irish history, in contrast to the powerful myths this history has generated'. The theme was obviously applicable to the growing interest and publication in women's history. As the Department of Modern History at Maynooth were the organisers of the conference, the opportunity was there to include a paper on women's history in the programme. And, within the field of women's history, the theme was particularly relevant to feminist activism. Here some important contributions were being made. Rosemary Cullen Owens' 1977 thesis on the Irish Suffrage movement was available at the time of the conference, and her* Smashing Times: A History of the Irish Women's Suffrage Movement 1889–1922 *was published in 1984. Margaret Ward's* Unmanageable Revolutionaries: Women and Irish Nationalism *was published in 1983. Anne O'Connor and Eibhlín Breathnach had written theses on the nineteenth-century campaigns for higher standards in girls' secondary education and for the admission of women to the universities. It appeared that Ireland had its own history of feminist action on a number of issues during the first-wave women's movement. For this article I found Richard J Evans' book,* The Feminists: Women's Emancipation Movements in Europe, America and Australasia 1840–1948 *(1977) very useful. As he did not deal with Ireland at all, I took it as a reference and starting point, and looked to see if there was evidence of action in*

Ireland in all or most of the different areas he examined. This approach proved to be useful, though I realised later, as research on the women's movement in Ireland developed, that in Ireland action on the different feminist issues had not followed the sequence Evans found elsewhere. It appeared that here action on suffrage emerged contemporaneously with that on married women's property, educational reform and the repeal of the Contagious Diseases Acts, and not after these had already developed. I also found that I had been mistaken in thinking that the suffrage campaign had occupied Irish feminists to the exclusion of other feminist concerns in the years immediately preceding 1922. They continued to see it both as a right in itself and as a necessary prerequisite to achieving many other feminist aims.

There has been little recent historical study of Irish feminism in the late nineteenth and early twentieth centuries. The studies that have been done have dealt with particular aspects of feminist activity[1] and there has not as yet been any overall survey. The aim of this article is to make a start in that direction by relating what we know of Irish feminist organisation to the context of international feminism, and by considering how one might attempt to determine what was 'radical' and what was not. In the present state of knowledge both objectives can be only partially achieved, but it is hoped that the study will do two things. It may indicate areas where research should be profitable. Also, while it is concluded here that the question in the title is the wrong question, it seems that the attempt to answer it helps to identify some of the right questions to deepen our understanding of Irish feminism.

The first essential is a perspective within which to place Irish feminist activity and against which to test it. This requirement is filled by Richard J. Evans's book, *The Feminists*.[2] It provides a broad comparative survey of feminist movements in Europe and most of the English-speaking world, while making no reference at all to Irish feminism. It also provides an explanatory hypothesis against which the Irish experience can be tested.

Evans first discusses the origins of nineteenth-century feminist movements, and then follows their development in the different countries he considers. Feminist movements he defines as organisations of women 'expressly created in order to fight for the emancipation of the female sex as a whole'.[3] Their origin he sees in an interaction between ideological and socio-economic forces.

The ideological basis he finds in the fusion of Enlightenment rationalism and the religious individualism of Protestantism, which resulted in nineteenth-century liberalism. The Enlightenment emphasis on the power of human reason to reform society, and also to criticise it and to legitimate criticism, had obvious potential for feminism. Much Enlightenment literature challenged lack of equality in various areas of human life, and a body of it supported the right of women, on the grounds of shared human reason, to equal education, equal access to employment and equal political rights. Evans sees the Protestant emphasis on the responsibility of individuals for their own salvation as also having clear, if latent, potential for feminism.

Liberalism saw the human race as developing and progressing by way of the removal of restrictions on individual development and achievement. Women were an obvious case where development and achievement were stunted by disabilities imposed on individuals on the basis of birth. In the name of *laissez faire* liberal individualism could be called on to support the equality of the sexes in terms of the removal of positive restrictions on one of them.

Indeed, the overt restrictions imposed on women amounted to a comprehensive man-made barrier to any possibility of economic, social or political equality between the sexes. While details might vary from country to country the overall pattern of discrimination was amazingly constant, so that Evans can advance a categorisation broadly applicable across all the countries with which he deals.[4] Women were excluded from participating in political life by holding public office, standing for election or voting. Restrictions on the holding of property and on involvement in business, trade and the professions barred them from economic independence. Denial of basic rights in civil and criminal law underlay many of the other disabilities and in itself gave men authority over women's lives. A moral double-standard made women the punishable party in cases of illegitimacy, prostitution and adultery. Finally, the objectives and practice of education differed for males and females, so that girls were specifically trained for domestication and subordination.

In spite of this artificially created and self-perpetuating dependency of women on men Evans does not think that the intellectual support that feminism could claim from liberal ideology is sufficient in itself to explain why feminist protest, not itself a novel phenomenon, should at this period have produced organised feminist movements. More than intellectual conviction was necessary, he argues, and he finds an answer in economic and social factors.

He identifies change in class structure as the dynamism behind the emergence of feminist movements.[5] By this he means the development of the middle classes in line with the expansion of trade, industry, administration and the professions. Within a rapidly-changing society the middle classes advanced in number, wealth, power, self-image and ambition. They abandoned earlier aspirations to rise to the ranks of the aristocracy, and redefined their aims and values in terms of an ethic of hard work and achievement, within which the individual was seen to succeed on the basis of personal merit.

This was an ethic whose practice was strictly confined to males. Indeed, as middle-class men increasingly built their self-esteem on their individual achievement in economic, social and political life, middle-class women were even more firmly than before debarred from the possibility of emulating them. The professionalisation of more and more desired occupations, which protected the interests of middle-class men, squeezed women out more completely than before. It correspondingly devalued the few occupations available to middle-class women. These developments, together with the separation of home and workplace, meant that within marriage also middle-class women found the actual and comparative content of their role as housewife seriously diminished. It became increasingly difficult for them to value either a relatively leisured life in the home or a precarious struggle for survival in the workplace in terms of their men's new ethic of work, achievement and success. Evans sees the first organised feminist movements as their response to this challenge, a demand by middle-class women that the theory and practice of liberalism be applied to women as well as to men.

Within any particular country Evans identifies the influences that helped or hindered the development of these movements. 'In favour were Protestant religion, liberal polity, bourgeois society, against were Catholic church, authoritarian constitution, feudalism and aristocracy'.[6] He also identifies a characteristic model or pattern of development followed by feminist movements,[7] a pattern from which particular movements might of course deviate to a lesser or greater extent. The pattern began with what was called 'moderate' feminism, which was concerned with economic, educational and legal rights, and then it developed into 'radical' feminism, concerned first with issues of moral reform of society and then, and more especially, with the franchise. The first essential prerequisite for full participation in society was economic independence. So feminists demanded for married women control over their own property and for single women access to higher education and the professions. In the next stage of moral reform they were particularly involved in the areas of temperance movements and sexual morality, both of which had something to offer both to women as a group and to middle-class interests generally. Evans sees involvement in these moral dimensions as having a radicalising effect on feminist aims and tactics, or, as he seems to mean, politicising them so that they turned to the demand for the vote as the means of access to political power to enforce their other objectives. The vote then rapidly acquired the status of a symbol of feminist demands generally, around which all feminists could rally and it became for many a basic objective in itself. After that stage was reached Evans sees organised feminism undergoing further vicissitudes, but this article is concerned with the model only up to that point in its development.

II

What we know of early organised feminism in Ireland seems to fit Evans's model. The membership of the groups involved appears to have been small and to have been drawn largely from Protestant middle-class women working closely with their English counterparts. Irishwomen and Englishwomen shared the same general disabilities under English law. They also shared similar problems in the discriminatory theory and practice of female education and in exclusion from the professions and political life. Within the United Kingdom they were both located within a liberal polity which tolerated organised dissent up to a point. In the early stages, when co-operation was closest, they sought redress from the same representative bourgeois parliament at Westminster.

On some issues Irish feminists seem to have shared a joint campaign with Englishwomen, as in that for the married women's property acts and the Social Purity Crusade. On others, as employment, education and the vote, it seems that they may have initially followed an English lead, but their campaigns were separate and developed differently. Differences inevitably arose from the colonial relationship between Britain and Ireland which increasingly faced feminists with diverging outside influences, problems and opportunities. When Home Rule became an imminent possibility, Irish feminists found themselves pressing for suffrage from the United Kingdom parliament and at the same time demanding its inclusion in any new constitutional arrangements in Ireland. Feminists themselves could differ on tactics and in their extra-feminist loyalties, as well as on the relative priority they gave the latter in relation to their strictly feminist objectives.

Feminist action on the linked issues of the employment and education of middle-class women was under way by the early 1860s at least with the foundation in 1861 of the Queen's Institute for the Training and Employment of Educated Women in

Dublin and in 1867 of the Ladies' Institute in Belfast. The inadequacy of the education of the 'educated women' pushed feminist action towards raising the general standard of middle-class female education. The employment motivation merged with the influence of the English movement to give girls as well as boys an education aimed at intellectual development as an aim in itself. Pioneering institutions were the Belfast High School for Girls, later known as Victoria College, founded in 1859, and Alexandra College for the Higher Education of Women founded in Dublin in 1866.[8] This development is seen as a major breakthrough in women's education as it produced the women teachers who could bring girls' secondary education up to the academic level of that of boys and provided a link between secondary and university education.[9]

The next major breakthrough came with the passing of the Intermediate Education Act in 1878 and the Royal University Act in 1879. Neither was in any way intended to contribute to the education of women. Both were *ad hoc* solutions to the British government's problem of finding some indirect method of subsidising male Catholic education in Ireland. The opportunity for women lay in the fact that the solution adopted in each case was to establish a purely examining and award-giving body and did not require compulsory attendance at any specified institutions. In each case the feminists recognised a golden opportunity, and lobbied successfully[10] to have girls and women included in the legislation.

So far all this had been achieved by a small body of Protestant feminists. Meanwhile development in the secondary education of Catholic girls had been in the direction of distinctly middle-class 'respectable' fee-paying convent schools as a response to the demands of

Catholic middle-class social aspirations.[11] The education provided in these by the religious orders was aimed at religious formation and preparation for domesticity. Academic and cultural subjects tended to be taught more at the level of accomplishments than as intellectual disciplines. But once the Protestant women had opened the door to new possibilities in female education the convent schools began to avail of the opportunities. As early as 1884 fifteen convent schools entered girls in the intermediate examinations, in spite of the indifference or hostility of many bishops. Catholic provision of education for university degrees followed and the Dominican St Mary's College, Merrion Square, and Loreto College, Stephen's Green, both in Dublin, were established among the leading women's colleges by the early 1890s. The driving force behind these developments was pressure from the Catholic middle class who made it clear that unless they got the educational provision they wanted in Catholic institutions they would seek it in Protestant equivalents.[12]

When the time came for the final settlement of the university question the feminists, now including Protestant and Catholic, had two organisations in the field to fight their case; the Central Association of Irish School Mistresses and the more recent Irish Association of Women Graduates. They both argued for fully co-educational institutions as the only way by which women could share in the higher standards made possible by endowments. Understandably the women's colleges, both Protestant and Catholic, fought to survive as teaching colleges affiliated to the universities and argued the benefits of the collegiate life they could provide. In the event they lost out while the feminist case triumphed. The Irish Universities Act of 1908 set up two institutions, Queen's University, Belfast, and the

National University of Ireland, comprising the other two Queen's Colleges and the Catholic University College. Compulsory attendance was imposed – no women's colleges were affiliated to either university – but women were admitted on equal terms with men to the teaching, degrees, honours and offices of both.[13]

Other areas of early Irish feminist activity await investigation, though it seems that there was activity on all the major issues in international feminism identified by Evans. There was an Irish input into the campaign for legislation to protect married women's property. The issue here was the right of married women to control over their own inherited and earned property, and so it affected women from all social classes. Feminists and others often saw it as concerning working-class and lower middle-class women most immediately in its relation to earnings, since the property of wealthy women could be protected by the legal stratagems developed by the courts of equity to allow propertied families to circumvent the common law. Anna Haslam,[14] a Quaker from Youghal living in Dublin, and Isabella Tod, of Presbyterian stock living in Belfast, both of whom seem to have been active in every branch of Irish feminist organisation, were involved in the campaign. Isabella Tod gave evidence before a select committee in 1868 on the advantages of such an act to working-class women in the Belfast area.[15] Petitions in favour of an act were organised in both Dublin and Belfast and there was a women's committee at work in Dublin.[16] Considerable progress in establishing the principle of spouses' separate property was achieved with the Married Womens' Property Acts of 1870, 1874, 1882 and 1907.

Irish feminists were also involved in the area of moral reform and sexual equality. Again both Anna Haslam and Isabella Tod were active in the Social Purity Crusade led by Josephine Butler. Haslam and her husband, also a feminist, became associated with Josephine Butler in 1869 and worked 'for ten years in this great fight, rousing public opinion by means of meetings, petitions and various forms of active propaganda'[17] until success was finally achieved. The campaign was aimed at repeal of the series of Contagious Diseases Acts, passed during the 1860s, which regulated prostitution in certain designated areas. They provided for compulsory registration of prostitutes as well as making them liable to compulsory medical examination and, if found to be suffering from venereal disease, to compulsory treatment. Three of the designated areas were in Ireland, the Curragh, Cork and Queenstown [Cobh]. For feminists there was a general moral issue in the tacit encouragement given to vice by any state regulation and a specifically feminist issue in the double standard which did not interfere with the men involved, but treated the women as commodities to be periodically cleansed and recycled as 'clean harlots for the army and navy'.[18]

Most areas of early feminist activity in Ireland still await exploration. Even a superficial testing of Evans's model indicates that most of the major issues attracted action. Petitions, public meetings, letters to newspapers and lobbying of politicians all point to organisation. Women's involvement in temperance movements,[19] abolition of slavery campaigns, women's committees within the churches and philanthropy of all kinds all need investigation. A comparative study of the activity of Catholic and Protestant women in these and other areas would add to our understanding of Irish feminism. Then we need a new look at nuns. The founding mothers of the religious orders of sisters were usually women in the heroic mould who themselves broke out of sex-role stereotyping and organised other women to follow suit.

Why did they or their successors turn these organisations into formal religious orders, thereby bringing them under the direct control of the male authority-structure of the Catholic Church? What are the implications for the history of Irish feminism of the availability to Catholic women of a career as a nun? Above all, perhaps, we need knowledge of the lives of as many individual women as possible. But we need biographies which do not concentrate simply on women's contribution to male-defined movements and goals. We need to ask how women saw their own lives, with their opportunities, aspirations and limitations and how they individually tried to reconcile these to their own best advantage in specific historical situations.

III

The early stages of the suffrage movement again seem to fit Evans's model. The first Irish suffrage society appeared some years after the emergence of feminist organisation on economic, educational and moral issues. Again Anna Haslam and Isabella Tod were in at the beginning, and Haslam founded the first independent Irish group, the Dublin Women's Suffrage Association, in 1876.[20] Its membership was predominantly Quaker, including men as well as women, and it worked by the usual methods of petitions, public lectures, letters to newspapers and lobbying of MPs. It expanded its range and changed its name to the Irishwomen's Suffrage and Local Government Association. Progress was slow, but in 1896 women became eligible as poor law guardians and in 1898 they won the local government franchise and the right to be district councillors.[21]

In the early years of the twentieth century a new generation of educated women, beneficiaries of the achievement of the earlier feminists and many of them

Catholic, arrived on the public scene. These women had been socialised in the cultural and political renaissance of the late nineteenth century. A more assertive, less patient and often nationalist-oriented type of feminist appeared, ready if necessary to use unconstitutional tactics. The Irish Women's Franchise League (IWFL), founded in 1908 by a group including Hanna Sheehy Skeffington and Margaret Cousins, was modelled on the militant English society, the Women's Social and Political Union (WSPU), whose 'spirited frontal attack on their government'[22] the Irishwomen greatly admired. But they were clear that the Irish situation demanded its own strategies and Irish leadership. Suffrage societies proliferated around the country in a growth and expansion achieved by no other Irish feminist movement. During the early stages of expansion the feminists succeeded in maintaining a united position in spite of individual unionist or nationalist sympathies. Their agreed policy was to support measures of female suffrage from whatever quarter they might come. But over the following years the mounting climax in the colonial relationship between Britain and Ireland imposed severe strain on the policy of 'Suffrage First – Above All Else!' and under it suffragist unity gradually disintegrated.

The immediate political context was the imminence of Home Rule after 1911. The priorities of the IWFL were to ensure that female suffrage was included in the Home Rule Bill and to pressurise Irish MPs to support any women's suffrage bill that came before parliament. Many members of the Irish Party were sympathetic, but when Redmond decided that their support might be detrimental to the interests of either Home Rule or the party itself they fell in line and voted against. In 1912 their opposition defeated an all party 'conciliation' bill which would have conceded a limited female suffrage.

The English WSPU retaliated by declaring opposition to Home Rule itself. Irish suffragists stepped up the pressure on the Irish Party to have suffrage included in the Home Rule Bill then before parliament. When Redmond remained immovable the feminists responded with a mass meeting of unprecedented size. Suffrage societies, unionist and nationalist, from all parts of the country, gathered in Dublin to demand that suffrage be included in the bill.[23] When this too was ignored the IWFL stepped up its militancy from organised heckling of political meetings to breaking windows in public buildings which led to a number of its members serving jail sentences. Between 1912 and 1914 thirty-five women were convicted for suffrage offences.[24]

Public reaction tended to see militant tactics as anti-Home Rule, anti-nationalist, or unwomanly behaviour, and sometimes all three. Such attitudes were reinforced by the intervention of the English WSPU, two of whose members threw a hatchet, variously described as 'small', 'blunt' and a 'toy', at the prime minister, Asquith, during his visit to Dublin in July 1912, and later tried to set fire to the Theatre Royal. The IWFL, blamed for the WSPU's activities as well as its own, suffered some bad press and some loss of membership.

Pressure on the alliance between unionist and nationalist suffragists was added to during a brief period of euphoria in 1913 when it seemed that the Ulster Unionist Council might commit itself to the inclusion of female suffrage in its plan for a provisional government to be set up if Home Rule became a reality. The English WSPU promptly established a branch in Belfast[25] which attracted Ulster suffragists whose own societies tended to be small and non-militant. Meanwhile the IWFL had little success in extending into Ulster because it was seen as being 'tainted with Nationalism'.[26] When Sir Edward

Carson made it clear that votes for women would not be included, the WSPU retaliated with large scale arson against unionist property.

The outbreak of war in 1914 increased the strain on suffragist unity. A core group remained committed to a 'Suffrage First – Above All Else!' position, while others decided that for the time being their unionist or nationalist loyalties must take precedence. Suffrage groups whose allegiance was to unionism tended to drop suffrage activity for the duration and turn to war work for the British cause. The gap between them and the suffrage-first position was widened by the pacifist stance of the suffrage newspaper, the *Irish Citizen*. The gap also widened between the suffrage-first position and those nationalist suffragists who believed that England's difficulty was Ireland's opportunity. By now there were women's organisations, the Ulster Women's Unionist Council (1911) and Cumann na mBan (1914), affiliated to the two male armed forces, the Ulster Volunteers and the Irish Volunteers, on either side of the political divide. These attracted many women who also supported women's suffrage.

The Home Rule bill had now become law, with its operation suspended until after the war and with the position of Ulster yet to be decided. John Redmond adopted a policy of support for Britain as being in the best interests of Home Rule. When the Irish Volunteers split, with the majority following Redmond, Cumann na mBan rejected his policy and opted for the revolutionary nationalist side.

The issues between the suffrage-first position and the nation-first position were fought in the pages of the *Irish Citizen*. They centred on how rather than whether suffrage should be achieved. One side argued that national freedom must come before that of a section, and the emancipation of women follow that of the nation. It also argued that in logic nationalists could not ask Britain for the vote. The *Irish Citizen* editorials insisted that feminists could not compromise on or postpone women's rights and deplored the fact that nationalist women accepted a status subordinate to that of men, the position of a 'slave woman' within the movement.[27]

In spite of these differences and the continuing decline of the suffrage movements in numbers and activity, there was a close relationship between the IWFL and the revolutionary nationalists which now gave the feminists a major victory. James Connolly was a feminist by conviction, and in turn many suffragists found that interaction with socialist ideas pushed their own aims beyond votes for 'ladies' to votes for 'women'. R.M. Fox in 1935 looked back to the days when the IWFL and the *Irish Citizen*

> formed a rallying point for all the best and most progressive elements in Dublin. In its pages the anti-conscription struggle, and other vital issues, received attention … Madame Markievicz, Connolly, Pearse, MacDonagh and many other pioneers of the Rebellion, used the platform of the Franchise League to express their views.[28]

The 1916 proclamation recognised women as full citizens and this recognition survived to find constitutional expression in 1922. This achievement is seen as jointly that of the pre-1916 suffrage campaign which 'forced the issue into the political vocabulary' of the revolutionary nationalist leadership, and of Cumann na mBan.[29] The latter became increasingly assertive of women's rights to equality during their 'years of strength'[30] between 1916 and 1921 and insisted on fulfilment of the commitment of 1916.

In a compromise between the Liberal and Conservative parties a limited measure of female suffrage, confined to women over thirty, was granted in 1918. While women in the new state of Northern Ireland had to wait until 1928 for full suffrage, this was given in the constitution of the Irish Free State in 1922. But by then the *Irish Citizen* had disappeared and the IWFL and organised feminism were becoming less visible on the public scene. Hanna Sheehy Skeffington, who herself personified the tensions imposed on so many women by the conflicting claims of feminism and nationalism, assessed the situation in the final issue of the *Citizen* in 1920. Ireland, she wrote, was now in 'a state of war', and, just as in other European countries during the recent great war,

> the women's movement merged into the national movement, temporarily, at least, and women became patriots rather than feminists, and heroes' wives or widows rather than human beings, so now in Ireland the national struggle overshadows all else.

Feminism could only mark time and wait. But in the meantime there

> can be no woman's paper without a woman's movement, without earnest and serious-minded women readers and thinkers – and these in Ireland have dwindled perceptibly of late, partly owing to the cause above mentioned, and partly because since a measure, however limited, of suffrage has been granted, women are forging out their own destiny in practical fields of endeavour.[31]

Organised Irish feminism had not disappeared by 1922. But it was reduced in numbers, had lost the incalculable contribution of a specifically feminist public voice in its own newspaper and was overshadowed in the public eye by the problems of the Free State. Above all, perhaps, it had lost the unifying but problematic presence of a single concrete issue like the vote. This loss would have forced reassessment and redirection in any case, even if the other factors had not been present. Feminists could rally round an object like the vote without being forced into serious analysis of longer-term aims or into examination of their possible internal differences with regard to these, including their reasons for wanting the vote itself. With the achievement of suffrage, Irish feminism, in line with the experience of feminism in other countries, entered a new phase and this too awaits historical investigation.

IV

Evans's book proved a useful starting-point for this tentative approach to an overview of Irish feminist organisation in the nineteenth and early twentieth centuries. In the first place it suggested where one might look for evidence of feminist activity. Then the fact that there *was* organised action of some kind on so many of the major issues does two things. It provides a foundation for further research on the Irish scene and it links Irish feminism directly to the international scene, a link which will obviously repay investigation.

It also seems clear that the testing of his analysis of the influences favouring and inhibiting feminist development against the Irish situation has potential for deepening our knowledge. Three interacting areas here seem immediately promising. One is his location of Protestantism on the side of the angels with Catholicism in the opposing camp. Another is the relationship between feminism and nationalism. The third is that between feminism and socialism.

The contribution of Quaker women – and men – in the early pioneering days is striking. We need to know more about the ways in which their religion facilitated the development or the articulation and assertion of feminist awareness in individual Protestant women.

Does the later involvement of Catholic women in the education struggle and the suffrage campaign constitute an exception to Evans's hypothesis or can it be satisfactorily explained within its terms?

Once Protestant women had forced a breach in the barricade surrounding the male educational preserve Catholic women showed little hesitation in following them. The relative speed with which they forced a revolution in convent secondary school education is impressive. In the final analysis it seems that the bishops capitulated because they set a higher priority on retaining control over the education of Catholic women than they did on refusing to compromise on the curriculum. Closer study of the various issues and participants in these developments should add considerably to our knowledge of Irish feminism and of the actual power and powerlessness of women in Irish Catholic society. How much of the pressure for change came from feminist awareness among Catholic women and how important was the economic potential of the new education? The role of economic incentives, the question of who was influenced by them, as well as the power structure and politics within Catholic families all need examination. If feminist awareness was a factor, what encouraged its articulation at this time? The extent and limitations of the revolution in convent-school education is also relevant. Did the new examination-orientated curriculum in fact foster changing self-awareness and how did it interact with values passed on in the hidden curriculum? How did the nuns who implemented the changes see the issues and their own position as women in a changing Irish society? What were their aspirations and what options did they see as available to themselves? Did the Catholic women who moved into leadership roles in the education and suffrage campaigns find problems in reconciling their feminism and their religion, and, if so, which had to yield most in the resolution?

Nationalism Evans found to be 'that profoundly ambiguous force'[32] in its relation to feminism, though he argues that the ideology of nationalism should favour female suffrage since it was based on the sovereignty of the people, which implied 'parliamentary sovereignty and the extension of the franchise'.[33] In Ireland the relationship between the two was certainly on the surface ambiguous. One group of nationalists held up the suffrage movement while another granted full suffrage some years before Britain. However, we need examination at a broader level of the contribution nineteenth-century Irish nationalism may have made to the development of feminism and feminist movements by way of a general legitimation of dissent and the provision of a vocabulary and models of constitutional and extra-constitutional pressure for civil and political demands. This might seem particularly relevant for Catholic women as nationalism and Catholicism became more closely linked. However, the fact that Irish nationalists also provided models and legitimation for the most militant English suffragists[34] suggests that the interactions may be more complex. At a more immediate level the interaction between feminism and socialism is intertwined with that between 'non-constitutional' feminists and revolutionary nationalists in the years leading up to 1916. Closer study of these relationships will add to our knowledge of Irish feminism.[35]

Evans's classification of feminist movements into 'moderate' and 'radical' raises problems. He sees feminism as proceeding from 'moderate' economic and educational demands to progressively more 'radical' stages of moral reform and the vote. This interpretation may be more useful in the controversy it raises than in a direct application of his model. He does not make it clear exactly what are the criteria of radicalism on which he bases his model. If the criterion of 'going to the root' of either a patriarchal or class structure of society is used, it is not easy to see a straight progress from moderate to radical along the stages indicated by Evans.

As has been seen, feminists faced a formidable array of economic, legal, political and social discriminations which effectively cut women off from the possibility of challenging men's dominance in all the areas of human activity claimed as 'naturally' male. The wide-ranging sweep of these restrictions, both geographically and effectively, can hardly be accepted as an accidental conglomeration of unrelated inequalities. Taken together they add up to an enforcement of conformity to a paradigm or model of male-female relations, a social construction of gender inequality whose very comprehensiveness queries its claim to a base in human 'nature'. The paradigm comprises a sex-based division of labour within a patriarchal value-system. Patriarchal values see men as 'naturally' superior to and more important than women and as naturally in authority over them. A patriarchal society structures itself accordingly. In this analysis the ultimate establishment under challenge by feminists was, and still is, the model in people's minds of what male-female relations are or should be. The model could find expression in legal, educational or political systems, in a church authority structure, a political party or a revolutionary movement. In the context of a patriarchal paradigm it seems difficult to rate suffrage as a more radical demand than, for example, economic independence. Classification along a scale from moderate to radical runs the risk of pushing feminist movements into artificially separate compartments which may obscure the complexity of interaction between ultimate aims and the available options for action.

Currently historians of feminism are reappraising the place of marriage and motherhood in the historical development of feminist thought. The thrust here is towards a holistic approach to the understanding of feminism and feminists in specific historical situations. For example, it is suggested that the history of English feminism is distorted if it is seen only in terms of efforts to gain access to the public and political spheres and if the 'immense concern' of feminists with the 'private and domestic lives' of women is ignored.[36] In the light of such reappraisal Evans's implication that acceptance of 'woman's primary role as housewife and mother' was necessarily conservative and non-radical[37] may be too limited an analysis to further the exploration of the full range of feminist thought. Examination of how these differing hypotheses fit the Irish experience will help us to determine whether the impetus behind Irish feminism can be adequately explained by the drive of middle-class women to join in the bourgeois work-achievement ethic.

If degrees of radicalism are determined by the extent to which feminist movements transcended class boundaries in objectives and practice, Evans's model of progression from moderate to radical again runs into some problems. As it applies to English feminism it has been challenged on the grounds that some of the progress was in fact in the reverse direction and that the suffrage movement actually marked the narrowing and moderation of earlier feminist objectives.[38] An issue 'of direct importance only to some middle-class women' replaced earlier concern with the 'problems of all women' as expressed in the campaigns for social purity and for married women's control of their property.[39] On the other hand, however, recent research indicates a higher working-class participation in the English suffrage movement than historians, including Evans himself, had previously suggested.[40] In Ireland the later suffrage movement showed considerable awareness of and concern for the problems of working-class women, though it seems there was little participation by the latter in the campaign for the vote.[41]

The issues raised are complex and need teasing out in each historical and geographical location. The task of assessing degrees of radicalism is further complicated by the growing consensus that the situation of women in any specific historical setting can be adequately explained only by an analysis that includes class and ethnic differences as well as the forms of patriarchy in the particular society.

Yet another strand in current historical criticism suggests possible difficulties with all interpretations, including Evans's, which locate feminist movements within particular historical and political contexts. The value of such location is not challenged, but concern is expressed that, given the inevitable patriarchal socialisation of today's historians, there is a danger that feminist thinking and feminist movements may be seen as purely derivative from predominantly male ideas and movements, when this may be an inadequate or distorted representation of the reality.[42]

The international scene in the writing of the history of feminism is an open and exciting one at present, and one in which more and more historians are joining. The value of a book like Evans's, especially when set in the context of current debate, for opening up an approach to Irish feminist history does not depend on the extent to which his models prove accurate for the Irish situation, but on the pointers it gives and the questions it raises. The extension and deepening of our knowledge of Irish feminists will probably be best served at this stage by trying to find as much information as possible on how they themselves, as individuals and as groups, saw their aspirations, opportunities, problems and limitations, how they related individual and group strategies to these, and how they differed among themselves on analysis and tactics. In other words, we need to aim at understanding as best we can the range of complexities, contradictions and differences that underlay the lives of the women who created Irish feminist movements.

from Patrick J. Corish (ed.), *Radicals, Rebels and Establishments* (Belfast, Appletree Press, 1985), pp 185–201.

NOTES

1   Rosemary Owens, 'Votes for Women: Irishwomen's Campaign for the Vote, 1876–1915' (MA thesis, UCD, 1977); Rosemary Owens, '"Votes for Ladies, Votes for Women"; Organised Labour and the Suffrage Movement, 1876–1922', *Saothar*, Vol. 9 (1983), pp 32–47; Rosemary Cullen Owens, *Smashing Times: A History of the Irish Women's Suffrage Movement* (Dublin, 1984); Anne O'Connor, 'Influences on Girls' Secondary Education in Ireland, 1860–1910' (MA thesis, UCD, 1981); Anne O'Connor, 'The Revolution in Girls' Secondary Education in Ireland, 1860–1910' in Mary Cullen (ed.), *Girls Don't Do Honours* (WEB/Arlen House, 1987); Eibhlín Breathnach, 'Women and Higher Education in Ireland, 1879–1914' (MA thesis, UCD, 1981); Eibhlín Breathnach, 'Women and Higher Education in Ireland, 1879–1914', *Crane Bag*, Vol. IV, No. 1 (1980), pp 47–54; Eibhlín Breathnach, 'Charting New Waters: The Experience of Women in Higher Education 1873–1912', in Cullen, *Girls Don't Do Honours*; Margaret Mac Curtain, 'Women, the Vote and Revolution' in Margaret Mac Curtain and Donncha Ó Corráin (ed.), *Women in Irish Society* (Dublin, 1978), pp 46–57; Margaret Ward, '"Suffrage First – Above all Else!"' An Account of the Irish Suffrage Movement', *Feminist Review,*

Vol. 10 (1982), pp 21–36; Margaret Ward, *Unmanageable Revolutionaries: Women and Irish Nationalism* (London and Dingle, 1983).

2   *The Feminists: Women's Emancipation Movements in Europe, America and Australasia 1840–1920* (London, 1977).

3   *Ibid.*, p. 13.

4   *Ibid.*, p. 22.

5   *Ibid.*, p. 28.

6   *Ibid.*, p. 238.

7   *Ibid.*, p. 34.

8   Breathnach, 'Women and Higher Education' (1980), p. 48.

9   O'Connor, 'Revolution in Girls' Education', pp 34–5.

10 *Englishwoman's Review*, Vol. XI (1880), pp 119–20.

11 O'Connor, 'Revolution in Girls' Education', pp 41–4.

12 *Ibid*, pp 45–6.

13 Breathnach, 'Women and Higher Education' (1980), pp 52–3.

14 Newspaper cutting, 23 August 1914, Historical Library, Religious Society of Friends, Eustace St., Dublin, Cup. B/65.

15 *Special Report from the Select Committee on the Married Women's Property Bill*, [4417], H.C. 1867–8, cccxxxix, 74–5.

16 *Ibid.*, p. 76.

17 *Irish Citizen*, 23 November 1915.

18 Evidence of Josephine Butler (*Report of the Royal Commission upon the Administration and Operation of the Contagious Diseases Acts, vol ii, Minutes of Evidence*, p. 440, H.C. 1871 (408–1), xix).

19 Isabella Tod had 'taken up the temperance question strongly' from early youth, *Englishwoman's Review*, Vol. XXVIII (1897), p. 60.

20 Owens, 'Votes for Women', pp 8–9.

21 *Ibid.*, pp 17–18.

22 Margaret Cousins in J.H. and M.E. Cousins, We *Two Together* (Madras, 1950), p. 164.

23 *Irish Citizen*, 8 June 1912.

24 Owens, 'Votes for Women', p. 126.

25 Ward, 'Suffrage First', pp 30–31.

26 Hanna Sheehy Skeffington, 'Reminiscences of an Irish Suffragette', in A.D. Sheehy Skeffington and R. Owens, *Votes for Women: Irishwomen's Struggle for the Vote* (Dublin, 1975), p. 16.

27 *Irish Citizen*, 11 April, 23 May 1914.

28 R.M. Fox, *Rebel Irishwomen* (Dublin, 1935), p. 138.

29   Ward, 'Suffrage First', p. 35.

30   Ward, *Unmanageable Revolutionaries,* pp 119–55.

31   *Irish Citizen,* September-December 1920.

32   Evans, *The Feminists,* p. 238.

33   *Ibid.*

34   *Ibid.,* p. 190.

35   This study has already begun with Owens, '"Votes for Ladies"'.

36   Barbara Caine, 'Feminism, Suffrage and the Nineteenth-Century English Women's Movement', *Women's Studies International Forum,* Vol. V (1982), p. 537.

37   Evans, *The Feminists,* p. 234.

38   Caine, 'Feminism, Suffrage', pp 549–50.

39   *Ibid.,* p. 550.

40   Joan Wallach Scott, 'Women in History: The Modern Period', survey article, *Past & Present,* No. 101 (1983), p. 148.

41   Owens, '"Votes for ladies"', p. 44.

42   Elizabeth Sarah, 'Finding a Feminist Historical Framework', *Women's Studies International Forum,* Vol. V (1982), pp 701–9.

BREADWINNERS AND PROVIDERS:
WOMEN IN THE HOUSEHOLD ECONOMY
OF LABOURING FAMILIES 1835–6

This essay was a contribution to Women Surviving: Studies in Irish
Women's History in the 19th and 20th Centuries, *published in 1989.*
The book was an important contribution to the development of women's
history in Ireland. The editors, Maria Luddy and Cliona Murphy, aimed at
a collection bringing together studies of 'a broad range of women in society,
the ordinary rather than the exceptional, to show how groups of
Irishwomen and individuals responded to society and the realities of their
everyday existence'. Contributions included studies of prostitution,
workhouses, domestic servants, family economy, religious women and
female spirituality, as well as suffrage and women in the Oireachtas
debates in the 1920s and 1930s. Overall the book brought out the resilience
and resourcefulness of the women studied, and made a major contribution
to the study of ordinary women. My essay looked at the role of women in
the economy of labouring and cottier families as this emerged in the Poor
Law Inquiry Reports of 1835–6. These families comprised about three-
quarters of the entire population and an impressive pattern of co-operative
survival strategies emerged. It was also a revelation to find how much
information on women could be found in sources focused for the most part
on men, compiled by men and based on evidence given almost exclusively
by men.

This article examines the role of women in the household
economy of labouring families as it emerges in the reports
of the commission of inquiry into the condition of the

poor in 1835–6. This shows that the labouring family operated as an interdependent economic unit where husband and wife – and children when they were old enough – contributed to family survival by paid and unpaid work. It establishes that the wife's contribution was a crucial one without which the economic unit could not have survived.

Labouring families adopted different strategies as their economic fortunes fluctuated. There were two main situations; in the first a family managed to live in more or less relative comfort, by its own independent labour; in the second its independent labour was not sufficient and supplementary methods had to be sought. In both situations a family continued to operate as an interdependent unit which maximised the economic potential of its different members.

In the relatively good times of survival by independent labour all able-bodied family members worked on the potato crop which provided their staple diet. All members also contributed earned income as opportunity allowed. In spite of the decline of domestic industry, in which they had been able to make substantial earnings, women still made a surprisingly large contribution to household income. This was in addition to their contribution through child rearing, food preparation and care of the home, activities to which the poor inquiry did not attach an economic value but which were vital to family survival.

When and if a family could no longer live by independent labour, a situation whose immediate cause was usually the husband's failure to get adequate employment, the wife regularly became the sole family breadwinner for the crisis period. In the economy of labouring families begging was women's work. She begged and by begging could support the entire family while it had no other resources. She could also support herself and her children over a period of months while her husband went to seek work and to try to save enough to re-establish the family at home.

Little of the evidence used here came from women themselves, and the inquiry showed little interest in their views or attitudes. It does not tell us much about how they experienced their lives or what they thought about them. It tells little directly about family relationships; about affection between wives, husbands and their children; or about autonomy and the location of decision-making and power. It does reveal a good deal about the structure of the family economy and of women's vital role in this, and, in doing so, raises questions about some of these issues.

This article is divided into four sections; a brief discussion of the source; an examination of women's explicitly economic contribution to the day-to-day survival of a family while it supported itself by independent labour; an examination of women's contribution to family survival when independent labour failed and it had to turn to combinations of labour, begging, migration and vagrancy; and a brief consideration of some of the implications of the findings.

The Poor Inquiry as Source

The brief given to the commissioners was 'to inquire into the condition of the poorer classes of your majesty's subjects in Ireland, and into the various institutions at present established by law for their relief'[1] and to suggest what further provisions might be made. In the process of carrying out this task the commissioners gathered an enormous amount of evidence about the conditions of life of the poor in Ireland.

They divided the evidence-gathering process into two sections. The first dealt with the *extent* of destitution and the various existing systems of providing relief and their effectiveness, while the second was concerned with the possible *causes* of destitution. The allocation of a social group to either category was made on the basis of preliminary enquiries which identified the aspects of poverty widely regarded as significant.

Women greatly outnumbered men among the destitute. Seven topics were included in the examination of the extent of destitution and the existing methods of relieving it. These were: deserted and orphan children; illegitimate children and their mothers; widows having families of young children; the impotent through age or other infirmity; the sick poor, who in health were capable of earning their subsistence; the able-bodied out of work; and vagrancy as a mode of relief.

The first topic obviously affected the lives of many more women than men. The second and third concerned groups comprised solely of women and children. The fourth and fifth included both women and men, but the evidence indicates there were more females than males, especially among the aged. The sixth dealt with unemployed men while the seventh showed that far higher numbers of women than men begged. These last two categories are to an extent inter-connected since many of the women counted among the vagrant beggars had husbands who were included in the able-bodied unemployed. Both these groups were relevant to the subject of this article.

The commissioners adopted two complementary methods of gathering information. The first was the time-honoured method of asking important people in the localities for their views. A set of 'statistical questions' was sent to clergy, magistrates, heads of police and 'educated persons'. This list immediately excluded the possibility of any woman being asked to fill in a questionnaire since there were no women clergy, magistrates or heads of police and the restrictions surrounding the education of women and girls[2] made it unlikely that any woman would qualify for selection as an 'educated person' as understood by the commissioners, themselves all male establishment figures. It further excluded all men who were not members of an elite group of the well-off and privileged.

Some 7,600 questionnaires were sent out and replies were received from about 3,100 witnesses covering 1,100 parishes. Two of the questions related to the earnings of women and children. Question 11 asked 'Are women and children usually employed in labour and at what rate of wages?' and question 14 asked:

> What in the whole might his (the labourer's) wife and four children, all of an age to work (the eldest not more than 16 years of age) earn within the year, obtaining as before an *average* amount of employment?

The fact that question 11 was confined to agricultural employment and did not include other sources of earnings limited its value for this article. Question 14 was potentially useful but did not turn out to be so for a number of reasons: respondents' answers differed wildly from one to another and an individual respondent's answer to the first question was frequently irreconcilable with his answer to the second. The cause of much of the confusion appears to have arisen from the location and wording of question 14, which led some respondents to understand they were asked to calculate the earnings of women and children on the assumption that they obtained the same average amount of employment as men, which was of course rarely, if ever, the case.[3]

There was another problem with the statistical question method which was duly noted by the commissioners. 'To obtain information sufficiently extensive in its range, and sufficiently impartial' in this way was 'obviously impossible'.[4] One man from a particular religious, social and economic class, however well informed, could not of his own knowledge supply full and accurate information on all aspects of the conditions of the poor in his locality. Equally important was the certainty that information on a topic as sensitive as the extent and causes of Irish poverty was going to encounter considerable problems of credibility if it was seen to come solely from clergy, magistrates, heads of police and 'educated persons'.

The idea of local examinations was based on the belief that the information most likely to be accurate and, equally important, most likely to be accepted as such by the greatest number of people, would be that which was seen to be agreed to by a wide cross section of Irish society. The method of achieving this was local enquiry sessions. These were to be presided over by two assistant commissioners sitting together, one Irish and one English, so that knowledge of the Irish scene and an outsider's objectivity could be combined in the conduct of the examinations. No-one else was to be allowed to preside or ask questions. Each 'grade in society ... each of the various religious persuasions ... each party in politics' was to be present. The testimony of each class was to be given equal attention, and the examination was to take place 'in the presence of all'. The names of those attending and giving evidence and, as far as possible, the actual words used by witnesses were to be recorded, the latter as a precaution against mis-interpretation. The assistant commissioners were to record the evidence and the impressions they themselves formed at the time. In the anticipation that there might be some conflicting evidence they were instructed to make it clear to all attending that a statement or opinion put forward by any witness and which was not challenged by anyone else would be considered to be accepted by all present as at least probably correct.[5]

Local examinations into the seven topics relating to destitution and modes of relief were held in one parish in every barony in seventeen counties; Galway, Mayo, Roscommon, Sligo, Carlow, Kildare, Longford, Westmeath, Wexford, Clare, Cork, Kerry, Limerick, Tipperary, Antrim, Donegal and Derry. Examinations into the topics identified as possible causes of poverty were held in thirty-two baronies in twenty-two counties; Galway, Leitrim, Mayo, Sligo, Dublin, Kilkenny, King's County, Louth, Meath, Queen's County, Wicklow, Clare, Kerry, Limerick, Tipperary, Waterford, Armagh, Cavan, Tyrone, Fermanagh, Down, and Monaghan. The evidence found most useful for this article came from the baronial examination into labourers' expenditure and into the earnings of women and children, and from the parochial examinations concerning the able-bodied out of work and vagrancy as a method of relief. The first two provided most of the information about women's contribution to the economy of a family living by independent labour. The second two revealed the nature and extent of women's contribution when a family could no longer so survive.

One strength of the local examinations as a source was their structure as laid down by the commissioners. The fact that witnesses from the various religious, political and class affiliations presented their evidence in each other's presence gave some confidence that information which was seriously inaccurate would have been challenged and have failed to find its way into the agreed consensus view on any topic. The efforts of the assistant commissioners at many of the examinations to establish general patterns agreed by all present were particularly useful. Where there was an explicit consensus it seemed safe to take this as a reasonably accurate approximation to the reality. Where no explicit consensus was forthcoming it was difficult to generalise on the basis of the testimony of the individual witnesses. These often contradicted each other, or used hyperbolic language, or their version diverged significantly from the consensus reached at the same examination.

Another strength was that the commissioners were concerned with the situation of the 'average' or 'typical' labourer rather than with extremes of either poverty or prosperity. While the number of baronial examinations was relatively small yet their geographical distribution covered much of the country and their objective was to find the general pattern of labouring families' household economy. This, of course, was what was needed to assess the extent and pattern of women's contribution.

Thirdly, the local examinations did in fact provide a considerable amount of information on women's economic activity. By using the agreed consensus views, and the opinions formed by the assistant commissioners themselves, it was possible to identify a pattern of women's economic contribution which was essentially similar in all parts of the country where examinations took place. It was possible to identify the main components of women's income-generating activity and the proportion of total family income their earnings constituted.

Having said this it must also be said that the evidence for women's contributions was not always readily recognised. The major reason for this was the paradigm of family economy underlying the structure of the report itself. The evidence was collected and presented within a frame of reference which saw the labourer-father as the family head and provider. All family income was regarded as his no matter which member of the family actually earned it. Since the English common law gave a husband a legal right to his wife's earnings there was, strictly speaking, no factual inaccuracy in this. As Blackstone explained, this depended on the fact that, in the eyes of the law

> the very being and existence of the woman is suspended during the coverture, or entirely merged or incorporated into that of the husband ... it follows, that whatever personal property belonged to the wife ... is absolutely vested in the husband.[6]

The resulting ambiguities created problems in identifying women's contributions. It was, for example, under the heading 'labourer's income' that the most detailed evidence of his wife's earnings was found. This sort of ambiguity is a recurring problem when searching for evidence of women's activity in source material compiled within terms of a patriarchal paradigm.

Women's Economic Contribution While the Family Lived by Independent Labour

At nineteen of the baronial examinations into 'labourer's expenditure' an agreed budget showing, in varying degrees of detail, the estimated yearly income of the typical labourer in the area was drawn up. These calculations of 'labourer's earnings' were the source which revealed the pattern of women's contributions and its importance to balancing the family budget. Those compiled in the baronies of Kells Upper and Lower, and Moyfenragh in County Meath, Talbotstown in County Wicklow, Portnahinch in Queen's County (Laois), and Dundalk Upper in County Louth were the most detailed and will be considered first. In all these baronies separate budgets for the yearly income and the yearly expenditure of both constantly employed and occasionally employed labourers were drawn up. In Kells, Portnahinch and Talbotstown the budgets for the occasionally employed were further subdivided according to the amount of employment the labourer obtained during the course of a year. These carefully itemised budgets were particularly useful for establishing the extent and value of women's contributions. They were based on a family of husband, wife and three or four young children.

1: Barony of Kells, Co. Meath

SUNDRY GAINS

	£ s d
Produce of 3 roods conacre potato ground, 45 barrels eating potatoes at 3s 4d plus 15 barrels small potatoes used for pig and seed	7 10 0
Profit on pig	1 10 0
Total £ 9 0 0	
Deduct rent of 2½ acres conacre tilled and manured by farmer at 7 per acre	4 7 6
	4 12 6
Remaining ½ rood rent free, being manured by pig manure mixed with ditch earth, bog stuff etc.	
Add net produce of fowls in eggs and chickens	0 10 0
Earnings of wife and children by field work, manufacture, gleaning, etc.	0 10 0
Total £5 12 6	

BUDGET FOR LABOURERS CONSTANTLY EMPLOYED

INCOME		EXPENDITURE	
Sundry gains as above	5 12 6	52 barrels potatoes	8 13 0
Deduct what he pays		Oatmeal	1 15 0
neighbour to assist him		Turf	0 10 0
and family in planting		Milk, Butter, etc called 'kitchen'	
and digging potatoes	1 0 0	at 6d per wk	1 6 0
	4 12 6	Tobacco	0 10 0
Labourer's Wages	12 0 0	Soap and candles	0 5 0
		Rent of cabin	2 0 0
	_____	Clothes	1 13 6
Total	£ 16 12 6	Total	£16 12 6

Budget for the First Class of Labourer
Occasionally Employed

Income		Expenditure	
Sundry gains as above	5 12 6	52 barrels potatoes	8 13 0
Labourer's wages	6 15 0	Meal for a few weeks at harvest	0 8 0
		Turf	0 10 0
		Kitchen at 3d a wk	0 13 0
		Rent of cabin	1 10 0
		Left for clothes, kitchen etc.	0 13 6
Total	£ 12 7 6	Total	£12 7 6

Budget for Second Class of Labourer
Occasionally Employed

Income		Expenditure	
Sundry gains as above	5 12 6	52 barrels potatoes	8 13 0
Labourer's wages	5 5 10	Rent of cabin	1 10 0
		Left for fuel, kitchen clothes	0 15 4
Total	£10 18 4	Total	£10 18 4

Budget for the Third Class of Labourer
Occasionally Employed

Income		Expenditure	
Sundry gains as above	5 12 6	52 barrels potatoes	8 13 0
Labourer's wages	3 6 4	Left for rent of cabin, fuel, kitchen, clothes	0 5 10
Total	£ 8 18 10	Total	£ 8 18 10

Source: *Poor Inquiry, First Report,* Appendix D, pp 100–1.

2: Barony of Portnahinch, Queen's County

BUDGET OF LABOURER
CONSTANTLY EMPLOYED

INCOME		EXPENDITURE	
Profit on pig	1 10 0	Rent 1 rood conacre potato	
Profit on fowls in eggs		land, tilled and manured	
and chickens	0 10 0	by farmer	2 10 0
Earnings by wife and		20 barrels eating potatoes	
children by field-work,		to supplement those grown	
gleaning, manufacture	0 10 0	by family for themselves	
Labourer's wages	9 10 0	and pig	4 0 0
		Rent of cabin	2 0 0
		Turf	0 12 6
		Kitchen	0 17 4
		Clothes	1 5 2
		Tobacco, soap,	
	_____	candles	0 15 0
Total	£ 12 0 0	Total £ 12 0 0	

BUDGET OF FIRST CLASS LABOURER
OCCASIONALLY EMPLOYED

INCOME		EXPENDITURE	
Profit on pig	1 10 0	Rent 1 rood conacre	
Profit on fowls in eggs		as above	2 10 0
and chickens	0 10 0	20 barrels eating potatoes	
Earnings by wife and		as above	4 0 0
children as above	0 10 0	Rent of cabin	1 15 0
Labourer's wages	8 1 4	Turf	0 10 0
		Kitchen	0 12 6
	_____	Left for clothes, etc.	1 3 10
Total	£ 10 11 4	Total	£ 10 11 4

BUDGET OF SECOND CLASS LABOURER OCCASIONALLY EMPLOYED

INCOME		EXPENDITURE	
Profit on pig	1 10 0	Rent 1 rood conacre	
Profit on fowls	0 10 0	as above	2 10 0
Earnings by wife and		16 barrels eating potatoes	
children as above	0 10 0	as above	3 4 0
Labourer's wages	5 19 8	Rent of cabin	1 10 0
		Left for turf, kitchen,	
		clothes, tobacco, etc.	1 5 8
Total	£8 9 8	Total	£ 8 9 8

BUDGET OF THIRD CLASS LABOURER OCCASIONALLY EMPLOYED

INCOME		EXPENDITURE	
Profit on pig	1 10 0	Rent 1 rood as above	2 10 0
Profit on fowls	0 10 0	10 barrels potatoes	
Earnings by wife and		as above	2 0 0
children as above	0 10 0	Rent of cabin	1 10 0
Labourer's wages	4 6 4	Left for everything else	0 16 4
Total	£ 6 16 4	Total	£ 6 16 4

Appendix D, p. 105

3: Barony of Talbotstown Upper, County Wicklow (16)

SUNDRY GAINS

Produce of 1/2 acre conacre potato ground, 25 barrels eating potatoes at 4s a barrel	5 0 0
7½ barrels small potatoes used for pig and seed, profit on pig	1 10 0
Total £	6 10 0
Deduct rent of 1½ roods potato ground tilled and manured by farmer at £2 15s a rood (ie. £11 an acre)	4 2 6
(the remaining half rood was rent free, manured by the pig)	
Total profit from potato ground, the work on it being by the labourer and his family	2 7 6
Profit from fowls in eggs and chickens	0 10 0
Earnings by wife and children by field work, manufacture, gleaning etc.	0 10 0
Total £	3 7 6

Budget of Labourer Constantly Employed

INCOME		EXPENDITURE	
Sundry gains as above	3 7 6	40 barrels at 4s a barrel	8 0 0
Labourer's wages	9 17 1	Rent of cabin	2 0 0
		Turf	0 10 0
		Kitchen, 4d a week	0 17 4
		Clothes	1 8 0
		Tobacco, soap, candles	0 10 1
Total	£ 13 5 5	Total	£ 13 5 5

Budget of First Class Labourer Occasionally Employed

INCOME		EXPENDITURE	
Sundry gains as above	3 7 6	37 barrels potatoes	7 8 0
Labourer's wages	7 14 0	Rent	1 15 0
		Kitchen, 3d a week	0 13 6
		Left for turf, clothes, soap, tobacco, etc.	1 5 0
Total	£ 11 1 6	Total	£ 11 1 6

Budget of Second Class of Labourer Occasionally Employed

INCOME		EXPENDITURE	
Sundry gains as above	3 7 6	34 barrels potatoes	6 16 0
Labourer's wages	5 11 6	Rent	1 10 0
		Left for kitchen, turf, clothes, soap, tobacco	0 13 2
Total	£ 8 19 2	Total	£ 8 19 2

Budget of Third Class of Labourer Occasionally Employed

INCOME		EXPENDITURE	
Sundry gains as above	3 7 6	26 barrels potatoes	5 4 0
Labourer's wages	3 17 0	Rent	1 5 0
		Left for everything else	0 15 6
Total	£ 7 4 6	Total	£ 7 4 6

Appendix D. p. 107.

4: Barony of Dundalk Upper, County Louth (17)

Sundry Gains

Produce of half acre potato ground, 30 barrels eating potatoes at 3s 6d per barrel	5	5	0
Also 10 barrels small potatoes, used for pig and seed; Profit on pig	11 0	0	
	£6 15	0	

Deduct rent 1 1/2 rood potato ground, tilled and manured by farmer at £2 rood, £3. Other ½ rood half price, manured by pig	3 10 0		
	3	5	0

Total profit on potato ground, the work on it being done by the labourer and his family when they would otherwise be unemployed	3	5	0
Net produce of fowls in eggs and chickens	0	10	0
Earnings of wife and children by field work, manufacturing, gleaning etc.	0 10 0		
Total	£4	5	0

Budget of Labourers
Constantly Employed

Income				Expenditure			
Sundry gains as above	4	5 0		52 barrels potatoes	9	2	0
Labourer's wages	9 15 0			Milk, butter etc., called 'kitchen' 6d a week	1	6	0
				Turf for fuel	0	10 0	
				Rent of cabin	2	0	0
				Left for clothes, tobacco, soap, candles etc.	1	2	0
Total	£ 14 0 0			Total	£14	0	0

Appendix D. p. 99.

5: Barony of Moyfenragh Lower, Co. Meath (18)

Sundry Gains

Produce of 3 roods conacre potato ground, 45 barrels eating potatoes at 3s 4d per barrel	7 10 0
Also 15 barrels small potatoes, used for pig and seed; Profit on pig	<u>1 10 0</u>
Total	£9 0 0
Deduct rent 2½ roods potato ground at £7 acre, tilled and manured by farmer. Other 1/2 rood rent free, manured by pig	<u>4 7 6</u>
	4 12 6
Total profit on potato ground, the work on it being done by labourer and family when they would otherwise be unemployed	4 12 6
Net produce of fowls in eggs and chickens	0 10 0
Earnings of wife and children by field work, manufacturing, gleaning, etc.	<u>0 10 0</u>
Total	£5 12 6

Budget of Labourers Constantly Employed

Income		Expenditure	
Sundry gains as above	5 12 6	52 barrels potatoes	8 13 0
Deduct for what labourer		Oatmeal	1 10 0
has to pay neighbour to		Turf for fuel	0 10 0
help with potato digging		Kitchen	1 6 0
and planting	<u>1 0 0</u>	Soap and candles	0 5 0
	4 12 6	Tobacco	0 10 0
Labourer's wages	11 10 0	Rent of cabin	1 15 0
	____	Clothes etc.	<u>1 13 6</u>
Total	£ 16 2 6	Total	£ 16 2 6

INCOME		EXPENDITURE	
Sundry gains	5 12 6	52 barrels potatoes	8 13 0
Labourer's wages	7 10 0	Meal for men, a few weeks at harvest and potato digging	0 13 0
		Turf	0 10 0
		Kitchen	0 13 0
		Rent of cabin	1 10 0
		Clothes etc.	1 3 6
Total	£ 13 2 6	Total	£ 13 2 6

Appendix D, pp 102–3.

At first glance the budgets suggest that the woman's only contribution was the small amount entered as occasional earnings. The general thrust of the evidence in this section is also to the effect that her contribution to household earned income was at best trifling. These comments by witnesses were usually made in reference to the reduced earnings by women in domestic industry, and contrasted with the remembered golden days when women's spinning had regularly paid the rent and determined the family's standard of living. They were accurate enough, but they obscured the reality that women were earning in other ways.

It is not until one turns to baronial examinations into the 'employment of women and children'[7] that the inclusion here of pigs and poultry provides explicit evidence that women in labouring families were generally recognised as the rearers of both, each of which made a substantial contribution to the family budget. The main reason why these are not immediately recognisable as women's contribution arises from the patriarchal paradigm already mentioned and the resulting ambiguity of language.

In almost every budget pigs and poultry are listed under labourer's income without attribution to the wife.

The only exception is the barony of Clonisk in Laois (see below). In the recorded words of witnesses both pigs and poultry are at times spoken of as being kept or reared by the labourer's wife and at others as being kept or reared by the labourer. Within the terms of reference of a patriarchal paradigm, or of the common law, this may not have been as contradictory as it seems at first sight, but it did make it more difficult to clearly identify women's income-earning activity.

Once the items contributed by women are identified the significance of their contribution can be examined more closely. The first point to be made is that the budgets pass the criteria for reliability. They were constructed on the consensus reached at the baronial examinations and supplemented by personal enquiries made by the assistant commissioners.

They establish that the wife in a labouring family contributed earned income to the family budget on a regular basis. These earnings are accepted as the pattern, and not as occasional or exceptional. They are a constant and unchanging component of every budget irrespective of the employment status of her husband. The value of sundry gains remains the same while his earnings are the variable factor.

Not only were her earnings a regular part of the budget but they represent a substantial percentage of total household income. Their value can be calculated by adding the profit from pigs and poultry and the occasional earnings of women and children. Since, in virtually every examination into the earnings of women and children, it was agreed that young children could earn nothing, allocating the whole to the wife cannot greatly overestimate her total earnings. Any small overestimation that might arise should be more than compensated for by the exclusion of the value of her contribution to the potato crop.

Assessed in this way, the woman's contribution to family income in these baronies ranges from fifteen per cent to twenty-five per cent when her husband was constantly employed to over thirty-five percent when he had very irregular employment. The budgets for yearly expenditure for these baronies show that her contribution more than equalled the rent of cabin and conacre in every case. It bridged the gap between relative comfort and distress, and was an important factor in the family's standard of living and in the difference between surviving and failing to survive by independent labour. If Kells is taken as an example the loss of the wife's total contribution of £2.10s would have eliminated much of the relative comfort enjoyed by the family of the constantly employed labourer. It would have reduced the income of the second class occasionally employed to the level of the third class and that of the third to below that of the fourth. The expenditure budgets demonstrate the seriousness of such a drop.

While none of the other baronial examinations produced a series of graded budgets, some did produce detailed typical budgets and, at others, a partial budget was drawn up or can be constructed from the report.

6: Barony of Kilconnel, County Galway[8]

Here the estimates were based on a family of husband, wife and three or four young children, renting a cabin and 1 acre for £2. With a family of this size they would also need 2 roods conacre at £3.15 rent, giving a fixed outlay of £5.15.

Earnings	£ s d
Profit on pig and fowl	0 15 0
200 days labour @ 6d a day	5 0 0
Oats grown on ½ land after potato crop	2 10 0
	Total £8 5 0

This left £2.10 for clothes, milk, kitchen and all other expenses and it was noted that few labourers could in fact grow grain on more than 6 or 7 perches.

7: Barony of Dromahair, Co. Leitrim[9]

The parish priest of Innismagrath presented the following average budget:

EARNINGS	£ s d	EXPENDITURE	£ s d
To wages, 2 days a wk.	3 10 0	Rent of conacre	4 0 0
Profit on pig, at highest	1 0 0	Salt	0 1 0
Sale of eggs and fowl	0 5 0	Herrings and other	
Sale of flax and yarn	0 13 0	'kitchen'	0 5 0
If near a town and	£ 5 8 0	Skimmed milk	0 10 0
allowed to sell turf,			£4 16 0
would make about	1 0 0	Balance/contingencies	0 12 0
Total	£ 6 8 0	Total	£5 8 0

8: Barony of Mohill, Co. Leitrim[10]

After 'much conflicting testimony on the subject' the estimate by Francis O'Beirne, a farmer 'whose circumstances afforded him much knowledge of the class' was adopted.

EARNINGS	£ s d	EXPENDITURE	£ s d
Labour, averaged 4 days		To rent of a cabin	1 0 0
a week @ 6d per day	5 4 0	Rent ½ acre conacre	4 0 0
Profit on pig	1 10 0	To fixed dues to clergy	0 2 0
Fowls, if permitted to		To 'kitchen' consisting	
keep them	0 5 0	chiefly of buttermilk, etc	1 14 8
Earnings of his wife and		Total	£ 6 16 8
children by spinning		Balance on clothes,	
Id per day at most	0 16 4	tobacco, meal in	
		summer etc.	0 18 8
Total	£ 7 15 4	Total	£ 7 15 4

9: Barony of Carbery, Co. Sligo[11]

It 'was found extremely difficult to obtain an average account of income applying to any large proportion of the labouring classes'. Eventually it was agreed to use the personal budget put forward by George Waters, a 'middle-aged man, having a family of a wife and four children', as an example of someone who got 'a fair share of employment during the year'. His budget for the last twelve months was:

EARNINGS	£ s d	EXPENDITURE	£ s d
To breaking stones @ 1d per barrel	2 5 0	Rent cabin and 1 rood	1 15 0
To labour in fields, chiefly in spring and harvest	1 0 0	Rent 1 rood conacre, manured and ploughed	1 15 0
Profit on pig	0 13 0	Bog	0 10 0
Profit on poultry	0 2 6	Grass for cow, May to May	1 10 0
Sale of 2 barrels surplus potatoes	1 0 0	Priest at Christmas	0 1 0
Sale of turf	0 10 0	Baptism of his child and churching of his wife	0 2 6
Sale of 2cwt. butter	1 10 0	Candles, soap, tobacco, kitchen	0 19 0
Value of wife's spinning	0 6 0	Total	£ 6 12 6
Total	£7 6 6	(He owes the priest 1s for Easter dues)	

This budget is the only one to include women's earnings by the sale of butter. Few labouring families could afford to keep a cow in the 1830s but the budget shows how profitable it could be.

10: Barony of Gowran, County Kilkenny[12]

EARNINGS OF COTTIER	£ s d	EARNINGS OF OCCASIONAL LABOURER	£ s d
Cottier's earnings at 6d a day, c. 260 days	6 10 0	Man's earnings at 7d a day, 180 days	5 5 0
Occasional earnings of wife and grown-up children	0 10 0	Earnings of wife and children, who have more leisure and opportunity than country cottier family	1 0 0
Profit on pig at most	2 0 0		
Total	£9 0 0	But no garden and so fewer pigs on worse terms	0 15 0
		Total £ 7 0 0	

It was noted that only the cottier family could afford to buy soap, candles, tobacco or kitchen.

11: Barony of Clonisk, King's County[13]

EARNINGS	£ s d
Earnings of labourer permanently employed	7 10 0
Earnings of wife by eggs and fowls	0 15 0
Earnings of wife by pig	1 10 0
Total £ 9 15 0	

12: Barony of Corcomroe, Co. Clare[14]

It was agreed that an 'ordinary labourer' constantly employed might work for 240 days per year, and this table was produced

INCOME	£ s d
240 days wages	8 0 0
Profit from eggs	0 5 0
Profit from pig	1 10 0
Total £ 9 15 0	

13: Barony of Iveragh, Co. Kerry[15]

INCOME	£	s	d
Wages from 200 days work	5	0	0
Profit from eggs	0	10	0
Profit from pig	<u>1</u>	<u>0</u>	<u>0</u>
Total	£6	10	0

14: Barony of Trugenackmy, Co. Kerry[16]

INCOME	£	s	d
Wages if constantly employed	6	13	4
Profit from pig	1	10	0
Profit from eggs	<u>0</u>	<u>15</u>	<u>0</u>
Total	£ 8	18	0

15: Barony of Conello Lower, Co. Limerick[17]

INCOME	£	s	d
Wages from 200 days work at 6d and food	5	0	0
Profit from pigs	<u>1</u>	<u>15</u>	<u>0</u>
Total	£6	15	0

16: Barony of Coshlea, Co. Limerick[18]

INCOME	£	s	d
Wages from 200 days work at 7d per day	7	0	0
Profit from pig	<u>2</u>	<u>0</u>	<u>0</u>
Total	£9	0	0

17: Barony of Middlethird, Co. Tipperary[19]

INCOME	£	s	d
Wages from 250 days work at 8d ('full average')	8	6	8
Profit from pigs	3	0	0
Profit from eggs 'a little'			<u> .</u>
Total	£11	6	8
		plus	

18: Barony of Decies without Drum, Co. Waterford[20]

INCOME	£	s	d
Wages for 220 days @ 6d and food	5	0	0
Profit from pig	2	0	0
Profit from eggs and fowl	0	10	0
Total	£8	0	0

19: Barony of Middlethird, Co. Waterford[21]

INCOME	£	s	d
Wages from 200 days work (no diet)	7	10	0
Profit from pig	2	0	0
Profit from eggs and fowl		10	0
Total	£10	0	0

	£	s	d
Wages for 250 days, with breakfast and dinner	6	5	0
Profit from pig	2	0	0
Profit from eggs	0	10	0
Total	£8	15	0

The report from the Ulster counties gives no actual or estimated 'typical' budgets agreed by all present at the baronial examination. However, any precise information that does emerge fits the general pattern of the budgets compiled in other parts of the country. In Iveagh Upper, County Down,[22] a budget of sorts emerged in a roundabout way which, incidentally, illustrates the difficulty in making any assessment of women's contribution in cases where no agreed average budget was produced. The assistant commissioners reported that all present agreed with the statement by one witness that a woman with four children 'could not do more than keep the home and family clean; she could not make as much as would buy soap to wash the children's clothes'. The commissioners then drew up a typical yearly expenditure account based on what witnesses said a labouring family would spend on different items during the year. This considerably exceeded the figures agreed as the average earnings of a typical labourer. When the discrepancy was pointed out the labourers present explained that the difference was made up by 'a pig, by some little spinning, and sometimes the husband went over at harvest time to England or Scotland, and earned as much as released the potatoes'.

In the barony of Lecale, Co. Down,[23] it was reported that the labourers saw their only certain source of income as the man's labour, valued at labour £10.8.0. per annum. In addition they might get £1.1.10. from a pig and 10s from the woman's labour.

The pattern of women's contribution in these budgets is strikingly similar to that in the graded budgets. The more detailed the budget the greater is the similarity. It is significant that every detailed budget includes earnings by the woman from pigs, poultry, and occasional labour, indicating how widespread and similar the pattern of her contribution was. A pig or pigs figured in every budget, detailed or not, and in the two County Down baronies. Poultry appeared in all except three budgets, and these three, Gowran, Conello and Coshlea were among the less detailed. In every case where a budget of any kind was produced, or where some sort of agreed budget can be extracted from the report, income earned by the wife was recorded and this ranged in value from 16 per cent to 37 per cent of total family earned income, with the more detailed budgets giving percentages in the 18 to 30 range.

In considering the budgets as evidence for women's contribution to the household economy of labouring families it has to be kept in mind that none of the budgets, even the most detailed, include *all* economic contributions. The unpaid work of women in the bearing and rearing of children, the care of home and the preparation of food is excluded, as it still is in most official calculations of gross national product, and in assessing the relative contributions of husbands and wives in relation to ownership rights relating to the family home and other property.

Clearly women's work in these unpaid and unevaluated areas made a real economic contribution. Reproduction and childcare was of direct economic significance to labouring parents. In the evidence given at the poor inquiry a frequently advanced explanation for the alleged early age of marriage among labourers was the expectation of producing children who would provide support for the parents' old age. Children can be seen as the only available form of pension investment for retirement. This is not to argue that the only reason labouring parents wanted children was their future economic potential, but that this does appear to have been a consideration for some people.

Women's work, in what would today be described as 'housework' in the sense of cleaning and washing house and furnishings, was probably not very time or labour consuming, since the material possessions of most labouring families were very limited. But, whatever about housekeeping in this sense, women did expend much time and labour in transforming the family potato crop into a meal for the family table. One witness said of this area of women's work:

> When they have dug the potatoes from the pits, they still have to collect fuel, and to wash them and boil them; in fact, between setting potatoes, digging potatoes, washing potatoes and boiling potatoes, they have hardly time to attend to anything else. They can never be clean or diligent at other matters until the nature of their food be changed.[24]

The labour involved in transforming the raw potatoes in the family pit to the steaming pot of potatoes for the family meal was as essential to family survival as the labour involved in growing them or in earning the means to purchase them. It may be noted that in some budgets the market value of the potatoes grown and consumed by the family is included in income.

What the budgets allow us to calculate is the extent of these women's contribution using the terms of reference of the dominant patriarchal paradigm for what was seen as having economic value. Even within these limited terms of reference the economic contribution of women was significant. They made a substantial and quantifiable contribution to household income in addition to their contribution in the home and in child rearing. This direct contribution is remarkably similar in content in all parts of the country covered.

It appears that, as their earning opportunities in domestic industry shrank, women in cottier-labouring families turned to new possibilities with considerable success. The rising number of pigs and poultry in rural Ireland was a response to the need of these families to increase their income.[25] Nearly one-third of the pigs raised in County Cork in 1841 were raised on holdings of less than one acre.[26] The development of steam navigation had opened the British market to 'many of the lesser articles of farming produce, formerly almost without a market, such as eggs, poultry, honey, etc'.[27]

Women's Begging as Family Survival Strategy
There were various stages in a family's slide from independent labour, to the need for some outside assistance, to the final stage when women took to the road as public beggars. Relatives or neighbours might offer help. Private application might be made to them, or

requests for work which were a disguised form of begging, or such strategies as happening to be in the vicinity at meal times could be adopted. Next came the stage where the wife, with or without the children, begged more openly in her own neighbourhood or at a distance. The final stage was reached when the entire family, or part of it, left their home for a period of weeks or months. In this last scenario the basic division of labour was that the wife supported herself and the children, and her husband saved to re-establish the family at home. He might remain at home to take what employment became available, or he might travel on his own to other parts of the country or to England or Scotland. He might also accompany his family 'on the road', taking any employment he could get on the way, and being supported by his wife's begging as necessary. The detailed budgets of income and expenditure graphically demonstrate how reduction in family income pushed a family down a sliding scale of deprivation which eventually reached starvation levels unless neighbours helped or the woman begged.

In the report from the Moyfenragh examination the assistant commissioners explained that the labourers' answers to questions as to how they survived were 'vague and contradictory'. When their children were young and numerous it was often 'next to impossible to discover how they live', but it was evident that both neighbours' help and begging by the wives and children were resorted to, and that the former was 'very prevalent'.[28] At Portnahinch the assistant commissioners calculated that the amount of potatoes available to the families of the constantly employed and of the first class of occasionally employed labourers was 'amply sufficient'. That available to the second class of the occasionally employed would suffice 'with strict economy'. The third class undergo great privation and distress during the time when potatoes are scarce and dear, unless, as is very generally the case among that class, their wives and children become beggars for the time, or the kindness of their charitable neighbours relieves their wants.[29]

The situation in Talbotstown was still more dire. Here the family of the constantly employed labourer had 'ample' potatoes and that of the first class of the occasionally employed 'sufficient with strict economy'. The families of the second class suffered 'more or less privation and distress' when potatoes were scarce and dear, and with the third class the

most dreadful misery prevails from the almost total want of employment, unless, as is very generally the case in or near Baltinglass, their wives and children 'take to the road', or, in other words, become beggars for the time …[30]

In the town of Ballina, where all witnesses agreed that unemployment among labourers was particularly high, a number of labourers described their own experience. Pat McNamara told how, in ten years as a landless labourer in Ballina with a conacre potato plot, in 'no one year has my earnings kept me up, but my wife has begged to support me and the children'. It was a story of day-to-day survival. Sometimes she begged, sometimes a friend helped, sometimes he got an occasional day's employment:

When we had no other means of living, she was able to keep the family up by her begging solely. Two and a half stone of potatoes each day would be scarce enough for my family; my wife would gather one stone or one and a half stone by begging, in summer; very seldom she has begged in winter, but when she has she has gathered two or three stone.

William Hanley, father of six children under sixteen, explained that his wife 'is out now begging, striving to gather a prog for myself and the children'.[31]

In Roscrea, County Tipperary, women's begging was an integral part of the family economy. The rent was generally paid from the labourer's wages or partly in labour. The profit from the pig paid for clothes. 'What remains of both wages and profit is set apart to buy potatoes, and if it be not enough, the wife must make up the difference by begging'.[32]

In the parish of Templemichael and Ballymacormac in County Longford work for labourers was scarce both in winter and summer. Survival was easier in winter, even for the family of a town labourer who had no stock or potatoes themselves since they had no conacre. However, in winter the small farmers had plenty of potatoes and the town labourers' wives took salt herrings to the country and exchanged them with the farmers for 'two or three times their value in potatoes'. In the summer when potatoes were scarce and distress was rife, the labourer's wife might reveal their plight to a better-off neighbour to seek help, or children might loiter around farm houses in the hope of being fed. Families also resorted to purchasing meal and potatoes on credit, or might pawn clothes or sell their pig. The final option was for the wife and children to beg while the husband went away to seek work.[33]

In County Antrim, where begging appears to have been less prevalent than in many other parts of the country, reports from about half the parishes said that the wives of unemployed labourers begged while half said they did not.

At Naas, County Kildare, it was said that when the Connaught labourers came to cut the harvest they accepted lower wages, thus putting the locals out of work with the inevitable result that the latter's 'wives and children are of course obliged to beg for their support'.[34]

At Burrishoole, County Mayo, it was reported that when

stocks of potatoes failed, the general rule is, that the wives and families beg in a remote part of the country. Strangers, similarly circumstanced, come into this parish; so that at certain seasons of the year there is nearly an exchange of paupers between parishes. The men generally remain at home and never beg, at least publicly.[35]

The summer months were the season of the year which saw the greatest family exodus. This was the period between the exhaustion of one year's potato crop and the readiness of the next. In many parts of the country it was also a season when employment was particularly scarce.

At the parochial examinations in all parts of the country witnesses agreed that the vast majority of the seasonal yearly invasion of strolling beggars in their locality was comprised of able-bodied women accompanied by young children. Some of these women were identified as widows but the majority were the 'wives of labourers'. Estimates of the proportion of all strolling beggars these women represented ranged from two-thirds to nine-tenths. So widespread was this pattern that one of the commissioners, G.E. Cornewall Lewis, pointed to a problem that would arise if vagrants were prosecuted:

It is ... observed, that the main body of vagrants in Ireland are the wives and children of able-bodied labourers, who beg in the summer when the stock of potatoes is exhausted; the husbands themselves rarely beg. Now, if the wife is apprehended and convicted for vagrancy, what will be done with the husband and children?[36]

Women's potential contribution through begging was taken into account in decisions to marry. In Ballina one labourer, claiming to speak for all present, explained that a poor man would marry early without any dowry with his bride. The couple married

without any fear of being worse off than before; for when he has no work, if he is ashamed to beg himself, the wife and children will beg and support him; or, if he chooses to take a fling out of the country to some other part of Ireland, or to the English harvest, they will support themselves by begging till he comes back.[37]

For the Poor Law commissioners begging, and particularly begging combined with vagrancy, was an undesirable mode of relief because it did not operate on the principle of distinguishing between the 'deserving' and the 'undeserving' poor, and for this reason they believed it contributed to the further spread of begging:

> The great cause of the extensive mendicancy which drains and impoverishes the small farmers of Ireland is their want of system and good judgment in bestowing relief. It is given by them without discrimination, without regard to the character, nay, without even knowledge of the circumstances of the applicant.[38]

From the point of view of the cottier-labourer population begging and vagrancy had the aspect more of a vast informal system of mutual insurance against unemployment. Indeed, the commissioners themselves recognised that women's begging played this role in the household economy of these families. In their first report they noted that one of the major problems facing them in their task was to gauge the extent of Irish poverty. This they found to include the vast majority of the population, a majority which was 'constantly fluctuating between mendicancy and independent labour'.[39] In their third report they noted that the

> wives and children of many are occasionally obliged to beg: they do so reluctantly, and with shame, and in general go to a distance from home that they may not be known.[40]

For the labouring family begging was a strategy for family survival when all efforts to do so by independent labour had failed. The evidence of the inquiry shows that it was an effective strategy. The constant report is that when independent labour failed families fell into serious distress unless they turned to begging. It is the families who refused to beg in such circumstances who were in real misery. The contrast led the assistant commissioners at Killaloe to comment that it was 'strange that the labourers do not envy the condition of the beggars'.[41] Begging as a family survival strategy was women's work and with it women took over the main, and sometimes the sole, breadwinner role in the family.

Conclusion

Since only a limited amount of the information collected in the poor inquiry has been considered here it would be premature to attempt an overall assessment of what it tells about the status and role of women in Irish society. However, the information used for this article does raise questions and suggest pointers.

In good times and bad labourers' wives shared the provider-breadwinner role with their husbands. If the location of status and power within families was determined by the economic contribution of their different members then the evidence of the poor inquiry suggests that men and women in labouring families should have enjoyed relatively equal status and power.

Contemporary commentators, usually observers from outside Ireland, did not believe that this was the case. They tended to see women in labouring families as a generally downtrodden group, overburdened with work, oppressed by their husbands and living in affectionless marriages.[42] At least one of the poor inquiry commissioners formed similar views. J.E. Bicheno argued that

> extreme poverty has a tendency to degrade the woman lower than the man, as may be inferred from her being worse clothed, and from her being the first to suffer privations; the very reverse of what happens in a better condition of life. She

is made the drudge and the slave. The man's pride will not suffer him to ask alms, but he sends forth his wife and children as beggars. In an improving district, shoes and stockings are first seen on the man. The woman's position before marriage being one of entire dependence, the same necessity of courting her affections does not exist as in countries where women can obtain the means of subsistence.[43]

George Nicholls, who presented his own separate report, observed that women's 'duties appear to be much more laborious than those of the same class in England. Their dress, too, is very inferior, and so likewise seems their general position in society'.[44] Bicheno's view that, while a woman in Ireland, 'does not take full status as a wife, she takes higher as a mother', supports this view to some extent while also qualifying it.

On the other hand, folklore sources indicate that marriage in Ireland conferred status as a 'full member of the community' on both men and women,[45] and that a wife was seen to have an 'absolute right as an independent money-earner, coupled with the right to dispose of the money earned as she wished'.[46]

The categories of the destitute in Irish society, listed above, indicate that the politics of gender, that is, the social, political and economic consequences for individuals which resulted from their being born male or female, were a factor in determining a person's status on the scale from rich to poor. For example, the reasons why illegitimate children and their mothers were found among the regularly destitute did not lie in any biological determinism. These reasons included a value-system that attached a label, either 'legitimate' or 'illegitimate', to every new-born infant, as well as a distribution of resources that placed the 'illegitimate' child and its mother, but not its father, in serious danger of destitution.

In the case of labourers' wives the paradigm of male-female relationships in the minds of the organisers of the poor inquiry obscured to the point of near invisibility the fact that these women were active breadwinners. From this it does not necessarily follow that labouring men or women did or did not share the same view of these relationships. However, if the commentators correctly interpreted what they observed, it suggests that a patriarchal paradigm did influence relationships between labouring men and women. If it did, it is likely to have distorted the operation of a direct causal relationship between economic contribution and status and power.

The role of begging in the household economy has implications regarding roles in labouring families. Apart from the question why the report does not give explicit recognition to the contribution of women's begging, there is the further question why able-bodied men rarely or never begged. Witnesses explained it on some logical grounds, such as that women earned more at begging than men, and that there was generally more work available for men. But perhaps the most frequently recurring explanation, and one on which there was universal consensus, was that men were more ashamed to beg than women. Men were said to have more feelings of 'independence'. They were reluctant to see their wives and children begging either but 'let' them when things got very bad. It appears that what men were ashamed of was not begging in principle – they did not after all refuse to live on its proceeds – but to be seen begging themselves. The issue seems to have been a somewhat vulnerable masculine identity based on the need to be seen *not* to be doing something. By contrast women could be seen as having more robust self-identity and to have been the realists who did what had to be done.

Begging combined with vagrancy raises questions about authority and autonomy. Here was an accepted pattern of family economy whereby women left their husbands, took their children with them and travelled to distant parts of the country where they were not known, and successfully earned enough to provide food, shelter and other necessities for themselves and their children for a period of weeks or months.[47] This is not a scenario which suggests that husbands exercised strict control over their wives' behaviour, sexual or otherwise, or over their freedom of movement. It strongly suggests that these women, whether or not they were oppressed by their husbands and by Irish society generally, as some observers believed, were also resourceful, independent and self-sufficient.

These issues and others await further research. However, the evidence from the poor inquiry considered here indicates that the politics of power, status, autonomy and decision-making in labouring families will not be fully and satisfactorily explained in terms of a single model, whether that of an oppressor-oppressed relationship between men and women, or of a one-to-one relationship between economic contribution on the one hand and power and status on the other.

The gender relationships specific to a particular group, time and place appear to develop from the interaction between the political, social and economic structures of the national and local society, the location within these of the group in question, and the currently prevailing paradigm of male-female relationships. As feminist historiography develops the evidence increasingly indicates that the obverse of this is also true, and that historical research into the structures of a society or the experience and contribution of individuals and groups requires the use of gender analysis in conjunction and interaction with other analytic approaches, such as, for example, those based on class, colour, race, religion, and many more.[48]

from Maria Luddy and Cliona Murphy (eds), *Women Surviving: Studies in Irish Women's History in the 19th and 20th Centuries* (Dublin, Poolbeg Press, 1989), pp 85–116.

NOTES

1   *Reports of His Majesty's Commissioners for Inquiring into the Condition of the Poorer Classes in Ireland,* (Hereafter *Poor Inquiry*) First report, H. C. 1835 (369) xxxii, pt. v.

2   See Anne V. O'Connor, 'The revolution in girls' secondary education in Ireland, 1860–1910' in Mary Cullen (ed.), *Girls Don't Do Honours: Irish Women in Education in the 19th and 20th Centuries* (Dublin, 1987), pp 31–54; Eibhlín Breathnach, Charting new waters; women's experience in higher education 1879–1908', in *ibid.,* pp 55–78.

3   *Poor Inquiry,* supplement to appendix D, H. C. 1836 (36), xxxi, p. 1. Joel Mokyr notes the 'rampant' confusion but uses the estimates by controlling for error. Idem, *Why Ireland Starved* (London, 1985), p. 25.

4   *Poor Inquiry,* p. viii.

5   *Ibid.,* pp ix–x.

6   Sir William Blackstone, *Commentaries on the Laws of England* (London, 1826), ii, p. 432.

7   *Poor Inquiry,* appendix D, pp 84–92.

8   *Ibid.,* p. 92.

9   *Ibid.*

10 *Ibid.,* p. 94.

11 *Ibid.,* p. 95.

12 *Ibid.,* p. 97.

13 *Ibid.,* p. 98.

14 *Ibid.,* p. 108.

15 *Ibid.*

16 *Ibid.,* p. 109.

17 *Ibid.*

18 *Ibid.*

19 *Ibid.*

20 *Ibid.,* p. 110.

21 *Ibid.,* p. 111.

22 *Ibid.,* p. 112.

23 *Ibid.*

24 *Ibid.,* p. 86.

25 L.M. Cullen, *Life in Ireland* (London, 1968), p. 121.

26 James S. Donnelly Jr. *The Land and the People of Nineteenth Century Cork* (London, 1975), p. 43.

27 *Report of the Select Committee on the State of the Poor in Ireland* H. C. 1830 (589) vii, p. 5.

28 *Poor Inquiry,* appendix D, p. 102.

29 *Ibid.*

30 *Ibid.,* p. 106.

31 *Ibid.,* appendix A, pp 367–9.

32 *Ibid.,* p. 454.

33 *Ibid.,* pp 405–6.

34 *Ibid.*

35 *Ibid.,* p. 371.

36 *Ibid.,* Remarks on the third report by George Cornewall Lewis Esq., H. C. 1837 (91) Ii, p. 18.

37 *Ibid.*

38 *Poor Inquiry,* Third Report, H. C. 1836 (43) xxx, p. 4.

39 *Poor Inquiry,* First Report, p. vi.

40 *Poor Inquiry,* Third Report, p. 4.

41 *Ibid.*

42 S.J. Connolly, 'Marriage in pre-Famine Ireland' in Art Cosgrove (ed.), *Marriage in Ireland* (Dublin, 1985), p. 89.

43 *Poor Inquiry,* H. C. 1836 (42) xxxiv, p. 19.

44 *Ibid.,* H. C. 1837 (69) ii, p. 28.

45 Caoimhín Ó Danachair, 'Marriage in Irish folk tradition' in Cosgrove, *op. cit.,* pp 99–100.

46 *Ibid.,* p. 46.

47 Potatoes were the usual currency of begging. They were the cheapest and most readily available items to the donor and they could be used to purchase lodgings and other necessities by barter or money exchange.

48 For the most recent review article see Gisela Bock, 'Women's history and gender history; aspects of an international debate', *Gender and History,* no. 1, vol. 1 (Spring 1989), pp 7–30.

HISTORY WOMEN AND HISTORY MEN:
THE POLITICS OF WOMEN'S HISTORY

This essay was a revised version of a paper given at the Desmond Greaves Summer School in 1993. Talking about women's history to an audience, many of them men, and few of whom had had much or any encounter with women's history, was educational for me. In the discussion that followed the paper most of the men who contributed spoke from a perspective that saw males as the driving force and significant actors in Irish history. While generally sympathetic to the story of feminist aims, they took for granted the civil and political rights enjoyed by men, and some spoke in terms of women needing to 'prove' their right to these, as for example, the right to vote. This discussion illustrated the power of the established versions of history we are exposed to, and how what is not there in those versions simply has not happened for most readers. I had to empathise with the audience's views, as I remembered that I myself had not challenged the gender roles and the explicit and implicit definitions of women's 'nature' and role in society in the history and literature I read as a child and young woman. And in my case, even though I knew it conflicted with my awareness of myself, I accepted it as 'the truth' and thought I was in some way out of line. For me, the discussion highlighted the debt we owe to those who make the first challenges to orthodox versions and ask new questions. The essay was published in Daltún Ó Ceallaigh, Reconsiderations of Irish History and Culture, *and a shorter version in* History Ireland *in 1994.*

Just as individual personal memory is vital to each of us if we are to make meaningful decisions about our lives, so knowledge of the history of the group or groups we belong to is also vital to those decisions. As Cicero said over two thousand years ago: 'Not to know what happened before you were born is to remain forever a child'. Historians are major custodians – or creators – of group memory, and as such, historians, for the most part, have not served women well.

Current developments in the research and writing of women's history did not just happen. They grew directly from the contemporary feminist movement. The roots of feminism lie in the roles and behaviours societies have prescribed for women and men. While these sex roles have differed over time and place, it appears that feminism has always grown from individual women's perception that the sex roles prescribed by their own society conflicted both with their knowledge of themselves and with their development as responsible adult persons. The new wave of feminism which emerged in Western society around 1960 challenged the prevailing stereotype which insisted that every female, by virtue of her sex, was best fulfilled as a person and made her best contribution to society in the role of wife and mother, subordinating to this the development of other talents and leaving responsibility for the organisation of society to males. This was the stereotype to which the American Betty Friedan gave the name the feminine mystique.[1] She was describing the model to which middle class women in the United States were socialised to conform, but women all around the globe recognised the model she described as corresponding in its essentials to those they knew in their own countries and cultures, and her book was translated into several languages within a few years.

The feminine mystique view of women has seldom been more publicly and clearly enunciated than in Article 41.2 of *Bunreacht na hÉireann*, the 1937 Irish Constitution: 'In particular, the State recognises that by her life within the home, woman gives to the State a support without which the common good cannot be achieved'. The use of the singular 'woman' instead of some or many 'women', and 'life' rather than 'work' within the home, moves this beyond a welcome recognition of the value to society of the work done by so many women in the home. It now becomes an assertion of an ideology that places all women on the basis of sex in a 'private' sphere from which they are to have no part in the 'public'.

Feminists found that their claim to take responsibility for decisions about their own lives instead of conforming to a model imposed by others was challenged in its turn by the counter-assertion that history showed that women had always been satisfied with the feminine mystique role. Their response was to turn to the history books to find what women actually had done.

The history books were of little help since they seldom mentioned women at all, with the exception of a few monarchs and revolutionaries whose lives and careers hardly conformed to the mystique model. So feminists turned themselves to the historical evidence with the question: what *did* women do? The answers which have come so far, and they are only the beginning, raise radical challenges to establishment history.

As feminist enquiry focuses on different areas of knowledge, history included, a number of stages can be discerned. The first is the seeing and saying that women are invisible in the knowledge and theory of the particular discipline. This is an essential stage. Until we recognise and acknowledge that we cannot see women we are unlikely to begin to look for them.

After this, the first research in a field is usually a search for 'great' women, individuals who have 'achieved' within terms of the criteria by which men are judged to be 'great' and to have achieved. For history Gerda Lerner has called this the 'compensatory' stage.[2]

The focus then moves from the exceptional individual to the contribution of a wider range of women to the political, social and intellectual movements and developments which underlie patterns of change and continuity in societies. For example, it has already been established that women played a much larger and more active role than had been realised in such movements as the United Irishmen, Young Ireland, the Fenians, the Land Movement, the 1916 rising, the war of independence and the civil war. While much of this scrutiny is directed towards movements already identified as 'important' in male-centred history, the research has broadened to look at women's contribution to social and intellectual movements, both independently and where they worked side by side with men. We now know that women made major contributions to many of the philanthropic reform movements of the 18th and 19th centuries which did so much to change perceptions of the responsibilities of society and state.[3] As these lines of enquiry expand they raise questions about causality in history, about how and by whom significant change is brought about. The driving force here is the hypothesis that women, and other groups far from the locations generally perceived to be the centres of power and the site of change, may have contributed to change in more fundamental ways than has been understood. These are significant developments which seem set to question many present assumptions and interpretations.

Following this, the next stage is to begin to see women as a distinct group, defined by their shared female sex, a group which has a history of continuity and change which demands the attention of historians.[4] This is a development in conceptualisation and analysis which has radical potential, and to which this essay will return later.

The ultimate stage should be the writing of a new kind of history which will incorporate the historical experiences of both sexes. This will be a venture into uncharted waters where inevitably new horizons and new landmarks will emerge and where it may be hoped a new inclusive human history will develop.

At this point it will be useful to consider one particular finding to emerge from research in women's history and its implications both for women's self-knowledge today and for what it tells us about how history is written. One of the early discoveries of the feminist historians was that of the women's emancipation movements of the 19th and early 20th centuries and the causes that gave rise to them.[5] It must be stressed that by using this example it is not intended to imply that the history of feminist movements is either the central theme of women's history or the most important aspect of it. But for the purposes of the argument being put forward at this stage it is particularly useful because it allows us to bypass one regularly repeated explanation of the invisibility of women in the history books. This is the assertion that, since women were not involved in the arena of public politics seen as central by so many historians, the latter could hardly be blamed for not dealing with them. The women's emancipation movement, a highly visible and international political movement, refutes this explanation.

While laws, regulations and customs were not identical in every country the position of women relative to men was fundamentally similar across the board. In virtually every country in Western society women were excluded from political life, whether by holding public office, or as elected representatives in parliamentary institutions where these existed, or as voters in the election of such representatives. They were barred from higher education and the professions. Titles and property passed to sons in preference to daughters. The home was seen as 'women's sphere'; yet, to take a representative example, under English common law, which was in force in Ireland, when a woman married she lost her legal identity which merged into that of her husband. Her property, whether earned or inherited, passed under his control to dispose of as he pleased and the law gave him extensive authority over her and their children. Divorce was considerably more difficult for a wife to obtain than it was for a husband, and if a woman left her husband his duty to maintain her lapsed while his right to her property did not. In sex-related offences such as adultery, prostitution and illegitimate birth, the law treated women as the more guilty and punishable party.

In organised and prolonged campaigns, which started around the middle of the 19th century and continued into the 1920s and 1930s, in country after country feminists succeeded in revolutionising the legal, political and social status of women The essence of this revolution was the removal of most of the overt and legally imposed civil and political disabilities based on sex. By any standards it was a sizeable achievement even if with hindsight we know that the underlying stereotypes of 'natural' or 'correct' feminine and masculine behaviour were harder to shift.

Two aspects of the significance of this rediscovered history of the women's emancipation movement are significant for the present discussion. The first is its relevance for women's self-knowledge today. It restores to women one part of their lost group memory. This restoration has both negative and positive implications.

On the negative side it tells them that they have not been paranoid in perceptions of oppression, and that the problem of sexism has older and deeper roots than many may have realised. Its significance in this regard is seen in the anger felt by many women when they first discover the nineteenth-century women's emancipation movement and the reasons for it, an anger also visible in the titles of some of the first pioneering books.[6]

On the positive side, the better sexism is understood the better is the chance of eliminating it. And, further on the credit side, the history of the women's emancipation movement establishes beyond argument that relations between the sexes, including relations of power, have not been eternally unchanging throughout history and dispels the belief that women have always conformed happily to a 'natural' role of passivity and subordination. It places feminist dissent today in context as one historically specific stage in a long historical process, instead of being the historical aberration sometimes suggested. This allows feminists today to start from the knowledge that at least some women before them also actively dissented from imposed patterns of behaviour and set about changing them. It frees them to build on what is already there in their history instead of spending years of mental energy in re-inventing the wheel in each new generation.

The other aspect is of course that it raises the question of why all this had to be rediscovered in the first place. Why had it ever been lost? Why had the women's emancipation movement and the reasons for it not been included in general histories of Ireland? Consideration of the possible answers to this adds to our understanding of the invisibility of women in the history books and of the way history is written.

Why then has the historical reality that the political, social and economic structures of Irish society included a systematic limitation of women's autonomy and freedom of action on the basis of their sex, where no similar limitation applied to men as a sex, not been recorded in histories of Irish society? There is no immediately obvious or satisfactory answer. It is difficult to see why an organisation of society which gave men a monopoly of access to political and economic power, and excluded women from virtually every avenue of approach to these, should be something that historians of Irish society have not seen as a significant or important aspect of that society. As for the exclusion of organised feminism, its objectives were the removal of the sweeping range of civil and political disabilities imposed on all women on the basis of their sex. It is not easy to find a convincing argument that could explain how these objectives could be regarded as more sectional, more trivial or less significant in their impact on society than, for example, those of nationalism or the labour movement.

It appears that the answers are to be found not in the content of the historical record but in the minds of the historians. If we dismiss a conspiracy theory of deliberate suppression, and most of us would dismiss it, the explanation can only be that most historians have not and still do not see women as important or 'significant' in the history of their societies. They have written history within the framework of a paradigm that sees men as the active agents in human societies, as the creators of the patterns of continuity and change historians look for. This paradigm does not see women as an integral part of human society. If it did these issues could not be so consistently overlooked. It sees women as peripheral and essentially outside history. Once the question 'What did women do?' was seriously asked and answers began to be found, it became clear that this patriarchal paradigm blinkered historians' vision and distorted both their findings and their interpretation.

This points to another strength in the contribution of women's history and feminist studies generally. They continually reiterate and insist that knowledge is not an objective given but is a human construct, created by the individual mind in interaction with its environment. The historian examines the available evidence and constructs the picture which, to his or her mind, is the best approximation to the reality of what must have happened. The historian does not exist in a vacuum but is a member of society, formed by it and influenced by its value systems. If a historian brings with him or her a way of looking at the world which sees males as the doers and leaders and females as the passive and followers that historian is unlikely to look for evidence of action or change brought about by female initiative, and may fail to recognise its significance when found.

This in turn raises the question of bias in the writing of history. History written from the perspective of groups distant from the centres which control access to power and privilege, such as women's history, labour history, Marxist history, black history, is often labelled as 'political' and liable to bias. Granted that the pitfalls of bias are real. I know that as a feminist historian I am likely to want to find certain things, and that there is always the temptation to search more assiduously for the evidence that supports one's hypothesis than for that which refutes it. 'By and large, the historian will get the kind of facts he [sic] wants'.[7] But I also think that knowing my bias puts me in a better position to be alert to the danger and to prevent myself falling into this trap. And others will also be more alert to see and tell me if I do so. It appears to me that historians who believe themselves to be value-free and 'neutral' are likely to be in more danger from bias. An assumption that the current political or intellectual status quo or orthodoxy is usually 'right' and all who dissent from it likely to be 'wrong' is as political a perspective as a feminist or Marxist one and, if unconsciously held, more likely to distort the way history is written. In my own case I am much more concerned about the biases and value-systems I must inevitably have, but of which I am *not* aware, than I am of my feminist sympathies.

At this point I want to return to the fourth stage in the development of feminist studies and women's history outlined above, the emerging realisation that women, the subset of society defined by their female sex, have a definable history displaying patterns of continuity and change. This realisation grew from the mounting evidence that differences in the relative position of men and women in societies could not all be attributed simply to 'nature' or 'biology'.

This can be illustrated by taking two examples from nineteenth-century Irish history: at one end of the social spectrum the landed family of the Parnells in County Wicklow in the second half of the century, and at the other end widowhood and illegitimate birth in the 1830s. The brother and sisters, Charles, Fanny and Anna Parnell were all committed and active nationalists.

Charles went to a public school and to Cambridge, inherited an estate, entered parliament and became the leader of a political party. All these stages in his life were open to him on the basis of his sex. As females his sisters could not go to a public school, could not go to Cambridge, could not enter parliament and could not become the leaders of political parties. The circumstances of Anna's leadership of the Ladies Land League vividly illustrate the difference. As females Fanny and Anna did not inherit estates but had incomes settled on them by their father and charged on the estate of another brother. These contrasts in the political, social and economic consequences of sex were not determined by 'biological' difference but by the laws, regulations and customs which determined what males and females could and could not do at that place and time in history.

At the other end of the social scale the Poor Inquiry of 1835–6 found among the categories of the destitute two which contained no men, but only women and children. These were widows with families of young children and illegitimate children and their mothers. Again, no direct biological imperative decreed that among the cottier and labouring classes widows, but not widowers, with young children, and illegitimate children and their mothers, but not their fathers, were highly likely to be destitute. Here also the causes must be sought in the distribution of resources at that time and place, in who controlled that distribution and in whose interests, and within terms of what paradigm of society, class structure and male-female relationships.

With the revelation that there have been real political, social and economic differences consequent on being born a male or a female at a specific time or place, and that these differences have varied from one society or culture to another and changed over time in reaction to change or conflict in society, sex emerged as a category of historical analysis. What was in question was not sex in the sense of any kind of biological determinism but sex in the way dominant groups in a society determined what it should mean in individuals' lives. The word 'gender' was drawn in to express this. In this meaning, gender denotes the social construction of sex and is based on the realisation that the implications of sex in an individual's life are not limited to the directly 'biological', but also and powerfully by the way societies create sex roles to which individuals are socialised or coerced to conform.

Used with precision within specific historical contexts gender is a valuable concept in historical research and interpretation. It focuses attention on the relationships between the sexes, and how these are structured and maintained as well as on how they are challenged, and on how they change over time and place.

In addition to relationships *between* the sexes, it also directs attention to differences in relationships *within* each sex, those between different groups of women and between different groups of men. It enables the historian to apply the discovery that sex has definable political, social and economic consequences widely in historical research and interpretation.

Historical specificity also makes it clear that gender cannot be claimed to stand on its own as the only important analysis. It interacts with other analyses such as those of class, colour, nationality, ethnic origin, political affiliation, religion, age, marital and parental situation and many more, in locating individuals or groups in their historical context. Feminist historians argue that, while gender is not the *only* essential analysis, it is *one* of the essential analyses, and consequently that, if gender is excluded, the picture drawn by the historian will be to a greater or lesser extent distorted.

Thus defined and used, gender analysis forestalls any reductionist interpretation that all women have shared the same history, or that women's history is simply a history of the oppression of all women by all men. Women have been oppressors both as individuals and as members of oppressing classes or nations. Men have been oppressed, both by other men and by women, as well as being oppressors. Women's history is far more than oppression and resistance to it, important as both these aspects are.

In a valuable article the German historian Gisela Bock has summarised some of the major developments in the writing of women's history during the past two decades. She discusses 'three dichotomies in traditional thought on gender relations', which have been both used and 'profoundly challenged' by feminist historians of the 1970s and 1980s. These dichotomies, or mutually exclusive opposites, are those of nature versus culture, work versus family, and public versus private.[8]

The nature versus culture dichotomy sees men and male activities as 'culture' and a proper subject of historical study, but sees women and female activities, especially those connected with 'sexuality between men and women, women's bodies and their capacity for pregnancy and motherhood' as 'nature', as unchanging over time and place, and so without a history and outside the historian's remit.

Feminist research has challenged this by showing that the words 'nature' and 'culture' have not had fixed immutable meanings but have meant different things at different times and places. Indeed, the idea of a nature/culture dichotomy itself appears specific to Western culture, and 'cultures' and 'natures' as defined in the dichotomies are revealed to be in reality interrelated and interdependent.

The work versus family dichotomy is an extension of the culture-nature opposition. Child bearing and rearing, and women's labour in the care of home and family, came to be seen as not 'work' but 'natural', Once historians turned serious attention to the lives of women they found that what

> had been seen as nature was now seen as work: bearing, rearing and caring for children, looking after the bread-winner husband and after other family members. To call this activity 'work' meant to challenge the dichotomy 'work and family' (because the family may mean work to women), but also 'work and leisure' (because men's leisure may be women's work), and 'working men and supported wives' (because wives support men through their work).[9]

This switches attention to the sexual division of labour in terms of whose work is more highly valued and more highly rewarded. The real dichotomy, Bock argues, turns out to be that between 'paid and unpaid work, between underpaid and decently paid work, between the superior and inferior value of men's work and women's work respectively'.[10]

The nineteenth-century Irish census reports allow us to observe in action a shift in the definition of work from meaning all contributions to the welfare and operation of society to a narrower definition based on a new idea of 'economic' activity as opposed to 'non-economic' activity which was no longer defined as 'work'. By 1861 the Irish census commissioners had developed a model which regarded virtually every person in the State as engaged in an occupation which contributed to society. Accordingly, married women who were full-time housewives were placed in the 'domestic' classification. But from 1871, on the instructions of the English census commissioners, housewives were moved from the 'domestic' class to the 'indefinite and non-productive' class, although domestic servants and others who worked for wages stayed in the 'domestic' class.

It appears that a change in the ideology of bourgeois men, for whom a 'leisured' and 'non-working' wife was becoming a status symbol, was adopted by officialdom and applied across the board to all women. It had little relevance to what most married women did except to obscure it and lead to the absurdity of today's use of the expression a 'working wife' to mean a married woman in paid employment.

Bock's third dichotomy, that of public versus private, pushes her analysis further. Feminist historians have challenged this also, and shown that the 'public' world of men and politics and power is not separate from the 'private' world or 'sphere' of women. Men cannot operate as they have traditionally done in the public world without the support of the private world. 'Male workers, male politicians and male scholars perform their tasks only because they are born, reared and cared for by women's labour'.[11] Also, far from women being unchallenged rulers of their 'sphere', until very modern times in most Western societies the law, backed by sanctions, gave men extensive authority over home, family and women.

In the other direction women have regularly crossed the boundary from private to public and from the female to the male role when it suited the interests of the established order. Instead of it being the case that men and women have occupied separate and parallel worlds which proceed side by side, there is only one world where the political, economic and social are interdependent, and where gender relations interact with all three.

History cannot avoid gender even if the historian ignores it. Wittingly or unwittingly, the writing of history is itself part of the historical construction of knowledge and theory. As the American historian Joan Wallach Scott has pointed out,[12] the way historians have written about, or not written about, women is itself part of the gender process, the social construction of sex, either reinforcing and perpetuating the dichotomies Gisela Bock refers to, or challenging or modifying them. The one thing the writing of history cannot be is neutral on the issue.

All this brings to the forefront the question which has been lurking in the background throughout the discussion so far, the question of men in history. While it is often said that history as it has been written so far is the history of men, it is more accurate to say it has been largely a history of the activities of privileged groups of men who occupied positions of public power. It has seldom concerned itself with men as a group, the subset of humanity defined by their male sex. And just as the history of women cannot be written without reference to gender relationships neither can the history of men.

Women's history has made it no longer tenable to see the male role in society as the human norm, from which women were for some reason, whether 'biological' inferiority, slower cultural development or whatever, left behind in human evolution and so had to try to catch up with men and attain the male role. The interdependence of the gender roles of the sexes rules out this interpretation.

We do not yet know the extent of the re-evaluations to which this will lead. As already noted, they will certainly focus attention on definitions of what is recognised as significant historical change and the respective contribution to such change by individuals or groups in positions of public power and by individuals and groups far distant from such positions.

They are likely to include re-assessment of the contribution of the full-time male politicians, intellectuals, artists, soldiers, revolutionaries or whatever who have been able to be all these full-time because of women's work. Male privilege, control of resources and freedom from daily family responsibility undermine theories which incorporate the idea of the 'naturalness' of male 'achievement' and which cite in support the relative paucity of similar female achievement.

Instead of asking why women have dissented, it will be seen to be more useful in terms of increasing our understanding of both the past and the present to ask why men, or male elites, have so consistently tried to keep control of wealth, education and political power as male monopolies. To what historical origins can we trace the continual efforts to limit women's freedom of action and to expand their child-bearing capacity into a life-time career devoted exclusively to care of family and home at the expense of any serious participation in the affairs of society at large or serious commitment to intellectual or artistic endeavour? Can the pronouncements by so many of the 'great masters' of Western philosophy on the intellectual and moral inferiority of women as compared to men continue to be dismissed as unimportant hiccups which do not affect the overall evaluation of their systems of thought? By whose instigation and in whose interests did the dualities and theories of opposites that have bedevilled Western thought about the sexes come into being? Why has male identity so often been built on being different to and having control over women? What impact have male sex-role stereotypes which see aggression and dominance as acceptable or desirable masculine characteristics had on the history of different societies?

There is of course another side to such re-evaluations. If historians of women argue successfully that women have made greater contributions to patterns of continuity and change in societies than has been recognised, this raises problems for interpretations which see males as bearing the sole responsibility for such recurring historical patterns as war or genocide.

These reconsiderations lead on to the big question of how a more embracingly 'human' history will be written. Incorporating women's history into the 'mainstream' may not be the best way of seeing the nature of the enterprise if we believe that 'human' history may turn out to involve much more than fitting women in as appropriate to the present orthodox account. An integrated history may be a better way of looking at it.

It is clear that seeing relationships between the sexes as an integral part of the history of a society will be central. Following on from this we may hope that women's history will carry into all areas of historical research its concern with the origin and operation of systems of power and control. In this context Joan Wallach Scott explains that she does not claim that gender will

> finally explain all inequality, all oppression, all history. My claim is more modest: that gender offers a good way of thinking about history, about the ways in which hierarchies of difference – inclusions and exclusions – have been constituted.[13]

We can also hope that women's history will bring to the new integrated history an openness to the complexities of human experience and to the danger of imposing absolutes and dichotomies, not only when dealing with women and men but throughout the search for the past. Gisela Bock, a leading exponent of this approach, suggests that historical knowledge will be best furthered by recognising ambivalences and uncertainties in the historical experience of individuals and groups and by the 'rejection of mutually exclusive hierarchies, and especially of either-or solutions, in favour of as-well-as solutions'.[14]

Who then is going to write the integrated history and when are they going to do it? One view is that before the enterprise is feasible we need to build a sufficient base of research and publication in women's history to provide a firm foundation.[15] In this scenario, once a critical mass of knowledge and theory has been developed the patriarchal paradigm at present in possession will collapse under the weight of the increasing mass of contrary evidence, and leave the way open for a new paradigm within which historians can rewrite history.

However, some recent developments suggest that in the meantime vigilance may be needed to prevent the radical potential of women's history being derailed or diverted into various blind alleys. These include a growing tendency to misuse 'gender' as a synonym for 'women', a misuse which allows the essence of gender analysis, that sex is a social construct, to be bypassed and allows men as a group to again elude the historian's scrutiny. This can produce a purely descriptive social history, valuable in the information it gives, but which does not ask the 'hows' and 'whys' which push social, economic and political history into engagement with each other.

Particularly ironic is the emergence in the United States of 'gender history' as a rival and alternative to 'women's history', with the former claimed to be more universal and less partial and biased. In light of the fact that women's history produced the concept of gender history, it is hardly surprising that this posing of yet another dichotomy is regarded by the sceptical as an attempt to neutralise the challenge of women's history by marginalising it as in some way less than fully academically respectable.

Here I believe the politics of women's history come into play. Today's women's history, which contributed the concept of gender, came from today's feminism, a political and intellectual movement which asserts women's autonomy as human persons and challenges male and female sex-role stereotypes which limit that autonomy and which incorporate male dominance over women. It sees such models as oppressive to women, dehumanising to both sexes, and above all as social constructs which can and must be changed. The diversionary movements described above appear either to fail to understand the concept of sex as a social construct, or to fail to engage with it. While they may be seen to some extent as the inevitable problems faced by a new and expanding field of history, at the same time they appear to display elements of an attempted counter-revolution which needs to be recognised and confronted.

Like women's history, many other major 'revisionisms' emerged from the contemporary politics of the historians' own period. Both labour history and black history did so. And the debate that at present monopolises the term 'revisionist history' for most people in Ireland grew from today's conflicting attitudes to the political issue of republicanism. Similarly the British revisionist debate about the origins of the English civil war in the 17th century and the role of parliament in British history has grown from today's political problems.

I think it is arguable that historians who do not understand what feminism today is about will have difficulty in accepting that women's history is 'real' history, and so a real part of human history, however well-intentioned and favourably disposed they may believe themselves to be. For example, this seems to me the most plausible explanation for the way two of the most recent and high profile histories of Ireland, by R.F. Foster and J.J. Lee respectively,[16] deal with the women's movement. Foster tells us in his annotated bibliography that Irish feminism of the late 19th and early 20th centuries is an 'important' topic, mentions feminists and feminism a number of times in the text, and yet gives the reader no information whatsoever as to what the objectives of feminism were, how feminists pursued them and what, if anything, they achieved. Lee makes no mention of feminism, whether in the 1912–22 period when it won the vote for women, or after the founding of the Free State when it faced a reactionary backlash, or when the new wave of feminism emerged in Ireland around 1970. The last is particularly surprising in a book ending in 1985, and whose cover states that it 'argues that Irish politics must be understood in the broad context of economic, social, administrative, cultural and intellectual history'.

It may be going too far to suggest that women's history and the new integrated human history can only be written by feminists, whether they be women or men. However, I am convinced that, if the potential of women's history to expand our understanding of the past and our understanding of ourselves as women and men today is to be realised, the historians concerned need to at least *understand* feminism today. They may agree or disagree with its analysis but they need to know what that analysis is. Unfortunately it appears that most historians, like most people generally, still fail to recognise feminism as a movement which concerns the whole of society, and instead see it as in essence women wanting to be like men, and so as a 'women's issue' which need not involve men. To believe this is of course an effective defence against having to think about feminism seriously, and in particular against having to think about its challenge to men and male stereotypes.

If the argument of this essay so far has any validity it follows that, in tandem and in dialogue with the work of research and its publication, we need to develop a debate about the nature of women's history, about methodologies and about politics. The objective will be to put debate about the politics of history in general, and the politics of women's history in particular, on the agenda of historians of women and from there to move it on to the agenda of the wider community of historians.

The dialogue between feminism and women's history should be part of this. The politics of today opened the door to the search for women's past and in return the discoveries of women's history bring back information and insights which expand and deepen feminist thinking, open up new vistas, often query the validity of some of today's assumptions, and insist that reality has been in the past and is today more complex, with more overlap and crossing of boundaries among categories and groups than we have understood.

By such a debate we can hope to prevent the blunting of the cutting edge that women's history has brought to established ways of looking at things. It may be that, in the process, historians of women will find that the challenge of pioneering the writing of the new integrated human history has fallen to them.

from Daltún Ó Ceallaigh (ed.), *Reconsiderations of Irish History and Culture: Selected Papers from the Desmond Greaves Summer School 1989–1993* (Dublin, Léirmheas, 1994), pp 113–139.

NOTES

1   Betty Friedan, *The Feminine Mystique* (Harmondsworth, Penguin, 1965; first published 1963).

2   Lerner, *The Majority Finds Its Past: Placing Women in History* (OUP, 1979), p. 145.

3   See Maria Luddy, *Women and Philanthropy in Nineteenth-Century Ireland* (Cambridge UP, 1995).

4   For a useful discussion of this see Gisela Bock, 'Women's History and Gender History: Aspects of an International Debate', *Gender and History*, i, 1 (Spring 1989), pp 7–30.

5   For the Irish women's emancipation movement, see Margaret Mac Curtain, 'Women, the Vote and Revolution' in Margaret Mac Curtain and Donncha Ó Corráin (eds), *Women in Irish Society: the Historical Dimension* (Dublin, Arlen House, 1978), pp 46–57; Margaret Ward, *Unmanageable Revolutionaries: Women and Irish Nationalism* (Dingle, Brandon, 1983); Rosemary Cullen Owens, *Smashing Times: The History of the Irish Women's Suffrage Movement 1889–1922* (Dublin, Attic, 1984); Mary Cullen, 'How Radical was Irish Feminism between 1860 and 1922?', in P.J. Corish (ed.) *Radicals, Rebels and Establishments* (Belfast, Appletree, 1985), pp 185–202; Cliona Murphy, *The Women's Suffrage Movement and Irish Society in the Early Twentieth Century* (New York and London, Harvester Wheatsheaf, 1989).

6   For example, Sheila Rowbotham, *Hidden From History: 300 Years of Women's Oppression and the Fight Against It* (London, Pluto, 1973).

7   E.H. Carr, *What Is History?* (Harmondsworth, Penguin) 1971, p. 23.

8   Gisela Bock, 'Challenging Dichotomies: Perspectives on Women's History', in K. Offen, R. Roach Pierson and J. Rendall (eds), *Writing Women's History: International Perspectives* (London, Macmillan, 1991), pp 1–23.

9   *Ibid.*, p. 3.

10   *Ibid.*, p. 4.

11   *Ibid.*

12   Joan Wallach Scott, *Gender and the Politics of History* (New York, Columbia UP, 1988), p. 9.

13   *Ibid.*, p. 10.

14   Bock, 'Challenging Dichotomies', p. 17.

15   As Margaret Mac Curtain and Mary O'Dowd suggest in M. Mac Curtain and M. O'Dowd (eds), *Women in Early Modern Ireland* (Dublin, Wolfhound, 1991), pp 13–14, and in 'An Agenda for Women's History in Ireland: Part 1', *Irish Historical Studies*, xxviii, 109 (May 1992), p. 9.

16   R.F. Foster, *Modern Ireland 1600–1972* (London, Allen Lane, Penguin, 1988); J.J. Lee, *Ireland 1912–1985: Politics and Society* (Cambridge UP, 1989).

ANNA MARIA HASLAM
(1829–1922)

As the body of publications in the history of Irish feminist activism grew, it became clear that we needed to know more about the women whose names kept emerging in the sources. Maria Luddy and I agreed that a collection of biographical studies of women who were active feminists in nineteenth and early twentieth-century Ireland would be useful in deepening our understanding of the historical development of feminist awareness and action. We first looked for contributors who had already researched or were currently researching women who 'were consciously feminist and played key roles in campaigns to improve the status of women'. We later broadened our criteria to include women who might not have seen themselves as part of the movement for the emancipation of women, yet whose lives and actions 'challenged and contributed to change' in accepted gender roles. Eventually we had enough studies for two books, one dealing with the nineteenth century and one with the twentieth. We ourselves looked at Anna Haslam and Isabella Tod, two key figures who kept appearing in all the different early feminist campaigns, and neither of whom had so far been the subject of a biography. Researching Anna Haslam was a rewarding experience. As well as emerging as a very likeable personality, the range and inclusiveness of her commitment to the 'advancement of women', the energy of her activism, the quality of her thinking and writing, opened my eyes to the enormity of the task she and her colleagues faced in the institutionalised patriarchy of mid-nineteenth-century Ireland, and the radical nature of their sustained challenge to its various manifestations. This essay appeared in the first collection, Women, Power and Consciousness in Nineteenth-Century Ireland: Eight Biographical Studies, *published by Attic Press in 1995. Since the essay was published the documents cited as in the care of the Irish Housewives Association have been deposited in the National Archives in Dublin. Also since then, Carmel Quinlan's study,* Genteel Revolutionaries: Anna and Thomas Haslam and the 19th Century Irish Women's Movement *(Cork University Press, 2002), gives the school Anna attended from 1842–1845 as the Quaker Castlegate School in York and the years of her teaching at Ackworth School as 1847–1848.*

Anna Haslam, 'one of the giants of the women's cause', as her colleagues described her,[1] became a legend in her own lifetime and the symbol of the women's movement, in particular the suffrage campaign, for a younger generation of Irish women in the early years of the twentieth century.

While much of her life's work was completed by the end of the nineteenth century, both her personality and her continuing vigour made a strong impact on the younger women and their descriptions bring her to life for us. Their affection and respect is the more telling since many of them strongly disagreed with her position on the conflict between nationalism and unionism. We know she took part in virtually every campaign for women's rights during the second half of the nineteenth century and that her organisational and leadership qualities were widely recognised. Yet, with the exception of women's suffrage, detailed information on her life and work is tantalisingly scarce. The sources so far available are largely public records such as minutes, speeches, leaflets and newspapers. This is the more frustrating since she and her husband, Thomas Haslam, arranged for the preservation of their papers, but few of these have been located.[2]

She was born Anna Maria Fisher into a middle-class Quaker family in Youghal, County Cork in April 1829, the second youngest of the seventeen children, nine girls and eight boys, of Abraham Fisher of Youghal and Jane Moore of Neath in southern Wales. Anna's great-grandfather, Reuben Fisher, had come from London to Youghal where he set up as a druggist in 1695, and married Margaret Shute of Youghal in 1705. Their grandson, Abraham (1783–1871), Anna's father, ran a corn milling business in Youghal.[3]

She herself saw both her religion and her family as significant influences in her formation as a future activist in the cause of women. The more a religious denomination emphasised individual conscience, the more favourable it appears to have been to the development of feminist consciousness. Where Roman Catholicism stood at the authoritarian extreme, the Religious Society of Friends, or Quakers, stood at the other, the most positive of the Protestant denominations. The central Quaker belief in the 'Inner Light', the voice of individual conscience which overrode every other authority, encouraged 'an attitude of individuality and responsibility'.[4] Quakers valued hard work and self-support above inherited ease and had a strong record of philanthropic activity. They also had a tradition of civil disobedience, such as refusal to take oaths or to bear arms, on grounds of religious principle.

In practice Quakers do not appear to have given women quite the same autonomy and authority they accorded to men. Quaker women, like women in other Protestant minority sects, did take leadership roles in the early days, in the case of Quakers after the foundation of the Society in the aftermath of the English civil war in the 1640s, but in all the sects women were later relegated to more subordinate and stereotypical female roles.[5] Yet, by comparison with women in other denominations, Quaker women were active and autonomous. Travelling ministers, who could be of either sex, kept groups in contact. There were both men's and women's monthly, quarterly and provincial meetings. While only the men's had executive authority, the women's dealt with such matters as the relief of the poor, and of widows and orphans, good behaviour, marriage and female dress, and the 'interaction between meetings and the idea of spiritual, if not executive, equality gave women important roles to play in this distinctive community'.[6] Haslam herself undoubtedly saw her religion as a training in sex equality. She noted that, like,

> my dear friend, Susan B Anthony,[7] I was brought up a member of the Society of Friends, and was accustomed to see women working side by side with their brothers, as Ministers, Elders, and Overseers, upon the footing of undisputed equality.[8]

As a Quaker she also received an education superior to that available to most contemporary middle-class girls. She attended the Quaker boarding school at Newtown in County Waterford from 1840–42, and then went to England to the famous Quaker School at Ackworth in Yorkshire which she left in 1845. Thus she was away from home at school for five years from age eleven to sixteen.

Quakers attached considerable importance to education for both boys and girls. Their schools aimed both to develop a sense of individual responsibility and to mould the pupils' wills through strict discipline and regulated lives.[9] Boarding schools were preferred to day schools as being more conducive to both objectives. Newtown, founded in 1798, was one of three Quaker provincial boarding schools in Ireland, the others being in Lisburn in Ulster and Mountmellick in Leinster. Originally intended to educate children from poorer Quaker families, girls for domestic service and boys for apprenticeships, at first they had a limited and practical curriculum. By the time Anna Fisher went to Newtown the provincial schools were also educating children from better-off families and expanding the curriculum to prepare students, or at least the male students, for careers in trade and commerce.

Many Quaker schools, including Newtown, were co-educational. However, the sexes attended separate classes, and girls had additional domestic tasks, learned spinning and other domestic skills, and received a more limited academic education.[10] Nevertheless, Quaker education for girls was highly rated by comparison with that available elsewhere, and Haslam herself was later described as one of 'the many workers whom the Society of Friends, with its solid and equal education for boys and girls', had given to the suffrage movement.[11]

Philanthropy is also seen as a nurturing ground of feminist consciousness. Haslam's parents engaged in a wide range of philanthropic activity.[12] The young Anna helped in the soup kitchen in Youghal during the Great Famine of 1845–9, and, like many other middle- and upper-class women, she and her sister started an industry, teaching poor girls fancy knitting and crochet, and arranging for the sale of their products. With what they earned many were able to emigrate. When the Fisher sisters left Youghal the Presentation nuns took over the industry and extended it to include embroidery and lace-making.[13]

Her parents also introduced her to the more political forms of philanthropy which are particularly linked with feminist activism. Abraham and Jane Fisher were involved in the anti-slavery movement, the temperance movement led by Fr Theobald Mathew and the international peace movement.[14] They 'entertained representatives of [the various philanthropic causes] at their home', so the young Anna would have met a number of these. She herself was certainly active in the peace movement, and in 1849 helped to start an Olive Leaf Circle and acted as its secretary.[15] These Circles grew from the Quaker London Peace Society founded in 1816. As the movement developed it stressed a connection between women, especially women as mothers, and peace. By the 1840s Olive Leaf Circles, inter-denominational groups of fifteen to twenty women, had emerged with monthly meetings and activities including discussions, correspondence with other Circles, and writing didactic stories for children. There was a strong link between peace movements and feminism in Britain, with early women peace polemicists championing women's rights.[16] Haslam saw a causal connection between her family upbringing and her feminism. She

> could not remember any time when she was not a believer
> in women's equality. It came to her naturally, and was
> always taken for granted in her household – a Quaker
> household, where nothing that was produced by slaves was
> allowed to be worn or eaten.[17]

It is highly probable that she was aware of the leading role played by Quakers in the developing women's movements in both Britain and the United States. The American Quaker minister and feminist Lucretia Mott (1793–1880) was in London for the 1840 anti-slavery world convention at which the American women delegates were refused full participation. This rejection led Mott and Elizabeth Cady Stanton (1815–1902) to organise the famous Seneca Falls convention on women's rights held in New York state in 1848. Mott visited Dublin and Belfast after the 1840 convention and Irish Quakers must have heard her account of what happened in London.[18]

In 1853 Anna Fisher returned to Yorkshire as a teacher at Ackworth School where another Irish Quaker, Thomas Haslam, had been teaching for some years. They came back to Ireland where they married in Cork in 1854 and then came to live in Dublin where Thomas Haslam worked as a book-keeper or accountant. Thomas Haslam was born in 1825 in Mountmellick in Laois (then Queen's County) and educated at the Quaker Leinster Provincial school in the town where he became an apprenticed teacher. By the time he met Anna Fisher he was already interested in 'the women's question', an interest he dated to his reading the British philosopher Herbert Spencer's aphorism: 'Equity knows no distinction of sex'.[19] Throughout their lives together he was to be his wife's co-worker and colleague in all the campaigns around women's rights.

The earliest description of Haslam comes from 1870 when she was in her early forties, and 'full of perseverance and buoyant energy'.[20] Most other descriptions date from her later years, and energy and vigour combined with vivacity and good-humour are the characteristics that keep recurring. Margaret Cousins, co-founder of the Irish Women's Franchise League in 1908, met the Haslams in 1906. They were, she wrote,

> a remarkable old pair, devoted to one another and dedicated to the cause of the advancement and enfranchisement of women. They were nearly seventy [in fact Anna had her 77th birthday and Thomas his 81st in 1906] when I met them; always in the best of health; she a dynamo of energy, small and sturdy; he intellectual, tall, rather like a university don, a good speaker, very refined and kindly.[21]

At the celebrations for the Haslams' sixtieth wedding anniversary in 1914 she was still making the same impression. She replied to the tributes 'in a very touching manner, and then most characteristically and amid applause, made a stirring appeal for further whole-hearted endeavour in the suffrage cause'. She went on to recite, 'by special request, and with surprising vigour', a poem she had learnt over seventy years earlier.[22] The report of another reception noted 'the inexhaustible verve and gaiety of Mrs Haslam, who concluded the evening by dancing Sir Roger de Coverley with Mr Haslam as her partner'.[23]

Extant photographs are all of the couple in their later years, their seventies or eighties, while the Sarah Purser portrait in the Municipal Gallery of Modern Art in Dublin was painted for their fiftieth wedding anniversary in 1904. In all of these she looks alert and vigorous, while he looks tall and thin, more serious and somewhat frail.

Accounts of their partnership in the cause of women speak of him as her assistant and helper and never the other way around. She herself said that marriage brought her 'a most valuable helper in her husband. She could never have undertaken what she did in later years if it were not for his sympathy and help'.[24]

Though he was the one who wrote feminist pamphlets and was in demand as a public speaker on feminist questions before she was, neither of them, nor anyone else, ever suggested that she was not the leader. At the anniversary celebrations in 1914 Thomas Haslam himself was explicit. For himself

> the most I can say is that, from time to time, I have rendered my wife some little help in her various efforts to raise her sex out of the many disabilities from which they are everywhere suffering ... for nearly sixty years she has lost no opportunity of promoting that object in whatever way it has come within her power.[25]

Their relationship experienced another reversal of accepted sex-roles when Anna Haslam became the family breadwinner. In 1866 Thomas Haslam's health broke down and he never again worked in paid employment. It is not clear what the nature of his illness was, or whether it was the reason the Haslams, both of whom came from large families, had no children. Whatever it was, Thomas Haslam lived a life which was active by most standards until his death at the age of ninety-two in 1917. A reader, writer and scholar, he was a member of the Rathmines Public Library Committee over many years and a 'great figure' at the weekly meetings of the Dublin Friends' Institute where he frequently read papers.[26] In the Dublin Women's Suffrage Association he attended all the committee meetings over the years, often spoke at its open meetings with three of his addresses being published as pamphlets, and was regularly a joint delegate with his wife, or accompanied her, to women's conferences in Britain.

When her husband's health broke down Anna Haslam opened a business described as a stationer's and 'fancy repository'[27] at 91 Rathmines Road, there 'maintaining her home and her invalid husband'.[28] True to Quaker principles she had no inhibitions about going into trade. She ran this business, which 'required her almost undivided attention', for the next forty years until the assistance of friends made it no longer necessary.[29] That she still managed to take an active part in so many campaigns, and a leadership role in some, is a testimony to the energy noted in descriptions of her. The other side of this, of course, was her husband's contribution to her activism. Without at least the sympathy of a husband it was difficult for a married woman in the mid-nineteenth century to play an active political role, and Haslam enjoyed a support from her husband, a feminist in his own right, that went beyond sympathy to active collaboration.

As a young married woman in Dublin, 'already alive to the questions of higher education and employment for women',[30] Haslam began her long career as a campaigner. Organised action was developing in Great Britain and Ireland on a number of issues; married women's property rights; improved female education and access to higher education; access to better paid and a wider variety of employments for middle-class women, including the professions; opposition to double sexual standards in the response to prostitution; and participation in political life, where the first step was the acquisition of the vote in central and local government. The early women's rights activists in Ireland had a close working relationship with their English counterparts. While the position of women was not identical in both countries, Irish women and English women shared the same general disabilities under English common law, and largely similar discrimination in education, employment and political life. Most reforms in either country required laws to be passed by the all-male parliament at Westminster. Lobbying members of that parliament was of necessity a central focus of feminist political action in both countries. On some issues there was joint action and on other quite separate campaigns. Irish nationalists tended to view women's rights campaigns with suspicion as an English importation.

As yet we do not know much about the first networks in Ireland, but it is clear that in all of these areas of action Haslam was among the pioneers, although, as noted, information about most of her work is frustratingly scanty.

Education was linked to women's self-development and self-esteem, as well as to widening employment opportunities for all women, and particularly for middle-class women. One major objective was to establish the principle of education as mental training for girls as well as boys, and to raise the content and quality of female education to the level of that of males.

Haslam was one of the group led by Anne Jellicoe[31] which founded the Irish Society for the Training and Employment of Educated Women, later called the Queen's Institute, in Dublin in 1861.[32] The Institute was a pioneering venture in the technical training of women and led in turn to Jellicoe's foundation of Alexandra College for the Higher Education of Women in 1866 and Alexandra High School for Girls in 1873. Haslam, though not one of the most prominent leaders, saw her work in education as one of her major activities.[33] She also played a part in the successful efforts to have the provisions of the Intermediate Education Act of 1878 and the Royal University Act of 1879 extended to girls and women. These Acts respectively opened public competitive school examinations to girls as well as boys and allowed women to take the degrees of the Royal University. When these achievements were mistakenly attributed solely to Haslam's efforts she disclaimed the unmerited laurel, incidentally confirming her contribution. Regarding the 'removal of some serious blots on the original drafting' of both Bills, she wrote she was only

> a co-worker with several others – and, more especially, Miss Tod, of Belfast, and Mrs Jellicoe of the Alexandra College – both of whom did admirable service in all questions affecting the educational and industrial interests of girls.[34]

In 1882 she was involved in setting up the Association of Schoolmistresses and Other Ladies Interested in Irish Education as a network to monitor and protect the educational interests of girls and women.

It aimed to build on what had been achieved while combating attempts to undermine it by such stratagems as the introduction of separate lower-level programmes for girls in the Intermediate examinations.[35]

During the 1860s and 1870s Haslam also made some input into the campaign to gain access for women to medical degrees and into the founding of the London School of Medicine for Women in 1874,[36] though again we do not have details of her contribution.

Under the Medical Registration Act of 1858 only registered persons could legally practice medicine in the United Kingdom. Since registration required the holding of a qualification from one of the specified British examining bodies, and since the latter barred women, women were effectively excluded from the practice of medicine. Women's accepted role as primary health-carers in the family and the local community and their long association with healing and medicine made the exclusion keenly felt.

A vigorous campaign resulted in an act of parliament in 1876 which allowed medical degrees to be conferred on women. The 'well-known sympathy of some of the leading members of the medical profession in Ireland' led to the King's and Queen's College of Physicians in Dublin being the first in the United Kingdom to allow women admission to medical degrees and thus to practise as physicians.[37]

Also during the 1860s and 1870s Haslam took part in the married women's property campaign.[38] The English common law, operative in Ireland, gave husbands full legal rights to the control and disposal of their wives' inherited or earned income, with the limitation that they could not actually dispose of property in land. Property rights for married women were a central issue for women's emancipationists. They affected the lives of women of all social classes. Lack of control drastically curtailed married women's power to make decisions about their own lives, and encouraged the education of middle-class girls to aim at the acquisition of accomplishments which maximised their chances of marriage to the wealthiest available male, rather than at self-development and economic independence.

The property of wealthy women could be protected by the system of trusts developed by the courts of equity to circumvent the common law. But this merely empowered trustees to 'protect' a woman's property against her husband. It did not give control to the woman herself and did not disturb the principle of patriarchal marriage. In any case the legal expense made trusts feasible only where fairly substantial property was involved.

Isabella Tod[39] of Belfast, a leading figure in the campaign, explained that the 'educated', by whom she meant middle-class, women in Belfast and Dublin involved in the campaign were primarily concerned about the position of the many poor married women working in the linen mills in the Belfast area. The law left their earnings, and those of their children, at the mercy of their husbands. The only satisfactory solution was a woman's full legal right to her own earnings. Middle-class women of limited means also needed this right since it was difficult for them to pay for a protective settlement or to find suitable trustees. A women's committee had been established in Dublin and petitions in favour of an act had been organised in both Dublin and Belfast.[40] Haslam was probably a member of the Dublin committee and one of the organisers of the Dublin petition.

The campaign succeeded by forcing one limited legislative reform after another in successive Acts between 1870 and 1907 by which time the principle of spouses' separate property was fully established.

More is known about Haslam's work in the campaign to repeal the Contagious Diseases Acts. She later said that this campaign held up suffrage activity for years because

> we were all so caught up in it. When it began, I remember one old friend saying, it was such an obviously just demand, that the moment people understood it, it would be granted; it could not be possible that such things should endure more than a few months. It took us eighteen years.[41]

Her comment highlights how small the number of activists was and how the same people were involved in all or most of the campaigns on different issues.

Passed during the 1860s, due to fear that venereal disease was undermining the British army, the acts provided for state regulation of prostitution in certain designated areas, including three in Ireland, the Curragh, Cork and Queenstown (Cobh). They introduced compulsory medical examination of any woman suspected of being a prostitute and compulsory medical treatment if she was found to be suffering from a venereal disease.

The National Association for the Repeal of the Contagious Diseases Acts and the Ladies' National Association (LNA) were founded in England in 1869 and had branches in Ireland. Isabella Tod in Belfast and Anna Haslam in Dublin were again involved from the start. Tod first, and after her Haslam, were members of the executive of the LNA. Membership in Ireland appears to have been small with subscribers never numbering more than forty-nine. The members appear to have been exclusively Protestant, with Quakers as usual to the fore.[42]

Work with prostitutes had always been high on the agenda of philanthropic women. Their opposition to the Acts was based first on the belief that state regulation gave recognition, and hence approval, to prostitution which they saw as a threat to family life. Feminists also rejected the double standard which did not interfere with the men involved, but treated the women as commodities to be periodically cleansed and recycled as 'clean harlots for the army and navy'.[43]

In 1870 Thomas Haslam published a vigorously argued eleven-page pamphlet[44] which, in view of the couple's close collaboration, it appears reasonable to see as representing his wife's views as well as his own. The thrust of the pamphlet, issued at an early stage of the campaign, was to place the blame for prostitution, 'one of the deadliest evils of our time', firmly on male injustice and licentiousness. It saw prostitutes themselves as women seduced and then abandoned by some man. Thomas Haslam argued that the law should concern itself with these guilty men, both the original seducers and the men who availed of prostitutes' services. The man who seduced 'a virgin girl' should be legally forced to marry her. If already married his guilt was worse as he betrayed two women, his children and society, and stringent penalties were called for. Turning to the 'compulsory celibates', soldiers and sailors, largely recruited from 'the dregs of our population', he suggested it might be better to have a volunteer force or attract a 'higher class of men' by better pay and encourage them to marry. Total suppression of brothels was not immediately feasible until 'the public conscience' had been better educated about the issues. In the meantime the Contagious Diseases Acts, by removing one of its 'natural penalties', venereal disease, encouraged rather than deterred prostitution. The Acts, he argued, must be repealed or radically amended.

Apart from seeing prostitutes as the victims of male seducers, the pamphlet said little about why women become prostitutes except to mention the lack of remunerative employment for all single women. This is probably because the immediate political purpose was to challenge the sexual double standards underlying the Acts.

Middle-class women had to breach many social and sexual taboos to campaign and speak at public meetings on an issue explicitly related to women's sexuality. As a result women's committees co-existed with mixed-sex committees. Anna Haslam, typically, took part in both, being secretary of the mixed-sex committee set up in Dublin in 1870, and treasurer of the women's committee set up a year later.[45] Thomas Haslam, for his part, collected the signatures of over one hundred doctors for a petition for repeal.[46]

The campaign continued with meetings and demonstrations in Belfast and Dublin over the years. In 1878 the English leader of the campaign, Josephine Butler, addressed a public meeting at the Rotunda in Dublin, which was disrupted by heckling medical students. Butler planned to return to England 'in chagrin', but Haslam and her husband promptly organised another meeting which Butler addressed and where she 'moved to tears some of the people who would not listen to her at the first'.[47] The Acts were eventually repealed in 1886. Haslam then became secretary of the Women's Vigilance Committee which was part of the Social Purity campaign which succeeded the Contagious Diseases campaign and worked for the 'health and safety of women and girls and the purification of the moral atmosphere of society'.[48]

The 1860s and 1870s also saw action on women's suffrage get under way. Participation in the making of laws was essential for women's citizenship. In 1866 the emerging circle of activists in Britain organised a petition to parliament to have women included on the same terms as men in the impending act to extend the male franchise. In the space of a fortnight the signatures of 1,499 women were gathered, and among the fifteen names with Irish addresses was that of Anna Haslam, who dated her involvement in the suffrage campaign from that time. The petition was followed a year later by a proposed amendment to the bill to replace the word 'man' by 'person'. When the amendment was rejected organised action began.

In England the National Society for Women's Suffrage was founded in 1867 and in Ireland the North of Ireland Society for Women's Suffrage was established in 1872. In the Dublin area Anne Robertson of Blackrock, County Dublin, was the first leading figure. She organised and spoke at meetings from 1866, and lobbied candidates in the 1868 general election urging support for women's suffrage. Anna Haslam recalled what she said at the first public suffrage meeting in Dublin in 1870, organised by Robertson, at which Millicent Garrett Fawcett, the English suffragist leader, spoke:

'I well remember', says Mrs Haslam, 'seeing Mrs Fawcett, a mere girl, leading her blind husband [F.C. Fawcett MP] on to the platform. 1 can see her now. That was the best meeting that ever was held in Dublin – no such names have been got together for any meeting since'. And she showed me the list of names on the platform – Sir Robert Kane, Sir William Wilde (father of Oscar Wilde), and his famous wife 'Speranza', Sir John Gray M.P. of the *Freeman's Journal*, whose statue stands in O'Connell Street, Provost Lloyd of Trinity College, Dr Ingram, Dr Shaw, Dr Mahaffy, and a host of other notabilites.[49]

Haslam herself was among the organisers of a suffrage meeting in Dublin in 1872 at which Isabella Tod was one of the speakers. It was in connection with this meeting that Helen Blackburn noted Haslam's 'perseverance and buoyant energy'. She added that the meeting led in 1876 to Haslam's founding the Dublin Women's Suffrage Association (DWSA), the first permanent suffrage organisation in Dublin.[50]

Meanwhile, in April, May and July 1874 Thomas Haslam wrote and published three issues of a periodical, *The Women's Advocate*. The first issue gives an insight into the Haslams' thinking on the suffrage question. It argued the case for women's suffrage as 'the moral right of properly qualified women to some share in the enactment of the laws which they are required to obey'. Women's claims are just in themselves, he asserted, and no convincing counter argument has appeared. Women demanded political and educational rights and 'to be treated as reasonable beings, who are personally responsible for the talents which have been confided to their care'. The second issue gave practical advice on how to organise local groups for effective political action. This advice was deemed so valuable that Lydia Becker, the English suffrage leader, ordered 5,000 copies for distribution.[51] The advice also corresponded closely to the methods adopted by the DWSA under Anna Haslam's energetic leadership.

Haslam was secretary of the DWSA from its foundation in 1876 until 1913 when she stood down and was elected life president. Throughout that entire period she did not miss a single meeting and was clearly the driving force in the organisation. The membership was predominantly Quaker, including men as well as women, though as the years went by women increasingly outnumbered the men. It worked to educate public opinion by writing to the newspapers and organising drawing room and public meetings, the latter whenever the opportunity of high-profile women speakers presented itself. It maintained contact with the movement in England and sent delegates, regularly both Haslams, to suffrage and other feminist conferences, and later to suffrage demonstrations and parades. It followed political developments in Ireland and Britain to avail of every favourable opportunity for lobbying in support of its objective. It organised petitions to the House of Commons. It sent deputations and letters to Irish MPs urging them to introduce or support bills or amendments to bills to enfranchise women. It exhorted 'influential' women in various parts of the country to lobby their MPs. It noted with approval advances in the various feminist campaigns, not surprisingly since Haslam was involved in all or most of them.

In 1884 women were yet again excluded from a reform act. This one extended the franchise to male agricultural labourers by making male household suffrage the basic vote, though a property qualification for lodgers still excluded a substantial proportion of men. After this private members' bills for women's suffrage were regularly introduced. These often received substantial support from MPs including the Irish members, who, according to Thomas Haslam, 'as a general rule ... voted preponderately upon our side in all questions relating to the interests of women'.[52] This support never translated into legislation both because the Conservative Party, generally opposed to women's suffrage, was in government almost continuously from 1885 to 1906, which enabled the leadership to use parliamentary procedures to dispose of unwelcome bills, and also because the Conservative majority in the House of Lords could quash any measure which passed the Commons.

The DWSA, like most suffrage organisations in the United Kingdom, demanded the vote for women on the same terms as men. In the mid-nineteenth century 'on the same terms as men' meant on a property qualification which also excluded most men. As the vote was extended to more categories of men by reducing the property qualification, the demand for women's suffrage correspondingly extended to more women. Every extension of the franchise to new groups of men while still excluding all women increased the grievance felt by the latter. Haslam wrote in 1886 that it

is not easy to keep our temper when we see the most illiterate labourer, with no two ideas in his head, exercising the very important function of self-government while educated women capable in every way of giving a rational vote are still debarred.[53]

Socialist feminists challenged suffragists as bourgeois women looking for votes for their own class. Taken in historical context neither the demand for parity with men nor the exasperation expressed by Haslam and others necessarily implied opposition to universal suffrage – so long as this included both sexes, and we may note that in 1916 Thomas Haslam's last pamphlet argued for universal suffrage for all women and men. Undoubtedly, some suffragists did see political participation as the preserve of the better-off, who had a corresponding duty to look after the poorer classes. Others may have simply made what they saw as being the only achievable demand in the social and political realities of the time. For similar reasons early suffrage demands applied only to unmarried women and widows, since married women did not control property and could not qualify for a property-related vote on the same terms as men. As married women gained property rights the suffragists demanded the removal of disqualification on the grounds of either sex or marriage.

Related issues emerged regarding the protection of women's interests in employment. Some middle-class philanthropic feminists moved beyond attempts to ameliorate the conditions of working-class women's employment to help in the organisation of women's trade unions which would be run by the workers themselves.[54] As with so many other aspects of feminism there was not a clear dividing line between the philanthropic and the self-help approaches, and Anna Haslam, who earned her own living, and whose Quaker principles gave her a respect for others who did the same, was involved with both. In the aftermath of the Trade Union Congress held in Dublin in 1880, two women's trade unions were established, the Dublin Tailoresses' Society and the Bookfolders and Sewers' Union. Both were branches of British unions and neither survived for long.[55] Haslam actively supported the venture, and also appears to have tried to link it to the suffrage campaign. With Rose McDowell, joint secretary of the DWSA, and acting against a decision of the DWSA committee,[56] she organised a public meeting in Dublin in support of women's suffrage where she was on the platform with women from the English Weavers' Union and the Shirt and Collar Makers' Union.[57]

Later in the 1890s Haslam entered a long association with the British-based National Union of Women Workers (NUWW), later the National Council of Women. The NUWW, which emerged during the 1880s, was not a trade union but a forum where women working for women could liaise and exchange information. Its first members were mainly middle-class women involved in philanthropic and religious work. By the end of the century it was promoting women in local government and on public bodies,[58] and women's trade unions were becoming affiliates.

Haslam and other DWSA delegates attended NUWW conferences over the years. Haslam was an enthusiastic supporter of the NUWW. In an account of the NUWW conference in Croydon in 1898, she emphasised the value she saw in the interchange of ideas at these meetings, and their particular benefit for Irish women who were 'so largely excluded from direct participation in the *mainstream* of human progress'.[59]

Meanwhile the numbers involved in the Irish suffrage campaign remained small. As late as 1896 the DWSA had only forty-three members.[60] As noted already, activity was sometimes interrupted by suffragists' participation in other feminist campaigns. At others unrest caused by the Land War and Home Rule agitation did the same. No executive meeting was held between April 1882 and June 1883 and the association 'did not feel that in the recent very excited condition of the country that the time was favourable for much action'.[61]

The Land War, while interrupting suffrage activity, gave a group of nationalist, and mostly Catholic, middle-class women the unique opportunity of running a nationwide political movement composed largely of men. Their experience in the Ladies' Land League[62] pushed many towards feminist consciousness. For Anna Haslam the possibility of Home Rule for Ireland was far from welcome and she became involved in counter-action. Around this time she helped to found a Dublin branch of the Women's Liberal Unionist Association and was also a member of both the Rathmines Liberal Association and the Central Unionist Committee. As was typical of Haslam she held office as secretary in the first two of these.[63]

To judge by a speech she made to a meeting of women in Dublin in 1888, she feared for the political and civil liberties of unionists under a Home Rule parliament. Ireland's present government, she claimed, while not perfect, was 'probably as good as that of any other great nation' and was improving rapidly. As evidence she pointed to Catholic Emancipation, the National Schools, the Poor Law System, the Royal University and the Intermediate Education System, the Industrial and Reformatory Schools, 'our admirable police force', and the extension of the vote to male householders, though she stressed the 'male'. She believed that all the main political leaders were committed to giving justice to Ireland, even if some made temporary mistakes, and that, with over one hundred Irish MPs to 'set them right', any serious injustice was impossible. The one threat to 'reasonable liberty' was the 'tyranny of the National League – the most unscrupulous body of men, I suppose, that have ever attempted to seize the reins of power in our land'. Home Rule would mean putting government in their hands, and they have 'refused to permit *one single Loyalist* to represent us in either of the three southern provinces', and the danger is that the Loyalists of Ireland 'will be politically extinguished'.[64]

Despite these views Haslam was committed to crossing barriers of religion and politics. The DWSA was explicitly non-party and Haslam consistently tried to widen its membership. She rejoiced in 1898 when the evidence of the polls showed that many women voters in Dublin had risen 'above all sectarian prejudices' and voted for a woman candidate of a different religion to their own 'simply because ... she can be absolutely trusted to do her duty' by the poor.[65] In the early decades of the twentieth century, when Home Rule was becoming an imminent probability, she actively encouraged women of nationalist sympathies and Catholic religion to become members. To the end of her life she was respected and held in real affection by feminists of very different political opinions. Indeed, in this speech her defence of the United Kingdom is based on what she sees as its record of justice to Ireland. She may also have been reassured by what the Haslams saw as the relatively good record of Home Rule MPs on women's interests.

In the later 1880s Irish suffragists turned their attention to local government. In England women had won the vote in municipal elections in 1869 and in 1887 the North of Ireland Suffrage Society did the same for Belfast. The poor law system, which had become an important part of the structure of Irish local government, was also under scrutiny. In England and Ireland women could vote in elections for Poor Law Guardians on the same property qualification as men, while women in England were also eligible for election as guardians. The office of Poor Law Guardian had obvious potential for women philanthropists as a move to participation in policy making. Haslam explained the failure of Irish suffragists to move on it earlier as due to the fact that election to the boards had almost from their establishment become an arena for political contest between male nationalists and unionists. It was conducted 'so on party lines and with so little regard for the well-being of our destitute poor that we were fairly excusable for taking little interest'.[66] Now the DWSA asked the Belfast MP, William Johnston, to introduce a bill and lobbied vigorously in support.[67] Participation by women in local government did not meet as strong opposition as did their access to parliament, and the Poor Law Guardians (Ireland) (Women) Act passed in 1896, providing that 'no person otherwise qualified ...

shall be disqualified by sex or marriage' from being elected or serving as a guardian.

The DWSA moved at once to consolidate this success and build on its potential. Haslam wrote to the newspapers and published leaflets explaining how women should ensure they were properly registered to vote and to stand for election, as well as writing to individual women around the country exhorting them to seek out suitable candidates and urge them to go forward. By 1898 there were seventeen women Poor Law Guardians, and by 1900 nearly one hundred.

This year of success, 1896, saw the death of Isabella Tod, the formidable Belfast campaigner for women's rights. Haslam considered Tod to have been

> one of the most effective speakers we have ever had in either Great Britain or Ireland, and her premature decease, in 1896, has been a serious loss to the cause of women in the northern province.

Tod and Haslam filled complementary roles as leaders in a number of campaigns. Haslam saw Tod as her 'great ally and co-worker in all the early fights',[68] and recognised a geographical divide, with Tod operating in Ulster, while Dublin activists were responsible for organising and inspiring women in 'our three southern provinces' as she often expressed it. While it was Haslam who later became a legend and inspiration to the next generation, Tod during her lifetime had the higher public profile as a speaker and writer while Haslam's talents lay more in organisation. While both women supported the union of Ireland with Great Britain, Haslam never saw herself as anything but Irish, and she saw the cause of women as crossing the boundaries of political and religious differences.

Eligibility as Poor Law Guardians was quickly followed by the achievement of all remaining local government franchises and eligibility for election to most local government bodies. The DWSA was again active in a campaign to include women in the forthcoming reorganisation of Irish local government, lobbying Irish MPs to support the relevant amendments. The Local Government (Ireland) Act of 1898 set up county councils and urban and rural district councils. It gave women all local government franchises on the same qualification as men, as well as making women eligible for election as urban and rural councillors, though eligibility as county councillors was withheld until 1911.

Again the DWSA published letters and leaflets to explain what had been achieved and how women could avail of it. In Anna Haslam's words the Act was

> the most signal political revolution that has taken place in the history of Irishwomen. We have, in round numbers, somewhere about one hundred thousand women ratepayers who are now invested with powers which they never possessed before.

As well as opening to women unprecedented opportunities of participation in public political life, the Act had an important psychological impact. The DWSA and Haslam saw it as a significant step to the parliamentary franchise. 'For the vast majority of our countrywomen in all our rural districts', Haslam wrote, 'their political education commences with the present year'. The experience of participation in local government 'will make them not only desire the Parliamentary vote, but willing to take some little trouble in order to obtain it'. She anticipated the spread of the suffrage movement which so far had 'never penetrated much beyond the outskirts of Dublin, Belfast and one or two other towns'.[69] This expansion had already begun and by 1898 the DWSA had branches in Tralee, Sligo, Skibbereen, Strokestown and Miltown

Malbay.[70] In line with these developments the Association now changed its name, first to the Dublin Women's Suffrage and Poor Law Guardian Association, then to the Dublin Women's Suffrage and Local Government Association, and finally to the Irish Women's Suffrage and Local Government Association (IWSLGA). The parliamentary franchise remained its core objective. However valuable in itself, the local government vote was not, insisted the Association, 'and never can be, a substitute for the parliamentary vote, to which all duly qualified women are morally as indubitably entitled as any male voters'.[71]

Anna Haslam's prophecy was proved true as the suffrage campaign grew internationally in the early years of the new century. In Ireland this expansion took place in the atmosphere of action and self-help that characterised the cultural and political renaissance of the late nineteenth and early twentieth centuries. Many of the new recruits to the suffrage cause were educated young women who had benefited by the earlier women's campaigns. Many were active in the cultural revival, some were nationalists and some sympathetic to the labour movement. Catholic women became involved in greater numbers than heretofore.

The long-established IWSLGA introduced many of the new suffragists to the movement. Anna Haslam continued to encourage educated women of all political and religious affiliations to join. Among IWSLGA members with well-known nationalist sympathies were Hanna Sheehy Skeffington and Margaret Cousins, the future founders of the Irish Women's Franchise League, Jennie Wyse Power, formerly of the Ladies' Land League and now on the executive of Sinn Féin, and Mary Hayden, professor of Irish History in University College Dublin.

In 1906 Thomas Haslam published another pamphlet on the suffrage question. Again his basic argument was that there is no sustainable argument against the principle of women's right to suffrage. He listed and rejected those which were usually trotted out; that women did not serve as policemen or soldiers; that the vote would lead to family disputes; that, because women outnumbered men in the United Kingdom men would be driven to forcibly prevent women from exercising their franchise; that women's delicacy and refinement would be put at risk. He proceeded to a succinct statement of the philosophy which permeated the thinking and statements of both Haslams on women's rights:

> Women have been brought into the world, like men, to cultivate their whole nature, physical, intellectual, moral, spiritual, political, and so on, in the way most conducive to their happiness, and the well-being of the world at large.[72]

As the suffrage movement grew internationally it began to employ new methods to use its size to political effect. Large scale street demonstrations with banners, slogans and colours became popular. Some suffragists moved further to what were called 'militant' methods, first to forms of passive civil disobedience such as refusal to pay tax, then to heckling and disrupting public meetings, and finally to physical violence such as damaging public property. This final level of militancy emerged in Britain and Ireland where suffrage had so long appeared just within reach but had never actually materialised. The name 'suffragette' was coined to designate the militants. In England the Women's Social and Political Union (WSPU), founded in 1903 by Emmeline Pankhurst and her daughters, was an explicitly militant organisation.

In June 1908 nine IWSLGA committee members, including both Haslams, 'under two appropriate banners', were among the Irish participants in a major suffrage demonstration in London.[73] However, the Association remained committed to action strictly within the law. Ireland's principal militant suffrage organisation, the Irish Women's Franchise League (IWFL), was established in 1908. The aim was a society on the model of the English WPSU but completely independent of any English society. Its founders, Hanna Sheehy Skeffington and Margaret Cousins, both members of the IWSLGA, were impatient for more assertive action. In recognition of the position Haslam held in the Irish suffrage movement, in November 1908 the founders of the new group went to

> ... the dear old leader of the constitutional suffragists, Mrs Anna Haslam, to inform her that we younger women were ready to start a new suffrage society on militant lines. She regretted what she felt to be a duplication of effort. She was also congenitally a person of peace, non-violent, law-abiding to the finger tips. But she sensed the Time Spirit, and we parted as friends, agreeing to differ on means, though united in aim and ideals.[74]

The IWFL, like the IWSLGA, demanded the vote for women on the same terms as men, and both organisations were non-party and open to members of all religions and political affiliations. Their constitutions differed in that the IWSLGA was committed to staying within the law while the IWFL was committed to breaking it if necessary. In practice there was another difference in that the leadership of the IWSLGA was unionist in sympathy and that of the IWFL was nationalist.

Other new suffrage societies were established in Ireland and by 1912 there were over three thousand active women suffragists, and the movement had attained a numerical strength far beyond any earlier feminist campaigns. The largest groups were the IWFL with over 1000 members, the IWSLGA with 700–800, an Irish branch of the Conservative and Unionist Women's Suffrage Association with 660, and the Irish Women's Suffrage Society, Belfast, originally a branch of the IWSLGA but now independent, with 'several hundred'.[75] The majority of suffragists were still middle-class and Protestant but the Catholic presence was much larger than before with the Catholic to non-Catholic ratio about one to two. Irish working-class suffragists appear to have remained few in number. A range of smaller organisations were affiliated to an umbrella network, the Irish Women's Suffrage Federation (IWSF) established in 1911. By 1913 it had fifteen affiliated societies, including nine from Ulster as well as the Munster Women's Franchise League (MWFL), which itself had branches.[76]

Home Rule for Ireland by now posed problems for suffragists. Once the Parliament Act of 1911 removed the power of the House of Lords to veto legislation the passing both of a women's suffrage act and a Home Rule act became more likely. In 1912 one of a number of what were called 'Conciliation Bills', women's suffrage bills agreed by members of the main political parties, failed to pass its second reading because the Irish Parliamentary Party did not support it. Its leader, John Redmond, himself an opponent of votes for women, feared that if the Bill passed it could lead to the fall of the Liberal government and so endanger Home Rule, and his party fell into line. The failure of this Conciliation Bill infuriated many suffragists in both Ireland and Britain. Interestingly, the IWSLGA, while sharing the anger, made some allowance for 'the tergiversation' of Irish MPs in the light of their fears for the Home Rule Bill,[77] an attitude which may reflect the presence in the IWSLGA of members like Mary Hayden who supported the Irish Parliamentary Party.

The suffrage organisations strove to remain united in action despite the contrary pull of nationalist and unionist loyalties and commitments to constitutional or militant action. The general policy was to support all measures of suffrage, whether a franchise bill for the whole United Kingdom or the inclusion of women's suffrage in a Home Rule Bill. However, some nationalist women argued that to ask the Westminster parliament for the vote was to recognise its authority over Ireland. They also claimed that there was no need to demand the inclusion of women's suffrage in a Home Rule Bill since this would be freely granted by nationalist men in a free Ireland.

When the third Home Rule Bill began its course through parliament in 1912 Redmond refused to endanger its passage by insisting on the inclusion of women's suffrage. Suffrage organisations of all political affiliations joined forces to demand its inclusion at a mass meeting presided over by Mary Hayden of the IWSLGA.[78] Redmond did not move and the IWFL turned to militancy. This was largely symbolic and publicity-directed. Members broke windows in a number of public buildings with the aim of being arrested, refusing to pay the fines imposed by the court and going to prison. Between 1912 and the outbreak of the First World War in 1914 thirty-five women had been convicted for suffrage militancy in Ireland.[79]

Haslam was in London at the time of the window-breaking. On her own initiative she wrote to the newspapers to publicly express the IWSLGA's disapproval of such action. She had been unable to summon her committee

... but I know that I am embodying their sentiments when I express my strong disapproval of the breaking of windows as a means of advancing our cause. It is my conviction that the adoption of such action by a section of our supporters was one of the chief contributory causes of the defeat of the Conciliation Bill, and I do not believe that it will promote the passing of a women's suffrage amendment to our Home Rule Bill, if carried. Our Association, which has been in existence since 1876, has always consistently disapproved of what are called militant methods in the advancement of our cause.[80]

Although the IWSLGA subsequently approved her action (although three members resigned in protest)[81] the attitude of both Haslam and her organisation was not one of blanket condemnation of militancy. Many suffragists who were themselves committed to constitutional methods could empathise with militancy provoked by the long denial to women of one of the basic rights of citizenship, and were angered by the hypocrisy of condemning actions by suffragists which, if carried out by male members of a political movement, would hardly have raised an eyebrow. Constitutional suffragists also conceded that militant methods sometimes succeeded where theirs did not. A few years earlier both Haslam and her friend and colleague in the IWSLGA, Lady Dockrell, had expressed sympathy and even approval of methods they would not themselves adopt. After clashes between some suffragists and police at a demonstration at Westminster in 1907, Dockrell admitted that she both sympathised and approved of militant action and that she thought it was the only way 'by which women will ever get anything'. Haslam smiled, said they could not really blame them, 'they are our sisters, after all', and gave it as her opinion that 'on the whole the campaign will do more good than harm'.[82] In 1910 the IWSLGA wryly noted that militancy had persuaded the Chief Secretary, Birrell, to receive a deputation when he had refused its own 'courteous request'.[83] Finally, we can note Hanna Sheehy Skeffington's account of Haslam's visit to her in Mountjoy Prison after the IWFL's window-breaking:

> Mrs Haslam came, with a difference: 'Don't think I approve – but here's a pot of verbena I brought you. I am not here in my official capacity, of course – the Irish Women's Suffrage and Local Government Association strongly disapprove of violence as pulling back the cause. But here's some loganberry jam – I made it myself.[84]

In 1913, at the age of eighty-four, Haslam resigned as secretary of the IWSLGA, becoming life-president instead. This, however, was far from signalling the end of her active role in the feminist movement. The outbreak of World War I in August 1914 made it difficult to maintain active suffrage campaigning. Irish organisations most closely associated with English groups tended to suspend suffrage action temporarily and turn to work in support of the British war effort. The *Irish Citizen*, the suffrage newspaper founded in 1912 in association with the IWFL, insisted, under the headline 'Votes for Women Now – Damn Your War', that suffragists must continue their campaign.[85] Both it and the IWFL took a pacifist position to the war itself. Other nationalist women, believing that England's difficulty was Ireland's opportunity and that for the time being the rights of the nation took precedence over women's rights, joined Cumann na mBan, the women's organisation set up in 1914 to work with the Irish Volunteers. The IWSLGA started a fund for the relief of Belgian refugees in Ireland,[86] and endowed a bed in the Dublin Castle Red Cross Hospital.[87] At the same time it initiated a Joint Committee, under Haslam, of delegates from women's societies in Dublin to co-ordinate efforts on women's issues other than suffrage.[88] One of the Joint Committee's activities was the setting up of patrols. The introduction of women police was a long-standing feminist objective and voluntary women patrols, working in conjunction with the police, were part of the campaign for professional women police.

Haslam, who, with Mary Hayden, was joint president of the Patrol Committee, reported in 1915 to the annual meeting of the Council of the Women's National Health Association of Ireland that there were twenty patrols, authorised by the police, in action in central Dublin. The patrols worked in couples, a Catholic and Protestant where possible, and needed more Catholic volunteers, as well as Catholic and Protestant clubs to which the patrols could direct girls who were walking about the streets.[89]

The *Irish Citizen* was uneasy about aspects of the patrols. While not disputing the need for women police in the exclusively male law-enforcement system, it feared that the patrols' method of removing women from the streets would in effect repeat the sexist method of policing women to protect men, and ignore the problem of rough treatment of women by the police.[90] It also queried the implications of such voluntary amateur services for demands for full entry by women into all the professions.[91] The *Irish Worker* challenged the middle-class composition of the Joint Committee and called on working-class parents to resent these 'well-to-do snobs'.[92]

1915 also saw the fulfilment of Anna Haslam's long-time aim to establish in Dublin a branch of the English-based National Union of Women Workers, of which the IWSLGA was already an affiliate.[93] This drew criticism from the *Irish Citizen* on the grounds it was unlikely to 'unite women of every shade of opinion' since the vice-presidents and committee appeared to be 'restricted practically to women of precisely the same shade of opinion', and expressed its disapproval of setting up Irish branches of British organisations.[94] Yet the nationalist Hayden was a member of the committee and the same issue of the *Irish Citizen* printed the full text of Thomas Haslam's address to a meeting of the IWFL.[95]

1916 brought the Easter Rising and the Proclamation of the Irish Republic which included full citizenship for all Irish men and women. In the following years, through the War of Independence to the Treaty and the establishment in 1922 of the Irish Free State, the IWFL, with Cumann na mBan and the Irish Women Workers' Union (IWWU), concentrated much of its attention on pressing Sinn Féin to include women in its own leadership and on ensuring that the citizenship of the 1916 Proclamation was delivered on in a future independent Ireland. This was an area where Haslam and the IWSLGA could have little input. What Haslam thought of the 1916 Rising is not recorded and the IWSLGA report for 1916 made no mention of it, instead focusing on the anticipated concession of women's suffrage by the UK government at the end of the war, and deciding to urge the inclusion of women in the new electoral register.

In 1916 Thomas Haslam, at the age of ninety, published his final suffrage pamphlet, *Some Last Words on Women's Suffrage*. In this he continued to argue that the essential for success was that enough women actively wanted it. He noted that the prime minister, Asquith, was committed to some measure after the war and that the extent of the suffrage then granted would depend on the attitude of women in the meantime. He called for full adult suffrage for both sexes, claiming that people with no property needed the protection of the vote more than people with property and that there was no justification for the present position which excluded all married women with the exception of those who were property owners in their own right. Women needed the vote more than men, he asserted, because generally they were poorer, paid less, victimised by inheritance laws, physically weaker, and their interests are also those of their children. He rejected the argument that it would be dangerous to give women the vote because women were constitutionally unable to take the broad view in national emergencies, though he conceded that in the short term women would follow their husbands and brothers until they acquired political experience which would give a sense of personal responsibility.

A year later, in 1917, Thomas Haslam died and was buried in the Friends' Cemetery at Temple Hill, Blackrock, County Dublin. What the breaking of this partnership of sixty-three years meant to Anna Haslam can only be imagined. If he had lived for another year he would have seen the culmination of their work for women's suffrage when his wife at last cast her vote in a parliamentary election.

In January 1918 the Representation of the People Act, a compromise between the Liberal and Conservative parties, gave a limited measure of female suffrage, confined to women over thirty, who themselves or whose husbands were householders or occupiers of land or premises of a minimum yearly value of £5. The restriction reflected the fears of all the parties as to how they would fare when women voted in the coming election. Even with these limitations both the Irish Party and the Unionists tried to prevent its extension to Ireland. In view of their past attitude to women's suffrage both had reason to feel apprehensive. Later in the year another Act made women eligible to stand as parliamentary candidates.

The general election was not held until December after the end of the war and, in the meantime, women's organisations were active on two main issues. In April 1918 the attempt to extend conscription to Ireland began, and in August a new government regulation of prostitution, similar to the Contagious Diseases Acts of the 1860s, was introduced in the Defence of the Realm Act (DORA). The IWSLGA took part in the campaign against DORA but not in the anti-conscription campaign, though members like Hayden did so in an individual capacity, while Cumann na mBan, the IWWU and the IWFL all took part in both.[96]

In December 1918 the first general election in which at least some women could vote and stand for election took place. The *Irish Citizen* noted that the declared voting intentions of some prominent feminist women refuted predictions that all women would vote the same way, all conservative or all radical. In Rathmines in Dublin, Mary Kettle, sister of Hanna Sheehy Skeffington, and Mary Hayden supported the Irish Party candidate, Anna Haslam the Conservative candidate, and Hanna Sheehy Skeffington the Sinn Féin candidate.[97] That these differences did not undermine the unique position Haslam held in the esteem and affections of Irish suffragists is shown in the IWFL's account:

On Election Day the League was represented with its banners and colours at joint demonstrations organised by the various suffrage and women's organisations for Mrs Haslam, the veteran Irish suffrage leader. She recorded her vote in the midst of an admiring feminine throng to cheer her, was presented with a bouquet in suffrage colours for the occasion ... It speaks well for the broadmindedness of the new women voters that women of all parties – Unionist, Irish Party and Sinn Féin – joined heartily to honour Mrs Haslam and suffrage.[98]

In the same month the IWSLGA changed its name to the Irish Women Citizens and Local Government Association to continue to work for sex equality in all franchises and opportunities for public service, to further the registration of women voters and the election of women at parliamentary and local levels, as well as the appointment of women to public offices.[99] It continued its efforts to promote combined action by the suffrage organisations at a series of conferences, but the IWFL reported that, 'owing to the disturbed state of the political atmosphere no common basis of agreement could be reached'.[100] The War of Independence, which began early in 1919, and the succeeding Treaty negotiations and debates dominated the following years. Haslam died at the age of ninety-three in November 1922, the year when the constitution of the new Irish Free State gave the vote and full citizenship to all women and men over twenty-one years of age.

Assessing Anna Haslam's contribution to Irish history is difficult. The energy and enthusiasm which made an impact on everyone she met brings her alive as a personality in a way that contrasts with the scarcity of information on most of her work, with the exception of women's suffrage.

One aspect that stands out is the sheer quality of her work. This is evidenced in particular by the thoroughly-researched pamphlets she wrote for the IWSLGA explaining in careful and accurate detail what women had gained in the poor law and local government legislation and how they could avail of this.

Her leadership qualities were also impressive. She had the ability both to inspire others and to work with them, as shown by her effective guidance of the suffrage association she founded in 1876 throughout her long tenure of its secretaryship. That the IWSLGA was not a one-woman show was demonstrated by its active survival when Haslam retired and after she died. Under its new name, the Irish Women Citizens and Local Government Association, it was quickly in the field in the early 1920s and played a leading role in feminist opposition to attempts by successive Free State governments to renege on aspects of women's full citizenship as established in the 1922 Constitution. This role continued until 1947 when the Women Citizens emerged with a new and vigorous group, the Irish Housewives' Association.[101]

In their claims for women's equality the arguments of both Anna Haslam and her husband are based mainly on the concept implicit in European Enlightenment thought that, on the basis of shared rational human nature, all persons had the right to autonomy and full citizenship. Both Haslams did at times speak of women's contribution as differing in some ways to that of men. For example, Anna referred to the need for women Guardians to improve the diet, the nursing and the training of children in many Poor Law Unions,[102] while Thomas saw women's participation in politics needed to solve the social problems of temperance, pauperism, prostitution and aggressive wars.[103] But neither urged these as the basis of their claims for equal rights.

Both placed much more emphasis on the equality of the sexes as persons. As has been seen, Thomas Haslam developed these arguments in his writings, both in *The Women's Advocate* and in his various pamphlets. While Anna Haslam did not expound her thinking as fully the same ideas permeate her speeches. In 1898 she spoke of the parliamentary franchise as *'a matter of the barest equitable right'*.[104] In 1907 she explained that 'we are still battling for a constitutional right which Mr Gladstone's government should have conceded to us when they passed their Reform Act of 1884'.[105] In the following year she emphasised that, in her opinion

> ... the elevation of women, the whole world over, to their rightful position in the social and political organism, is one of the most important problems, if not, indeed, the *most* important, that is confronting us at the present day. Our parliamentary enfranchisement is only the first step in its practical realisation; but it is the first, and the *most indispensable* to the realisation of the rest.[106]

The thinking of both Haslams on women's rights can be summed up in the quotation from Herbert Spencer which was printed under the title of each issue of *The Women's Advocate:* 'Equity knows no difference of sex. The law of equal freedom applies to the whole race – female as well as male', and in Thomas Haslam's comment: 'Ethically speaking, that principle covers all that needs to be said upon the subject'.[107]

Research on Irish feminist organisations has tended to concentrate on the relationship between feminism and nationalism in the early decades of the twentieth century. The work of Haslam and her contemporaries extends our perspective, backwards to at least the mid-nineteenth-century and forwards with the organisation she founded into the Inter-War years and after. The feminism-nationalism nexus is then seen as one aspect of a multi-faceted engagement of feminism with unionism and with nationalism, with Catholicism and with Protestantism, and with socialism and the Labour movement. A more complex picture emerges, within which feminism actively influenced other movements and ways of seeing the world as well as being in turn influenced by them.

Haslam and her Protestant middle-class colleagues created the first organised Irish feminist campaigns and changed the legal position of women in Irish society in a number of significant ways. The specific contribution of Haslam herself included her clarity of thinking and expression, her long presence as an articulate and confident voice steadily and consistently asserting the self-evident truth of women's claims, and, perhaps most of all, her inclusive concept of Irishness. This last quality, allied to her warm and lively personality, must have been a major factor in encouraging the participation of Catholic and nationalist women in organised feminist action, particularly the Irish suffrage movement, in the early twentieth century. It was to this quality that a leading Irish feminist paid tribute in 1913, when she wrote:

> [T]he Society of Friends is as prominent in the history of suffrage in Ireland as it is in every other good work. Many have sought to help Ireland and have only earned the distrust of the Irish: to the Friends alone it has been given to win the trust and love of the Catholic south and the Protestant north, and so we find the name of Mrs Haslam in the list of suffrage work.[108]

from Mary Cullen and Maria Luddy (eds), *Women, Power and Consciousness in Nineteenth-Century Ireland: Eight Biographical Studies* (Dublin, Attic Press, 1995), pp 161–196.

NOTES

1   *Report of the Executive of the Irish Women's Suffrage and Poor Law Association for 1917* [Hereafter *IWSLGA Report*] (Dublin, 1918), p. 4.

2   Thomas Haslam's obituary stated that the Haslams had deposited their collected papers in the National Library, Dublin, but the National Library has no trace of them. A few items in the custody of the Irish Housewives' Association (hereafter IHA) are now deposited in the National Archives.

3   Genealogical information from the Religious Society of Friends' Historical Library, Swanbrook House, Dublin (Hereafter FHL).

4   Cyril G. Brannigan, 'Quaker Education in 18th and 19th Century Ireland', *Irish Educational Studies,* Vol. IV, No. 1 (1984), p. 57.

5   Phil Kilroy, 'Women and the Reformation in Seventeenth-Century Ireland', in Margaret Mac Curtain and Mary O'Dowd (eds), *Women in Early Modern Ireland* (Dublin, 1991), p. 192; David Hempton and Myrtle Hill, 'Women and Protestant Minorities in Eighteenth-Century Ireland', *ibid.,* p. 198.

6   Hempton and Hill, 'Women and Protestant Minorities', p. 200.

7   The American Quaker feminist, born in 1820, and for many years co-leader with Elizabeth Cady Stanton of the US women's movement. She visited Ireland in 1884.

8   Typescript of speech given by Haslam, no date, IHA.

9   Cyril Gerard Brannigan, 'Quaker Education in Ireland 1680–1840', MA thesis, St. Patrick's College, Maynooth, 1992.

10 *Newtown School Centenary Record* (Waterford, 1898), passim and p. 76.

11 Helen Blackburn, *A Record of the Women's Suffrage Movement in the British Isles* (London, 1902), p. 129.

12 MS note, IHA.

13 *Irish Citizen,* 21 March 1914, p. 347 and 28 March 1914, p. 355.

14 *Ibid* and newspaper cutting, 5 April 1909, FHL.

15 Typescript of speech, 1886, IHA.

16 Jill Liddington, *The Long Road to Greenham: Feminism and Anti-Militarism in Britain since 1820* (London, 1989), p. 16.

17 *Irish Citizen,* 21 March 1914, p. 347.

18 Frederick B. Tolles (ed.), *Slavery and 'the Woman Question': Lucretia Mott's Diary 1840* (London and New York, 1952). Mott made a pithy comment on Quaker education in one Dublin school: 'his boys forward in arithmetic – girls sampler work – stitching and other nonsense', p. 64.

19 *Irish Citizen,* 21 March 1914, p. 347.

20 Blackburn, *Record,* p. 129.

21 J.H. and M.E. Cousins, *We Two Together* (Madras, 1950), p. 129.

22 *Irish Citizen,* 4 April 1914, p. 366.

23 *Ibid.*, p. 361.

24 MS note, IHA.

25 *Irish Citizen*, 4 April 1914, p. 366.

26 Obituary of T.J. Haslam by Professor C.H. Oldham, FHL.

27 *Slater's Commercial Directory of Ireland* (London, 1870), p. 120.

28 Obituary by Oldlam, FHL.

29 Speech by Thomas Haslam at function in honour of Anna Haslam's eightieth birthday, newspaper cutting, 5 April 1909, FHL.

30 Blackburn, *Record,* p. 129.

31 See Anne V. O'Connor, 'Anne Jellicoe' in Cullen and Luddy, *Women, Power and Consciousness*, pp 125–160.

32 *Final Report of the Royal Irish Association for Promoting the Training and Employment of Women* (Dublin, 1904), p. 10.

33 *Irish Citizen*, 12 March 1914, p. 347.

34 *Ibid.*, 28 March 1914, p. 355.

35 Anne V. O'Connor and Susan B. Parkes, *Gladly Learn and Gladly Teach: A History of Alexandra College and School, Dublin 1886–1996* (Dublin, 1983), pp 46–7.

36 MS list of campaigns in which Haslam had been involved, IHA.

37 *Englishwoman's Review,* 15 March 1877, p. 132 and 14 April 1877, pp 150–1.

38 *Irish Citizen*, 21 March 1914, p. 347.

39 See Maria Luddy, 'Isabella M.S. Tod' in Cullen and Luddy, *Women, Power and Consciousness*, pp 197–230.

40 *Special Report from the Select Committee on the Married Women's Property Bill* [4417], H.C. 1867-8, cccxxxix, 74–5.

41 *Irish Citizen*, 21 March 1914, p. 347.

42 Maria Luddy, 'Irish Women and the Contagious Diseases Acts', *History Ireland,* Vol. I, No. l (Spring 1993), pp 32–4.

43 Evidence of Josephine Butler (*Report of the Royal Commission upon the Administration and Operation of the Contagious Diseases Acts, vol ii, Minutes of Evidence*, p. 440, H.C. 1871 (408–1), xix).

44 T.J. Haslam, *A Few Words on Prostitution and the Contagious Diseases Acts* (Dublin, 1870).

45 *Annual Report of the National Association for the Repeal of the Contagious Diseases Acts 1870–1*, p. 4.

46 *Irish Citizen*, 21 March 1914, p. 347.

47 *Ibid.*

48 *The Shield*, 5 June 1886.

49   *Irish Citizen*, 21 March 1914, p. 347.

50   Blackburn, *Record*, p. 129.

51   *Irish Citizen*, 21 March 1914, p. 347.

52   T.J. Haslam, *Women's Suffrage from a Masculine Viewpoint* (Dublin, 1906), p. 15.

53   Typescript of speech, 1886, IHA.

54   Ellen Mappen, *Helping Women at Work: The Women's Industrial Council 1889–1914* (London, 1985), p. 13.

55   Theresa Moriarty, *Work in Progress: Episodes from the History of Irish Women's Trade Unionism* (Dublin and Belfast, 1994), p. 2.

56   Minutes of DWSA executive committee (hereafter DWSA Minutes), 4 November 1880, IHA.

57   *Women's Suffrage Journal,* 1 October 1880.

58   Patricia Hollis, *Ladies Elect: Women in English Local Government 1865–1914* (London, 1987), pp 25–6.

59   MS notebook, IHA.

60   Rosemary Cullen Owens, *Smashing Times: A History of the Irish Women's Suffrage Movement 1889–1922* (Dublin, 1984), p. 25.

61   DWSA Minutes, 27 June 1883, IHA.

62   See Jane McL Côté and Dana Hearne, 'Anna Parnell', in Cullen and Luddy, *Women, Power and Consciousness*, pp 263–293.

63   MS list of societies Anna Haslam was connected with, IHA.

64   MS text of speech, IHA.

65   *Ibid.,* p. 222.

66   *Englishwoman's Review,* 10 October 1898, p. 221.

67   *Report of the Executive Committee of the Dublin Women's Suffrage and Poor Law Guardians Association for 1896* (Dublin, 1897), p. 3. (Hereafter *IWSLGA Report*).

68   *Irish Citizen*, 28 March 1914, p. 347.

69   *Englishwoman's Review,* 15 October 1898, pp 223–5.

70   *IWSLGA Report for 1898,* p. 8.

71   *IWSLGA Report for 1900,* p. 11.

72   Haslam, *Women's Suffrage.*

73   *IWSLGA Report for 1908,* p. 7.

74   Cousins, *We Two Together,* p. l64.

75   *Irish Citizen*, 25 May 1912, p. 7.

76   Cullen Owens, *Smashing Times*, p. 43.

77   *IWSLGA Report for 1912,* p. 5.

78   Cullen Owens, *Smashing Times,* pp 51–3. While the IWSLGA is not mentioned among the organisations represented, Hayden presided and Anna Haslam sent a message.

79   *Ibid.,* p. 64.

80   *Irish Citizen,* 22 June 1912, p. 39.

81   IWSLGA minutes, 12 September 1912, IHA.

82   *Evening Mail,* 15 February 1907.

83   *IWSLGA Report for 1910,* pp 12–3.

84   Hanna Sheehy Skeffington, 'Reminiscences of an Irish Suffragette', in Andree Sheehy Skeffington and Rosemary Owens, *Votes for Women* (Dublin, 1975), p. 21.

85   Cullen Owens, *Smashing Times,* p. 95.

86   *IWSLGA Report for 1914,* p. 7.

87   *IWSLGA Report for 1915,* p. 5.

88   *IWSLGA Report for 1914,* p. 4.

89   *Irish Times,* 15 April 1915.

90   *Irish Citizen,* 2 January 1915, p. 253.

91   *Ibid.,* 9 January 1915, p. 258.

92   *Ibid.,* 16 January 1915, p. 267.

93   *IWSLGA Report for 1915,* p. 8.

94   *Irish Citizen,* 20 November 1915, p. 165.

95   *Ibid.,* p. 171.

96   Cullen Owens, *Smashing Times,* p. 76.

97   *Irish Citizen,* December 1918, p. 633.

98   *Ibid,* January 1919, p. 643.

99   Meeting 12 November 1918, *IWSLGA Report for 1918,* pp 8–9.

100 *Irish Citizen,* April 1919, p. 655.

101 Hilda Tweedy, *A Link in the Chain: The Story of the Irish Housewives' Association 1942–1992* (Dublin, Attic, 1992), p. 22.

102 *Englishwoman's Review,* 15 October 1898, p. 222.

103 Haslam, *Some Last Words on Women's Suffrage,* p. 17.

104 Speech to the National Union of Women Workers, Croydon, October 1898, IHA.

105 Typescript of speech delivered at Manchester, IHA.

106 Typescript of speech to International Suffrage Congress meeting in England, 1908, IHA.

107 Haslam, *Last Words,* p. 4.

108 Dora Mellone quoted in Cliona Murphy, *The Women's Suffrage Movement and Irish Society in the Early Twentieth Century* (New York and London, 1989), p. 17.

TOWARDS A NEW IRELAND:
WOMEN, FEMINISM AND THE PEACE PROCESS

Women and Irish History *(1997) was a collection of essays in honour of Margaret Mac Curtain, edited by Maryann Valiulis and Mary O'Dowd. It was a fitting tribute to a pioneer in the writing of women's history in Ireland. The subject of my essay was an area I had been interested in for many years. In Northern Ireland the emergence of second wave feminism coincided with the emergence of the Northern Ireland civil rights movement, and inevitably interacted with it. Over the years it continued to interact with the rising tension between nationalists and unionists, the intervention of the British government and the arrival of British troops, the long years of conflict between the latter and the IRA, the various attempts to end that conflict, the IRA ceasefire of 1994, followed by the ups and downs of the Peace Process. The Peace Process negotiations focused on nationalist versus unionist differences, and on achieving a workable compromise acceptable to both sides. By the time this essay was written, in Northern Ireland Clár na mBan had been set up in 1994 to push feminist claims within the republican movement, and in 1996 the Northern Ireland Women's Coalition had been established by women from both sides of the political divide. The Coalition aimed to win itself a place at the negotiating table and to work there to ensure that any agreement reached was fair to all interests and traditions, and that women's concerns were on the agenda and integral to that agreement. The northern situation also impacted on feminism in the Republic and gave rise to ongoing debate and argument. This essay was an attempt to sort out my thinking on the role that feminism in Ireland north and south might play in achieving a solution.*

As a feminist, I have been particularly interested in two features of the peace process over the past few years: the claims for women's participation in the public negotiations and the grassroots arena where community groups and women's groups have developed their own politics. I was privileged to be present at the first Clár na mBan conference in March 1994 where nationalist and republican women expressed openly their concern at the exclusively male and secretive nature of the negotiations then in progress, and their insistence that any agreed new Ireland must take on board a much broader range of discriminations and conflicting interests than simply those of the nationalist-unionist nexus. Since then, I have taken part in many debates about the relationship between women and the peace process, and have watched with interest and sympathy the emergence of the Northern Ireland Women's Coalition which crossed the conventional political divides and won itself a place at the negotiating table.

It has become increasingly clear that the peace process, as presently structured, has no space for serious discussion of a new Ireland in any holistic sense. Its remit is to deal with nationalist/unionist conflict within a narrow green versus orange model of Irish politics. I also believe that it is feminism rather than women *per se* that has the potential to make a radical contribution to debate about a new Ireland. Putting these two together, it appears to me that the best way feminists can try to ensure that this potential is realised, and, paradoxically, the best way we can support the women actively participating in the peace process is by working outside the process to develop a serious internal debate about feminism itself and between feminists and other groups interested in radical change in society. In this article I try to explain and justify this conclusion.

When we talk about women and the peace process, we need to be clear whether we mean the right to take part in the negotiations, or the contribution women might make to them, or both of these. One claim that women should participate equally with men in the process is based on the argument that women are as fully citizens as men are, and that the dearth of women among the negotiators is due to discrimination based on sex. This does not necessarily imply that women would act differently than men as negotiators, but neither does it exclude the possibility that they might. Another claim to participation includes an explicit or implicit argument that women's contribution is different to men's but equally valuable.

If we think women have a different contribution to make, we need to ask in what way it is different. We might think women in general are more capable of resolving conflict by negotiation and compromise than men in general, and less inclined to use force of any kind to impose a solution. Or our view might be that women are in general more inclined towards peace at any price, even if that includes leaving an issue of perceived injustice unresolved. On the contrary, we might believe women are *more* interested than men in a just solution that seeks to provide for the legitimate needs of all parties, where men tend to opt for a winner and loser situation.

If we believe any of these things, we have to ask on what grounds we do so. One explanation would be that women and men are in some way biologically programmed to think and act differently. Another is that the different social experience of being a female or a male teaches the sexes different values and/or strategies. Yet another would argue that the sex-role stereotypes to which we are socialised to conform, condone, foster or encourage different ways of thinking and acting for each sex.

The whole question of male and female 'human nature' is fraught with uncertainties and unresolved questions. Whatever 'biological' differences may exist between the sexes in ways of perceiving and interpreting the environment, and acting to change it, over the centuries these have been so interwoven with social and political interventions that disentangling them is no easy task. Observed differences in general patterns of behaviour between the sexes, in particular with regard to male 'dominance' and female 'subordination', have yet to be explained. Explanations indeed abound but all have the standing of hypotheses, and none has established itself beyond challenge.

Nor is the evidence of history decisive. More physical violence has been and is perpetrated by men than by women, and this cannot be fully explained by saying that in general men are physically stronger, and so more often in a position where they can exercise physical violence at little risk to themselves. This might apply to violence by men against women, but not to violence between men or to violence against children. The role of masculine stereotypes which include aggression and the use of physical force need evaluation. To what extent do these stereotypes reflect the real 'nature' of males or are they essentially socially-constructed models to which males are pressurised to conform? On the other hand, it is difficult to maintain that women are inherently more committed to peace than men. Women are obviously capable of aggressive behaviour and the use of verbal and physical force. It could be argued that the lesser use of force by women is the result of both lesser opportunity *and* the power of social stereotypes of appropriate female behaviour. Nor does history show a consistent pattern of women as a group actively opposing war. It shows instead that the majority of women, like the majority of men, have supported their own group or country and helped in its war effort. While men have for the most part been the front-line combatants, women have played active and essential roles in war.

When we turn to the longer-term project of building political, social and economic structures that might create conditions favourable to lasting justice and peace, there are few grounds for believing that all women will share the same view as to what sort of structures would be most likely to create a just society. The historical evidence does not show women consistently supporting different political policies than men. In Ireland today, women involved in politics, like men involved in politics, are members of parties and movements which have very different views as to the political structures and social and economic policies that would best serve the community at large.

I believe a stronger case can be made for feminism having an identifiable contribution to make. This starts with definitions of feminism. The roots of feminism lie in the roles and behaviours societies prescribe for women and men. Women are not a separate homogeneous group in society, but comprise half of every race and nation, half of every colour and creed, of every ethnic group and every age group and so on. Women, like men, have been oppressors as well as oppressed, slave owners as well as slaves, colonisers as well as colonised. Yet, within such categories as the rich and the powerful, men are over-represented and women under-represented. And, within all groups and categories, women and men seldom share the same access to resources, power and opportunities. The lifestyle and opportunities of the daughter of a wealthy middle-class family in suburban Dublin in the late nineteenth century and of a married woman rearing a family in a slum in the same city at the same time might seem so different as to have no point of contact. Yet in each case, the lifestyle and opportunities of the woman were affected by her sex as well as by her class, wealth, education, age and marital status, and were observably different to and more restricted than those of her brother or husband. Throughout recorded history the sex of an individual has always cut across and interacted with all other divisions within society.

Feminist theorists argue that the political, social and economic consequences of one's sex cannot be explained by a simple biological determinism, but by the ways in which societies have constructed political, social and economic roles around biological sex. The theorists have given the name 'gender' to this social construction of sex. Our sex, whether female or male, and the gender roles in our society, together comprise one factor which interacts with many more to locate each of us in our time and place and to define the challenges, opportunities and difficulties that face us in our growth to self-realisation.

While men as well as women have been and are oppressed by the unequal distribution of authority, resources, personal autonomy and freedom to explore different areas of human activity, the specific oppression of women arises from the interaction of sex with this unequal distribution. While concepts of what it means to be human have differed over time and place and society, it appears that women, in comparison with men in the same family, class, ethnic or national group, religious or political organisation, have seldom shared the same degree of autonomy and choice in their personal lives, or the same access to the arenas of public power and decision-making. Societies identified as patriarchal by feminists have sought to control women's lives and define women's 'nature' or 'role' in terms of a male-centred perspective which served the interests of a dominant elite.

While we need to be historically specific and avoid sliding into reductionism or unsustainable generalisation, and while actual gender roles have differed over place and time, it appears that feminism has always grown from individual women's perception that the roles imposed by their own society conflicted both with their knowledge of themselves and with their development as self-directed adult persons. This was, for example, the analysis of Mary Wollstonecraft, daughter of the Enlightenment and the radical republicanism of the late eighteenth century. She rejected Rousseau's dictum in *Émile* that women's role in society was to serve men and that consequently women should be educated in subordination. She insisted that women were rational beings as men were, with the same right and duty to develop and use reasoned judgement. For the thinkers of her day, including Wollstonecraft herself, reason and virtue were closely linked. 'How grossly do they insult us who thus advise us only to render ourselves gentle, domestic brutes', she wrote, insisting that 'it is a farce to call any being virtuous whose virtues do not result from the exercise of its own reason'.[1]

The basis, justification and ultimate driving force of feminism is the conviction that sex roles which limit women's control over their own lives, and which subordinate women to men, and women's needs to men's needs, deny women's full humanity and are based on a model of relationships which is oppressive to women, dehumanising to both sexes and detrimental to society as a whole. From this it follows that the feminist project is to try to understand the oppression of women, what it consists of and how it operates, and to identify the conditions which would eliminate it. This is not an easy task. When women reject existing female stereotypes, the only models to hand of self-determination and personal autonomy derive from the male stereotype. The very language of self-determination and autonomy which we use comes from this male model. To a dawning feminist awareness, it is not always immediately obvious that women can hardly aspire to a stereotype which further feminist reflection reveals to be itself oppressive and which includes dominance over women. Indeed, a main ingredient of the macho-male stereotype of today is the negative one of not behaving like a woman. Feminist theory and strategy face the challenge of breaking one defective mould without creating another equally unacceptable. This presents difficulties, since creating a space for women to exercise autonomy, and to experiment with new models, requires as an essential first step the assertion of equal rights with men in all areas of society, and this can all too easily be equated with acting as men do.

Feminism seldom arrives in our lives complete with a ready-made new human model or a comprehensive theory of how society should be organised. Most of us move towards feminism as a result of a personal experience of discrimination or oppression which is only gradually recognised as part of a wider phenomenon. I remember my own growing awareness as a very young girl and then as a young woman, that society saw me and my life and activities as being restricted and curtailed in ways that did not apply to boys and men. The message was that males were the doers and the leaders and the shapers and changers of society, while females were the followers. Departures from the pattern were exceptions which did not disturb the norm. To me, as a child in a middle-class family in my time and place in history, the powerful sanction behind the norm appeared to lie in the combined weight of how history presented the past, the paradigm of male-female relationships in the books I read, the lives of the people around me, the apparent dominance by males of the worlds of art, literature, music, science and politics, and the fact that no one appeared to explicitly challenge any of this. I knew that the female model conflicted both with how I experienced myself and with my aspirations for the future, and I remember my growing feelings of injustice and powerlessness. After years of partial denial and sporadic attempts to conform, as a young adult I finally rejected the model. Even then my first rationalisation was to see myself as an odd one out who did not fit the pattern, and to look for a personal accommodation within my own situation. Only later did I realise that many other girls and women felt as I did, and that the problem was not one of individual maladjustment, but of how sexism was incorporated into the structures of society and that real change would not come from finding loopholes to allow individuals to slip through the net.

When we face our discovery that the personal is political, and begin to try to understand the politics of sexism, we each start from our own place in a particular niche in a particular society at a specific time. Just as we encounter gender roles first as an unquestioned part of the world, only later to be analysed and resisted, so we encounter as given the other structures of our society, its economic base, its social hierarchies and its political system. These too some of us later come to question and reject. Feminist theory develops in interaction with other analyses of the dynamics and structures of human societies, and the different proposals of philosophers and political thinkers over the centuries as to the ideal forms of political, economic and social organisation. This interaction gives rise to areas of agreement and disagreement, of challenge and dispute, of partial acceptance and partial rejection. From all these emerge different feminist analyses, none of which has as yet established itself as a definitive orthodoxy.

An understanding of the development of Irish feminism over the past century and a half, its interaction with political and ecclesiastical establishments, as well as with other radical movements, and its thinking about the kind of society that would best accommodate feminist objectives could be the starting point for today's debate. The writing of the history of Irish feminism is still at a relatively early stage, and in particular has not yet developed a sustained historical analysis of its theoretical base or bases. Nevertheless, it seems useful to attempt an overview, however sketchy, if only to suggest what may emerge from more in-depth research and analysis. For a model, I have used the American political scientist Alison Jaggar's study of feminist theories and the organisation of human society.[2] Jaggar describes four main strands of western feminist theory today, which she calls liberal feminism, traditional Marxism, radical feminism and socialist feminism.[3] Underlying each strand of feminism she identifies an explicit or implicit theory of human nature and its needs, which in turn informs the kind of changes in society each strand seeks to bring about. Both liberal and Marxist feminism developed during the period of organised feminist campaigns in the nineteenth century, while radical and late-twentieth-century socialist feminism emerged during the new wave of activity which began with the women's liberation movement in the 1960s.

Liberal feminism emphasises the similarities between the sexes and minimises the differences. Nineteenth-century liberalism grew from the eighteenth-century Enlightenment emphasis on the rational human nature shared by all human beings. Liberal political theory sees human beings as essentially rational agents, each determining what it wants from life. The State should protect the individual's right to autonomy and self-fulfilment but otherwise interfere as little as possible in the individual's life. All barriers to individuals using their reasoned judgement should be removed, including restrictions based on birth, colour, religion and so on. Liberal feminism calls for the removal of sex-based restrictions and for equal rights and equal opportunities for women to compete in all areas of human society.

Jaggar sees liberal feminism as having achieved a lot for women, but sees limitations in a feminism which, explicitly or implicitly, aims at the full incorporation of women into a society based on competition for success, wealth and status. In emphasising the similar nature and potential of women and men, and minimising the biological differences, it tends to overlook the structural nature of the barriers to women's full participation posed by existing patterns of childbearing and rearing, and by the existing organisation of paid work. The paradoxical result is that liberal feminism has had to increasingly contradict liberal principles by looking for State intervention to create a level playing field in the competitive liberal world in the form of State provision of childcare, anti-discrimination laws, affirmative action and so on. Further, she argues, in a competitive system the playing field will not stay level. In each generation some men and some women will rise to top positions and so give their children a head start in the next round. So in each generation, further State intervention is needed to try to restore the equal starting point in the competition for the glittering prizes.

Marxist analysis does not see human nature as static but as changing as it creates itself by meaningful work, or praxis. The key to understanding any given society is its system of production. This determines the productive activity, and the social conditions of different groups of people. These in turn influence the development of physical and personality characteristics. The poor may be smaller in physique than the wealthy because they eat less nourishing food. The rich child may be encouraged to develop artistic and intellectual potential, while the poor child may get little opportunity to do so. Changes in human nature and in forms of social organisation can only come with revolutionary change in the mode of production in a society. Where capitalism makes people see each other as potential rivals or enemies, in a socialist system society as a whole would own the means of production and the goal of social organisation would be the full development of all human potential.

Marxism criticised liberal feminist campaigns as benefiting middle-class women only. However, Jaggar argues that Marxism's own analysis of the position of women was inadequate. It claimed that the oppression of women would disappear with the overthrow of capitalism but remained vague about the details. It saw women's incorporation into the labour force as the way to emancipation, but did not develop a political analysis of reproduction, both childbearing and rearing, and domestic work, thus ignoring a central arena of power relations between the sexes.

Radical feminism emerged in the late 1960s and its analysis differed from both liberal feminism and Marxist feminism. In contrast to liberal feminism, radical feminism saw both biological sex *and* socially-constructed gender as core issues. Sexual relationships were central and their influence more pervasive than had been realised. Sexuality, lovemaking, childbearing and child-rearing, areas of human life which most political analysts had seen as 'natural' and outside political analysis, were in reality a crucial arena for political analysis and transformation.

Jaggar sees radical feminist theory as composed of many strands, all emphasising the centrality of both biological sex *and* the social construction of gender roles. Overall the 'contemporary radical feminism movement is characterised by a general celebration of womanhood, a striking contrast to the devaluation of women that pervades the wider society'.[4] Lesbian feminism forms one powerful strand. Some radical feminists advocate the development of a women's culture, separate from mainstream culture and uncontaminated by its misogyny.

Jaggar sees radical feminism making a major contribution to feminist thinking by stressing the significance of both biology and gender and rejecting any aim of making women 'equal' to men. She sees a potential weakness in a tendency to universalism and a failure to be historically specific in analysis, which can slide into a biological determinism. She also believes that a separate women's culture can never become more than a minority movement and so cannot transform the lives of all or the majority of women.

Finally, Jaggar describes socialist feminism as it has developed in the late twentieth century, which she sees as a synthesis of insights drawn from Marxism and radical feminism. The new socialist feminists agree with radical feminists that both gender and biology are political issues of central importance. They agree with Marxists on the value of historical materialism in understanding human nature and human society. Applying the historical materialist method of analysis to sexuality, childbearing and childrearing, and the care and maintenance of family members, they argue that the struggle to control productive forces has always included the control of both women's reproductive capacity and domestic work. Of the four types of feminism she identifies, Jaggar sees contemporary socialist feminism as having the greatest potential to achieve feminist objectives.

Analyses like Jaggar's of the potential and limitations of different feminist theories indicate how much can be learned from a historical-analytical approach. Needless to say, few individuals fit neatly and precisely into any ideal category and most combine elements of a number in their thinking. The nineteenth-century Irish women's emancipation campaigns developed within a liberal political ethos. Most of the activists appear to have shared this ethos to a large extent, though they do not exactly fit the classic liberal model. They claimed women's right to full citizenship on the basis of both similarities *and* differences between the sexes. They argued the Enlightenment case that women and men shared the same rational human nature and the same right to develop and use it. They also accepted that women and men had different roles and contributions, and saw these differences as a strength. Women's experience as mothers and household managers gave them qualities of sympathy, empathy and budgeting skills that few men shared. Yet another claim was based on the moral superiority of women. The Victorian definition of women, unlike previous definitions such as those of Aristotle or the early Church fathers, lauded them as morally superior to men and gave them responsibility for the moral behaviour of family and society. Opponents of women's emancipation argued that this superiority was so fragile that it would disintegrate if women were exposed to the corruption of political life and the 'public sphere'. Feminists, however, used it in support of their contention that women's contribution to the organisation of society's affairs was urgently needed, and that to make it women needed full equality with men.

Emancipationists challenged laws, regulations and customs which severely limited the areas of human activity open to women. During the second half of the nineteenth century they co-operated with British women to win married women's control of their own property, and the repeal of the Contagious Diseases Acts which regulated prostitution on a basis of sexual double standards. Separate Irish campaigns achieved improved standards in girls' secondary education and opened university education to women. They instigated a long struggle for entry to political life, which by the end of the century had gained access to local government both as voters and elected representatives, though it had not yet won the parliamentary vote.

The methods they used were for the most part rational argument and the education of public opinion. They lobbied politicians and governments, wrote letters to the newspapers, organised meetings and petitions. The women who participated in the early campaigns were mostly middle-class, Protestant in religion and in politics supporters of the union. Among the leading figures were the Quaker Anna Haslam[5] in Dublin, and the Presbyterian Isabella Tod[6] in Belfast. They tended to be relatively comfortably well-off and economically independent, either as widows or spinsters who could use their time and money as they wished, or married women whose husbands supported their political activism. Many came to feminism through middle-class philanthropic activity. Most women philanthropists, like most of their male colleagues, believed that the 'educated' classes had a duty to the less well-off, and aimed to improve the lot of the poor within the existing political and economic structures. Only a minority moved on to tackle discrimination against women. Of those who did, many accepted that political and other rights for women would in most cases be of immediate benefit to middle-class women, who would have the responsibility of using their new powers for the benefit of poorer women.

With hindsight these feminists are often seen as conservative in their demands. From a class point of view this is correct, and they did not seek radical change in the political and economic organisation of society. The language they used, of 'women's rights' and the 'advancement' and 'emancipation' of women, might imply an objective of achieving equality with men within the existing structures. Yet they did not see equality as simply an end in itself. They believed that it would be a force for change to a more moral and caring society. Also, to assert the equality of women with men as human beings, to insist on the importance of women's work in the home, and to organise political campaigns to achieve equal participation in education, politics and the professions, was hardly conservative from a gender perspective. This is a separate issue to any judgment as to whether or not their campaigns could have achieved emancipation for all women. There is a danger of being anachronistic and ahistorical if the demands and campaigns are not seen in the context of their own time and place.

Nor is it accurate to see the campaigns as motivated solely by selfish middle-class interests. While most of today's feminists would challenge the maternalistic attitude of nineteenth-century middle-class feminists to poorer women, within its terms they were right in thinking they had to free themselves before they could effectively carry out their duty to help less advantaged women. In addition, they saw gains such as married women's control of their own property as being of real and immediate benefit to working-class women whose earnings were legally at the disposal of their husbands. During the nineteenth century in Ireland, no vigorous Marxist or socialist feminist analysis emerged to challenge the middle-class women's movement on ideological or strategic grounds. The example of Anna Wheeler shows that the potential existed. Wheeler, an Irish woman, became a respected member of the Saint-Simonian co-operative movement in France and the Owenite co-operative movement in England. In 1825, she co-authored with William Thompson from west Cork a sustained exposition of an ideal society based on mutual co-operation and the elimination of sexism.[7] However, in Ireland itself a strong and sizeable socialist movement within which socialist women could argue and develop their case did not develop. The socialist parties which emerged in Ireland at the end of the nineteenth century and the early years of the twentieth were small in membership.

By the turn of the century, more nationalist and Catholic women were joining the suffrage campaign, now the central focus of feminist action.[8] Among the new organisations was the Irish Women's Franchise League (IWFL), founded in 1908, which was nationalist in sympathy but not prepared to put women's demands on hold pending the achievement of independence. Irish feminism and Irish socialism both became entwined in the complexities of the growing nationalist-unionist conflict and in the divergence between Home Rule and separatist nationalists. Despite their other political sympathies, or in some cases affiliations, the suffrage organisations aimed to combine their efforts to achieve the vote. This became increasingly difficult. For nationalist feminists, the question of whether national independence or women's suffrage took priority came to the fore. Those who put the freedom of the nation first included members of Cumann na mBan, founded in 1914 as a women's auxiliary to the Irish Volunteers, while the IWFL insisted that women's citizenship could not be relegated to second place. To date there is little published information on the interaction between feminism and unionism. The Ulster Women's Unionist Council (UWUC), founded in 1911 to support the male Ulster Unionist Council in opposing Home Rule, attracted many thousands of members. While the UWUC explicitly gave maintaining the union precedence over any other objectives, it did have feminist members and it appears that in the long run their politicisation in unionist politics contributed positively to the suffrage movement.[9] The outbreak of the First World War in August 1914 inevitably made it difficult for all suffrage organisations to maintain previous levels of activity, although some, notably the IWFL, tried to continue.

Some feminists supported the British war effort, others fought in the 1916 rising, and there was also a strong pacifist strand in Irish feminism. In 1915, the International Committee of Women for Permanent Peace, renamed in 1919 as the Women's International League for Peace and Freedom (WILPF), was founded directly from the International Woman Suffrage Alliance. The Irish Women's Reform League (IWRL), founded by the feminist, pacifist and trade-unionist Louie Bennett, and the IWFL with its associated suffrage newspaper, *The Irish Citizen* (1912–20), were to the fore among Irish feminist pacifists and an Irish branch of WILPF was established.

At the same time co-operation and dialogue was developing between the labour movement led by James Larkin and James Connolly and feminists with socialist and nationalist sympathies. The Irish Women Workers' Union (IWWU) was founded in 1911 with the participation of both. Louie Bennett's IWRL explicitly worked for the social and economic interests of working-class women as well as for the vote, and Bennett took over the general-secretaryship of the IWWU in 1916. Many feminists gave active support to the ITGWU during the 1913 lockout, and the labour connection forced the question of class, and specifically whether the vote was for 'women' or for 'ladies', higher on the feminist agenda. Some leading nationalist feminists, including Constance Markievicz and Hanna Sheehy Skeffington, one of the founders of the IWFL, were socialists, and *The Irish Citizen* carried articles and discussion on socialist issues.

The combined efforts of the feminists of the IWFL, many of whom were nationalists, and the nationalists of Cumann na mBan, many of whom were feminists, extracted from the separatist-nationalist leadership a feminist as well as a socialist commitment in the 1916 proclamation of the Irish republic. However, after the execution of the proclamation signatories and the emergence of a new leadership, between 1916 and 1922 much of the energy of republican feminists was spent on keeping up the pressure on the men to accept women as equal colleagues, and to deliver on the 1916 commitment to women's full citizenship in the coming independent Ireland. In the last issue of *The Irish Citizen* in late 1920 Hanna Sheehy Skeffington commented sadly on how the struggle for national independence had overshadowed and sidelined feminist debate.

In 1918, influenced both by women's contribution to the war effort and by fear of the resurgence of suffrage campaigning, the United Kingdom parliament passed a limited measure of women's franchise, confined to women over thirty. In 1922 Article 3 of the constitution of the Irish Free State explicitly endorsed the full and equal citizenship of all women and men over twenty-one: 'Every person, without distinction of sex ... shall enjoy the privileges and be subject to the obligations of such citizenship'. Women in Northern Ireland had to wait until 1928 for full adult suffrage. However, as other contributors to this volume have shown, during the 1920s and 1930s the politicians who took office in the new southern state, both those who had supported and those who had opposed the Treaty, sought to withdraw various aspects of women's citizenship. During the 1920s women were exempted from jury service and excluded from competition for higher posts in the civil service, while the 1930s saw the introduction of a ban on married women as teachers in national schools and in the civil service as well as a government power to limit the numbers of women in a given industry or exclude them completely. This trend culminated in the 1937 Constitution. Feminist protests succeeded in removing or modifying a number of clauses which either infringed or had the potential to infringe full equality of citizenship, but did not succeed in changing the wording of Article 41.2.1: 'by her life within the home, woman gives to the state a support without which the common good cannot be achieved'. The use of the singular and inclusive 'woman' rather than 'many women', and of 'life' rather than 'work', changed this from a welcome recognition of the value of the work of the majority of women to an insistence on a division between 'public' and 'private' spheres which confined women strictly to the latter.

The feminist organisations which publicly contested the anti-women policies of Cumann na nGaedheal and Fianna Fail governments during the inter-war years generally campaigned for women's rights to full citizenship within the existing system.[12] They included the Irish Women's Citizens Association, first founded by Anna Haslam as the Dublin Women's Suffrage Association in 1876, and the women graduates' associations of both the National University and Trinity College. The minority of feminists who were socialists tended for the most part to be republicans who opted out of participation in the political structures of the new state. Some found themselves torn between a number of often conflicting loyalties, including feminism, republicanism, pacifism and socialism. The dissident republicans were committed to undermining the authority of the new state and establishing a republic based on the second Dáil of 1921. They were themselves, both men and women, divided as to whether that republic should be socialist. Pacifist feminists also experienced divisive tension on the question of whether pacifism could or could not include a war of defence against aggression. The Irish labour movement was now essentially conservative and the male membership at best ambivalent and at worst hostile to such claims as equal employment opportunities and equal pay for women. The female membership itself, both leaders and rank and file, faced problems in reconciling demands for full equality in employment with the social realities of Irish working-class life. Equal pay might be attractive to a single woman, but if she married, a 'family wage' for her husband might take priority.[13] The ethos of the Free State was increasingly Catholic and specifically anti-communist and anti-socialist. In these circumstances, it is hardly surprising that no systematic debate about feminist objectives and what organisation of Irish society was most likely to satisfy them appears to have developed. However, historians have only very recently begun to examine Irish feminism in the inter-war years and in the 1940s and 1950s. Information on feminism in Northern Ireland during this period is particularly scarce. When the full history comes to be written, we are likely to find that there exists a more multi-faceted legacy of Irish feminist thinking than we now realise.

In Ireland, as elsewhere, the demographic, economic and social conditions of the 1960s opened the way to a new upsurgence of feminist activism. In the southern state the existing organisations, led by the Irish Housewives Association (1942) and the Business and Professional Women's Federation (1965), achieved a break-through with the appointment of the government commission on the status of women in 1970.[14] With the acceptance and publication of its report, the government committed itself publicly to the principle, if not necessarily the practice, of formal equality. At the same time the Irish Women's Liberation Movement (IWLM) emerged, inspired by the women's liberation movement in the United States.[15] With hindsight it had become clear that self-determination for women and full equality of citizenship between the sexes required more than simply the removal of legal barriers to women's full participation in all aspects of society. Barriers of 'tradition' and custom, as well as deeply entrenched stereotypes, could be as strong as or stronger than legal prohibitions and in some cases could outlast the latter.

Where the longer-established women's organisations worked through committees and lobbying, the IWLM aimed at sweeping change by way of a mass non-hierarchical movement which sought both to raise and politicise women's consciousness of their own oppression and to jolt public opinion in general into awareness of that oppression. The movement sparked off a nationwide response, and consciousness-raising and action groups sprang up all around the country. Both socialist and republican activists, as well as liberal feminists, were involved in the central IWLM group which gradually broke up due to internal differences. It was succeeded in 1975 by Irishwomen United (IU) whose membership was strongly left-wing. It too disintegrated after a year or so, and with it attempts to establish a mass movement around a central core group.

The movement has developed in a wide variety of directions and forms. Joining forces with the longer-established groups, both the IWLM and IU helped to push through a range of laws improving the position of women. New organisations providing services by women for women sprang up, to support rape victims and single parents, to offer legal advice, to set up refuges from domestic violence, to offer women-centred health care, providing contraception and non-directive pregnancy counselling, including information on abortion. A strong radical feminist strand emerged with links to lesbian feminism. Feminist publishing houses made available a wealth of writing by and about women. Women's caucuses appeared in political movements and parties along with a new drive to bring women into political life and office. Later developments have included the widespread emergence of women's community-based groups, combining action on both local and women's concerns, the growth and expansion of Women's Studies, a specifically Christian feminism with nuns to the fore, and a flourishing of creative art.

In Northern Ireland,[16] the new wave of feminism emerged against the background of the civil rights movement of the 1960s, and developed during the years of conflict which followed. Many women came to feminist awareness through participation in housing allocation campaigns and then in the civil rights movement. In contrast to the sudden emergence of a highly visible central group in the south, a range of individual groups emerged. Community-based groups, combining local and women's concerns, have been a strong feature from the early years. Reproductive issues, including the extension to Northern Ireland of British legislation on abortion, have been to the fore. Women's Aid, providing support and refuges for victims of domestic violence, has also been particularly vigorous. The Northern Ireland Women's Rights Movement was set up in 1975 to ensure that United Kingdom anti-sex-discrimination legislation was extended to Northern Ireland. It developed into an umbrella organisation aiming to co-ordinate the efforts of a wide range of groups. Socialist feminist and lesbian feminist groups also emerged during the 1970s.

The context in which the new feminism in the north developed had elements of the all-Ireland situation in the early decades of the century. Feminists were again torn between conflicting allegiances to orange and green. The pressure not to rock the boat, and to give unionism or nationalism priority over feminism was strong. Among nationalist women there was debate and disagreement on issues such as the feminist response to the strip-searching of republican women prisoners, and to an extent nationalist/feminist debate was so prominent that it inhibited some unionist women from becoming active feminists.

The 1980s witnessed the emergence of more groups and increasing efforts to achieve unity and understanding across political and religious divides. In the 1990s this developed into a concerted campaign to put gender inequality and women's demands on the agenda at all discussions of solutions to the problems of Northern Ireland, and continued efforts to build a feminist movement that crossed political, religious and class divides.[17] Both Clár na mBan and the Northern Ireland Women's Coalition emerged from these imperatives. The 1994 ceasefires also gave a new impetus to the efforts which have been repeated throughout the 1970s, 1980s and 1990s to build an all-Ireland feminist movement.

Today, it seems fair to say that feminism is an important aspect of the lives of more women in Ireland north and south than ever before. It has also become a household word which everybody recognises and thinks they understand. Yet, to judge from media coverage, the general public's perception is that feminism is solely a liberal feminist demand for equal rights and equal opportunities for women within existing political, economic and social structures. Those of us who believe that feminism has something more radical, and more subversive, to offer to building a new Ireland face a major challenge in getting the potential of feminist thinking onto the agenda of public debate. In the early stages of the current phase of feminism in the 1970s, there was vigorous debate both north and south about the meaning and objectives of different feminist theories and the changes in society needed to implement them. Today's strategy could be to first revive and cultivate a broad and inclusive internal debate around these issues, and then to initiate constructive dialogue with other movements working for change.

The historical perspective provides a good starting point. It shows us that Irish feminism has never been the preserve of any group or section. It has crossed religious and political boundaries, and challenged religious and political establishments. Feminists have been unionists and nationalists, Protestants and Catholics, capitalists and socialists, soldiers and pacifists. They have dealt with the problem of conflicting loyalties in different ways. Some have brought their feminist thinking into dialogue with their other political beliefs. Some have at times put their feminist convictions on hold. Feminists and feminism do not exist in a vacuum. Both are what they are as a result of the interaction of individuals with the societies of which they are part. This does not mean that all actions and analyses in the past were of equal value or equal validity. It means that we can begin to see how Irish feminists in the past saw the options open to them and why they chose as they did. It helps us to understand how we ourselves have come to hold our particular brand of feminism and presses us to analyse both its potential and its limitations.

Analysis of the changes in society that could deliver our various feminist objectives could be the starting point for both internal feminist debate and engagement with other movements. One example of this would be that middle-class feminists like myself would seriously engage with the thinking of women in community groups in working-class areas in Dublin and other cities, particularly in areas of high male and female unemployment and in those where there is a high traffic in drugs. We would consider our response as feminists to their analysis and the steps they propose to begin a process of change. Their views of what they see as the current middle-class feminist agenda would be another useful debating point. Another debate could concern the role of State-provided child care. Do we see this as the ultimate solution to women's problems in combining family with work outside the home or as a temporary expedient to provide equality of opportunity for women pending a radical overhaul of the organisation of paid employment so that it is no longer based on hours and timetables suited to a man who has a wife to look after home and family? Do we want to rethink family roles to allow more active parenting by fathers as well as mothers? If there is a value for most children in the early experience of good pre-school education, how does this fit in? Such questions in turn lead to another debate: whether feminist objectives can be achieved within a global economy and politics based on free-market competition, or only within one based in some way on socialist principles.

With regard to dialogue with other movements working for change in Irish society, the challenge is to develop a forum for meaningful engagement. As noted already, the peace process in its present form does not provide space for a holistic approach to discussion of a new Ireland, and is unlikely to move in that direction without serious pressure. One possible way to apply this pressure would be the development of a parallel debate about a new Ireland. This would challenge the parties and the two governments to broaden and deepen their analysis of the issues involved and their perception of the interests that should be represented at the talks. It would give the women and men involved, both within the negotiating rooms and within the political parties, a source of support, terms of reference and a pool of ideas on which they could draw and with which they could engage. Irrespective of the outcome of the current peace process, a constructive response to its limitations in the form of a wide-ranging, multi-faceted and inclusive debate about a new Ireland could build towards the future.

from Maryann Valiulis and Mary O'Dowd (eds), *Women and Irish History* (Dublin, Wolfhound, 1997), pp 260–277.

NOTES

1   Mary Wollstonecraft, *A Vindication of the Rights of Woman* (London, 1982; first published 1792), pp 23–5.

2   Alison Jaggar, *Feminist Politics and Human Nature* (Totowa, New Jersey, 1983).

3   *Ibid.*, p. 9.

4   *Ibid.*, p. 95.

5   See Mary Cullen, 'Anna Maria Haslam', in Mary Cullen and Maria Luddy (eds), *Women, Power and Consciousness in Nineteenth-Century Ireland: Eight Biographical Studies* (Dublin, 1995), pp 161–96.

6   See Maria Luddy, 'Isabella M.S. Tod' in *ibid.*, pp 197–230.

7   William Thompson, *Appeal of One Half of the Human Race, Women, Against the Pretensions of the Other Half, Men, to Retain Them in Political, and Thence in Civil and Domestic Slavery* (London, 1983). For Wheeler, see Dolores Dooley, 'Anna Doyle Wheeler', in Cullen and Luddy, *Women, Power and Consciousness*, pp 19–53.

8   See Margaret Mac Curtain, 'Women, the Vote and Revolution' in M. Mac Curtain and Donncha Ó Corrain (eds), *Women in Irish Society: The Historical Dimension* (Dublin, 1978), pp 46–57; Rosemary Cullen Owens, *Smashing Times: The History of the Irish Women's Suffrage Movement 1889–1922* (Dublin, 1984); Margaret Ward, *Unmanageable Revolutionaries: Women and Irish Nationalism* (Dingle, 1983); Beth McKillen, 'Irish feminism and national separatism' in *Eire/Ireland*, xii (1982), 3, pp 52–67; 4, pp 72–90; Mary Cullen, 'How radical was Irish feminism between 1876 and 1922?', in P.J. Corish (ed.), *Radicals, Rebels and Establishments* (Belfast, 1985), pp 185–201; Cliona Murphy, *The Women's Suffrage Movement and Irish Society in the Early Twentieth Century* (Brighton, 1989); Carol Coulter, *The Hidden Tradition: Women, Feminism and Nationalism* (Cork, 1993).

9   Diane Urquhart, '"The female of the species is more deadlier than the male"? The Ulster Women's Unionist Council, 1911–1940' in Janice Holmes and Diane Urquhart (eds), *Coming into the Light: The Work, Politics and Religion of Women in Ulster*

1840–1940 (Belfast, 1994), p. 95. See also Diane Urquhart, 'Women and politics in Ulster, 1880–1940' (Ph.D. thesis, Queen's University Belfast, 1996).

10 See Rosemary Cullen Owens, 'Women and Pacificism in Ireland, 1915–1932', in Maryann Valiulis and Mary O'Dowd (eds), Women and Irish History (Dublin, 1997), pp 220–238.

11 See Rosemary Cullen Owens, '"Votes for women, votes for ladies": organised labour and the suffrage movement' in Saothar, ix (1983), pp 32–47.

12 See Maryann Gialanella Valiulis, 'Defining their role in the new state: Irishwomen's protest against the Juries Act of 1927' in Canadian Journal of Women's Studies, xviii, 1 (July 1992), pp 43–60; 'Power, gender and identity in the Irish Free State' in Journal of Women's History, 6.4 and 7.1 (Winter/spring 1995), pp 117–36.

13 For a discussion of some of the issues involved see Mary E. Daly, 'Women and trade-unionism in Ireland' in Margaret Mac Curtain and Donncha Ó Corráin (eds), Women in Irish Society: The Historical Dimension (Dublin, 1978), pp 71–81; Ellen Hazelkorn, 'The social and political views of Louie Bennett 1870–1956' in Saothar, 13 (1988), pp 32–44; Mary Jones, These Obstreperous Lassies: The History of the Irish Women Workers' Union (Dublin, 1988).

14 For the genesis of the commission see Hilda Tweedy, A Link in the Chain: The History of the Irish Housewives Association 1942–92 (Dublin, 1992).

15 See June Levine, Sisters: The Personal Story of an Irish Feminist (Swords, 1982); June Levine, 'Women and politics, 1970–1980' in Field Day Anthology of Irish Writing, vol. iv (Cork/New York); Catherine Rose, The Female Experience: The Story of the Woman Movement in Ireland (Galway, 1975); Ailbhe Smyth, 'The women's movement in the republic of Ireland 1970–1990' in Ailbhe Smyth (ed.), Irish Women's Studies Reader (Dublin, 1993), pp 245–69; Linda Connolly, 'The women's movement in Ireland: a social movement's analysis' in Irish Journal of Feminist Studies, i (March 1996), pp 43–77.

16 See Margaret Ward and Joanna McMinn (eds), A Difficult, Dangerous Honesty: Ten Years of Feminism in Northern Ireland (Belfast, 1986); Eileen Evason, Against the Grain: The Contemporary Women's Movement in Northern Ireland (Dublin, 1991); Catherine B. Shannon, 'Women in Northern Ireland' in

Mary O'Dowd and Sabine Wichert (eds), *Chattel, Servant or Citizen: Women's Status in Church, State and Society* (Belfast, 1995), pp 238–47; Monica McWilliams, 'The church, the state and the women's movement in Northern Ireland' in Smyth, *Irish Women's Studies Reader*, pp 79–100; and 'Struggling for peace and justice: reflections on women's activism in Northern Ireland' in *Journal of Women's History*, vol. 6, no. 4/vol. 7, no. 1 (Winter/spring 1995), pp 13–39; Eilish Rooney, 'Political division, practical alliance: problems for women in conflict' in *ibid.*, pp 40–48; Lynda Walker, *Grandmothers and Mentors: Women, Politics and Education in Northern Ireland* (Belfast, 1996).

17   Monica McWilliams, 'Struggling for peace and justice', pp 29–30.

PARTNERS IN STRUGGLE:
THE WOMEN OF 1798

The bicentenary of the 1798 rising stimulated a surge of new publications on a range of aspects, including the political thought of the late eighteenth century, the influence of the American war of independence and of the French revolution, the origins of the United Irishmen and the 1798 rebellion itself. The reality that women had been involved in United Irish activity at all levels from political thought to actual combat revealed the complexity of gender relationships. At each level, from intellectual debate to organisation, propaganda and physical combat, women as well as men had been involved. At every level indeed gender roles and divisions had operated, but there was no absolute line of demarcation. As is usually the case, there is little information on the thinking and motivation of women and men outside the leadership figures. In this context I later realised that I had missed some that did exist in relation to Anne Devlin. In 2003, when preparing a talk about her for a series of lectures organised by the Robert Emmet Society, I read Brother Luke Cullen's account of his interviews with her in the 1840s, some forty years after the Emmet rising. He aimed to reproduce her own words as far as possible and, even though he did not ask her about what she herself thought and what motivated her, his sympathy and the length and detail of his record convey something both of her personality and her understanding of and engagement with the politics of the period.

So far relatively little has been published dealing specifically with women and 1798. Helena Concannon's *Women of 'ninety-eight* was published in 1919, and in this bicentenary year we welcome *The Women of 1798* edited by Dáire Keogh and Nicholas Furlong in which ten authors examine a range of different aspects of the subject. Obviously further research will reveal much more, yet already, drawing on these and other published work, it can be argued with some confidence that women as well as men were active in all aspects of 1798.

When addressing this topic one is faced by two main problems. The first is that, as always, the better off and better educated have left more records of what they did and thought than have the poorer and less well educated. The second is that such sources as exist have usually been compiled within a mindset that sees males as the active agents of change in human history and females almost solely in support and follower roles. The second problem is compounded by the fact that many historians still work within a somewhat similar mindset.

The foundation of the United Irishmen grew directly from the broad eighteenth-century debate around Enlightenment emphasis on the rational nature of all human beings and republican emphasis on virtuous government in which both the interests and the voice of the people as a whole could be expressed. It seems clear that women were more active participants in this political debate than has usually been recognised.

A recent study of British politics during the period found that aristocratic women were increasingly influential. While they might actually *say* that women were not suited to politics, in reality many were actively involved in on-going political discussion with other women and with men, offering political opinions and advice through letter writing, salons, *tête-à-têtes*, discussions, and so on. Many had a solid educational base and 'many were widely read, particularly in the works of the French Enlightenment ... in history and to some extent in English and Scottish moral philosophy and political economy'.[1] Indeed, it appears that these women were often more widely read, especially in Enlightenment literature, than the men.

In the light of this we can note Stella Tillyard's assessment of Emily duchess of Leinster. The duchess was clearly a powerful influence on her favourite surviving son, Lord Edward Fitzgerald, one of the most radical and egalitarian of the United Irish leaders. English by birth and upbringing she quickly developed an active interest in Irish politics. She appears to have read more widely in politics than her husband who 'turned [political pamphlets] over to Emily',[2] and in their correspondence she offered political advice while excusing her interference. She moved from a family-based interest centred on the liberal politics of her husband, her brother-in-law, Henry Fox, and her nephew, Charles James Fox, to more radical constitutional issues including the relationship of king, parliament and people and whether parliament existed for king or people. Tillyard sees her as becoming increasingly more radical,

> not only idealistically interested in liberty, but also prepared to countenance civil rights – access to offices, courts, information and religious emancipation – for a far wider section of the people than enjoyed them at the time.[3]

She seems to have supported Edward's political stance up to mid-1794, and even his wish to see the French example followed in Ireland. When she realised that the United Irishmen and radicalism were now heading for rebellion her enthusiasm waned, though not her political sympathies. She made a significant statement of these sympathies after Edward's death. On the cover sheet binding a bundle of his last letters she copied a passage from a political pamphlet written by Joseph Priestley in

1768, and underlined some of his phrases. In *An essay on the first principles of government; and on the nature of political, civil and religious liberty* Priestley argued that rebellion was justified if a government was oppressive and hence unconstitutional:

> if the bold attempt be precipitate and unsuccessful the government will be sure to term it rebellion, but the censure cannot make *the thing itself less glorious*. The memory of such brave tho' unfortunate friends of liberty and of the rights of Mankind as that of Harmodious and Aristogeiton among the Athenians and Russell and Sidney in our own country, will be held in everlasting honour by their grateful fellow citizens, and *History will speak another language than laws*.[4]

When we turn to what little is known so far about the political thinking of middle-class women in United Irish circles we find them making no pretence that women were not interested in or suited to politics. Martha McTier was an informed and vigorous contributor to debate and discussion. Her letters to her brother William Drennan of the United Irishmen are regularly used by historians as a source for what happened and what people thought. For example, when discussing the extraordinarily enthusiastic reception in Ireland of Tom Paine's writings *Common Sense* and *The Rights of Man*, David Dickson quotes Martha McTier's comment on *The Rights of Man* as catching the essence of the enthusiasm:

> I never liked kings and Paine has said of them what I always suspected, truth seems to dart from him in such plain and pregnant terms, that he, or *she* who runs may read.[5]

We probably know more about Mary Ann McCracken than any of the other women in United Irish circles thanks to Mary McNeill's biography.[6] A member of a middle-class Belfast Presbyterian merchant family, she was well-educated, attending with her brothers a progressive co-educational school. The McCracken home was a centre of United Irish political discussion and planning. She was particularly close to her brother Henry, and Nancy Curtin notes that she seemed 'quite comfortable lecturing her elder brother on the subject of politics' and appears to have been far better read than he in the classic republican and radical texts.[7] In a recent article John Gray argues that her commitment to United Irish aims was deeper and tougher than it appears in McNeill's biography.[8] Gray queries the basis for believing she cherished an unrequited love for Thomas Russell, and sees her continued and active support of Russell and Robert Emmet after the execution of her brother Henry as politically rather than romantically driven.

The political activity of Margaret Bond brought her to the attention of Dublin Castle.[9] The Leinster directory of the United Irishmen, of which her husband Oliver was a member, often met in the Bonds' house. So formidable was her reputation that in 1898 when a grandniece of Oliver Bond wished to distance her great-uncle from the United Irishmen she did so by asserting that Margaret Bond had been a 'rampant rebel' who held United Irish meetings on her husband's property against his wishes.[10] She is also famed for smuggling writing materials, newspapers and communications from friends into the United Irish leaders in Kilmainham Jail hidden beneath the crust of a freshly baked pie.

Another recent article broadens the participation of women in the radical political debate to include women like Mary Leadbeater of Ballitore and her circle of Quaker women friends. Kevin O'Neill notes that while Quakers were of more recent English descent than most Irish Protestants and maintained their English links more than most, yet

[f]rom a Catholic perspective the Friends of Ballitore were neither landlords, magistrates, soldiers or tithe collectors – the normal rural functions of the Anglo-Irish. Instead they were farmers, teachers, millers and most of all, neighbours.[11]

While Quakers were completely opposed to the use of violence by either the government or its opponents they strongly supported the ideas of liberty, equality and fraternity and agreed with the United Irish in placing the blame for the miseries of Ireland firmly on the shoulders of its government. Quakers, both men and women, were actively involved in the political debate in the years preceding 1798. Leadbeater herself read widely in French and English political philosophers from Edmund Burke to Mary Wollstonecraft, and William Godwin's *Political Justice* was the most quoted work in her diaries in the 1790s. Both she and her husband were on terms of intimate friendship with their neighbour Malachi Delaney during the early 1790s, and while he was actively recruiting for the United Irishmen in 1796 and 1797. Delaney led the United Irish in the fighting in the Ballitore area in the following year. 'During those years, in word and action, she was an advocate of radical equality in Irish society'.[12]

The same factors that fostered United Irish republicanism also stimulated feminist assertion. Enlightenment and republican thinking encouraged challenges to the long-standing model of women's role which defined women in terms of relationship and service to men, as wives, mothers, daughters or sisters. The impetus underlying feminism has always been to challenge such reductionism and assert the autonomy of women as self-directed human persons. Both the American and French revolutions encouraged demands for practical as well as intellectual change. In late eighteenth-century Ireland women, in common with women in western societies in general, had few civil or political rights. A central issue was the position of married women. Under the English common law when a woman married she lost her separate legal identity which merged with that of her husband. Both her person and her property came under his full legal control. Within a system based on the principle that only those who were economically and socially in a position to exercise independent judgement could be trusted with political rights the legal position of married women ruled them out. In practice all women were excluded from holding public office, sitting in parliament or voting in parliamentary elections.

Among the best known feminist writings was Mary Wollstonecraft's *A Vindication of the Rights of Woman* (1792) which argued that women as well as men shared rational human nature, and so should be educated to become responsible and autonomous adults who made responsible and virtuous decisions about their lives and actions. In revolutionary France quite a few radical women went further to assert the right to full political participation but were rejected and suppressed by the male leadership. In Ireland, where growing calls for reform and more radical change provided an opening, it appears likely that many United Irish women would have urged feminist claims. Wollstonecraft's book was widely read and discussed by both women and men. Certainly Mary Ann McCracken is on record as having put the challenge to the United Irishmen. A wonderful letter of 16 March 1797 to her brother Henry in Kilmainham Jail links a number of aspects of her thinking. First she tells him of local political developments, including the growth of support for the United Irishmen. Then she mentions the Societies of United Irishwomen:

I have a great curiosity to visit some female societies in this Town (though I should like them better were they promiscuous, as there can be no other reason for having them separate but keeping the women in the dark and certainly it is equally ungenerous and incandid to make tools of them without confiding in them). I wish to know if they have any rational ideas of liberty and equality for themselves or whether they are contented with their present abject and dependent situation, degraded by custom and education beneath the rank in society in which they were originally placed; for if we suppose woman was created for a companion for man she must of course be his equal in understanding, as without equality of mind there can be no friendship and without friendship there can be no happiness in society. If indeed we were to reason from analogy we would rather be inclined to suppose that women were destined for superior understandings, their bodies being more delicately framed and less fit for labour than that of man does it not naturally follow that they were more peculiarly intended for study and retirement, as to any necessary connection between strength of mind and strength of body, a little examination will soon overturn that idea, I have only to place the McCombs, Val Joice and our worthy Sovereign opposite Mr O'Connor, Mr Tone and our dear departed Friend Dr Bell (three little men possessing genius) to show the futility of such an argument ... I hope the present Era will produce some women of sufficient talents to inspire the rest with a genuine love of Liberty and just sense of her value without which their efforts will be impotent and unavailing ... I think the reign of prejudice is nearly at an end, and that the truth and justice of our cause alone is sufficient to support it, as there can be no argument produced in favour of the slavery of woman that has not been used in favour of general slavery and which have been successfully combated by many able writers. I therefore hope it is reserved for the Irish nation to strike out something new and to shew an example of candour generosity and justice superior to any that have gone before them – as it is about two o'clock in the morning I have only time to bid you goodnight – Believe me – Yours affectionately Mary.[13]

It will be interesting to see how this picture develops as information on a larger number of women emerges. For instance, Mary Leadbeater and some of her Quaker women friends were actively involved in printing and circulating anti-slavery literature,[14] and participation in the anti-slavery movement is recognised as a breeding ground for feminist awareness. As for the United Irishmen themselves, Nancy Curtin sees their republican ideology as excluding women as full citizens while seeing them as having a supporting role in the republican campaign. However, it appears that individual men may have pondered and perhaps supported women's claims. For example, in 1793 Thomas Russell, travelling in County Antrim to organise the United Irish movement, gave the question some thought. A diary entry for 11 July reads:

> Should women be learn[e]d? Is their a difference of mind? Why not as of body? Has it ever occur[r]ed to anatomists to observe is their any difference in the brains of men and women children [sic]? Women in public offices as clever as men. Queens, poetesses, etc., etc. In merchants' houses keep the accoun[t]s as well as men. Why not mathematicians?[15]

The support given to United Irishmen by their wives, mothers and sisters is the central theme of Helena Concannon's book. In view of the model of women's role noted above, many historians of women are understandably uneasy with looking at women only in the context of their relationship with men. Yet male-female relationships and sex-based divisions of labour need to be re-examined and analysed rather than ignored. One flaw in the model is that it tends to see 'men's work' and 'women's work' as mutually exclusive, with men's work regarded as the more important. Another is to see women's work and support of family members as 'natural' and instinctive rather than an active, self-directed and positive contribution without which a political or social movement could not have functioned.

In this context Nancy Curtin notes the sheer physical and mental strength involved in Matilda Tone's sacrifice of a normal domestic life, her acceptance of her husband's long absences, her shouldering of the full responsibility for their children and the worries about money, her unfailing support of her husband's undertakings which she carried to the extent of concealing the fact that she was pregnant when he left America for France on behalf of the United Irishmen.[16] Recognition of the importance of this type of contribution to any movement and its incorporation into historical analysis will be one key component in writing a more inclusive history. At the same time this recognition should not obscure Matilda Tone's personal contribution to political discussion and United Irish thinking and planning.

Mary Ann McCracken too gave a sister's support to her brother right to the scaffold. When Henry Joy McCracken was in hiding after the Battle of Antrim she found him and organised help in food and clothing. She arranged for his escape to America by ship but he was arrested on his way to the appointed rendezvous. She visited him in Belfast Jail and was present at his trial for treason. She was with him in his cell on the day of his death and walked with him, her arm in his, to his place of execution before the Market House on 17 July. She only left then because he could not bear that she should witness his death. She later brought up his illegitimate daughter Maria who became her close companion.

Nancy Curtin mentions three main ways in which women participated in the United Irish movement; as members of oath-bound Societies of United Irishwomen; as active recruiters; and as passive recruiters in the role of symbols of endangered Irish womanhood. She describes the United Irishwomen as

> a kind of female auxiliary which attended to fund raising and providing amenities for imprisoned United Irishmen and their families. These women might also undertake the dangerous business of gathering information and carrying secret messages within the vast network of local United Irish societies. Women as well as children were certainly required to take the United Irish oath of secrecy, forbidding the swearer to reveal the secrets of the organisation and the identity of its members. Such an oath was also a prerequisite for membership of the organisation.[17]

Rose McGladdery, Mary Ann McCracken's sister-in-law, is said to have been a sworn United Irishwoman before her marriage to William McCracken. She carried intelligence then, and later brought information in and out of Kilmainham when William and Henry were imprisoned with other United Irish leaders.[18]

Further research may throw more light on these societies, their number and the number of members, their location and more on their activities. As noted above, Mary Ann McCracken was suspicious of separate male and female societies on the grounds that the men were not keeping the women fully informed or involved. However separate 'auxiliary' female organisations often contribute more substantially than is recognised to a cause and participation in them can increase political awareness and lead some of the women involved to question contemporary gender roles.

There were different grades of oaths and it appears possible that some women may have been sworn into the central United Irishmen.[19] Miss Moore of Thomas Street in Dublin told Dr Madden that she took the United Irish oath and that, to her own knowledge, several women were sworn members. She herself administered the oath to William James MacNeven. Her father James Moore was a United Irishman and a friend of Lord Edward Fitzgerald. Fitzgerald stayed at the Moores' house more than once while in hiding and she carried messages for him. He was there around 16 May 1798 when a carpenter at Dublin Castle heard that James Moore's house was to be searched. He carried the warning and James Moore went into hiding, leaving responsibility for the safety of the commander-in-chief to his wife and daughter. Miss Moore arranged to bring him to a house on Usher's Island belonging to Francis Magan, who, unknown to the United Irish, had become an informer. Both women set out with Fitzgerald and an escort of two male companions for an evening stroll. They were met by Major Sirr and his men, informed by Magan. Lord Edward and Miss Moore escaped and she took him instead to the house of Murphy the feather merchant. When the next day Magan came to ask why his visitor had not arrived, she told him what had happened, and that evening Fitzgerald was taken.[20]

Recruiting for the United Irishmen was a specific female activity. One way in which this could be done was by persuading militiamen to change their allegiance. Curtin quotes a militia officer in Derry complaining of a 'practice of having an intrigue with a girl and swearing the man to secrecy when the matter [the aims and goals of the United Irishmen] should be divulged in confidence'.[21] Another way was by exerting moral pressure. Charles Teeling, of the Antrim Catholic family who were forgers of links between the United Irish and the Defenders, wrote that

the enthusiasm of the females exceeded the ardour of the men; in many of the higher circles, and in all the rustic festivities, that youth met with a cold and forbidding reception from the partner of his choice, who, whether from apathy or timidity, had not yet subscribed to the test of union.[22]

Overall information on the activities of women in the broad United Irish and Defender movements is scattered and scarce. That women were active is clear but the information comes in glimpses or snapshots through passing references. One report will tell of women supporters of the United Irish going through towns and villages singing seditious song. Another will speak of women wearing green ribbons, handkerchiefs and shoe laces to show their political allegiance. So far we have no records in their own words of what these women did and what they thought. This is all the more frustrating as research is showing that the Defenders were far more politically aware and politically motivated than had been realised.

When we come to the rebellion itself there is a striking contrast between United Irish ideology of women's role and popular memory as recorded in story and ballad. The first portrayed women as symbols of Ireland, or as heroic mothers urging on their sons for the cause, or as beautiful maidens turned into wandering maniacs by the brutality of the soldiery.[23] It never represented them as actual combatants. Popular memory, on the other hand, has remembered individual women who took part in physical combat as heroines, and often as Joans of Arc leading the men into battle. This contrast raises some interesting questions for historians.

Best known of all is Betsy Grey who fought at the Battle of Ballynahinch in County Down:

The popular memory has preserved a vision of her, a bright-faced, beautiful girl, dressed in green silk, mounted on her gallant mare, and brandishing her burnished sword above her head, while side by side with Munro she led one victorious charge after another.[24]

According to Concannon, her lover Willie Boal and brother George Grey were sworn United Irishmen, and it is believed that Betsy was also. The story as told to Madden by Mary Ann McCracken is that Betsy Grey went to the camp on the Saturday before the battle with some supplies for her brother and sweetheart and insisted on staying to live or die with them. They procured her a pony and she went into action on it bearing a green flag. After the defeat they were overtaken in flight by a party of Hillsborough yeomanry who killed all three.[25]

Molly Weston of Westmeath who fought and died at the Battle of Tara was famed for recruiting United Irishmen. Folk memory recalls a handsome and accomplished horsewoman, dressed in a green riding costume with gold braid and a green cocked hat with a white plume. Armed with sword and pistols she rode to battle with her four brothers. She too is remembered as a leader, rallying the pikemen and leading repeated charges. Her four brothers were reported killed but Molly Weston was never seen again.[26]

Mary Doyle, who appears to have seen lengthy military service in Wexford, is remembered for a specific military achievement. When the rebel army attacked New Ross it was defeated and reduced to a tattered remnant. Immense amounts of ammunition and powder had been used and hundreds of guns and pikes lost. Only one of the artillery pieces was saved and that by the 'heroic efforts' of Mary Doyle.[27]

Many other women fell in active combat. The names of some are remembered, such as that of Ruth Hackett who was killed at Prosperous in County Kildare,[28] but many others are not. For instance, at the battle of Vinegar Hill the women were not content to leave the fighting to the men. They mingled with them, encouraging them and fought with fury themselves. Several were found slain among the fighting men, where they had fallen in crowds, felled by the delayed bursting of the bomb shells.[29]

Obviously the participation of women in war goes far beyond the actual wielding of pike or gun in battle. The rebel camps contained large numbers of women. For example, that under Fr John Murphy at Oulart Hill in County Wexford held four and five thousand people, one thousand fighting men, and the rest women, children and the elderly.[30] The work done by the women in these camps has yet to be recorded in a systematic way but some indications of their activities survive. Anna Kinsella records that cutting the cross belts from the bodies of fallen dragoons was 'a common task for camp followers, many of them apparently women', and that women also appear to have made gun-powder in the camps.[31] Some, like Suzy Toole, the 'moving magazine' of County Wicklow, 'secured ball cartridge and ammunition from disaffected soldiers ... [and] provided intelligence on the movements of the King's troops'.[32]

Such activities as acquiring and supplying combatants with food, arms, ammunition and other supplies, carrying messages and gathering information, providing hiding places and safe houses, the dangerous harbouring and hiding of rebels on the run, collecting and burying dead bodies from the field of battle are all seen as part of soldiers' work when done by men in all-male armies. Many individual cases of all these activities being carried out by women are remembered in various parts of the country. The work going on during this bicentenary year in compiling and collating local knowledge and folk memory may provide the basis for more systematic analysis.

Occasional glimpses of rebel women may be found in sources such as the written accounts by seven loyalist or neutral Protestant women in County Wexford of their experiences during the rebellion.[33] Even though some were written or rewritten many decades later, and despite divides of class, religion and political sympathy, these accounts do aim to describe what witnesses actually observed. They show rebel women as independent actors, and in some instances as acting differently to and in opposition to their men. Dinah Goff described one instance where her father was threatened by a company of rebels. As they hesitated as to who would strike the first blow 'some women came in great agitation through the crowd, clinging to their husbands and dragging them away'. On another occasion, where a United Irish officer prevented some rebel soldiers from looting the Goffs' house, she saw 'many wicked-looking women ... [who] made frightful faces and shook their hands at us as we stood at the windows'.[34] There is some suggestion that rebel women may have been at least as ready as their men to throw off the bonds of traditional deference. Jane Barber described how a rebel woman, Molly Martin, mother of one of the Barbers' servants, dressed in new clothes whose source she declined in less than deferential language to explain, nevertheless brought Jane to where her father lay dead, killed by the rebels, and then, with the help of a rebel man, brought her safely home when another rebel man began to beat her. Jane Addams recounted an incident where four women having breakfast in a Wexford alehouse refused to get her a glass of water when she fainted and she had to wait until two men arrived.

On another aspect of the experience of rebel women the brief and ambivalent comment of Elizabeth Richards on the rape of local women by the English and Hessian troops who crushed the rebellion evokes the horror more vividly than many lengthy descriptions: '... all the morning we listened to the shrieks, the complainings of female rebels. They almost turned my joy into sorrow'.[35]

One woman's own voice does reach us even if at second hand. In 1842 Dr Madden found Anne Devlin living in poverty in Dublin. In 1803 at the age of 25 or 26 she acted as housekeeper in the house near Rathfarnham rented by Robert Emmet as a base for planning the proposed rising of that year. She was arrested there after the rising, threatened and tortured with bayonets and half-hanging to make her tell what she knew. She revealed nothing in response to torture, bribes and imprisonment. She was particularly badly treated and her health undermined in Kilmainham Jail where she remained until 1806. In Madden's record of her words the force of personality and the depth of anger which enabled her to survive break through. She regularly abused her chief tormentor, Dr Trevor, the Superintendent of Kilmainham, to his face. 'She knew he was everything that was vile and bad, and it eased her mind to tell him what she thought'.[36] She attributed her survival to an Englishwoman, the wife of a gaoler, who, in Trevor's absence, 'would bring her to her own apartments for an hour or two at a time, and give her wine and nourishing things'. Once Trevor discovered this and 'his rage was dreadful. He cursed her, and she returned his maledictions curse for curse'.[37] In 1843 when Anne Devlin and Dr Madden found the house rented by Emmet she showed not terror but 'as lively a remembrance of the wrongs and outrages that had been inflicted on her as if they had been endured but the day before'.[38]

Already it is clear that looking at the participation of women in 1798 will add to our knowledge of the whole United Irish and Defender movements and of what actually happened in 1798. The United Irish and Defender alliance spanned all classes and creeds in a political movement inspired by the idea of republican government. By simply asking the question 'what did women do?' we find that even the limited and scattered information so far available points to their active participation with men across the board. This participation stretches from the intellectual powerhouse through organisation and planning to partnership in rebellion. The search for answers to the question also broadens the focus from concentration on a relatively small number of male leaders to include the scale of the contribution at every level by the men and women of all classes who are not seen as 'leaders'. Above all it challenges us to find out more about who these women were, what they did and why they did it.

from Cathal Póirtéir (ed.), *The Great Irish Rebellion of 1798* (Cork, Mercier, 1998), pp 146–159.

NOTES

1   P.J. Jupp, 'The roles of royal and aristocratic women in British politics 1782–1832' in Mary O'Dowd and Sabine Wichert (eds), *Chattel, Servant or Citizen: women's status in church, state and society* (Belfast, 1995), pp 105–6.

2   Stella Tillyard, *Aristocrats: Caroline, Emily, Louisa and Sarah Lennox 1740–1832* (London, 1994), p. 69.

3   Ibid., p. 71.

4   *Ibid.*, p. 395.

5   David Dickson, 'Paine and Ireland', in D. Dickson, D. Keogh and K. Whelan (eds), *The United Irishmen: republicanism, radicalism and rebellion* (Dublin, 1993), p. 140.

6   Mary McNeill, *The Life and Times of Mary Ann McCracken 1770–1866: a Belfast panorama* (Belfast, 1986; facsimile of first edition 1960).

7 Nancy Curtin, 'Women and eighteenth-century Irish republicanism', in Margaret Mac Curtain and Mary O'Dowd (eds), *Women in Early Modern Ireland* (Dublin, 1991), p. 140.

8 John Gray, 'Mary Ann McCracken: Belfast revolutionary and pioneer of feminism', in Dáire Keogh and Nicholas Furlong (eds), *The Women of 1798* (Dublin, 1998), pp 47–63.

9 Dáire Keogh, The women of 1798: representation and realities', in Mary Cullen (ed.), *1798: 200 Years of Resonance* (Dublin, 1998), p. 65.

10 Anna Kinsella, 'Nineteenth-century perspectives: the women of 1798 in folk memory and ballads', in Keogh and Furlong, *The Women of 1798*, p. 196.

11 Kevin O'Neill, 'Mary Shackleton Leadbeater: peaceful rebel', *ibid.*, p. 142.

12 *Ibid.*, p. 162.

13 McNeill, *Mary Ann McCracken*, pp 126–8.

14 O'Neill, 'Mary Leadbeater', pp 150–3.

15 *Journals and memoirs of Thomas Russell 1791–5*, edited by C.J. Woods (Dublin, 1991), p. 86.

16 Nancy Curtin, 'Matilda Tone and virtuous republican femininity', in Keogh and Furlong, *The Women of 1798*, pp 26–46.

17 Curtin, 'Women and republicanism', p. 134.

18 Helena Concannon, *Women of 'ninety eight* (Dublin, 2nd edition, 1920), p. xiii; McNeill, *Mary Ann McCracken*, p. 129.

19 Kinsella, 'Women in folk memory', p. 188.

20 Concannon, *Women of 'ninety eight*, pp 299–300.

21 Curtin, 'Women and republicanism', pp 134–5.

22 Quoted in Concannon, *Women of 'ninety eight*, p. xii.

23 Mary Helen Thuente, 'Liberty, Hibernia and Mary Le More: United Irish images of women', in Keogh and Furlong, *The Women of 1798*, pp 9–25.

24 Concannon, *Women of 'ninety eight*, pp 297–8.

25 R.R. Madden, *Antrim and Down in '98* (Glasgow, nd), p. 244.

26 Kinsella, 'Women in folk memory', pp 192–3.

27 Daniel Gahan, *The people's rising: Wexford 1798* (Dublin, 1995), p. 132.

28 Peadar Mac Suibhne, *Kildare in 1798* (Naas, 1978) p. 61.

29 Nicholas Furlong, *Fr John Murphy of Boolavogue 1753–1798* (Dublin, 1991), p. 133.

30 *Ibid.*, pp 53–4.

31 Kinsella, 'Women in folk memory', p. 191.

32 *Ibid.*, p. 192.

33 John Beatty, 'Protestant women of County Wexford and their narratives of the rebellion of 1798' in Keogh and Furlong, *The Women of 1798*, pp 113–36.

34 *Ibid.*, p. 120.

35 *Ibid.*, p. 118.

36 R.R. Madden, *The United Irishmen: their lives and times*, 3rd series, iii (Dublin, 1846), p. 182.

37 *Ibid.*

38 *Ibid.*, p. 187.

'RATIONAL CREATURES AND FREE CITIZENS':
REPUBLICANISM, FEMINISM AND THE WRITING OF HISTORY

The second half of the eighteenth century is seen as the period that saw the origins of modern Irish republicanism. It is also the period where historians locate the origins of modern feminism. This essay was published in The Republic, *the journal of the Ireland Institute for Historical and Cultural Studies. The Institute was established in 1997 with the aim of studying and promoting republican thinking. Over the following years* The Republic *published a broad range of contributions examining different aspects of republican thinking as well as looking at issues in today's Ireland from a republican perspective. Writing this essay raised for me the engagement of feminism with political thought, first with republicanism and Enlightenment thinking in the late eighteenth century, and then with developing liberalism and socialism in the nineteenth.*

Modern republicanism and modern feminism both trace their roots back to the eighteenth-century European Enlightenment and the American and French revolutions. The scientific revolution of the seventeenth century had caught the imagination of intellectual Europe, marking a further stage in the move from reliance on received authority to reliance on the power of the human mind, allied to systematic observation, to discover truth about the material world and the universe. Enlightenment thinkers applied the admired scientific methods to human beings and the organisation of human societies. At the level of the individual, they emphasised the rational aspect of human nature, the ability to think and reason, to decide between good and evil, and to make responsible and moral decisions about individuals' own lives. Since reason was an attribute of every human being rather than a monopoly in the hands of the high-born, they queried the allocation of resources, power and privilege, on the basis of arbitrary differences like birth. Hereditary monarchy and all forms of hereditary access to privilege and power came under critical scrutiny. At the level of society, Enlightenment thinkers looked for universal laws controlling human behaviour, as Newton had looked for the laws governing the movement of the planets.

Republican thinking was stimulated by Enlightenment ideas, and by both the American revolution in the 1770s and the French revolution from 1789. These fed into the long tradition of European republican thought, based on the classical education universally enjoyed by the better-off, with its knowledge of the political ideas of Greece and Rome. From this came the concept of the classical republic, the res publica or public thing, with the virtuous and active citizens at the centre of political life. However, this citizenship was confined to male heads of households, and excluded all dependents, including women and slaves. Enlightenment values deepened the democratic values of republicanism, stressing that good government must be in the interests of all the people and must be one in which all the people had a say. Writers, like Thomas Paine, advocated putting the principles of freedom and equality into practice on the ground, through political action. The French revolution saw one of the major European states attempt to do just that. Republican writings were widely read in late eighteenth-century

Ireland, especially Paine's latest work, *The Rights of Man* (1791–2), which defended the French revolution, and presented a detailed Enlightenment and republican critique of the structure of British government.

Both the Enlightenment and the French revolution created a space and a climate which encouraged the assertion of claims for women's equality with men. In eighteenth-century Europe, for the small number of women – and men – who voiced such ideas, equality meant equality in terms of moral and rational worth, freedom to fulfil individual potential, and recognition as full members of the human race, instead of the second class membership allocated to women. The emphasis was not on equal work, but on recognition of the value of different work and roles. In Enlightenment debate, the position of women in western Europe was analysed in new terms, not of what God had ordained, but of 'nature', what was 'natural' for their sex. Nevertheless, women's nature and role continued to be defined by most male thinkers, in the context of their view of the relationship between the sexes. That role was famously defined by Jean-Jacques Rousseau in 1762. The education of a woman, he wrote, must be planned in relation to man:

> To be pleasing in his sight, to win his respect and love, to train him in childhood, to tend him in manhood, to counsel and console, to make his life pleasant and happy, these are the duties of woman for all time, and this is what she should be taught when young.[1]

The view accepted by most Enlightenment thinkers of women's nature fitted this role. Women were essentially non-rational, guided by emotion and feelings rather than moral judgment, and needing the guidance and control of rational men to find the path to virtue.

The language of reason, and of revolution and citizenship, became familiar to all sections of society, and disadvantaged groups expressed old concerns in new political terms. In France, for some years after 1789, radical women, mostly middle-class, pressed for specific reforms, formed clubs, marshalled their arguments, and began to petition the National Assembly. Demands included marriage reform, divorce, better employment, education, political liberty, and a general equality of rights. One of the best known, Olympe de Gouges, in 1791 published *Les Droits de la Femme*, demanding complete equality in the public sphere. In 1793 the *Club des citoyennes républicaines révolutionnaires* was founded, but, in October of that year, the revolutionary government outlawed all women's clubs, and told women their contribution to the republic lay strictly within the home, where they could rear good republican citizens. The Assembly did pass some reforms in the area of divorce and property rights, but not on education or the public role of women.

While Britain did not experience a revolution, the early years of the French revolution made radical political change seem a real possibility and in this heightened atmosphere Mary Wollstonecraft published *A Vindication of the Rights of Woman* in 1792. A writer and intellectual, unequivocally committed to the values of the Enlightenment and republicanism and who had already published a book on the rights of men in response to Edmund Burke's *Reflections on the Revolution in France*, she now argued the case for women's equality in the terms of republican citizenship. Her main target was the basic contradiction underlying Rousseau's views on the education of women already noted. Either women were rational human creatures who should be both educated and expected to act as such, or men should declare openly that they did not believe women were fully human. For Wollstonecraft, as for most Enlightenment thinkers, reason and virtue were closely linked. To be virtuous one had to be free to act as reason dictated. According to Rousseau, a woman 'will always be in subjection to a man, or men's judgment, and she will never be free to set her own opinion above his'.[2] Wollstonecraft responded:

> In fact, it is a farce to call any being virtuous whose virtues do not result from the exercise of its own reason. That was Rousseau's opinion respecting men; I extend it to women.[3]

While she argued that all knowledge and occupations should be open to both sexes, she saw women as being primarily occupied as wives and mothers. To be good as either, they must first be self-determining virtuous human beings. The political, social and economic structures of society forced women into dependence on men, and hence into subordination. This then made it an economic necessity for women to seek to attract a man who would support them. It was useless to expect virtue from women while they were so dependent on men. If women were recognised as free, independent citizens, they could then be expected, as other citizens were expected, to work, and to work to acceptable standards. Being wives and mothers would then be seen as real work by citizens, contributing to society, and a revolution in the quality of mothering would follow. 'Make women rational creatures and free citizens, and they will quickly become good wives and mothers'.[4]

Some Enlightenment writers, female and male, supported improved education for women on the grounds of improved motherhood. Wollstonecraft was one of the few who justified the rights of women on the same grounds as the rights of men, on shared human reason:

> Speaking of women at large, their first duty is to themselves
> as rational creatures, and the next, in point of importance,
> as citizens, is that, which includes so many, of a mother.[5]

She went further still in seeing motherhood in terms of citizenship, rejecting any absolute division between the private and public spheres.

Ireland did see a rebellion, but not one which, like the French revolution, led to a new constitution and a new state. The defeat of the United Irishmen in 1798 was followed by the passing of the Act of Union in 1800. We do not know what sort of state would have followed success. Nor do we, as of now, know how widespread demands for women's citizenship were among the women in the movement. However, we do know that some at least had developed opinions. Mary Ann McCracken (1770–1866), writing from Belfast to her brother and leading United Irishman, Henry Joy McCracken in Kilmainham Prison in Dublin on 16 March 1797 put the case in language and ideas reminiscent of Wollstonecraft (who was widely read in Ireland), and with the added edge of the French *citoyennes*. She wrote of the dignity of women's nature and their current situation, 'degraded by custom and education'; if woman was intended as man's companion, she 'must of course be his equal in understanding'; women must take responsibility for their own liberation:

> is it not almost time … that the female part of creation as
> well as the male should throw off the fetters with which
> they have been so long mentally bound and rise … to the
> situation for which they were designed.

They must believe that 'rational ideas of liberty and equality' applied to themselves as well as to men and must cultivate a 'genuine love of Liberty and just sense of her value', if their support of liberty for others is to be of value. Like the women activists of the French revolution she urges that a new Irish constitution should include women as citizens, and hopes

> it is reserved for the Irish nation to strike out something new and to shew an example of candour, generosity and justice superior to any that have gone before them.[6]

It was not to be. Sixteen months later almost to the day, she walked with her brother, her arm through his, to his execution in Belfast. The rebellion had been crushed, and there was no new Ireland in the building.

A number of points arise relevant to our understanding of how history is written. Mary Wollstonecraft, Mary Ann McCracken and the radical Frenchwomen were not outsiders pressing claims on movements of which they were not a part. They were all active participants who from within tried to broaden the intellectual base. Olympe de Gouges and the French women who urged women's rights to full citizenship on the revolutionary leadership were active revolutionaries themselves. Wollstonecraft's writings, including the *Vindication*, are part of the body of Enlightenment and republican thought. McCracken, while not a sworn member of the United Irishmen, was active in the broad movement. Nancy Curtin, one of the leading historians of the United Irishmen, describes her as taking 'the radicals' notion of the natural rights of man to self-government to its logical conclusion – the extension of these rights to women', and notes that she 'seems to have been far better read in the classic republican and radical texts than her brother'.[7] These women took part in the mainstream development of republican thinking and practice, and, in addition, argued for a more inclusive concept of republican citizenship. By any criteria this would seem a significant contribution. Yet, few histories of the Enlightenment, the French revolution or the radical politics of 1790s Ireland see women as part of the action or see the feminist challenge as part of the political thinking of the period.

Most survey histories of societies have been written from a perspective that sees males as the active agents in human history, dominating the 'public' sphere of political, macro-economic, intellectual and cultural affairs and as the instigators of the patterns of change and continuity that historians study. Women are implicitly seen as passive spectators or followers in the public sphere and as in control in their special domain of the 'private' or domestic sphere. The two spheres are seen to operate separately and independently.

A major factor in this perspective is that few historians have seen the relationships between men and women as a part of history. Instead, relationships between the sexes appear to have been taken for granted, as 'natural', biologically based, essentially the same across societies and over time, unchanging and unchangeable, and so outside the remit of the historian.

To see these relationships as solely 'natural' and outside history seems extraordinary once attention is drawn to them. In eighteenth-century Ireland, as elsewhere in Europe, access to resources and power was directed to males, rather than females, through a combination of laws, regulations, and customs. These involved inheritance laws, marriage laws including husbands' legal control of their wives' persons and property, and double sexual standards in law and daily life, as well as the exclusion of women from the universities, the professions and political life. It is difficult to see how all these together could be explained as occurring 'naturally', without any purposeful human intervention. Yet, few historians have seen them as needing to be even adverted to or described, let alone analysed or explained as significant aspects of the history of a society.

If historians do not see relationships between the sexes as part of history, then feminist argument and campaigns have no reference point. If historians do not see the historical realities that provoked them, they appear to come from nowhere. This blindness of the historians appears to be the main reason why survey histories, when they do mention women's rights campaigns, which is seldom, almost never consider their origins, their significance, their interaction with other movements or the light they throw on other developments.

The 'discovery' of these relationships, as the proper subject for historical research and interpretation, came in response to a simple question: what did women do in history? This question came to be asked when the current growth in women's history developed under the impetus of the new wave of the women's movement in the 1960s. It arose because opponents argued that women had always lived happily in a purely domestic sphere. Attempts to answer it uncovered, among other things, both earlier assertions of women's right to autonomy and the structures of societies which gave rise to them. It became clear that male-female relationships in history could not be ascribed solely to a simple biological determinism. It was necessary to distinguish between, on the one hand, whatever biological differences exist between the sexes and on the other, the roles societies prescribe and enforce for males and females. These roles involve the political, social and economic consequences experienced by an individual in any particular society, at any particular time, depending on birth as male or female. Feminist theorists took the word 'gender' and gave it a new meaning to denote this social construction of sex.

This highlights the significance of both the questions historians ask and the questions they do not ask. Women's emancipation campaigns, and the reasons for them were fully visible in the historical evidence. It was historians' perceptions of who and what was significant that made it irrelevant to ask: what did women do? This reminds us that we all bring our political and other beliefs to the writing and reading of history. While this is inevitable, it also indicates the importance of listening to new questions, and paying less attention to who is asking them, and more to how we try to answer them. New questions may be politically motivated in various ways, but that does not invalidate a question that opens up hitherto unexplored areas of human experience. We may also ponder what conscious or unconscious motivations contribute to the various blindspots of historians, as well as what questions remain as yet unasked.

Gender analysis is a powerful tool in historical research and interpretation, and it is ironic, to say the least, that before its value has been recognised and exploited on any broad scale, popular usage has translated it into a synonym for sex and so drained it of its value. However, whatever name we use for it, it is important that the concept itself and the reality it names do not become invisible again. Once the relationships between women and men are brought under historical scrutiny, sex takes its place with other categories of analysis, such as class, colour, race, religion, nationality, wealth or access to resources. The interaction of all these determines the location of individuals in time and place, and influences the opportunities and choices open to them. Seeing this interaction eliminates the danger of a reductionism that sees all women as always oppressed by all men. For example, the interaction of class and sex will find some women exercising power over men and other women. Women as well as men can be oppressors. The reality is that we have human beings, female and male, grappling with their situation, with varying degrees of altruism and self-interest, awareness and muddled thinking, within the constraints of sex, class, and the other categories.

Women's history in Ireland, while not as fully developed as elsewhere, is rooted and growing. Relevant to the discussion here is its discovery of women's emancipation activism in the nineteenth and early twentieth centuries. Nineteenth-century campaigns, some of them conducted in close co-operation with British activists, and other separate Irish endeavours, achieved a number of substantial reforms: improved standards in the education of girls and women including admission to universities and degrees; married women's control of their own property; wider employment opportunities; and the local government vote and eligibility for election to most local government bodies. The early twentieth-century campaign for parliamentary suffrage, as well as continued pressure on other fronts won full citizenship, including full political participation, for women in the 1922 Constitution of the Irish Free State. After 1922 activism continued, albeit with a lower public profile, as feminists tried, with varying degrees of success, to counter the general hostility of the conservative Free State governments of the 1920s, 1930s and 1940s to women's participation in the public sphere.

These findings have yet to infiltrate the 'mainstream' survey histories of Ireland. To be fair, there is not, as yet, a sustained and comprehensive overview of the history of the Irish women's movement. There are a few good monographs on the suffrage movement and quite a wide range of collections and scattered articles on various aspects. It may be that an inclusive overview or overviews are needed before the breakthrough will come. Be that as it may, for a group, society, or nation, history plays the role that personal memory does for the individual. What is not recorded by the historian has not existed for the reader. So effective can the memory loss be, that when the new wave of the women's movement, Women's Liberation, burst very publicly onto the scene in 1970, few of the participants were aware that Irish activism went back at least to the 1860s. Even today, knowledge of the history of Irish feminist organisation is confined to a small group of the interested, and has made little inroad into the awareness of the public at large or popular political debate. This is only too evident in the very limited perception of feminism generally portrayed in the media, where it is seen as a 'women's issue' and essentially a matter of women trying to compete on equal terms with men within the existing structures of society.

So, the cycle of reinventing the wheel continues. Time and energy, which could be spent in critical self-analysis and reflection on what could be learned from the earlier experience, are instead used in rediscovering information and insights. Equally, of course, successive generations of men have lost the memory that male-dominated societies imposed such restrictions on the areas of human activity they allowed women to enter, and have not had to ponder the implications. How many other distortions of our shared past have yet to be recognised?

However, once we see the relationships between the sexes as part of history, this brings feminist thinking unequivocally into the arena of political thought where it makes its own contribution to debate. In practice, of course feminism has always engaged in political debate and argument with other analyses. Again, because the political, social, and economic relationships between the sexes have been overlooked, so too the contribution of feminism to debate has – until very recently – been largely ignored in discussion of political thought. At the international level, a large body of critical feminist theory has developed over the past 20 years or so, and is beginning to find its way into some histories of political thought.[8] In Ireland, so far there has been only a limited amount of publication on political thought and feminism is not included.

Feminism does not produce a blueprint for the ideal society. Its contribution to political thought is to insist that the political, social and economic relationships between the sexes be scrutinised. It argues that sex-roles which limit women's control over their own lives and which subordinate women to men and women's needs to men's needs are oppressive to women, dehumanising to both sexes and damaging to society as a whole. In interaction with other analyses of the dynamics and structures of societies, various feminist political theories have developed and so far none has become recognised as the definitive orthodoxy.

Nineteenth-century liberalism, itself a product of the Enlightenment emphasis on reason, sees human beings as autonomous, rational individuals, competing for success, wealth and status. The state's role is to create a level playing field by removing obstacles based on factors such as birth, religion or ethnicity. Other than this, it should interfere as little as possible. However, in a liberal democracy, like Ireland today, feminists, whether or not they agree with the liberal world-view, find they have to call for continuing state intervention to remove obstacles based on sex. The social construction of sex, including the unequal division of domestic labour, the smaller earning power of women and the distribution of power within families which determines whose interests get priority, inhibits equal competition between the sexes within the worlds of paid work and politics. Feminists argue that a liberal democracy, which aims to treat all citizens equally, will have to exercise active discrimination. To achieve equal treatment, account must be taken of the differences in the life situation of different groups, and the balance of advantage and disadvantage has to be redressed. This may be done in various ways, for instance by providing child-care services to free women to compete on equal terms, by insisting on a quota of women on boards or by anti-discrimination legislation.

These arguments are valid and important, but have limitations if the aim is to radically change society. In the first place, measures that aim to adjust the balance *between* the sexes often overlook the differences *within* each sex. Freeing women from various domestic responsibilities may allow more affluent women to compete with more affluent men, but may make little difference to poorer women and poorer men whose participation may be inhibited by other factors, such as lower educational achievement, lack of a car, etc. Secondly, it can easily slide into an assumption that the objective of feminism is solely equal rights and equal opportunities between the sexes. Equal participation of women with men in political, social and economic life will only create a more inclusive and equitable society across the board if women *per se* are more committed to such values and to devising policies to promote them. Neither the historical record nor today's world show women consistently supporting different political policies to men. Like men, women involved in politics are, and have been, members of parties and movements whose policies differ fundamentally. In any case, there is a contradiction at the core of a view that sees women's rights as solely concerned with women attaining the position and privileges men enjoy. If we reject sex-role models which see women as subordinate to men and which limit women's autonomy and control over their own lives, the corollary must be rejection of a male model of dominance and authority. The logic of the feminist starting point is the need to develop new and more fully human models for both sexes.

Marxist analysis also drew on the Enlightenment, in its case on the search for the laws governing human behaviour and societies. It believes that capitalism, based on private ownership and competition for profits, produces an unjust society with high levels of deprivation and unhappiness. Marxism and socialism argue that society as a whole should control the entire economic and political systems, which should be developed in a non-competitive way in the interests of the welfare of all. Feminisms which accept Marxist and socialist views criticise liberal feminism as bourgeois and interested only in middle-class women. In Marxist and socialist analysis, *all* women will only be fully liberated the class issue is resolved and capitalism replaced by socialism. In turn, feminists challenge Marxism and socialism that gender analysis must be incorporated with their class analysis if women are to benefit from a class revolution.

Radical feminism emerged in the 1960s and took yet another approach. It saw both biological sex *and* socially constructed sex-roles as crucial issues. Sexuality and sexual activity, as well as childbearing and rearing, were areas for political scrutiny and analysis. It rejected any aim of making women 'equal' to men and celebrated women's difference.

There are many feminisms, many feminist theories with many variations and interactions. Few people's thinking fits neatly into any one theory and most combine elements from a number.

All this points to the potential of dialogue between republicanism and feminism to contribute to radical change in society. Feminist awareness of the need to recognise social difference when trying to create conditions of equality and freedom can engage with republicanism's insistence that good government must be concerned with the welfare of all citizens and must facilitate the participation of all citizens. Feminism also brings its insight that current models of masculinity and femininity may be obstacles to creating the republic; in particular the macho model with its reluctance to admit error and its obsession with saving face. If socialist principles are included in the dialogue, a critical approach to the existing organisation of the world, socially, economically and politically, could follow. The present organisation and structures subordinate people to profits. This may favour male participation over female, but it does not aim to facilitate the human development, welfare and happiness of either sex. Instead of trying to fit women into this model we could ask what forms of economic organisation would best suit the real needs of women, men and children. The same question could be addressed to political participation. The dialogue could also seek ways to counter the inhuman aspects of the current global, free-market economy where many of the issues that concern feminism and republicanism arise in new forms. Critics of globalisation stress the need to counter the belief that a competitive and unregulated free market, divorced from social responsibility, will best serve the interests of people everywhere because it is the most effective way of increasing wealth. It may increase wealth, but that wealth will benefit the few and not the many, unless some form of global regulation is devised to protect individuals from bearing the costs of unchecked competition, through job insecurity, the breakdown of communities, increasing wealth for some, accompanied by the increasing alienation of others, or destruction of the environment.[9]

Feminism, republicanism, and democracy are concerned with combining individual freedom and social responsibility. Feminism is not a 'women's issue'. It is a human issue with implications for society as a whole and it addresses fundamental questions concerning the definition of a human being and a citizen. Perhaps because the logic of its analysis leads to critical scrutiny of masculinity as well as femininity, male thinkers have been slow to accept this. The emphasis of the women's rights argument in the 1790s was on a number of concerns: inclusiveness; the need to recognise and respect diversity among individuals and roles; the responsibilities as well as the rights of citizenship; and the need for education for good citizenship. All these have an applicability that is not confined to women and can engage constructively with the republican values of liberty, equality and fraternity/ sorority. The writing of history, just as it played a role in losing the memory of feminist challenges to patriarchal societies, can now play a role in helping to retrieve some of that lost memory. If we can start by recovering the interaction of republicanism and women's emancipation in the 1790s and incorporating it into the written histories of the period, we can prepare the ground for ongoing engagement in the present day. If history is what the evidence forces us to believe, the first task must be to make that evidence so visible that it cannot be ignored. This is part of the project of writing a more inclusive human history. The challenge here is to historians and perhaps particularly to historians of women.

from *The Republic: A Journal of Contemporary and Historical Debate,* No. 1 (June 2000), pp 60–70.

NOTES

1   J.J. Rousseau, *Émile* (London, Dent, 1974), p. 321.

2   *Ibid.*, p. 333.

3   Mary Wollstonecraft, *A Vindication of the Rights of Woman* (London, Dent, 1982), p. 25.

4   *Ibid.*, p. 213

5   *Ibid.*, p. 159.

6   Mary McNeill, *The Life and Times of Mary Ann McCracken 1770–1866: A Belfast Panorama* (Belfast, Blackstaff, 1988), pp 126–8.

7   Nancy Curtin, 'Women and Eighteenth-Century Irish Republicanism', in Margaret Mac Curtain and Mary O'Dowd (eds), *Women in Early Modern Ireland* (Edinburgh, Edinburgh University Press, 1991), pp 138–40.

8   See, for example, John Morrow, *History of Political Thought: A Thematic Introduction* (Basingstoke and London, Macmillan, 1998).

9   See, for example, John Gray, *False Dawn: The Delusions of Global Capitalism* (London, Granta Books, 1999).

WIDOWS IN IRELAND, 1830–1970

The publication of Vols IV and V of the Field Day Anthology of Irish Writing *was a landmark in the development of feminist scholarship and writing. In response to concerns that the first three volumes, published in 1991, had contained little work by women, Field Day invited some women scholars to edit a volume devoted to women's writing. The eight-woman editorial group set out to make 'their history, culture and traditions' available to Irish women. They found it impossible to do justice in one volume to the 'flowering of women's writing, political activism, and feminist scholarship in Ireland' since the 1970s, and so two volumes, running to over 3000 pages, were published in 2002. They included material dating from 600 to the time of publication, both writings by women and texts that centred on women, and covered a wide and wonderfully rich variety of subjects. Political activists, journalists, theologians, poets and novelists, as well as scholars, were among the large number of contributing editors. This essay was the introduction to the section on widows.*

The economic situation of widows is easier to document than widowhood's emotional impact, which must have varied enormously from individual to individual. During the period 1830–1970 most Irish women who lived to late middle age or old age became widows. While most were in the older age groups, there were significant numbers in the age range 30 to 54, those likely to have dependent children. Widows, but not widowers, were seen to be vulnerable to poverty. The

1835–6 Poor Law Inquiry identified widows with families of young children as a group highly likely to be destitute. Witnesses explained that this was not because care of children or home prevented them from earning, but because the remuneration for women's work, however hard or long they worked, would not support a family. At agricultural labour, for example, women generally earned half the male wage. Yet during the nineteenth century most widows supported themselves by their own efforts.

The 1871 census showed over 59 per cent of widows as having occupations other than home duties. Information from the census indicates that farming dominated the working lives of widows, as it did those of married women. Other work performed by widows fell into the category of 'traditional' women's work, such as work in the textile and needle trades, and domestic service. Widows also managed businesses in which they had worked during their husbands' lifetimes. Continuing a business after her husband's death gave a widow the best chance of earning a 'family wage'. Reliance on earnings in occupations traditionally open to women would, in most cases, lower the family's standard of living.

For widows who could not maintain themselves from their own resources, family support was important. Common law and custom obliged children to provide for parents. In farming families, when parents handed over control to one of their children, usually a son, the parents were guaranteed life-long maintenance rights. The son then married and other children were provided for with the proceeds of the incoming bride's dowry. Among cottier and labouring families, marriage and parenthood were seen as the only available form of insurance for old age.

During the second half of the nineteenth century, economic and social change increased the number of families solely dependent on a male wage. Suburban lifestyles were adopted by middle-class and skilled artisan families. Separation of workplace and home made it difficult for wives to maintain former involvement in their husbands' work, and very few were well placed to take over a family business as widows.

In response to these changes, insurance grew in importance. Increasingly widowhood was provided for by life assurance policies taken out by a husband. Occupational groups ran their own schemes, while the state increasingly accepted responsibility for social welfare, including provision of widows' and children's pensions for state employees such as the Royal Irish Constabulary.

The state also began to provide for people who fell outside insurance schemes. The first such provision for widows had come in the Poor Law of 1838. Widows were treated like everyone else and, if able-bodied, had to prove destitution to be considered for relief. Pressure on the system during the 1845–9 Famine forced modifications in the regulations. Poor Law guardians were empowered to give relief outside the workhouse to specified groups, including destitute widows with two or more dependent children, the first – and limited – state provision for widows as a specific group. Workhouse provision for widows was criticised by middle-class philanthropists as contrary to family life and to the growing bourgeois ideology of women's economic dependence on men.

The numbers of widows helped by the Poor Law was never large. For example, in 1889 there were 3,980 widows and their 12,855 children in receipt of outdoor relief in the half year ended 25 March. Voluntary charitable organisations also provided support. The 1901 census recorded a total of 3,737 females and 1,255 males in charitable institutions in the country. The stigma attached to charity and the Poor Law made people reluctant to use either. The 1906 *Report of the Viceregal Commission on Poor Law Reform in Ireland* (3 vols) noted that while there were

> only 60 respectable widows with one child in the workhouses in Ireland ... [this] may safely be taken as an indication that there are many more out of workhouses making perhaps too hard a struggle to remain independent.[1]

The introduction in 1908 of state old age pensions at age seventy was of real benefit to widows, since they comprised such a high percentage of the population in the relevant age group. In 1924 workhouses in the Irish Free State were abolished and replaced by home assistance, outdoor relief under a new name. A commission in 1927 found witnesses favoured taking widows with children out of the Poor Law as it was 'hurtful to the self-respect of these women to be compelled to parade their poverty every week at the office of the Assistance Officer'.[2]

In 1935 the Widows and Orphans Act introduced both contributory and non-contributory widows' pension schemes. The former provided for the better-off working class by a compulsory pension financed by contributions from employees, employers and government. The latter provided for those not insured. To qualify, a widow had to be between sixty and seventy (the old age pension threshold), or have a dependent child under fourteen. Neither pension was payable if the widow remarried or cohabited with a man. Widows who fell outside both pension criteria could seek a discretionary payment called home assistance. After

1935 the age limit and the children under fourteen requirements for the non-contributory pension were gradually phased out. The trend has also been to reduce restrictions generally so that the numbers receiving contributory pensions have grown and those receiving non-contributory ones have decreased.

Thus, from 1838 until 1935 state assistance to widows was confined to impoverished mothers with dependent children. After 1935 state support was gradually extended to widows without dependent children, and also to unmarried mothers and deserted wives. This shows a move from the principle that only status as a mother of dependent children entitled a widow to support to one where widowhood *per se* was a qualification. The move reflected the increasing proportion of married women dependent on their husband's earnings and not in a position to earn their own living if he died.

The evidence suggests that the cause of widows' poverty lay in the lower earning power of women as compared to men. This was as true in the twentieth century as it had been in the nineteenth. In 1951 widows who depended on their labour in the market-place were still relatively poor. The 1951 census showed over 58 per cent of all widowers 'at work', compared with 30 per cent of widows, and significantly higher proportions of widowers in higher status and better paid areas such as the professions and skilled manual work. A comparison of industrial workers in 1966, 1971 and 1976 showed the disposable income of female breadwinners, both widows and single women, to be substantially lower than that of married or single men.[3]

The National Association of Widows in Ireland, founded in 1967, has asserted that widows' primary need is 'a decent living allowance'. A widow did not want charity or pity but 'the chance to carry on and hold on to that which she and her husband had started out to do together', and she asked of the state and society only that they stopped making the obstacles she has to overcome 'greater and greater'.[4]

from Angela Bourke, Siobhán Kilfeather, Maria Luddy, Margaret Mac Curtain, Gerardine Meaney, Máirín Ní Dhonnchadha, Mary O'Dowd, and Clair Wills, (eds), *The Field Day Anthology of Irish Writing: Vol V: Irish Women's Writing and Traditions* (Cork, Cork University Press, 2002), pp 609–10.

NOTES

1   *Report of the Viceregal Commission on Poor Law Reform in Ireland*, Vol. 1, Report, 1906 (Cd. 3202), 1i, p. 349; Vol. 2, Appendix to Report, 1906 (Cd. 3203), 1i, p. 441; Vol. 3, Evidence and Index, 1906 (Cd. 3204), lii, p. 1.

2   *Report of the Commission on the Relief of the Sick and Destitute Poor, Including the Insane Poor* (Dublin, Stationery Office, 1928), p. 57.

3   *National Economic and Social Council Report 25: Towards a Social Report* (Dublin, NESC, 1976), pp. 149-51.

4   Eileen Proctor, 'Our Association, Its Story', *Women, Wives, Widows*, Vol. 1, No. 1 (June 1971).

WOMEN, EMANCIPATION AND POLITICS, 1860–1984

A New History of Ireland was a major undertaking in Irish history publication. It aimed to provide an overview or synthesis of the current state of research, from prehistory and geological and archaeological evidence to 1984, with a wide range of contributors. Publication started in the 1970s and continued into the early twenty-first century, and comprised nine volumes in all. During the 1970s and 1980s women's history was growing rapidly, and by the 1990s the New History editors decided to include chapters on women in Vols VI and VII, covering the periods 1860– 1921 and 1921–84 respectively. I was invited to contribute these. The first chapter was not completed in time for the publication of Vol VI, and it was agreed that a longer chapter combining the periods dealt with by the two volumes would appear in Vol VII. The attempt to provide a fairly succinct overview that did justice to the ever increasing volume of research and publication was challenging but rewarding. There was an added angle as I was an active feminist, and had been a panellist on the 1971 Late Late television show devoted to the Women's Liberation Movement. Writing the chapter deepened my appreciation of the range and quality of work being done in the field.

The women's emancipation movement that emerged in Ireland in the second half of the nineteenth century was part of a wider phenomenon in western society. At a time when greater rights and opportunities for middle- and working-class men were being demanded, there were those who contended that women too had rights and should be accorded greater autonomy or even full equality with men. Such a claim was not entirely new, but the nineteenth century witnessed sustained pressure on a number of different fronts.

While laws, regulations, and customs differed from country to country, the restrictions imposed on women's autonomy in the early nineteenth century were essentially similar. With some aristocratic and royal exceptions, women were excluded from positions of formal power. They could not hold public office, sit on representative parliamentary bodies, or vote in parliamentary elections. Virtually all well-paid employments, including the expanding professions, were closed to them, as were the universities. For those middle- and upper-class women who had to earn their own living, the only socially acceptable employments were poorly paid and low-status occupations such as governessing or needlework. At secondary level, girls' education aimed largely at accomplishment-level learning. While the family was regarded as women's 'sphere', within it laws placed authority and control of resources firmly in male hands. Under English common law, operative in Ireland, married women 'had no civil existence: they owned no personal property, they could neither sue nor be sued, they could not divorce their husbands, or claim any rights over their children'.[1] If a woman left her husband, his duty to maintain her lapsed but (assuming that her property was not held in trust) he retained control of her property, including any income she might earn after separation. In sex-related offences such as adultery, prostitution, and illegitimate births women were the guilty and punishable party in the eyes of society.

Among the intellectual and philosophical influences that contributed to the emergence of the women's emancipation movement, historians have noted the European enlightenment, the French revolution, and evangelical religion. Enlightenment emphasis on a common rational human nature encouraged women's claims, despite little support from male thinkers. So did the French revolution's calls for liberty, equality, and fraternity, again despite male scepticism. Evangelical religion, influential across all denominations, stressed a mother's responsibility for the moral welfare of the family, and by extension the wider community. This gave religious backing to improved female education and a concept of women as in some ways morally superior to men. Other philosophical developments, too, encouraged challenges to accepted models of male-female relations, particularly within left-wing and socialist movements. The radical tradition that emphasised utility as the guiding force in political economy was one such influence, giving primacy to the principle of the greatest happiness of the greatest number. The cooperative movement produced, in the joint work of an Irish woman and an Irish man, one of the most cogently argued cases for the full equality of the sexes in all spheres of life, including the political.[2] Within the Marxist tradition Engels's contention,[3] that the ideology of the father-dominated family originated in male control of private property, challenged claims that patriarchal authority protected women and children. Theories of evolution gave scientific support to arguments that women's moral and intellectual character could be improved by better education, upgraded legal status, and the shouldering of political and civil responsibility in place of being shielded from 'the world' in a perpetual childhood. Drawing on these various sources, nineteenth-century emancipationists used two main lines of argument in support of their cause. The first began with the individual, irrespective of sex, and claimed women's full emancipation as a human right based on the rational human nature shared by all persons. The second started from a concept of difference and complementarity between male and female. It saw the contribution of women to society as different from that of men, but equally important and equally essential. To make their contribution women needed and had the right to participate in society at all levels.

Organised action in Ireland emerged first among small groups of middle-class Protestant women. Many of these pioneers came from the considerable number of women, married and single, who had already found their way to contribute to society outside the confines of the immediate family circle. Inspired by religious zeal and humanitarian concern, and mandated by the now recognised responsibility of women as custodians of morality and dispensers of charity, well-off women in the late eighteenth and nineteenth centuries poured energy and commitment into work for the moral and physical betterment of the poor.

This philanthropy developed beyond the activity of benevolent individuals to the formation of organisations to carry out specific work. Women moved from fund-raising for charities run by men to establishing and running their own societies.[4] Magdalen asylums – refuges for prostitutes, that gave shelter, protection, and encouragement to find alternative means of support – were among the first enterprises. So were visiting the poor in their homes and visiting prisons to teach women inmates to read, write, and sew. This was followed by aftercare in the form of refuges where ex-prisoners could learn domestic skills and be prepared for a new life, often through emigration. Creation of employment for poor women was a constant activity through the setting up of local industries and sale of the products. Foundations included orphanages, hospitals, schools, and asylums. Such work brought philanthropists into interaction with the 'public' sphere of administration, where they could observe its workings and analyse its inadequacies. They learned for themselves how the poor lived. Work with prostitutes, the sick poor, and impoverished mothers trying to earn money to feed and clothe their children, demolished the myth that women were a favoured species supported and 'protected' by men.

The philanthropists laid the foundations for many services that were later taken over by the state. As governments became more involved in education, health services, and provision for the poor, women's exclusion from the public political process came to be seen as a serious restriction on their work. Some became convinced that women needed access to public decision-making if they were to be effective in their mission to help the underprivileged and raise the moral level of society.

A minority of philanthropic women moved beyond the idea of alleviating the symptoms of poverty, and helping the poor to cope within the existing system, to tackling causes of social inequality and injustice. Working and organising in groups also encouraged analysis of their own position as women in society. Some gained political experience of campaigning to change the law by participation in such movements as the abolition of slavery and the temperance movement. Claiming the rights and duties of citizenship for other excluded groups highlighted women's own lack of civil rights. The slowness of some male colleagues to support women's full citizenship or to treat women as equal partners in other campaigns was often educational. The notorious refusal of the English anti-slavery movement to allow American women delegates to participate in the world anti-slavery convention in London in 1840 was a major impetus behind the first women's rights convention held in Seneca Falls, New York State, in 1848, and the lesson was not lost on women in other countries.[5] While only a minority of women went on to organise campaigns for female citizenship, a larger number with experience in philanthropy comprised a pool of female knowledge and concern about a broad range of social problems. Many of them shared the conviction that what women had to offer society was valuable and badly needed, and they were ready to move into new areas of activity opened up by feminist action.[6]

As to the relevance of religion, the Christian churches on the one hand tended to approve women's spiritual mission while on the other in varying degrees they emphasised submission to authority and self-effacement as virtues particularly pleasing in females. In general terms the more importance a church gave to private judgement and the less hierarchical its authority structure, the more it appears to have favoured, or the less it hindered, demands for emancipation. Protestantism generally allowed the individual conscience more autonomy than did Catholicism. While no church gave women equal status with men in decision-making roles,[7] the Quaker doctrine of the inner light appears to have been particularly favourable. The Catholic Church, whose exclusively male priesthood reserved to itself the right to interpret God's revelation and will for the laity, and which had no remembered tradition of women preachers or teachers, lay at the other extreme. For Catholic women to assert claims to personal autonomy and equal citizenship must have involved a more radical challenge to their church than was required of women from other denominations. Moreover, in Ireland the perception that women's emancipation was a foreign, and specifically an English, import posed problems for nationalist women, most of whom were Catholics.

Any assessment of Catholic women's engagement with women's issues in nineteenth-century Ireland must take into account the growing appeal of the religious orders after the relaxation of the penal laws. While middle-class Catholic lay women were involved in the philanthropic movement from its beginnings in the eighteenth century, by the middle of the nineteenth their work had largely been taken over by nuns. The number of nuns in Ireland grew from 120 in 1800 to 1,500 in 1851 and over 8,000 in 1901; exact numbers are difficult to ascertain because some women religious were classified as nurses or teachers.[8] By 1926 the number exceeded 9,000 in the twenty-six counties of the Irish Free State. The number of convents grew from 11 in 1800 to 91 in 1850 and to 368 in 1900.

The Poor Clares (1629), Dominicans (1644), and Carmelites (1690) were already established. The Ursulines came to Cork in 1771 at the request of Nano Nagle, and subsequently from the late eighteenth century to the middle of the nineteenth there was a growth of new Irish congregations working for the most part with the poor. Most of these began as groups of lay philanthropists which later transformed themselves into religious congregations. Nano Nagle's Presentation Sisters, founded first as the Sisters of the Charitable Institution of the Sacred Heart of Jesus in Cork in 1775, Mary Aikenhead's Irish Sisters of Charity (1815), Frances Ball's Irish branch of the Loreto order (1822), and Catherine McAuley's Sisters of Mercy (1831) all made this transition. Margaret Aylward's first major undertaking (1850) was the establishment of the Ladies' Association of Charity of St Vincent de Paul to undertake the visitation of the sick poor in north Dublin city; this lay group formed the core management of St Brigid's outdoor orphanage and poor schools. A most reluctant foundress, Aylward came under pressure from Archbishop Paul Cullen to transform her fellow workers into a religious community. Accordingly, in order to ensure the continuation of these charities, Aylward established the Holy Faith congregation (sanctioned 1867).[9] Certain bishops played a key role in respect of new foundations: in 1807 Bishop Daniel Delany of Kildare and Leighlin initiated the restoration of the ancient Order of St Bridget, while Thomas Furlong, bishop of Ferns, facilitated the foundation of the Sisters of St John of God in 1871 by a group of Irish women who had been members of the Sisters of Bon Secours in Paris.

From the middle of the nineteenth century there was an influx of French teaching congregations, which recruited Irish women. These included the Sacred Heart (1842), the Faithful Companions of Jesus (1843), St Louis (1859), St Joseph of Cluny (1860), and the Marists (1873). Such congregations supplemented the work of the Dominicans and Ursulines, who had a long record of catering for the education of the daughters of better-off Catholics. The new indigenous Irish foundations, by contrast, were more preoccupied with the education and catechesis of the poor.

The contribution of nuns to Irish life was impressive. They undertook an enormous range and variety of social work. Schools, orphanages, refuges, asylums, and hospitals were among the institutions founded and run by nuns to serve the needs of the poor, and later of the better-off. By the end of the nineteenth century they had established an immense network of institutions, which had become indispensable to the functioning of the Irish church and society.[10] By welfare-state standards the regimes in some of these institutions, such as the refuges for 'fallen women', were harsh. However, the commitment, orderliness, and cleanliness the nuns brought to their undertakings raised standards across the board and did much to make nursing in particular an acceptable career for middle-class women. Their work was regarded with respect and admiration by English feminists.

Recent scholarship has been reassessing the vocation of nun in the context of the work and choices available to Irish women.[11] The historical context was the challenge faced by the Catholic Church in retaining the adherence of rapidly expanding populations, especially among the poor in cities and towns. This gave the opportunity for a new form of religious life for women in which they moved outside the convent enclosure and engaged in active ministry. The founding mothers were women of formidable character and vision, but also of wealth and social standing who, as single women or widows, had control over the use of their property, and could decide to use their money and position to establish the new organisations. These organisations had an obvious attraction for women who wanted to contribute to society in substantial ways outside the confines of their immediate family, and to exercise initiative and management skills not usually allowed to women. Their growth also reflected the relatively low marriage rate in post-famine Ireland.

In many respects the way of life of nuns might appear well suited to the emergence of feminist awareness. Nuns lived in all-women communities with female authority figures, and were engaged in demanding work, which required organisation and cooperation. They ran their own convents and institutions. The fact that they were in varying degrees under the authority of the bishop, and there was always the possibility, and sometimes the reality, of clerical regulation might have acted as a stimulus to assertions of female autonomy. Yet only one Irish nun appears to have produced anything resembling a critical analysis of women's position in society, and even she (the outspoken Margaret Anna Cusack, the 'Nun of Kenmare') accepted that God had ordained the subordination of wives to husbands, and appears to have subscribed to the view that women were in some respects less intelligent than men.[12]

Nor did convents produce critiques of poverty and inequality in society or proposals for social revolution. On the contrary nuns won the grudging approval of state officials (who were sometimes ill-disposed to the very idea of Catholic nuns) because they were seen to train the young of the poorer classes to accept social inequality. In the education of young women of more privileged backgrounds there is the apparent paradox of nuns, the successors of pioneering women who themselves broke through the conventions of appropriate female behaviour, training generations of young Irish women of all classes, including later generations of novices, to conform to a model of feminine meekness and docility as well as piety. It appears that once the founding mothers had won their first battles, the women who followed them did not have to challenge convention as did lay women who organised and ran philanthropic institutions. It also has to be remembered that most women entered religious life primarily for religious reasons; the constant struggle to overcome self and self-will that was an integral part of religious life scarcely encouraged radical critiques of contemporary society. Moreover, although the phenomenon of nuns undertaking a wide range of social, educational, and philanthropic roles now seems unremarkable, in the nineteenth century the tradition that women could only contribute to the Catholic Church's mission through their role in the family, or in enclosed orders, still commanded much support among the church authorities. From this perspective, the main challenge facing the religious orders was to gain acceptance from the church authorities for their role.[13] This they achieved, thanks in part to the contribution the religious orders were able to make in helping to impose post-Tridentine Catholic standards on the whole of Catholic Ireland.

The early stages of feminist organisation in Ireland have yet to be fully researched. However, by the 1860s action was emerging around the issues of married women's property, education and employment for middle-class women, double sexual standards, and the parliamentary vote on the same terms as men. Membership of the first groups was small, middle-class, and Protestant, with Quakers particularly prominent. Two of the leading pioneers, who appear to have been to the fore in all areas of action, were Anna Haslam (1829–1922)[14] in Dublin and Isabella Tod (1836–96)[15] in Belfast. Haslam, born Anna Fisher, came from a Quaker family in Youghal involved in philanthropy and the anti-slavery movement. She helped in a soup kitchen during the famine of the 1840s and with her sister set up a crochet and knitting industry for poor women. Isabella Tod, born in Edinburgh, was a Presbyterian with a background in philanthropy and a lifelong commitment to women's involvement in the temperance movement. Both shared with other feminist pioneers relative financial independence and freedom from family opposition. Tod was unmarried while Haslam had no children; her husband was her lifelong co-worker in the women's movement.

The position of married women under common law was a crucial issue. Lack of control over inherited or earned property was fundamental. This affected the lives of women of all social classes, those of married women directly and those of single women indirectly. It severely limited married women's control over their own lives, and, linked with women's exclusion from most lucrative occupations, encouraged girls' education to aim at acquiring the accomplishments that would lead to marriage, rather than towards intellectual development and economic independence. The property of wealthy wives could be protected by the system of trusts developed by the courts of equity to circumvent the common law. This empowered trustees to 'protect' a woman's property against her husband, but did not necessarily give control to the woman herself and did not disturb the principle of patriarchal marriage. In any case, trusts were only feasible where substantial property was involved.

Isabella Tod and Anna Haslam were both involved in this campaign. Tod organised a Belfast branch of the London-based Married Women's Property Committee for reform of the law; she was the only woman to give evidence before the Select Committee of the House of Commons in 1868. She explained that 'educated' women in Belfast and Dublin had taken up property-law reform primarily to help the many poor married women working in the linen mills in the Belfast area. The pay was too low to make such work worth their while unless their husbands' 'ill-health or bad conduct' made it imperative. The law left their earnings, and those of their children, at the mercy of their husbands. Tod argued that protection orders were not the answer and that the only satisfactory solution was a woman's full legal right to her own earnings. She explained that middle-class women of limited means also needed this right since it was difficult for them to pay for a protective settlement or to find suitable trustees. She pointed out that a women's committee had been established in Dublin, and petitions in favour of reform had been organised in both Dublin and Belfast.[16] Tod went on to serve on the executive committee of the central Married Women's Property Committee in England during 1873–4.[17] Opponents of the campaign argued that married women's control of their own property would undermine the authority of husbands, to the consequent peril of the family and society. Reform proceeded gradually, with successive acts of parliament in 1870, 1874, 1882, and 1907, by which time the principle of spouses' separate property had been established.[18]

There was also Irish participation in the campaign to repeal the Contagious Diseases Acts, which had been passed in the 1860s amid fears that venereal disease was undermining the health of the British army and navy.[19] They provided for state regulation of prostitution in certain designated areas, of which three were in Ireland: Cork, Queenstown (Cobh), and the Curragh in County Kildare. The acts allowed the arrest of a woman on suspicion of being a prostitute and, if she was found to be suffering from venereal disease, her detention in a lock-hospital for up to nine months. Work for prostitutes had always been high on the agenda of philanthropic women. While the objective was to 'rescue' the 'fallen' woman and help her to a better life, the emancipationists understood the economic realities underpinning prostitution and its link to the low level of payment in all 'respectable' female employments. They opposed state regulation of prostitution on two main grounds. The first was that in practice it gave state sanction to a major threat to family life. The second was that it applied a double standard, which did not interfere with the men involved but treated the women as commodities to be periodically cleansed and recycled as 'clean harlots for the army and navy'.[20]

The Ladies' National Association (LNA) and the National Association for the Repeal of the Contagious Diseases Acts, both founded in England in 1869, had branches in Ireland. First Tod and subsequently Haslam were members of the LNA executive, and branches were established in Belfast, Dublin, and Cork. Numbers were never large. The members appear to have been exclusively Protestant, with Quakers as usual to the fore. Campaigning and speaking at public meetings on an issue explicitly related to women's sexuality broke new ground for middle-class women, who were expected to know little about prostitution and venereal disease, much less make public speeches about them. The smallness of the numbers involved reflects the strength of the taboo, as does the existence of separate women's committees side by side with mixed-sex committees. Haslam, typically, took part in both, becoming secretary of the mixed-sex committee set up in Dublin in 1870, and treasurer of the women's committee set up a year later. Meetings and demonstrations were held in Belfast and Dublin over the years, and petitions were organised.

Participation provided experience of the rough-and-tumble of public politics from which so many men were anxious to shield women's delicacy. In 1878 the English social reformer Josephine Butler addressed a public meeting at the Rotunda in Dublin, which had to be abandoned when it was disrupted by heckling medical students demanding that women be ejected. Haslam and her husband promptly organised another meeting, which Butler successfully addressed, winning over many of the former hecklers. The Contagious Diseases Acts were eventually repealed in 1886. Anna Haslam's comment that the eighteen-year campaign 'threw the suffrage movement, back for ten years as we were all so absorbed in it'[21] indicates how small was the number of active emancipationists; so many of the same people were involved in the different campaigns.

Education was another key area for women's emancipation, not merely for the improved employment opportunities it would bring, but as developing and confirming women's intellectual abilities. Educational provision for girls beyond primary level was limited. In 1871 the number of boys and girls attending primary schools was almost equal, while there were no women at all in the universities. Secondary schools were not yet fully differentiated as a separate category, but all educational establishments that taught at least one of the subjects Latin, Greek, modern languages, or mathematics were defined in the census reports as providing 'superior' education. Among those receiving a superior education males outnumbered females by more than five to three, but it was differences in the kind and quality of the education of the two sexes that was the first concern of feminists. Few girls studied Greek, Latin, or mathematics. The vast majority receiving a superior education did so on the basis of learning French, and the census commissioners were sceptical about the standards involved: 'From time immemorial the acquirement of some knowledge – very superficial for the greater part – of foreign living languages has entered into the instructions of females rather as an accomplishment – like music, or drawing, or embroidery – than as a study'.[22] The reforming pioneers included Margaret Byers (1832–1912), a Presbyterian from County Down, who founded the Ladies Collegiate School (later called Victoria College) in Belfast in 1859; Anne Jellicoe (1823–80), a Quaker from Queen's County (Laois), closely involved in founding the Queen's Institute for the Training and Employment of Educated Women (1861), Alexandra College (1866), the Governess Association of Ireland (1869), and Alexandra School (1873), all in Dublin; and Isabella Tod, who was involved in setting up both the Ladies' Institute in Belfast in 1867 and the Ulster Schoolmistresses' Association in 1881.[23]

Anne Jellicoe's work highlights some of the problems encountered in raising standards. The Queen's Institute organised training for sewing machinists, law writers, telegraph clerks, and commercial clerks. It also provided classes in ornamental writing, lithography, and wood and metal engraving.[24] The list indicates the limited range of careers seen by the pioneers as realistic aspirations for genteel women. And there were barriers to be overcome to achieve entry even to some of these. The Queen's Institute lobbied successfully for the opening of examinations for commercial certificates to women on the same terms as men in 1861, and for the opening of the first civil service jobs to women as telegraph clerks in 1870.[25] The basic education of the supposedly 'educated' students of the Institute was found to be so poor that Jellicoe proceeded to the foundation in 1866 of Alexandra College for the Higher Education of Women, with the primary purpose of producing teachers and governesses who could raise standards in girls' education. In turn, deficiencies in the education of the students entering the college led to the founding of Alexandra High School in 1873 to act as a feeder. Not surprisingly both Jellicoe and Byers had to turn to male dons and graduates to provide teaching in the early stages of their projects.

The prospectus of Alexandra College offered

an education more sound and solid, more systematically imparted and better tested than is at present easily to be obtained by women of the middle and upper classes in this country.

Victoria College in Belfast aimed 'to afford girls the same opportunities for sound scholarship that were given to their brothers in the best boys' schools'. These new developments were based on a belief in

public examinations as a means of raising standards, the inclusion of mathematics and Latin in the curriculum, a close liaison between secondary schools and university, and the belief that the education of boys and girls should, as far as possible, be the same.[26]

The universities, too, were pressed to admit women. The first response was the provision of special classes for females, but the reformers wanted full admission to degrees and classes on the same terms as men. Meanwhile they achieved some important objectives through the Intermediate Education Act in 1878 and the Irish University Act, under which the Royal University of Ireland was established, in 1879.[27] Both acts were designed to wean middle-class Catholics away from home rule by extending opportunities for male Catholics to obtain qualifications. In each case a purely examining and award-giving body was established; no compulsory attendance at any specified institutions was required. The emancipationists, who, with Isabella Tod to the fore, kept a careful watch on legislation to further women's interests, recognised the potential and in each case carried out a successful lobby of politicians in London, with the result that when passed both acts had been amended to extend their provisions to girls and women. The Intermediate Board held competitive examinations yearly. Pupils were awarded prizes and exhibitions, and schools received per capita payments according to the number of subjects passed by their pupils. For girls' schools access to Intermediate examinations allowed the testing of standards alongside those of boys' schools, and gave an incentive to introduce such subjects as Latin and mathematics. Qualifications achieved by competitive examination also opened the way to new employment possibilities. This was particularly relevant to the growth of clerical work in the civil service and the expanding commercial sector.

Meanwhile in the secondary education of Catholic girls a trend had emerged towards fee-paying convent schools to meet the social aspirations of the Catholic middle classes. At the top of the social hierarchy were convent boarding schools, affordable only by the well-off, and these were dominated numerically and socially by the French religious teaching orders from the 1850s on. The majority of convent boarding schools were run by these orders, and they set the general tone and educational standards. French language, emphasis on politeness, order, general good conduct, and the development of good taste (*le goût*) in literature and art were among the French traditions emphasised. For the less wealthy, two of the Irish teaching orders, the Mercy and Presentation, provided fee-paying day schools for those who could not afford boarding schools. In addition, some convent national schools provided subjects beyond the basic three Rs, thereby allowing some upward social mobility for poorer girls. The Catholic middle classes were quick to see the employment potential of the Intermediate examinations for their daughters and to demand that the convent schools prepare their pupils for them. The nuns responded: the number of convent schools entering pupils was 29 in 1893 and 45 in 1898.[28] The nationalist press added a political dimension by urging the convents to compete for results with their Protestant counterparts. The Catholic bishops, initially unenthusiastic for the most part, saw where things were heading and began to voice encouragement instead of disapproval.

At university level the problem for women, excluded from the universities, was to find the teaching to prepare them for the Royal examinations. Alexandra College in Dublin immediately began to provide classes and Victoria College in Belfast followed, as did a number of other northern institutions. Organisations were set up to protect what had been achieved and to push forward. The Ulster Schoolmistresses' Association (1881) and the Dublin-based Central Association of Schoolmistresses and Other Ladies Interested in Education (1882) merged to form an umbrella organisation, to which a Cork branch and corresponding members in Derry and Galway were added. Pressure on the universities to admit women to degree courses increased. The Queen's Colleges were the first to respond: Belfast in 1882, Cork in 1886, and Galway in 1888 (Galway's concession somewhat marred by the Catholic bishop forbidding Catholic women to attend). In Dublin both Trinity College and the Catholic University, renamed 'University College' in 1882 and under Jesuit control from 1883, held out against full admission for many years. In spite of the difficulties the first nine women graduated from the Royal University in 1884, to general feminist acclaim.[29]

Catholic institutions were slower to provide the teaching necessary to prepare girls for university. In Dublin many Catholic women studied at Alexandra College; for their part, both the Loreto and Dominican sisters were eager to set up university establishments. Archbishop William Walsh was persuaded by the Dominicans to cooperate in the opening of a Catholic women's college, St Mary's University College on Merrion Square in Dublin in 1893. The Loreto order on its own initiative promptly established a university centre at St Stephen's Green in 1894. In the same year the Ursulines in Cork began to provide university teaching.[30]

By the early years of the twentieth century the long-expected resolution of the Irish university situation was imminent.[31] The Royal University had been intended as a stop-gap pending a final solution, and women had no assurance of their position in new structures, which would almost certainly make attendance at specified institutions a prerequisite for degrees. Two government commissions were set up, the Robertson in 1901 on the Royal University and the Fry in 1906 on Trinity College. The women educationists gave their views to both. The Central Association of Irish School Mistresses and the more recent Irish Association of Women Graduates (1902) pressed for fully coeducational institutions, arguing that this was the only way for women to share in the higher standards made possible by endowments, and the only way for women's degrees to be accepted as equal with men's. The women's colleges, both Protestant and Catholic, understandably wanted to survive as recognised teaching colleges affiliated to the universities, and argued the benefits of the collegiate life they could provide. The pros and cons of single-sex education were vigorously debated. But the campaign for coeducation was led by the women's colleges' own alumnae, who were adamant they did not want women 'to be shut into women's colleges'.[32] Then, while the arguments were in progress, both University College and Trinity College finally agreed to admit women. The enthusiasm with which students from both Catholic and Protestant women's colleges took advantage of this development further weakened the single-sex case.

The Irish Universities Act of 1908[33] set up two new institutions, the National University of Ireland – comprising University College, Cork, and University College, Galway (formerly Queen's Colleges), together with University College, Dublin – and the Queen's University of Belfast, the third former Queen's College. Attendance was compulsory. Women's colleges were not given recognised college status in either university, but women were admitted on equal terms with men to the teaching, degrees, honours, and offices of both.

Access to degrees did not remove all barriers to the admission of women to the higher professions. In the United Kingdom the rise of 'scientific' medicine, monopolised by men, had culminated in the Medical Registration Act of 1858. This made registration a prerequisite for medical practice, and registration required a qualification from one of the specified British examining or licensing bodies, thus excluding women. Feminist campaigning led to an act of parliament of 1876, which allowed, but did not require, United Kingdom governing bodies to award medical degrees to women.[34] There was some Irish participation in this campaign: Anna Haslam was one of those involved. The cause had the support not only of Irish feminists but also of some Irish doctors. Hence it was that the Royal College of Physicians of Ireland became the first institution in the United Kingdom to admit women to the examinations for their licentiate; the first contingent of pioneering English and Scottish women were registered as licentiates in 1877. This allowed them to gain admission to the medical register and hence to practise.[35] Full admission to all professions had to wait until the Sex Disqualification (Removal) Act, 1919.[36]

Meanwhile organised efforts to obtain the parliamentary vote had been under way in Ireland since the 1860s.[37] The explicit exclusion of women by the introduction of the words 'male person' in the reform act of 1832,[38] which extended the parliamentary franchise to middle-class men, was in itself evidence of developing feminist claims. Anna Haslam was one of the signatories to the famous petition for women's suffrage presented to the United Kingdom parliament by John Stuart Mill and Henry Fawcett in 1866. This asked for the inclusion of women in the 1867 reform act which extended the franchise to householders in boroughs and to rural and urban occupiers, subject to a property qualification.[39] Its rejection sparked off organised action in England and Ireland. During the late 1860s and early 1870s public and drawing-room meetings were held in various parts of Ireland. In the Dublin area Anne Robertson of Blackrock was a leading organiser, while in 1872 in Belfast Isabella Tod established the North of Ireland Society for Women's

Suffrage, affiliated to the London Women's Suffrage Society. Tod became one of the most effective public speakers for suffrage and other feminist causes, and was in demand for public meetings in both Ireland and England. Anna Haslam and her husband founded the Dublin Women's Suffrage Association (DWSA) in 1876.

The numbers involved in the suffrage campaign remained small until the end of the century, and Anna Haslam noted that it 'never penetrated much beyond the outskirts of Dublin, Belfast, and one or two other towns'. The DWSA itself, the organisation about which most is known, had only forty-three members in 1896.[40] Its membership was predominantly middle-class, Protestant, and Quaker, and included men as well as women. Haslam's husband, Thomas J. Haslam, also from a Quaker family and a life-long collaborator with his wife in the women's movement, published three issues of a periodical, the *Women's Advocate*, in April, May, and July 1874. The first issue argued the classic Enlightenment case for suffrage as 'the moral right of properly qualified women to some share in the enactment of the laws which they are required to obey'. The second gave practical advice on how to organise local groups for effective political action, advice followed by the association itself over many years under the energetic secretaryship of Anna Haslam, who continued as secretary and central organiser until 1913 when she became life president. Members worked to educate public opinion by writing to the newspapers and organising drawing-room and public meetings, the latter whenever the opportunity of high-profile or effective speakers arose. The DWSA maintained contact with the movement in England and sent delegates, regularly both Haslams, to suffrage and other feminist congresses. It kept a watchful eye on political developments in Ireland as well as in Britain to exploit favourable opportunities to lobby. It organised petitions to the House of Commons. It sent deputations and wrote letters to Irish MPs urging them to introduce or support bills or amendments to bills to enfranchise women. It wrote to 'influential' women around the country exhorting them to lobby MPs. It noted with approval advances in the various emancipation campaigns, understandably since Haslam was involved in most or all of them.

Private members' bills for women's suffrage were introduced regularly from 1884, when women were yet again refused inclusion in a reform act.[41] This act extended the franchise to all male agricultural labourers who were householders, though a property qualification for lodgers still excluded a substantial proportion of men. Women's suffrage regularly attracted considerable support, sometimes majorities, in the House of Commons, but never translated into legislation. This was partly because the Conservative party, generally opposed to women's suffrage, was in government almost continuously from 1885 to 1906; and partly because the Conservative majority in the House of Lords could quash any measure that passed the Commons.

Suffrage activity was sometimes interrupted by members' participation in other feminist campaigns. It was also interrupted by the Land War. The DWSA, for instance, held no executive meeting between April 1882 and June 1883. Although it distracted from the suffrage campaign, the land movement was to afford a unique opportunity for middle-class nationalist women to exercise political leadership in the Ladies' Land League.[42]

Participation in community-based politics was nothing new for Irish women. During the nineteenth century some had also been active, as individuals, in such organisations as the Repeal Association, Young Ireland, and the Fenians On the unionist side, by the end of the century there were women's unionist associations. Isabella Tod, a particularly committed unionist, organised a Liberal Women's Unionist Association in Belfast, while Anna Haslam established a branch in Dublin.[43] As far as the Land League was concerned, women had taken an early part in the League's activities. They were essential participants – and often in the van – in the boycotting, preventing of evictions, and repossession of holdings that were the sanctions behind the League's policy.[44] Women who were tenant farmers in their own right (mostly widows) were eligible for League membership, and some took an active part. But the Ladies' Land League, an organisation of middle-class women that for a time ran a national campaign composed largely of men, was a new venture.

Michael Davitt, while in America, had been impressed by what he saw of the Ladies' Land League, an effective fund-raising and propaganda organisation initiated by Fanny Parnell, sister of Anna and Charles, in October 1880. He suggested a similar organisation in Ireland to dispense League funds to evicted families and families of arrested men (the typical work of a women's auxiliary organisation), but also to keep the League going in the expected event of the male leaders being imprisoned. In spite of the misgivings of the rest of the male leadership, including C.S. Parnell, the Ladies' Land League was established – on the male leaders' initiative – in January 1881 with Anna Parnell as organising secretary.

There appears to have been some lack of clarity as to what exactly the male leaders wanted the Ladies' Land League to do, and what the women understood them to want. In the event, the women found themselves in charge of spending League funds according to existing League policy, that of 'rent at the point of a bayonet'. The women came to believe that this was a counterproductive policy, since in most cases the rent was eventually paid, at great expense to the League and little benefit to the cause: in other words, 'a great sham'. When the male leaders were imprisoned and the Land League suppressed in October 1881 the women found themselves in charge of the entire movement. This included administering a new policy, the 'No rent manifesto', issued from Kilmainham, calling for the suspension of rent payments until the leaders were released. The Ladies' Land League's conduct of affairs at this point became the subject of some dispute. It appears that the women were not aware that the manifesto was essentially a political face-saver, which the men did not expect to be put into effect. Accordingly, they tried to implement a policy that was enormously expensive, and for which it would probably have been impossible to gain effective support from the tenants as a body. Anna Parnell came to believe that the male leadership had involved the women on false pretences.

When the men were released in May 1882 the Ladies' Land League leaders wanted to disband and hand back the management of League policy to the men. According to Anna Parnell, the men wanted the women to continue to do the unpopular work of handling the tenants' claims, as 'a perpetual petticoat screen behind which they [the men] could shelter, not from the government, but from the people'.[45] Her brother, however, is recorded as having been anxious for the Ladies' Land League to be suppressed. In any case, by this time the Ladies' Land League was a proscribed organisation. C.S. Parnell ensured that there would be no repetition of such clashes by excluding women from the Irish National League with which he replaced the Land League in October 1882.[46]

Despite all this the Ladies' Land League left a legacy of pride and achievement as a pioneering development in women's political organisation in Ireland. By July 1881 there were over 400 branches of various sizes throughout the country, with rank-and-file membership drawn largely from the Catholic tenant-farmer class. The central leadership was composed mainly of middle-class women, Catholic and Protestant. At central and local level women filled public leadership positions. Some travelled around the country organising local activities, conduct regarded as a particular breach of conventional middle-class female behaviour. They organised the building of Land League huts for the dispossessed, addressed huge outdoor public meetings, and defied official suppression of the Ladies' Land League. Some were arrested and went to prison.

Catholic members of the Ladies' Land League had to brave considerable criticism for invading a male sphere. The Catholic archbishop of Dublin, Edward McCabe, in a pastoral letter read in all the parishes of his diocese, spoke of the modesty and chastity by which Irish women had brought glory to their country and which were now 'to be laid aside' on a false 'pretext of charity'. He urged his flock not to tolerate in their sodalities 'the woman who so far disavows her birthright of modesty as to parade herself before the public gaze'.[47] This was balanced by Archbishop T.W. Croke of Cashel who commended the women as praiseworthy nationalists.

In the closing years of the century the suffrage movement was back in full action and achieved some tangible results. In the 1880s local government reform was on the political agenda in Britain and Ireland. English women had won the municipal franchise in 1869 and the omens were promising for an Irish initiative. A campaign led by Isabella Tod and the local women's suffrage society succeeded in winning the municipal franchise for female: householders in Belfast in 1887. Eligibility of women to serve as Poor Law Guardians now moved to the top of the suffragists' agenda. Women ratepayers already had the vote for guardians on the same terms as men, while in Britain women were also eligible for election as guardians. The office of Poor Law Guardian had obvious interest for women philanthropists anxious to participate in policy-making. Anna Haslam attributed the Irish suffragists' earlier neglect of this issue to the fact that election to the boards had early on become an arena for political contests between male nationalists and unionists. It was conducted so much on 'party lines and with so little regard to the well-being of our destitute poor, that we were fairly excusable for taking little interest in it'.[48] Now it gave them their first major breakthrough. The Belfast MP William Johnston, who had introduced the Belfast municipal franchise bill, introduced a bill that became law as the Poor Law Guardians (Ireland) (Women) Act, 1896.[49] It provided that no person otherwise qualified 'shall be disqualified by sex or marriage' from being elected or serving as a guardian. The DWSA wrote to the newspapers and published leaflets explaining how women could ensure that they were properly registered to vote and to stand for election. Individual women all around the country were exhorted to seek out suitable candidates and urge them to go forward. By 1898 there were seventeen women Poor Law Guardians, and by 1900 nearly 100; enough to hold a conference to share experience and ideas.

Isabella Tod died in 1896, without seeing the full results of her work. During her lifetime Tod had one of the highest profiles of any Irish feminist and was one of the leaders in every aspect of feminist activity. For the next generation it was Anna Haslam whose name became synonymous with pioneering Irish feminism. Haslam lived till 1922, retained her boundless energy, enthusiasm, and organising ability, and continued as an active suffragist well into the second decade of the twentieth century.

The next success came with the 1898 Local Government Act, which set up county councils and urban and rural district councils. Women gained all the remaining local government franchises on the same terms as men, as well as eligibility to become district councillors and town commissioners. Eligibility for membership of county and borough councils was withheld till 1911. These developments were seen by the DWSA as 'the most signal political revolution that has taken place in the history of Irishwomen. We have, in round numbers, somewhere about one hundred thousand women ratepayers who are now invested with powers which they never possessed before'. Again the DWSA published letters and leaflets to explain what had been achieved and how to exercise it. Anna Haslam saw the 1898 act as a political educator that would greatly strengthen the drive for the parliamentary vote. She envisaged the spread of the suffrage movement far beyond its current limits in Dublin, Belfast, and one or two other towns. 'For the great majority of our countrywomen in all our rural districts their political education commences with the present year'. The experience of participation in local government will 'make them not only desire the parliamentary vote, but willing to take some little trouble in order to obtain it'.[50] In response to these developments the DWSA changed its name first to the Dublin Women's Suffrage and Local Government Association and then to the Irish Women's Suffrage and Local Government Association (IWSLGA). While these local government advances were real achievements in themselves, Irish women were essentially catching up with what women in England had already gained; serious opposition, though real, was limited. The right to vote for and sit in parliament was unlikely to be so readily won. This became the central feminist campaign of the next two decades.

By the turn of the century a new generation of educated Irish women, beneficiaries of the achievements of the earlier feminists, was emerging on the public scene. By 1881 in the age group 15–24 the literacy rate of females had overtaken and outstripped that of males, and in school attendance rates for the 5–9 age group girls had nearly caught up with boys.[51] By 1901 at secondary level, though boys outnumbered girls by nearly two to one, the curriculum in girls' schools was more academically demanding than it had been. And while the census recorded 3,101 male undergraduates to just 91 females, the very existence of women undergraduates and graduates, as well as a women graduates association (founded in 1902), was an important development for the women's movement and the suffrage campaign. In the new ferment of cultural and political activity and the surge of optimism and self-help, many women became actively involved in the language and cultural movements, in politics, organised labour, and agricultural improvement. When they found themselves excluded from an organisation, a regular response was to establish a women's organisation. An implicit feminist awareness appears to have informed most of these developments even when the objectives were not explicitly feminist.

The structure of Irish society suggested that the majority of feminist activists would continue to be middle-class women. Few working-class women worked in situations conducive to feminist politicisation and organisation. Outside the north-east, large-scale factory work was limited. Census reports continued to record most women as housewives classified under 'indefinite and non-productive' occupations. The big areas of paid employment were still domestic service, agriculture, and cloth and garment manufacture. Young women from the poorer classes expressed their dissatisfaction with what Ireland had to offer them by emigrating in large numbers.

Employment opportunities for educated middle-class women remained few. Teaching was by far the largest professional occupation: the 1911 census recorded 11,667 schoolmistresses and assistants, and 2,265 teachers, lecturers, and governesses. Clerical work was beginning to expand, with 2,804 women in the civil service as 'officers and clerks' and 7,849 commercial clerks. Nuns, at 8,887, came next. Nursing, developing as a career for educated women, had moved out of domestic service to professional status with 4,516 women in 'subordinate medical service' and 1,006 'hospital certificated nurses', showing the trend towards training and recognised qualifications.[52] Among the 'higher' professions only medicine was effectively open to women, and the number entering was small; only 33 were recorded as 'physicians, surgeons, and general practitioners'.

The first fully autonomous organisation of nationalist women, Inghinidhe na hÉireann (Daughters of Ireland),[53] was founded in Dublin in October 1900 with Maud Gonne as the first president.[54] An ad hoc women's committee had come together to organise a 'patriotic children's treat' to counter an official free children's outing marking Queen Victoria's visit to Ireland in 1900. This committee went on to form a permanent national women's organisation. The objectives of the Inghinidhe were:

The re-establishment of the complete independence of Ireland.

To encourage the study of Gaelic, of Irish literature, history, music and art, especially among the young, by organising the teaching of classes for the above subjects.

To support and popularise Irish manufacture.

To discourage the reading and circulation of low English literature, the singing of English songs, the attending of vulgar English entertainments at the theatres and music hall, and to combat in every way English influence which is doing so much injury to the artistic taste and refinement of the Irish people.

To form a fund called the National Purposes Fund, for the furtherance of the above objects.[55]

The Inghinidhe brought to their work a style and flair that epitomised the enthusiasm and high spirits of the broad cultural-nationalist milieu of the period. Among the members were poets, writers, actresses, and feminists, including such diverse personalities as Jennie Wyse Power, formerly of the Ladies' Land League; Alice Milligan, the Presbyterian nationalist and poet who with the poet Anna Johnston ('Ethna Carbery') edited the nationalist paper *Shan Van Vocht* in Belfast from 1896 to 1899; and Constance Markievicz, daughter of the landed Gore-Booth family in Sligo, and a convert to nationalism and socialism.

From 1908 to 1911 the Inghinidhe published the first Irish women's paper, *Bean na hÉireann*, a 'woman's paper advocating militancy, separatism, and feminism',[56] which attracted a wide spectrum of readers and writers of both sexes. They also ran children's classes, organised céilís, and staged *tableaux-vivants* and plays, including W.B. Yeats's 'Cathleen Ni Houlihan', written for Maud Gonne to play the title role. Their work in these areas contributed to the emergence of the Abbey Theatre, some of whose leading actresses, including Máire Nic Shiubhlaigh and Helena Molony, were members. On the political side, the Inghinidhe were also active in the foundation in 1905 of Sinn Féin,[57] the first nationalist organisation in which women held executive office alongside men. In pursuit of their political aims the Inghinidhe also patrolled the streets of Dublin to dissuade young Irish women from consorting with British soldiers.

In the area of rural development 1910 saw the foundation of what was to become the largest and most long-lived of all Irish women's organisations, the United Irishwomen (later known as the Irish Countrywomen's Association). The first branch was founded in 1910 by Anita Lett, a farmer, in Bree, County Wexford, following a lively correspondence in the pages of the *Irish Homestead* on the drabness of rural life for young women. A major impetus came from interaction with the cooperative movement of Sir Horace Plunkett and the Irish Agricultural Organisation Society (1894). Registered as a friendly society and affiliated to the IAOS, the United Irishwomen sought to supply a dimension missing from the work of the former. The aim was to animate country living by encouraging rural women, of all classes, religions and politics, to develop a 'healthy and progressive community life' which would reduce both emigration and the flight from country to city.

The society was organised on hierarchical lines with an executive in Dublin. Branches were to be established at parish level and affiliated to county organisations, and through these to the central body. Officeholders were drawn from the middle and upper classes, Protestant and Catholic, with the Catholic Lady Fingall serving as president from 1912 to 1942 in succession to the Protestant Anita Lett. But the society aimed at a membership of all classes and denominations and saw itself as 'strongly national' from the start.[58]

The United Irishwomen's work covered agriculture and industry, domestic economy, and social and intellectual development. Some of its first campaigns targeted health education for women and the provision of qualified district nurses and doctors. Other activities included instruction in household economy, horticulture, bee-keeping, poultry and egg production, and the holding of local shows. Dances, music, and drama were also important; and by 1912 there were twenty-one branches in Counties Antrim, Carlow, Clare Donegal, Galway, Kildare, Kilkenny, Limerick, Louth, Mayo, Wicklow, and Wexford.

While the society did not describe itself as a feminist organisation, it did aim to have women's voices and actions felt in the development of the new Ireland. According to its first organiser, writing in 1911, the United Irishwomen

> consider it essential that women in Ireland should make their wishes known if they want them to be gratified, and they feel that they have somewhat neglected their own and each other's interests by not putting them before the public more prominently than they have done. For this reason they intend to seek for better representation on public bodies, so as to be able to make their point of view known in public affairs.[59]

Organisation and activity were disrupted by the first world war, the 1916 rising, the war of independence, and the civil war. But expansion began again in the 1920s, and in 1935 the society reorganised and changed its name to the Irish Countrywomen's Association.

Meanwhile the suffrage campaign was expanding rapidly, fulfilling Anna Haslam's prophecy. Internationally it was becoming a large-scale movement and adopting new campaigning methods. In the later decades of the nineteenth century large-scale street demonstrations with banners, slogans, and colours had appeared in countries where governments tolerated such public expressions of dissent. Some women moved to more assertive methods, first to passive civil disobedience such as refusing to pay tax, then to heckling and disrupting public meetings, and finally to physical violence such as damaging public property. This final level of what was termed 'militancy' emerged in Britain and Ireland where suffrage had for so long appeared within reach but had not yet been attained. The name 'suffragette' was coined to distinguish the 'militants' from the 'constitutional' suffragists who believed the cause was best served by campaigning strictly within the law. In England militancy was associated with the Women's Social and Political Union (WSPU), founded in 1903 and led by the Pankhursts, in contrast to the constitutional National Union of Women's Suffrage Societies (NUWSS).

In Ireland the Irish Women's Franchise League (IWFL) was founded in 1908 as a society prepared to use militant methods if necessary, by a group led by Hanna Sheehy Skeffington[60] and Margaret Cousins.[61] Both women had begun their suffrage careers in the IWSLGA, and their respect and affection for Anna Haslam remained strong. But although the IWSLGA was explicitly non-aligned to any political party, and had many nationalist members, the new group wanted a suffrage society that was more assertive and more distinctly Irish. The IWFL (also non-aligned to any political party) modelled its militancy on that of the English WSPU, whose 'spirited frontal attack on their government' the Irish women greatly admired.[62] But it was committed to complete independence of any English organisation. It grew rapidly, and it appears that a large proportion of Catholic suffragists joined its ranks.

Further new suffrage organisations followed, and the movement attained a numerical strength and scale far beyond that of any earlier feminist campaign. Membership was still predominantly middle-class and Protestant, but a growing proportion – about one-third – were Catholics.[63] In 1912 it was calculated (perhaps optimistically) that there were over 3,000 active suffragists in Ireland. The largest groups were the long-established IWSLGA with 700–800 members; the IWFL with over 1,000; an Irish branch of the Conservative and Unionist Women's Franchise Association with 660, and the Irish Women's Suffrage Society (IWSS) in Belfast, with several hundred.[64] There was also the umbrella Irish Women's Suffrage Federation (IWSF) founded in 1911 to link the smaller groups in a network. The Federation included the Irish Women's Reform League (IWRL), founded by Louie Bennett with a remit that included the social and economic interests of working-class women as well as the vote. By 1913 there were well over a dozen societies affiliated to the IWSF, including nine in Ulster as well as the Munster Women's Franchise League (MWFL), which had its own branches.[65] Some groups had specific political or religious, affiliations, and in 1915 the Irish Catholic Women's Suffrage Association was founded, which had about 167 members in 1917.

Political developments in the early twentieth century created tensions within the suffrage movement. The 1911 limitation on the powers of the House of Lords improved the prospects for legislation on both Home Rule and women's suffrage. Suffragists now had to contemplate the likelihood of two parliaments. A women's suffrage act passed by the UK parliament might enfranchise women in both Britain and Ireland, but it was important that women should have the vote for any Home Rule parliament. Despite their politically mixed composition, the suffrage societies maintained a united policy of supporting all measures of female suffrage. Unionist suffragists opposed Home Rule, but if it should come wanted it to include votes for women. So did British suffragists, since this would make it more difficult to refuse the vote for women in the UK.[66] The attitude of the Irish Home Rule MPs was important to all suffragists, since it could be crucial to the success of a UK as well as a Home Rule suffrage measure.

Nationalist women experienced some tensions over the suffrage issue. The nationally minded IWFL was to the fore in pressing that female suffrage be included in any Home Rule bill, and also urged Irish MPs to support any UK suffrage bill that came before parliament. Other nationalist women, often themselves suffragists, argued that on principle nationalists should not give legitimacy to the UK parliament's claim to authority over Ireland by asking it for the vote. They also argued that women should wait until the Home Rule Bill was safely passed before pressing for women's suffrage in a new Irish parliament. The Inghinidhe na hÉireann paper *Bean na hÉireann* posited a golden era in Ireland's past when women and men had been fully equal, and argued that equality would automatically be restored once independence was achieved. Another claim was that, by virtue of their equal status with men in the Gaelic League, Sinn Féin, and the industrial movement, women already effectively had the franchise in Irish Ireland. Such optimism was criticised by 'suffrage first' activists as doomed to disillusionment. Hanna Sheehy Skeffington cautioned that until 'the parliamentarian and the Sinn Féin woman alike possess the vote, the keystone of citizenship, she will count but little with either party'.[67] Unionist women also faced political choices. The Ulster Women's Unionist Council (UWUC) was established in January 1911 to support the Ulster Unionist Council's opposition to Home Rule. Within a year it recorded 40,000–50,000 members. While the UWUC insisted that maintenance of the union took priority over any other commitment, the political experience gained by its members appears to have been a positive one for the suffrage movement in the longer run.[68]

While many members of the Irish Parliamentary Party individually supported women's franchise, they fell into line whenever Redmond decided that backing it might harm the prospects for Home Rule. Looking back Hanna Sheehy Skeffington commented that to 'the powerful Irish Party and its machine, backed by such organisations as the sectarian Ancient Order of Hibernians of Joseph Devlin ... we were a pestilential red herring across the trail of home rule'.[69] The situation was similar to that in the United States, where some had opposed women's suffrage on the grounds that it might delay votes for freed male slaves, or in Britain, where it might hold up extensions of the franchise to new classes of men. The suffragists' frustration was not lessened by the knowledge that Redmond himself and the Liberal prime minister Asquith were both personally opposed to women's franchise.

Because newspaper coverage of suffrage and other feminist concerns was so inadequate, in 1912 a fortnightly suffrage paper, the *Irish Citizen*, was founded in association with the IWFL, with Francis Sheehy Skeffington and James Cousins as editors, carrying on its masthead the motto: 'For men and women equally the rights of citizenship; from men and women equally the duties of citizenship'. The *Irish Citizen* supported the suffrage-first position, but it carried news on all suffrage activity and provided a forum for debate on a range of feminist concerns. This debate demonstrated the continuing broad agenda of the Irish feminist movement. Working-class women's conditions and their need for trade union organisation; equal pay; domestic and sexual violence against women and children; and the need for women jurors, lawyers, police and judges were among the issues discussed The paper continued till 1920 and became one of the best sources of information on the women's movement during that period.

In 1912 one of a series of 'conciliation' bills, which by agreement between the main political parties would have conceded a limited female franchise, confined to householders, was defeated when the Irish Party failed to support it. Redmond feared its passing might jeopardise the Liberal government thus endangering Home Rule. The English WSPU retaliated by declaring opposition to Home Rule itself on the principle 'No Suffrage – no Home Rule'. Irish suffragists increased the pressure on the Irish Party to have suffrage included in the Home Rule Bill then before parliament. The IWFL had already begun to use more militant methods against the Irish Party, heckling and disrupting its public meetings. Redmond remained obdurate, and the combined suffrage movement responded with a mass meeting in Dublin. Mary Hayden, professor of Irish history at UCD, chaired the meeting in the Antient Concert Rooms. The hall was packed with suffragists of all creeds and politics as well as nationalist and labour women. The meeting sent an agreed resolution to cabinet ministers and to all Irish MPs:

That while expressing no opinion on the general question of home rule, this mass meeting of delegates from the Irish suffrage societies and other women's organisations, representing all shades of political and religious opinion, profoundly regrets the proposal to establish a new constitution in Ireland on a purely male franchise, and calls upon the government to amend the home rule bill in committee by adopting the local government register (which includes women) as the basis for the new parliament.[70]

When this still failed to elicit a response the IWFL moved up the scale of militancy to an organised breaking of windows in Dublin Castle and other public buildings. Several Irish suffragists had already been imprisoned for militant suffrage activities in England, and the Dublin incidents now led to a number of suffragists being arrested, charged, fined, refusing to pay, and being sent to prison. Down to this point, public reaction to the Irish suffrage movement had been mixed. Now the IWFL's militant tactics, which were regarded as unwomanly, attracted widespread criticism. Nationalists also worried about the implications for Home Rule. Of course, many of the critics opposed votes for women even when advocated by constitutional suffragists. The constitutional IWSLGA publicly criticised the IWFL's militancy as counterproductive, but it rejected the double standards that attacked the IWFL for largely symbolic actions which would hardly have raised an eyebrow if carried out by any male organisation. Anna Haslam, herself a liberal unionist and now aged 83, visited Hanna Sheehy Skeffington in Mountjoy prison:

> Don't think I approve – but here's a pot of verbena I brought you. I am not here in my official capacity, of course – the Irish Women [sic] Suffrage and Local Government Association strongly disapprove of violence as pulling back the cause. But here's some loganberry jam – I made it myself.[71]

During Prime Minister Asquith's visit to Dublin in July 1912 three members of the English WSPU travelled to Dublin without the knowledge of the Irish suffragists. One of them threw a hatchet, 'small ... blunt and meant symbolically, but that didn't help much', according to Hanna Sheehy Skeffington, at Asquith's carriage. It missed him and grazed Redmond. The following day two of the women set fire to curtains at a box in the Theatre Royal, and this was followed by a small explosion. Amid public outrage Mary Leigh and Gladys Evans were each sentenced to five years penal servitude. Refused political prisoner status, they went on hunger strike and were forcibly fed. The IWFL was annoyed at this unauthorised intervention in Ireland, but did not condemn the action itself; the League was, however, blamed by a hostile press and members of the public for the WSPU's activities. Some members resigned and there were serious physical attacks on their public meetings. The *Irish Citizen* defended the Englishwomen, and Sheehy Skeffington and others in prison at the same time went on sympathetic hunger strike.

Militancy died down in Dublin towards the latter part of 1913, but it flared up in the north. Suffrage societies in the north had tended to be quite small and non-militant, and the IWFL had found it difficult to get a foothold there because it was seen as a nationalist body. However, the English WSPU established a branch in Belfast to press for the inclusion of women's suffrage in the Ulster Unionist Council's plan to set up a provisional government if Home Rule became a reality. But in March 1914 Sir Edward Carson made it clear that he was no more prepared than Redmond to commit himself to the potentially divisive policy of votes for women. The WSPU retaliated with violence that went beyond the largely symbolic actions of the IWFL, setting fire to privately owned unionist property and planting a bomb at Lisburn cathedral. Between March and August 1914 thirteen women were arrested.[72]

At the same time the suffrage movement was interacting with socialism and the labour movement. For many socialists, the initiative in social revolution must come from the workers, not the middle or upper classes. Socialist feminism had emerged most strongly in Germany under the leadership of Clara Zetkin and in association with the Social Democratic Party (SPD) in the 1890s.[73] Socialist feminists argued that working-class women would not benefit from the removal of discrimination based on sex unless the class issue was first resolved.

The nineteenth-century Irish emancipation movement, like the American and British movements, had developed within a liberal-individualist ethos. It sought the vote for women on the same terms as men, which in the mid nineteenth century still meant a property qualification. For socialist feminists this turned the campaign into a 'bourgeois' one, concerned mainly with emancipation for middle-class women. In the early decades of the twentieth century some links developed between the nationalist and syndicalist trade union movement, led by James Larkin and James Connolly, and the suffrage organisations sympathetic to nationalism and socialism, the IWFL and the IWRL. Connolly was a feminist by conviction, who unequivocally supported women's right to the franchise and their right to use it against him if they wished, and who encouraged militant demands for the vote. The Irish Socialist Republican party he had founded in 1896 had included universal suffrage in its manifesto. Later, he became national organiser of the Socialist Party of Ireland, of which both Sheehy Skeffingtons were members. Connolly was regularly available to speak on IWFL platforms.[74]

In the early 1900s some of the young feminists in the suffrage movement had socialist and labour sympathies. Louie Bennett's IWRL explicitly linked labour issues with suffrage, and both *Bean na hÉireann* and the *Irish Citizen* advocated the organisation of women workers. Trade unions were more difficult to organise among women than among men. Homemaking, the majority occupation, was ill adapted to unionisation, and so were those major areas of women's paid employment, domestic service and agriculture. Marriage added a further complication. A young single employed woman might want equal pay with men, but once she married higher pay for men might become preferable. Factory work was the most favourable to unionisation, but many women in the clothing industries worked at home as outworkers.

Moves to develop women's trade unions in Ireland had begun at least as early as 1880[75] and had attracted the support of middle-class feminists, including Anna Haslam. In the aftermath of the Trade Union Congress held in Dublin in 1880, two unions were formed, the

Dublin Tailoresses' Society and the Bookfolders and Sewers' Union, but both were shortlived. In 1893 the Textile Operatives Society of Ireland was established in Belfast. Mary Galway, who became its secretary in 1897, later became the first woman vice-president of the Irish Trade Union Congress. In August 1911 3,000 Dublin women struck for better pay at Jacob's biscuit factory. In the same year the Irish Women Workers' Union (IWWU) was established in Dublin as a general union for all women workers. Towards the end of the first world war it grew rapidly; by 1918 its members included printers, laundresses, and general workers.

The IWWU emerged within the socialist and nationalist labour movement led by Larkin and Connolly, and with the encouragement and support of many feminists. Constance Markievicz and Hanna Sheehy Skeffington were platform speakers at the IWWU's inaugural meeting. Markievicz reminded her audience that they could achieve nothing without organisation, and urged them, amid laughter, to join the union, which would help them to gain the vote 'and make men of you all'.[76] The first general secretary was Delia Larkin, sister of James, who was succeeded by Helena Molony,[77] and in 1916 by Louie Bennett.[78]

During the 1913 lockout Sheehy Skeffington and other IWFL members helped in the soup kitchen in Liberty Hall, presided over by Markievicz, while Bennett and the IWRL gave support to strikers' families. The Irish Citizen Army, set up by Larkin and Connolly to protect the workers, enrolled women on equal terms with men. All this encouraged debates about adult suffrage as opposed to women's suffrage, and forged bonds between labour and feminism, at least at leadership level. It is less clear how close the links were at rank and file level. Looking back in 1930 Helena Molony wrote that the women's movement had 'passed over the head of the Irish working woman and left her untouched'.[79]

The growing political tension over Home Rule saw the emergence of a new women's organisation and more problems for feminists. The Ulster Women's Unionist Council engaged in vigorous propaganda and demonstrations against Home Rule, and (when women were barred from signing the Ulster covenant in September 1912) organised a women's declaration which collected more signatures than the men's covenant. When the Ulster Volunteer Force was set up in 1913, the UWUC actively supported it. It appears that far larger numbers of women could be rallied for unionist causes than for either nationalism or suffrage.[80] On the nationalist side in April 1914 Cumann na mBan (Association of Women) was established in Dublin as an auxiliary to the Irish Volunteers. Cumann na mBan's constitution stated its aims as:

> To advance the cause of Irish liberty.
>
> To organise Irishwomen in furtherance of this object.
>
> To assist in arming and equipping a body of Irishmen for the defence of Ireland.
>
> To form a fund for these purposes to be called the 'Defence of Ireland Fund'.[81]

Both the UWUC and Cumann na mBan attracted many women who supported women's suffrage. Argument among nationalist feminists over priorities broke out immediately. The issue was how, rather than whether, suffrage should be achieved. Cumann na mBan women supported the separatist view that England's difficulty in the imminent war would be Ireland's opportunity, and argued that national freedom must come first, with the emancipation of women following that of the nation. The IWFL and the *Irish Citizen* maintained that suffrage must remain the first priority;

they also adopted a pacifist position. *Irish Citizen* editorials insisted that feminists should not compromise on women's rights, and deplored the fact that nationalist women accepted a status subordinate to that of the men in the Volunteers. Cumann na mBan retorted that they were not the servants of the Volunteers but their colleagues and co-workers.

Britain's entry into war in August 1914 faced unionist feminists with their own questions about priorities. In Britain most suffrage societies, including the militant WSPU, suspended campaigning and lined up behind the war effort. In Ireland, suffrage groups linked to British organisations tended to suspend suffrage activity and turn to relief work. For many suffragists who looked to the UK parliament for the vote, war work gave women the opportunity to prove their entitlement to the vote by their ability to carry out men's work. The IWSLGA, whose members included both nationalists and unionists, subscribed to a Red Cross hospital bed, collected funds to help refugees, and tried to coordinate feminist action on issues other than suffrage. Allegiances were often strained. Individual members of Cumann na mBan cooperated with Lady Aberdeen (wife of the viceroy) and the Women's National Health Association (1907) to form an Irish branch of the Red Cross after the outbreak of war;[82] but when the Munster Women's Franchise League donated an ambulance to the war effort, Mary MacSwiney, a nationalist and member of Cumann na mBan, resigned. The IWFL and the *Irish Citizen* continued to urge that suffrage must remain the first priority.

A Home Rule Bill passed in September 1914, but with its operation suspended till the war ended, and with the future of the Ulster counties still unclear. When John Redmond, hoping to promote Home Rule, adopted a policy of support for Britain, the Irish Volunteers split, with the majority following Redmond into the National Volunteers and many from there to the trenches, and the minority retaining the original name and the hope that Ireland's opportunity might be imminent. Cumann na mBan also split; the majority of the executive rejected Redmond's policy and opted for the separatist side.

The relationship between feminists, war, and pacifism was now to the fore. Women, and particularly feminists, had long been active in peace movements. In Ireland, for example, Anna Haslam's first public activity had been in the Olive Leaf Circle, a Quaker peace organisation. Now a women's peace movement emerged from the international women's movement, with which Irish feminists had long-established contacts. In 1888 the International Council of Women had been established to link national councils of women's organisations in different countries. Not all were supporters of women's suffrage, and so a separate International Woman Suffrage Alliance (usually called the International Alliance) was founded in 1904. Since its early years the IWSLGA had maintained links with the movement, and in 1906 Thomas Haslam was a delegate from the IWSLGA to the International Alliance congress in London.[83] In 1913 Hanna Sheehy Skeffington from the IWFL, Louie Bennett from the IWSF, and Lady Dockrell from the IWSLGA attended the congress in Budapest.[84] By 1914 the International Alliance had extended its membership to women's organisations in twenty-four countries around the world. By 1920 its aims had expanded to include, besides suffrage, equal pay, the right to work, the improved legal status of wives and mothers, abolition of slavery and child marriage, and the control of dangerous drugs.

As war approached the Alliance was divided over whether to take a strict pacifist stance. The International Committee of Women for Permanent Peace (ICWPP), known from 1919 as the Women's International League for Peace and Freedom (WILPF), was founded by pacifist feminists after an international congress at The Hague in April 1915.[85] Pacifism was a controversial issue both for feminists who supported their own government's participation in the war and for those who upheld the right of armed insurrection. In Ireland as elsewhere pacifist feminists were in a minority. At this period they appear to have been drawn largely from the IWFL and the IWSF, with vigorous support from the *Irish Citizen*. An Irish committee was established, which nominated seven delegates to attend The Hague conference. The British government, like others, was opposed to pacifism and tried to obstruct attendance. Of the Irish delegates only Louie Bennett obtained a permit and she, like most of the English women, was prevented from attending by the British admiralty's banning of passenger traffic on the crucial day. The Irish committee continued in being, at first as part of the British branch. However, it sought separate representation, and in January 1916 an independent Irish branch was set up, with the name 'Irishwomen's International League' (IIL), which by December was recognised by the ICWPP. Its objectives were to work for the 'complete enfranchisement of women', a 'just and reasonable' settlement of the Irish question by promoting 'goodwill and a better understanding', and cooperation with women of other countries with the aim of 'permanent international peace'.[86]

In the turmoil of political events the suffrage movement inevitably declined in numbers and vigour, yet the close relationship between the IWFL, Cumann na mBan, and the republican male leaders led to the public endorsement of women's full citizenship in the 1916 proclamation. R.M. Fox in 1935 looked back to the days when the IWFL and the *Irish Citizen* formed a rallying point for all the best and most progressive elements in Dublin ... In its pages the anti-conscription struggle, and other vital issues, received attention ... Madame Markievicz, Connolly, Pearse, MacDonagh, and many other pioneers of the rebellion used the platform of the Franchise League to express their views.[87]

The 1916 proclamation asserted that the

Irish Republic is entitled to, and hereby claims, the allegiance of every Irishman and Irishwoman. The Republic guarantees religious and civil liberty, equal rights, and equal opportunities to all its citizens.

Kathleen Clarke recalled how on the night the proclamation was signed her husband told her 'it represented the views of all except one, who thought equal opportunities should not be given to women'. She went on: 'Except to say that Tom [Clarke] was not that one, my lips are sealed'.[88] James Connolly, too, indicated that only one of the seven signatories had disagreed with the commitment to equality.[89] The proclamation, together with women's participation in the rising, accordingly became the basis for nationalist women's demand for full equality of citizenship in an independent Ireland.

Despite the confusion resulting from the countermanding of the orders for Easter Sunday, over 200 women took part in the 1916 rising, most of them in Dublin. A few were involved in active combat, others in liaison and dispatch-carrying, more in nursing, first aid, and cooking, and yet others in bringing food, arms, and equipment to the various posts.[90] The particularly difficult task of acting as Pearse's envoy during the surrender was carried out by Elizabeth O'Farrell, a member of the Inghinidhe na hÉireann branch of Cumann na mBan. In general, Citizen Army women appear to have found it easier to be accepted as equals by their male colleagues, and to take an active part in the fighting. Constance Markievicz fought as second-in-command to Michael

Mallin at St Stephen's Green and the College of Surgeons. She was court-martialled and sentenced to death, though this was commuted to a life sentence. Helena Molony took part in the attack on Dublin Castle, and she too was imprisoned after the rising. Dr Kathleen Lynn, another leading feminist member of the Citizen Army, served as medical officer. Cumann na mBan women had a more mixed experience, some finding that they were not readily allowed to join the men and those that did discovering that they were apt to be treated very much as auxiliaries.

In the later months of 1916 women such as Kathleen Clarke played a central role in the emergence of Sinn Féin as an umbrella organisation for a broad range of nationalists. They organised help for the republican prisoners and relief for their families, developed an amnesty movement, and raised the profile of the rising and kept it constantly before the public eye. As the revitalised Sinn Féin became established, 'nation-first' and 'suffrage-first' feminists came together to press their male colleagues to share leadership with women. Cumann na mBan no longer believed that nationalist men would of their own accord accept women as equal political partners. Like Sinn Féin, Cumann na mBan grew significantly in numbers during this period.

The IWFL, while maintaining its suffrage-first position, was also concerned to assert women's rights within the new nationalist structures. Hanna Sheehy Skeffington, whose husband had been summarily executed by British soldiers during the rising, was also becoming a leading public speaker in support of nationalist claims for full independence. The two organisations found a new unity of purpose in which they also cooperated with the IWWU,[91] now under the leadership of Louie Bennett, who remained an uncompromising pacifist but who was also a strong supporter of Irish independence and a committed feminist.

A new organisation, Cumann na dTeachtaire (Society of Delegates), comprising women delegates to all republican bodies and conferences, was set up to press for adequate representation for women in republican structures, to promote women's rights in general, and where possible to cooperate with other women's organisations. Accordingly, during 1918 Cumann na mBan, the IWWU, and the IWFL combined in opposition to conscription, and the IWSLGA joined them to oppose the regulation of prostitution in the Defence of the Realm Consolidation Act of 1914.[92] Nationalist women, and the IWWU in particular, played an important part in the resistance to conscription. Their refusal to accept industrial conscription (the recruitment of women to fill the jobs vacated by conscripted men) was essential to the success of the campaign.

At this time too the first instalment of parliamentary suffrage was finally achieved. In February 1918 the Representation of the People Act,[93] a compromise acceptable to the Liberal and Conservative parties, was passed. This gave a limited measure of female suffrage, confined to women over 30 who themselves or whose husbands were householders or occupiers of land or premises of a minimum yearly value of £5, a restriction that reflected the fears of most political parties as to how women would use their votes in the coming election. Both the Irish Parliamentary Party and the Unionists tried to prevent the extension of the limited franchise act to Ireland. In view of their record on women's suffrage both had reason to feel apprehensive. In November 1918 a further act[94] made women eligible for election to parliament. When the general election was held in December 1918, suffragists of all political hues came together to honour the veteran Anna Haslam who finally cast her vote after over forty years of campaigning. The IWSLGA now changed its name again, to the Irish Women Citizens and Local Government Association (IWCLGA), and continued to promote women's citizenship.[95]

For republican women the election results brought mixed messages. On the one hand it appeared that women's votes and campaign work had had a significant impact on the outcome. Also, the combined efforts of Cumann na mBan, the IWWU, the IWFL, and Sinn Féin had succeeded in getting Constance Markievicz (herself in Holloway Prison – 'an excellent election address', as she wrote to her supporters) returned for a seat in Dublin, the first woman to be elected to the Westminster parliament. Yet to have returned only one woman was a poor result. It had proved difficult to get the parties to adopt women candidates. Only Sinn Féin ran any women: Markievicz, and Winifred Carney in Belfast, though Louie Bennett had declined an offer to stand for Labour. Nor did the feminists believe that the men in Sinn Féin had pulled their weight in trying to get women elected. The *Irish Citizen* expressed the feeling of betrayal:

> Under the new dispensation the majority sex in Ireland has secured one representative. This is the measure of our boasted sex equality. The lesson the election teaches is that reaction has not died out with the Irish party.[96]

It appears that unionist women also felt let down by the lack of recognition from male colleagues; the UWUC was becoming increasingly dissatisfied with control by the male council. The unionist political campaign had been suspended during the war, but the women's organisation sought to keep it going through the efforts of individual members. The UWUC also actively supported the extension of conscription to Ireland, and during the

1918 election campaign worked to get the unionist women's vote out.[97]

When the Sinn Féin members boycotted Westminster and set up Dáil Éireann and alternative government structures in 1919, again there were some welcome, if very few, female advances. When the Dáil met after the release of the republican prisoners and de Valera was elected president, Markievicz was appointed Minister for Labour, a European first for women. This too had to be fought for, as Kathleen Clarke recounts:

> I asked her how she had managed it, as I had noticed that the present leaders were not over-eager to put women into places of honour or power, even though they had earned the right to both as well as the men had, having responded to every call made upon them throughout the struggle for freedom. She told me she had had to bully them; she claimed she had earned the right to be a minister as well as any of the men, and was equally well fitted for it, educationally and every other way, and if she was not made a minister she would go over to the Labour Party.[98]

Clarke herself was chosen to chair the north-city republican courts in Dublin. In the 1920 local elections Sinn Féin swept the board despite the introduction of a proportional representation voting system. In Dublin five women were elected to the corporation: Jennie Wyse Power, Kathleen Clarke, Hanna Sheehy Skeffington, Margaret McGarry, and Anne Ashton.[99] Again the result was gratifying, but felt far short of real equality.

As the War of Independence escalated in 1920, the services of Cumann na mBan were essential in the ensuing guerrilla war. A much more active role was taken than had been possible in 1916, and the importance of this contribution was recognised by male colleagues. The work in support of the West Cork IRA, for instance, was described as 'indispensable to the army, nursing the wounded and sick, carrying dispatches, scouting, acting as intelligence agents, arranging billets, raising funds, knitting, washing, cooking for the active service men, and burying our dead'.[100] This participation gave added authority to the demand for women to be accorded full citizenship in the future settlement.

For the feminist movement the War of Independence was seriously disruptive. A major loss was the *Irish Citizen*, which had managed to survive thus far despite lack of funds and personnel. Louie Bennett offered to take it over and turn it into a trade union paper, but Hanna Sheehy Skeffington refused. During 1920 it appeared irregularly and carried repeated requests for new writers. The last issue was for September-December 1920, and contained a review by Sheehy Skeffington of the current position of feminism. She compared Ireland (now in 'a state of war') with other European countries during the recent war, in which

> the woman's movement merged into the national movement, temporarily at least, and women became patriots rather than feminists, and heroes' wives or widows rather than human beings, so now in Ireland the national struggle overshadows all else.

Feminism, she said, could only mark time. But in the meantime there could be no woman's paper

> without a woman's movement, without earnest and serious-minded women readers and thinkers – and these in Ireland have dwindled perceptibly of late, partly owing to the cause above mentioned, and partly because since a measure, however limited, of suffrage has been granted, women are forging out their own destiny in practical fields of endeavour ... We still believe we have a mission and a message for Irishwomen as a purely feminist paper and emboldened in that belief we shall carry on.[101]

Soon after this, the police smashed the printing equipment and publication ceased.[102]

In the general elections held in May 1921 under the Government of Ireland Act, the Sinn Féin candidates in the twenty-six counties were all returned unopposed. They included six women: Markievicz, Kathleen Clarke, Margaret Pearse (mother of Patrick), Mary MacSwiney, Katherine O'Callaghan, and Dr Ada English. In the Treaty debates all six opposed the Treaty and voted against it. In March 1922 O'Callaghan, invoking the 1916 proclamation and women's role in the War of Independence, proposed that women be immediately admitted to the parliamentary franchise on the same terms as men. Anti-treaty deputies showed support for this position, while pro-treaty deputies opposed it, apparently for fear of its effects on the prospects of the Treaty in any election in which younger women had the vote. In the event the Dáil rejected the proposal by 47 to 38 votes, and the election was held in June 1922 with women under 30 still disfranchised. The delay was only temporary, and within months full political and civil rights were extended to women in article 3 of the constitution of the Irish Free State:

Every person, without distinction of sex, domiciled in the area of the jurisdiction of the Irish Free State [Saorstát Éireann] at the time of the coming into operation of this constitution, who was born in Ireland ... shall ... enjoy the privileges and be subject to the obligations of such citizenship.

Taken in conjunction with the UK Sex Disqualification (Removal) Act, 1919,[103] which outlawed disqualification on grounds of sex or marriage for civil professions and jury service, the Free State constitution established the full formal equality of the sexes in the new state. Women in Northern Ireland and Great Britain had to wait till 1928 for similar equality.

Thus by 1922 the women's emancipation movement had succeeded in removing virtually all legal barriers to women's personal autonomy and citizenship. However, during the campaigns there had been signs that formal equality might not remove less visible barriers of custom, tradition, and entrenched paradigms of male and female roles. How the new constitutional position of women would translate into practice remained to be seen.

In the decades following the Anglo-Irish Treaty, attitudes became if anything more resistant to women moving into 'non-traditional' roles and occupations. Here both the Irish Free State and Northern Ireland were in line with the general European trend in the 1920s and early 1930s. In reaction against the extension of women's roles during the first world war, and in order to safeguard employment for men, the prevailing mood now looked back to pre-war values, stressing the role of women in the home. The teachings of both the Catholic and Protestant Churches, north and south, reinforced this. In neither part of Ireland was there a powerful socialist or liberal movement to act as a counteracting force, while the all-male church authorities could call on a body of educated intellectuals and a propaganda network that included control of the primary and secondary educational systems, and the weekly sermon in the parish church.[104]

Accordingly, north and south, the majority of Irish women continued to work as houseworkers and child-rearers in their own homes, and their unpaid work continued to be regarded by officialdom as economically 'non-productive'. Most of those in 'gainful employment' worked in occupations characterised by low pay and status. In 1926 the largest areas of women's employment in the Irish Free State were still domestic service, agriculture and textile and clothing manufacture.[105] Participation in professional work had increased; teaching and nursing were now dominated by women, though neither brought the financial rewards or public prestige of such male-dominated professions as medicine and law. The law had only recently been opened to women by the 1919 Removal of Sex Disqualification Act, and there were very few women lawyers. In Northern Ireland the pattern was much the same. Women comprised over two-thirds of teachers in Dublin and Belfast, but only 13 per cent of Dublin doctors and 14 per cent of Belfast doctors were women. There were still fewer in other professions. Only 2 per cent of dentists in Dublin and 1 per cent in Belfast were women, and there were no female engineers or surveyors in either city. Belfast had no female accountants, though there were a few in Dublin.[106]

Women's participation in public political life followed this general pattern. Politics in both parts of the island remained overwhelmingly a male preserve. In the Irish Free State and the Republic of Ireland between 1923 and 1969 women comprised between 1.9 per cent and 2.9 per cent of the total number of Dáil candidates, and between 1.9 per cent and 3.4 per cent of elected deputies. There were five women in the Dáil in 1923 and only three in 1943. Numbers did not begin to rise significantly till the 1980s. By 1989 14.1 per cent of candidates and 7.8 per cent of elected deputies (thirteen in all) were women.[107] In Northern Ireland, the first woman was elected to the Northern Ireland parliament in 1921, but in all only seventeen women stood as candidates between 1921 and 1972, no more than nine of whom were ever elected, mostly for the QUB seats. The first woman to be elected to the UK parliament for Northern Ireland was Patricia Ford (Down North) in 1953. In the Irish Free State such low participation on the part of women may seem surprising, in view of the high profile achieved by nationalist women between 1916 and 1922. But that relative breakthrough had not taken place within the established political structures, rather within a revolutionary movement, where traditional taboos regarding acceptable female behaviour were more readily broken, at least temporarily. Once the revolutionary movement became the new ruling establishment, the usual historical patterns suggests that equal participation by the sexes in the public political life of the new state would have been problematic even in the most favourable circumstances. As it was, one of the most striking features of post-Treaty politics in the Irish Free Scale was the sudden disappearance from the public political arena of many of the women who had become prominent there. Some of these women opposed the treaty, and some did not recognise the legitimacy of the new state and therefore refused to participate in its political structures. However, most of them continued to participate in republican, socialist, feminist, or pacifist activities, though these have received little attention from historians.

The general election in June 1922 gave pro-Treaty Sinn Féin fifty-eight seats against thirty-six for anti-Treaty Sinn Féin. Only two women were elected, both in strongly anti-treaty areas: Mary MacSwiney in Cork and Kate O'Callaghan in Limerick. Of the five women elected to Dáil Éireann in 1923, four – Constance Markievicz, Mary MacSwiney, Kathleen Lynn, and Caitlín Brugha – opposed the Treaty and did not take their seats, which left Margaret Collins-O'Driscoll, sister of Michael Collins and member of Cumann na nGaedheal, as the only woman deputy in the Dáil. MacSwiney and Lynn lost their seats in the 1927 election and Caitlín Brugha left politics. Constance Markievicz remained active in local politics as a member of Rathmines Urban District Council, and was particularly concerned with housing, public health, and child-welfare issues. She published a pamphlet in 1924 reconciling James Connolly's socialist views with Catholic teaching. She joined Fianna Fáil in 1926, drawn by its programme of national economic self-sufficiency and tariff barriers, and was elected to the Dáil in June 1927 but died in July before Fianna Fáil entered the Dáil.

Hanna Sheehy Skeffington opposed the Treaty and was active in Sinn Féin and the Women's Prisoners' Defence League set up by Maud Gonne and Charlotte Despard in 1922. Attracted by the return to participation in the Dáil, she became a member of the Fianna Fáil executive, but resigned when de Valera signed the oath of allegiance. She then threw her energy into socialist republicanism and feminism, as assistant editor of *An Phoblacht*, and in organisations including the Friends of Soviet Russia and the Women's International League for Peace and Freedom (WILPF). She supported the idea of a women's political party in the 1930s and stood as a Dáil candidate for the Women's Social and Progressive League in 1943.

The two prominent nationalist-feminist women who stayed in public political life moved further towards a republican position as time went on. Kathleen Clarke opposed the Treaty, joined Fianna Fáil, won and lost a Dáil seat in the two elections of 1927, and became a Fianna Fáil senator in 1928. Disillusioned by what she saw as Fianna Fáil's abandonment of its policies on partition and the Irish language, she openly criticised the 1937 constitution for its attitude to women. An unsuccessful attempt was made to expel her from the party for this protest. She became the first woman to be elected Lord Mayor of Dublin and served a two-year term, 1939–41. She subsequently resigned from Fianna Fáil, stood unsuccessfully for both the Dáil and Seanad as an independent, and for Clann na Poblachta in 1948.

Jennie Wyse Power, one of the small minority in Cumann na mBan who supported the Treaty, became a senator, nominated by Dublin Corporation and appointed by W.T. Cosgrave. Disappointed with Cumann na nGaedheal's stand on the boundary commission in 1924, she voted against the government. She resigned from the party, became an independent senator, and later, attracted by the Fianna Fáil policy of dismantling the Treaty, joined that party and was elected as a Fianna Fáil senator in 1934. She remained an outspoken supporter of feminist causes throughout her career.[108]

The women who entered the Dáil did so through a system where, in terms of winning and retaining a seat, party support was more important than commitment to feminist issues. An assessment written in 1978 noted that, while the women TDs were competent and successful, as evidenced by regular re-election, they generally toed the party line; none 'has ever defied the party whip, taken a major initiative on women's rights or championed any significant legislation against the wishes of the party'.[109] By contrast, in the Seanad some of the women senators were prepared, when necessary, to oppose a government over feminist issues.[110] These included Eileen Costello (Cumann na nGaedheal senator, 1922–34), Kathleen Clarke (Fianna Fáil senator, 1928–36), and, in particular, Jennie Wyse Power, from 1922 to 1936 successively a Cumann na nGaedheal, Independent, and Fianna Fáil senator.

When the Civil War broke out Cumann na mBan split, as did the IRA, but unlike the IRA a large majority voted to take the anti-treaty side. As in the War of Independence, Cumann na mBan again took an active role, carrying arms and dispatches, finding safe houses, and hiding IRA men. Some hundreds were arrested and imprisoned in Kilmainham gaol. When the war ended Cumann na mBan did not recognise the legitimacy of the Free State government.[111] It declined in numbers and experienced further divisions in the 1930s over the question of a workers' republic. Individual members such as Sheila Humphries joined Saor Éire, the socialist republican organisation founded in 1931, while others, such as Mary MacSwiney, regarded socialist republicanism as unduly divisive. Maud Gonne MacBride, Charlotte Despard, Rosamond Jacob, Nora Connolly O'Brien, and Helena Molony (together with Hanna Sheehy Skeffington) were among republican women active in organisations such as the Friends of Soviet Russia, the Indian-Irish Independence League, and the League against Imperialism and for National Defence. Cumann na mBan participated in marches and demonstrations in support of several of these causes, but appears to have remained generally aloof from feminist opposition to discriminatory policies in the Irish Free State.

A number of republican women continued to be active in the peace movement during the 1920s. From the outset there had been different emphases placed on the relationship between 'peace' and 'freedom' by members of the IIL, specifically as to whether pacifism was compatible with support for a defensive war or resistance to oppression. The 1921 Treaty and the civil war increased these internal tensions. Most of the Free State supporters resigned from the IIL, while republicans such as Hanna Sheehy Skeffington, Rosamond Jacob, Maud Gonne MacBride, and Charlotte Despard remained active members, alongside pacifists such as Louie Bennett, Helen Chenevix, and Lucy Kingston who held that pacifism ruled out the use of force in any circumstances. Tensions continued throughout the 1920s and were apparent when the WILPF held its fifth international congress in Dublin in 1926 at the invitation of the Irish committee. It was a major public event, with 2,000 people attending the public meeting in the Mansion House addressed by Jane Addams, the American president of WILPF, on the subject of 'next steps towards world peace'. Topics discussed included colonial and economic imperialism, women and world peace, the relationship between majorities and minorities, and conciliation, arbitration, and disarmament. The Irish section presented a report on minority problems in Ireland. The tensions within the IIL led to further dissension when some of the republican women used the opportunity of a large international presence for demonstrations in support of republican political prisoners. Continuing disagreements over precisely what pacifism involved in practice eventually led to the disintegration of the IIL in 1931. Some members continued to participate in WILPF as individuals, and some were active in the disarmament movement of the 1930s.[112]

As far as specifically feminist interests were concerned, the national and international climate in post-war Europe did little to encourage the emergence of a new generation of activists. By and large it was groups founded earlier that carried on the campaign. Both the IWCLGA and the women's graduate associations (the IAWG had split in 1914 into the National University, Dublin University, and Queen's University women graduate associations) were to the fore. Cross-party cooperation continued, and while numbers were smaller than in the suffrage campaign, many high-profile women were involved. For instance, both Senator Jennie Wyse Power and Mary Hayden, professor of Modern Irish History at University College, Dublin, were longstanding members of the IWCLGA. Hayden also served as president of the National Council of Women and of the NUWGA. Hanna Sheehy Skeffington, Mary Macken, professor of German, and Agnes O'Farrelly, professor of Modern Irish, were all prominent members of the latter.[113] Contact with the international women's movement continued. The International Alliance had lobbied at the Paris peace conference after the armistice to have women's interests taken into account. It set up an office in Geneva and worked to have women's equality recognised and supported by the authority of the League of Nations, which was bound by its charter to uphold equal opportunity for women in its own appointments. In 1926 the Alliance changed its name to the International Alliance of Women for Suffrage and Equality. In the Irish Free State the National Council of Women in Ireland was founded in 1924 to affiliate to both the International Council of Women and the International Alliance, and 'to promote joint action ... and to stimulate thought and cooperation on all questions of social interest'. Affiliates to the National Council included the two graduate associations; the Women's National Health Association (1907); the IWWU; the IWCLGA; the United Irishwomen (1910); Saor an Leanbh (the Irish branch of Save the Children, founded in 1920); the Irish Matrons' Association (1904); the Irish Girls' Friendly Society (1877); and the Irish Union of Assistant Mistresses in Secondary Schools. Northern affiliates included the Belfast Women Citizens Union (1911), first established as a suffrage society.[114]

Feminists soon found themselves in conflict, first with the Cumann na nGaedheal governments in the 1920s and later with the Fianna Fáil governments in the 1930s, as each in turn tried to dismantle aspects of the political and economic equality of the sexes guaranteed by the 1922 constitution.[115] There was no shortage of issues to concern feminists. Women's liability for jury service had been established only in 1919 by the Removal of Sex Disqualification Act. In 1924 the government proposed to remove women from jury service on the grounds that 'the woman juror has not been an outstanding success'. It was alleged that 'the insertion of women's names in the jury book leads to nothing but trouble; the women do not turn up, or they get themselves excused, or they are objected to'.[116] Although this proposal apparently incurred no opposition in Dáil or Seanad, the feminist organisations saw it as likely to stifle the growth of women's citizenship before it could take root. The IWCLGA argued that women had no right to evade the duties of citizenship, and that to allow them to do so was unfair to men and degrading to women. The Women's Independent Association claimed that it was a reactionary step, which would discourage women's acceptance of civic responsibility. Kevin O'Higgins, Minister for Justice, dismissed the 1919 act as a measure that only applied in Ireland 'because we were at that time part and parcel of the political system of Great Britain'.[117] This was a revealing comment in view of earlier expectations of some nationalist feminists that their male colleagues would give women full equality in an independent Ireland. The feminists won a limited compromise in that the 1924 Juries Act[118] retained women as jurors while allowing any woman who was qualified and liable for jury service to opt to be registered as exempt.

In 1927 the government returned to the subject. Awareness of its significance had increased since 1924. The IWCLGA was again in action, as well as the Women's Equality League and the IWWU, and on this occasion they found allies in the Dáil, Seanad, and other political and civic groups. O'Higgins claimed that the vast majority of women would be grateful to be relieved of jury service, that the system could work without them, that women had obligations to home and children, and that the state would save money by not having to provide separate bathroom facilities. He described the women who opposed him as unrepresentative 'self-appointed spokeswomen'. Ultimately, it seemed, he and the government knew what was best for women:

> We find ourselves frequently in the position of preventing people getting something which they pretend they want, and which would not be good for them. Politically and

economically, that seems to be our chronic position. In this matter I am really the champion of women in the state, but I never expect to get any gratitude for that.[119]

Certainly the feminists were not grateful. Instead they suggested that the bill was in breach of Article 3 of the constitution. They asked whether, if the duties of citizenship were curtailed, the rights would also be cut, and they saw sinister implications in the extension of this benevolence to women but not to men. They urged that petty economies should not be put in the balance against common justice and public duty, and that arguments based on women's unwillingness to serve were dishonest in the light of women's very recent access to jury service and of the regular practice in the courts by which women jurors were asked to stand aside. Again the result was a compromise, but the new position was significantly worse than in 1924. The 1927 act[120] placed all women in the category of persons exempted but entitled to serve on application, which made it highly unlikely that many women would see this as part of their duties as citizens.

In 1926 the Civil Service Regulation (Amendment) Act[121] amended a 1924 act[122] to legalise a sex bar by allowing competitive examinations for positions in the civil service to be confined to people 'qualified in respect of sex, age, health, character, knowledge and ability for such situation'. In the Dáil there was no opposition to the bill, and Margaret Collins-O'Driscoll actively supported it. The IWCLGA, the National University Women Graduates Association, and other women's organisations campaigned against it, as did Senators Eileen Costello and Jennie Wyse Power. Wyse Power reminded the Seanad that no men 'in a fight for freedom ever had such loyal cooperation from their women as the men who now compose the present executive council', and who now proposed such discriminatory legislation.[123] The bill was defeated in the Seanad, but was passed by the Dáil after the required constitutional delay and became law.

The question of divorce also arose in the 1920s. In 1925 the government moved that standing orders be changed so as to prevent the introduction of divorce bills. The United Kingdom Matrimonial Causes Act of 1857,[124] which had allowed divorce to be pursued through the courts, had not been extended to Ireland, and divorce required legislative approval for a private members bill. Opposition came chiefly from male Protestants in the Seanad. It is not clear whether or to what extent divorce was seen as a feminist concern at this time. The government action was in line with Catholic teaching, and in the interests of the socially and politically powerful farming class, for whom divorce raised difficult questions concerning property. Moreover, most married women were dependent on their husbands for their livelihood and thus were unlikely to be enthusiastic for divorce. Some of the double standards involved in the provisions were noted by feminists. In relation to the definition of a wife's domicile as that of her husband even if they lived in different continents, Lucy Kingston, a Quaker member of the IWCLGA, commented that the Dáil debate was

> very unsatisfactory. No divorce (*a vinculo matrimomia*) but judicial separation without remarriage possible. Divorce possible only if husband changes domicile – not possible at all therefore to the wife.[125]

Birth control literature was banned under the Censorship of Publications act of 1929.[126] There appears to have been no discussion in the Oireachtas of the merits or demerits of contraception. There was feminist concern about the bill, but it is not clear to what extent the women's organisations saw birth control as a feminist issue. Both the IWCLGA and the Irish branch of the

WILPF took part in the public debate on birth control that preceded the censorship measure, and the former campaigned against some aspects of the bill. Lucy Kingston's diaries suggest that birth control was debated in the context of control of world population, and when the bill appeared she noted it as 'an insidious move against birth control'.[127]

The year 1932 witnessed a major political shift when Fianna Fáil came to power under Eamon de Valera. It quickly became apparent that this would produce little change in attitudes to women. Shortly before the 1932 general election, when Cumann na nGaedheal was still in government, the Department of Education informed the Irish National Teachers Organisation (INTO) that it proposed to introduce compulsory retirement on marriage for women national teachers. The election intervened and the INTO executive complained to the new Fianna Fáil government that the regulation was unconstitutional, contending that married women were especially suitable as teachers of young children and were favoured by parents.[128] The government proceeded with the ban, arguing that married women teachers meant some loss either to the school or the home, and that the double-income families of comparatively well-paid teachers gave rise to jealousy. Both the government and the INTO referred the question to the Catholic hierarchy, which decided to express no opinion, effectively giving it tacit approval.

Sexuality issues arose again with the Criminal Law Amendment Bill of 1934 The 1931 Carrigan report on sexual offences, which was not published but was in part reported in the *Irish Press*, contained several proposals, including raising the age of consent in respect of carnal knowledge to 18, making prostitutes' clients as well as prostitutes liable to prosecution, setting up a women's police force, recruiting more women probation officers, and placing jury service for women on the same terms as for men. The subsequent government bill (which passed in 1935)[129] raised the age of consent from 13 to 15 in cases of unlawful carnal knowledge classed as felonies, and from 16 to 17 in cases classed as misdemeanours. Ignoring the commission's other recommendations, it proposed to control prostitution by imposing a fine of up to 40 shillings for a first conviction for soliciting, and imprisonment for up to six months for subsequent offences. It also banned the sale or importation of contraceptives.

In the Oireachtas the three women TDs made no intervention on any of the issues in the bill, but there was opposition in the Seanad, which set up a special committee to examine it. Kathleen Clarke opposed the ban on contraception on the grounds that it would be counter-productive. Oliver St John Gogarty in the Seanad and R.J. Rowlette in the Dáil argued in favour of contraception, both pointing to the pressures on the poor and the dangers of infanticide. The Seanad committee deleted the ban, but the house then accepted a government amendment to reinstate it. On prostitution the committee proposed to replace 'every common prostitute' with a wording that made men as well as women chargeable for soliciting or importuning a member of the opposite sex. The government opposed the proposal and the Seanad accepted the government amendment by a single vote. The Seanad accepted its own committee's proposal to raise the age of consent from 15 to 18 in the case of indecent assault, but subsequently yielded to government representations and agreed to drop it.[130]

Outside the Oireachtas there was a strong feminist response. A Joint Committee of Women's Societies and

Social Workers was established in March 1935. The attendance at the early meetings included W.R. O'Hegarty, Hanna Sheehy Skeffington and her sister Mary Kettle, Helen Chenevix, Louie Bennett, and Maud Gonne MacBride. The committee was composed of delegates from independent societies and had two aims: to study social legislation affecting women and children and to recommend necessary reforms.[131] Early affiliates included the Irish Girls Friendly Society, the Girl Guides, the Irish Countrywomen's Association (ICA), the Irish Matrons' Association, Saor an Leanbh, the Irish School Mistresses Association, the IWWU, the National Council of Women in Ireland, the Dublin University Women Graduates Association, the IWCLGA, the Women's National Health Association, the Mothers' Union, the Holy Child Association, the SPCC, and the Legion of Mary.[132] Many of these, as noted above, were also affiliates of the National Council of Women.

The Joint Committee immediately lobbied to have the bill amended in line with the Carrigan proposals, although it does not appear to have protested against the ban on contraceptives. Again, the reason for not taking up the contraceptive issue is not clear. The 1930s witnessed a strengthening of the Catholic ethos in the Irish Free State, which created difficulties for some feminists. Lucy Kingston noted that she had worked 'comfortably' with Catholics on committees and mixed socially with them prior to 1932, the year of the Eucharistic Congress in Dublin, but afterwards, and through the 1940s and 1950s, she was more aware of tensions on certain issues, especially when anti-communism was at its height.[133] But it may be that contraception did not become a serious feminist demand until the introduction of the contraceptive pill in the 1960s made available an effective woman-controlled method of birth control.

Later in 1935, in the context of economic depression and high male unemployment, the Conditions of Employment Bill proposed to control the entry of women to various skilled trades. Seán Lemass, Minister for Industry and Commerce, used the protectionist argument that some types of work were unsuitable for women. There was no opposition from the three women TDs. In the Seanad both Jennie Wyse Power and Kathleen Clarke opposed the bill, the former recalling the dashed hopes of the young girls who had been dismissed from their employment after the 1916 rising, and the latter calling on the united trade union movement to support equal pay. In response to the accusation that 'the feminists have run riot' over the Conditions of Employment Bill, Clarke replied that, although she was sympathetic to the feminist movement, her opposition was specifically based on the 1916 proclamation.[134]

The women's organisations lobbied vigorously, and the IWWU representatives met Lemass to try to influence the bill. They found neither government nor male trade unionists in general sympathetic to their case. Under pressure, the ICTU reluctantly passed a resolution supporting 'equal democratic opportunities for all citizens and equal pay for equal work'.[135]

In spite of the objections, the Conditions of Employment Act as passed[136] authorised the minister to prohibit the employment of women in any form of industrial work and to impose a limit on the female proportion of the workforce in any particular industry. In a case where the minister made such regulations it was illegal for an employer to breach them. The problems experienced by the IWWU in opposing this legislation highlight some of the difficulties faced by a women's trade union. The union wanted to support both the interests of the labour movement as a whole and women's interests within that movement. The very question of a separate women's union was controversial. But male trade unionists generally had little interest in the problems of women's employment, and many were mainly concerned with any threat to men's employment. Wage differentials in favour of men were defended, though the fact that lower pay for women could lead employers to favour them in preference to men was deplored. Women workers themselves were not united on all issues. Many women agreed with the prevailing ethos that women's place was ideally in the home with an adequate family wage paid to the male breadwinner. In the light of these complexities it is not difficult to understand why the views on such issues expressed at different times by IWWU leaders appeared contradictory.

Undoubtedly the contribution of the IWWU to the labour movement as a whole was positive and substantial. It insisted on raising issues of sex equality and led the way in the unionisation of Irish women. It defended the right of women to work in all employments while accepting that men and women had different roles and functions in society. It won many victories for its members, and played a leading part in winning improvements in working conditions, including paid holidays, shorter working hours, and tea breaks, for all workers, men as well as women.[137]

In 1937 the draft of de Valera's proposed new constitution incorporated several of the principles underlying the various pieces of legislation that the feminist organisations had been challenging since the birth of the state. Article 3 of the 1922 constitution had given full and equal citizenship 'without distinction of sex', while article 14 stated that

all citizens of the Irish Free State [Saorstát Éireann] without distinction of sex, who have reached the age of twenty-one years and who comply with the provisions of the prevailing electoral laws, shall have the right to vote for members of Dáil Éireann …

The new draft constitution replaced this unambiguous equality with a qualified one. Its text read that the 'acquisition and loss of Irish nationality and citizenship shall be determined in accordance with law' (Article 9.1), while 'every citizen who has reached the age of twenty-one years, and who is not placed under disability or incapacity by this constitution or by law, shall be eligible for membership of Dáil Éireann' (16.1.1). A similar qualification was attached to the right to vote (16.1.2).

Article 41.2.1 recognised the work of housewives: 'In particular, the state recognises that by her life within the home, woman gives to the state a support without which the common good cannot be achieved'. But the use of the singular 'woman' rather than some or many 'women', and 'life' rather than 'work', went beyond recognition of the value to society of the work done by so many women to express an ideology that placed all women on the basis of their sex in a 'private' or domestic sphere. Article 41.2.2 followed with an undertaking that 'the state shall, therefore, endeavour to ensure that mothers shall not be obliged by economic necessity to engage in labour to the neglect of their duties in the home'. Article 45.4.1 pledged the state

> to safeguard with especial care the economic interests of the weaker sections of the community, and, where necessary, to contribute to the support of the infirm, the widow, the orphan and the aged.

Article 40.1 guaranteed equality before the law for all citizens but added the qualification that this 'shall not be held to mean that the state shall not in its enactments have due regard to differences of capacity, physical and moral, and of social function'. Article 45.4.2 was more explicit:

The state shall endeavour to ensure that the inadequate strength of women and the tender age of children shall not be abused, and that women or children shall not be forced by economic necessity to enter avocations unsuited to their sex, age or strength.[138]

Taken together, and interpreted in the light of government policy towards women over the previous fifteen years, these clauses appeared to feminists as an attempt to reverse much of what women had achieved in 1922. The Joint Committee of Women's Societies lobbied de Valera to reinstate equal citizenship 'without distinction of sex', but he argued that, now that women were fully equal, they no longer needed a clause that reminded them that they had not always been so. Since their fear was that they might not in fact remain so for much longer, they were not impressed. Eventually de Valera agreed to the reinstatement, and gave a commitment that no other article would be used to curtail women's citizenship (Article 9.1.3). He refused to change the other suspect clauses, and the feminists turned to a campaign to win public support.

In letters to the newspapers Mary Kettle, who chaired the Joint Committee, explained the need for an explicit commitment to women's equality in the light of recent history. Women who read Articles 40, 41, and 45 in context would realise that if they became law 'no woman who works – be it in trade, factory, or profession – will have any security whatever'. Article 40.1 would give the state 'dangerous' powers of legislating on sex or class lines, while 41.2.2 could sanction further limitation of women's work opportunities. The Committee wanted article 45.4.2 deleted on similar grounds and asked who was to make decisions under these articles. With technology eliminating heavy work in industry, it was in the home that many women faced really heavy work. The suspicion was that protection would not be used to help women where they needed it, but to exclude them from work where they threatened the interests of men.[139] For her part, Hanna Sheehy Skeffington roundly asserted that the equal citizenship of 1916 was

being scrapped for a fascist model, where women are relegated to permanent inferiority, their vocations and choice of callings limited because, apparently, of an implied permanent invalidism as the weaker sex.

The changes were in line with the Cosgrave government's policy on jury service, the civil service, and the 1936 employment act. Now the 1916 proclamation was being nullified. Having been a colleague of de Valera for many years, she claimed that concerning women, he and other cabinet members shared the 'fascist ideal now working under Mussolini and Hitler'.[140]

Articles 40, 41, and 45 were of particular concern to the Joint Committee. What did it mean that mothers should not be forced by economic necessity to work, and could it be used to deny employment to married women? The Joint Committee was also suspicious of the clauses concerning women's employment. It particularly wanted the removal of phrases such as 'the inadequate strength of women'. Again de Valera defended his wording vigorously. Like Kevin O'Higgins before him he claimed he was doing women a service for which he deserved gratitude rather than reproach. He seemed particularly concerned about women's 'inadequate strength', a phrase he managed to repeat six times in one paragraph of a Dáil speech.[141]

An IWWU delegation eventually succeeded in winning a commitment to amend Article 45.4.2, which eventually read:

The state shall endeavour to ensure that the strength and health of workers, men and women, and the tender age of children shall not be abused and that citizens shall not be forced by economic necessity to enter avocations unsuited to their sex, age or strength.

Having won this, the IWWU dropped its opposition and withdrew from the campaign to amend the constitution.

The Seanad had been abolished in 1936, so Oireachtas debate was confined to the Dáil. Of the three women deputies, Margaret Pearse made no contribution, Bridget Redmond did so only under pressure, and, perhaps most significantly, Helena Concannon, a member of the National University Women Graduates Association, itself a leading participant in the feminist campaign, supported the draft constitution, putting her party before feminist politics. The Joint Committee continued its campaign but gained no further changes. Feminists were now a small group of activists, and no significant body of public opinion emerged to support their case. Of the newspapers, editorials in the *Irish Times* and the *Irish Independent* took a neutral, if not negative, stance on feminist concerns, while the *Irish Press* vigorously supported de Valera.[142] The feminists campaigned for a no vote in the subsequent referendum on the constitution, which in the event was passed by a fairly narrow majority.

The Joint Committee's work gives an indication of the issues on which the constituent organisations joined forces, if not of the full range of the latter's concerns. The committee continued to campaign for women police, a longstanding feminist aim. In 1936 it lobbied for a 50 per cent representation of women in the new Seanad, to be chosen on vocational rather than party lines. During the 1940s it worked to amend the married women's maintenance act and the law on adoption, to replace institutional care of deprived children by a boarding-out system, and for the appropriate training of social workers.

During the debates over the constitution the idea of a women's political party was mooted, and as a result a meeting of women's associations on 24 November 1937 founded the Women's Social and Political League to 'promote and protect the political, social and economic status of women and to further their work and usefulness as citizens'. It aimed to organise women voters, to secure equal opportunities and pay, put forward independent women candidates for the Dáil, Seanad, and other public bodies, and secure the appointment of women to government commissions. The women members of the Dáil had shown that they did not see themselves as campaigners for women's rights. The new party would try to change this, and to challenge entrenched ideas of separate spheres for women and men. In the event the problems of sustaining a political party, including the ban on civil servants joining one, proved too formidable. In 1938 the league changed its name to 'Women's Social and Progressive League', but continued to work for the same objectives'.[143]

During the 1938 general election campaign the League raised a range of feminist concerns. These included women's jury service, pay differentials between men and women in secondary-school teaching, the civil service, and the professions in general, and the enforced retirement of women primary-school teachers at 60, recently introduced by the Fianna Fáil government to provide more jobs for a surplus of trained teachers,[144] which deprived women teachers of full pension rights. In the 1943 general election the League put forward its president Hanna Sheehy Skeffington as an independent candidate, and backed three other women candidates, but none of them was elected.

Between 1939 and 1943 the Commission on Vocational Organisation was at work. In April 1940 representatives of several women's organisations set up a committee to prepare a memorandum and give evidence if required. Three organisations, the National Council of Women in Ireland, the Joint Committee of Women's Societies, and the Catholic Women's Federation of Secondary School Unions, presented a joint memorandum and gave oral evidence together. They proposed the direct representation of home-makers' on vocation-based assemblies at local or national level. Home-makers, most of whom were female, included those returned in the census as engaged in home duties (1,301 men and 552,176 women) and domestic servants (2,282 men and 86,102 women), altogether comprising over 25 per cent of the adult population.

Despite the 1937 constitution's emphasis on the importance to society of the contribution of women in the home, the commission refused to endorse this proposal. Its chairman, Michael Browne, bishop of Galway, was disparaging when W.R. O'Hegarty, Lucy Franks, and Mrs V. Dempsey appeared before the commission. He noted that it was 'quite easy to organise a number of philanthropic ladies of leisure' but more difficult 'in the case of most working women and domestic servants …'. When challenged on the 'ladies of leisure', he said that he had used the expression in the technical sense meaning those who did not have to work for a living, to which O'Hegarty replied that many of the committee members worked for their living. The bishop's response is indicative of the attitudes the women's movement encountered during these years.[145]

The Irish Countrywomen's Association also presented a memorandum to the commission, advocating the provision of village halls and more cooperation between the Departments of Primary and Vocational Education and of Agriculture, as well as the direct representation of countrywomen in any scheme of vocational organisation. The association, when still known as the United Irishwomen, had been growing again since the mid 1920s,[146] largely owing to the work of Lucy Franks, who was a founder member in 1928 of the Associated Countrywomen of the World. From 1926 the Royal Dublin Society provided space for UI exhibitions and craft demonstrations. An annual summer school began in 1929 and An Grianán, a residential college at Termonfeckin in County Louth, was established in 1953. In 1935 a new and more democratic structure was adopted, which replaced the central executive and branches by self-managing guilds and a national council of guilds. The organisation could no longer be registered as a friendly society and was no longer affiliated to the Irish Agricultural Organisation Society. To avoid confusion with the United Ireland Party (Fine Gael) of 1933, the UI became the Irish Countrywomen's Association. It grew in size, and by the 1990s had 1,000 guilds and over 22,000 members. Continuing the original commitment to 'a healthy and progressive community life' and to making rural life lively and enjoyable, it combined development of members' skills from housewifery to art and drama, with research and lobbying on such issues as rural water supply and electrification.[147] It was an affiliate of the Joint Committee of Women's Societies, and its interest in some specifically feminist concerns, such as the jury service issue, continued.

In 1942 a new organisation, the Irish Housewives' Association (IHA), was founded by a group of young married women, all Protestant and middle class. Some had links with the preceding generation of feminists;

members included Andrée Sheehy Skeffington, daughter-in-law of Hanna, and Susan Manning, a sister of Louie Bennett. Membership soon crossed religious divides, but despite strenuous efforts did not succeed in crossing class barriers: the IHA remained a largely middle-class organisation.

The IHA's first concern was the fair and efficient provision of food and other scarce commodities during the second world war. Its work and substantial research, and particularly that on the milk and beef industries, led to the founding of the Consumers' Association of Ireland. Its agenda soon included specifically feminist goals, as shown in the statement of objectives from its 1946 constitution:

(a) to unite housewives so that they shall recognise, and gain recognition for, their right to play an active part in all spheres of planning for the community;

(b) to secure all such reforms as are necessary to establish a real equality of liberties, status, and opportunity for all persons;

(c) the aims and general policy shall be to defend consumers' rights as they are affected by supply, distribution and price of essential commodities, to suggest legislation or take practical steps to safeguard their interests, as well as generally to deal with matters affecting the home;

(d) to take steps to defend consumers against all taxation on necessary food, fuel and clothing.[148]

The IHA also took part in the campaign to elect Hanna Sheehy Skeffington to the Dáil in 1943. In 1947 the IWCLGA merged with the IHA, thus bringing the latter into affiliation with the International Alliance of Women (IAW).

During the 1950s government attempts to claw back aspects of women's equal citizenship passed their peak. The 1956 Civil Service Commissioners Act[149] explicitly continued the marriage and sex bars. However, Irish society was about to enter a period of dramatic change, which was to have profound consequences for women and the women's movement. During the economic boom of the 1960s, the population grew and emigration trends were reversed. The proportion of women completing second-level education and going on to third-level increased. Under the influence of the second Vatican Council, Irish Catholicism was also changing. One analysis sees Irish Catholics moving away from a

> legalistic acceptance of the Church's rules and regulations to a more Protestant, do-it-yourself type of religious ethic in which they are making up their own minds about what is right and wrong.

Another suggests that 'Irish people have become more optimistic, more adventurous ... and more ready to accept criticism from themselves and from others'.[150] The link between unquestioning acceptance of Catholic Church teaching and genuine 'Irishness' was diminishing.

At the same time Irish demographic patterns began to approach the European norm. Marriage age fell, marriage rates rose, and the number of children per family dropped, while the percentage of married women in employment outside the home grew, though it remained well below the western European average. More Irish women than ever before had a direct interest in issues such as equal pay and employment for married women. The advent of the contraceptive pill, which gave women control over their fertility, prompted a new interest in birth control; this despite the fact that even after Vatican II the Catholic Church still frowned on artificial methods of contraception.

The year 1968 saw the start of a new campaign to press for full equality of citizenship. The impetus came from the international women's movement. Irish Housewives' Association delegates had attended International Alliance of Women's conferences over the years, with Hilda Tweedy serving on the IAW board from 1961 to 1964 and from 1973 to 1989. The 1961 alliance congress was held in Dublin, where the changed times found President de Valera acting as patron to the congress while Archbishop McQuaid of Dublin made the Institute of Catholic Sociology available as a venue for plenary sessions.

The IAW had developed links with the United Nations, as it had earlier with the League of Nations.[151] In 1967 the UN Commission on the Status of Women issued a directive to women's international organisations to instruct affiliated groups to examine the status of women in their own countries and, where necessary, urge governments to set up national commissions. In Ireland the Federation of Business and Professional Women's Clubs, recently established in 1965, and the IHA both received this instruction and jointly called a meeting of women's organisations in January 1968. An ad hoc committee was set up to work for a national commission. Permanent members of the committee included, besides the two aforementioned bodies, representatives of the Association of Widows in Ireland, the ICA, the Soroptimists, the two associations of women graduates, and the Women's International Zionist Organisation.

The ad hoc committee identified issues for particular attention, including equal pay for equal work, discrimination against married women in employment and taxation, and girls' education. In October 1968 a memorandum was sent to the taoiseach, Jack Lynch, and after a year's lobbying by the committee the government set up the first Commission on the Status of Women. It met in 1970 to

> examine and report on the status of women in Irish society, to make recommendations on the steps necessary to ensure the participation of women on equal terms with men in the

political, social, cultural and economic life of the country, and to indicate the implications generally – including the estimated cost – of such recommendations.

The aid hoc committee ensured that the commission would be composed of equal numbers of women and men, and chaired by a woman of the committee's choice, Dr Thekla Beere.[152]

The Commission's report, published in 1973, noted the stereotyped role that was assigned to women, and the transmission to both boys and girls in their formative years of firm views about distinct and separate roles for the sexes.[153] Girls were encouraged to think in terms of a relatively short period of gainful employment, followed by marriage and responsibilities for home care and child rearing. Yet the women workers interviewed were dissatisfied with jobs involving repetitive action and low skill levels. They wanted recognition as individual workers rather than as 'a group of women workers'.[154] The report recommended the removal of discrimination based on sex and marriage in access to employment, pay, taxation, social security and pension schemes. It advocated improved provision for deserted wives, unmarried mothers, widows and wives of prisoners. It proposed equal liability of the sexes for jury service, the appointment of more women to statutory and other bodies, coeducation and encouragement to study 'non-traditional' subjects. It advocated marriage-counselling services and family-planning advice centres that would respect the moral and personal attitudes of every married couple.

The setting up of the Commission and the publication of the report suggested a dramatic change in the attitude of Irish governments to the role of women in society. These moves, however, had largely come about through UN pressure. It did not follow that Irish governments either actively desired the proposed reforms or would take steps to put them into effect. Accordingly, in 1973 the women's organisations established the Council for the Status of Women to ensure the implementation of the report's recommendations. The Council was subsequently granted government funding and consultative status on draft legislation concerning women. By 1980 it had over thirty-five member organisations.

Even as the existing women's organisations were achieving this unprecedented public recognition, a new wave of the women's movement was appearing on the public scene in Ireland. The Irish Women's Liberation Movement (IWLM) began in 1970 with a meeting in Bewley's cafe in Westmoreland Street, Dublin, of five women who were all involved in left-wing radical activities in the 1960s. Their inspiration came from the women's liberation movement in the United States.[155] So low was the public profile of feminism in Ireland at the time that the younger women did not at first regard the longer-established women's groups as feminist, but as part of the establishment. Whereas the existing feminist organisations used a gradualist approach, operating through committees, mandated leaders, and lobbying, the women's liberation movement aimed at sweeping change by means of a non-hierarchical movement intended both to change women themselves and to jolt and shock public opinion into awareness of discrimination. The new international wave of feminism contained a number of strands, including the liberal feminist emphasis on equal rights, the 'radical' feminist insistence on the importance of sexuality, and a new socialist feminism that linked Marxism to radical feminist insights. All these strands were present in Ireland.

Three groups were prominent in the IWLM: 'political women (mainly left-wing and republican activists), women in the media, and professional/university-educated women'.[156] From the outset the movement achieved unprecedented publicity. In March 1971, *The Late Late Show*, the television series that had become compulsive viewing, devoted a whole show to 'women's lib'. This was followed in April by a public meeting that packed the Mansion House in Dublin; long queues of women formed to express their views. Then came the 'contraceptive train' in May, when a group of thirty women travelled by train to Belfast where they purchased condoms and other contraceptives and brought these back to Dublin amid maximum publicity.

The first stated objectives of the new movement were very similar to those of the longer established groups. The 1970 IWLM manifesto, *Chains or Change? The Civil Wrongs of Irish Women*, set out a number of areas of discrimination: inequities in law; the lack of equal pay for equal work; differences in the education of boys and girls which effectively closed many areas of well-paid employment to women; discrimination at work and job bars to women; inequitable treatment of widows, deserted wives, unmarried mothers and single women; laws against family planning and lack of child-care facilities, playgrounds, retraining; unfair taxation of women. These concerns were essentially the same as those addressed in the report of the first Commission on the Status of Women. Finally it pointed to the advantages of 'living in sin' as opposed to marriage: women could keep their jobs; they would not have to pay extra tax; they could retain their business identity; and they could leave a bad relationship.

As the original group expanded, internal differences emerged. Socialist women wanted 'the entire fabric of society changed from the bottom up' while others wanted piecemeal reforms. Some favoured action while others wanted discussion and consciousness-raising. Some argued for setting up a national movement immediately while others doubted the group's ability to run one. All were talking a new language, a 'language of personal political power'.[157] In an account written several years later, the point was made that

> [a] sober, sensible, structured organisation would never have given the jolt that was necessary, would never have grabbed the headlines, would never have shocked men and women into awareness of the inferior legal and social status of women. They may have disliked much of what was going on, but they could not ignore it. Most importantly, the movement provided a breeding ground for the many pressure groups which emerged throughout the seventies.[158]

Yet publicity and style by themselves could not have accounted for the impact made by women's liberation if its message had not struck a chord with many women in all parts of the country. In highlighting discrimination against women the new movement identified the individual as the central focus for change, with personal awareness leading to personal liberation and then to change in society. This appears to have been the new factor that made the message relevant to so many women in the Ireland of the 1960s and 1970s, in a way never achieved by the older established organisations. Women's consciousness-raising groups and action groups began to spring up around the country. 'The personal is political' expressed the belief that individuals' perceptions of personal oppression must be accepted as real experiences but then must be analysed and the underlying social structures changed.

Having achieved the initial response the central IWLM group faced the problem of how to proceed. Was it to be a mass movement or a small pressure group? If a mass movement, how would it be organised – indeed, should it be organised? Should it confine itself specifically to women's issues or take on others?

Under these pressures the central IWLM gradually

disintegrated, and 1975 saw the foundation of Irish Women United (IWU), another attempt to establish a nationwide women's movement. Few members of the IWLM were involved in this strongly left-wing grouping, which had links to the Movement for a Socialist Republic, the Communist Party of Ireland, an emerging gay women's movement, and the trade union movement, as well as having a strong student membership.[159] Its charter covered many of the established goals, though it expressed these in a socialist language and context. It broke new ground in sex-related areas, being more explicit with regard to contraception and adding abortion and lesbian rights to its main demands, which included the removal of all legal and bureaucratic obstacles to equality; free legal contraception, with birth-control clinics and the right to free, legal, and safe abortion; equality in education, with state-funded, secular, co-educational schools with community control, and women's studies programmes at second and third level; equal pay for equal work and a minimum wage for low-paid, mainly female jobs; state funding for women's centres; the right of all women to a self-determined sexuality. This charter is particularly interesting, since now for the first time the majority in the Irish women's movement came from Catholic backgrounds. Despite the taboos on public discussion of sex and sexuality in the Republic, and Catholic teaching that 'unnatural' birth control and single-sex relationships were sinful, these issues were now appearing in feminist manifestos. Liberation for Irish Lesbians (LIL) was founded in 1978.

Internal tensions caused IWU in its turn to fragment in 1977, even as all-Ireland feminist conferences in Belfast and Dublin and the trade union women's forum were endorsing the need for an all-Ireland women's movement. Although this was to prove elusive – and there were major difficulties in reconciling national organisation with the ideal of an unstructured mass movement – the highly publicised activities of both groups also helped the longer-established women's organisations in getting many of the recommendations of the Commission on the Status of Women put into effect. The 1970s saw growing mutual recognition and cooperation between old and new feminists with fruitful results.

The Civil Service (Employment of Married Women) Act, 1973, removed the power to bar married women from competing for appointments, and ended the requirement that women had to retire from the civil service on marriage. In a 1974 test case the Supreme Court ruled that the ban on the importation of contraceptives was illegal. In 1976 a new juries act overturned the 1927 compromise and made qualification and liability for jury service the same for both sexes. European Community membership put pressure on Irish governments to introduce equality legislation. Sex-differentiated pay scales were removed in 1973 and marriage-differentiated scales in 1974. The Anti-Discrimination (Pay) Act, 1974, brought the principles of 'equal pay for like work' and 'equal pay for work of equal value' into Irish labour law. The Employment Equality Act, 1977, prohibited discrimination on grounds of sex or marital status in recruitment, training, or provision of opportunities for promotion. The Unfair Dismissals Act, 1977, prohibited dismissal on grounds of pregnancy except in specified circumstances, and the Maternity Protection of Employees Act, 1981, introduced the right to fourteen weeks paid maternity-leave. The Health (Family Planning) Act, 1979, allowed the sale of contraceptives, but only to married couples.[160] Not until 1992 was it permissible to sell contraceptives to unmarried persons aged 17 or over.

In 1976 the Family Law (Maintenance of Spouses and Children) Act made it possible to apply to the courts for maintenance, while the Family Home Protection Act of that year provided that a spouse could not normally sell the family home without the consent of the other spouse. Within the social welfare system various differences between the treatment of women and men were removed. In addition, the Social Welfare Act, 1973, introduced an unmarried mother's allowance. The Social Welfare Act, 1974, gave the legal title to children's allowances to mothers rather than fathers, and the Social Welfare Act (no. 2) 1974, introduced an allowance for wives of prisoners.[161]

Both IWLM and IWU members contributed to the emergence of an impressive range of single-issue organisations during the 1970s. A network of self-help services developed, provided for women by women, often recruiting those who had themselves come for help. The Women's Progressive Association (1971), which became the Women's Political Association in 1973, fostered entry to public and political life. ALLY (1971) established a service for pregnant women, single or married. The following year saw the foundation of AIM for family law advice and reform; of Family Planning Services, a company providing contraceptives; and of Cherish, an organisation for single parents; and in Cork a federation of women's organisations was established. ADAPT, an association for deserted wives and husbands, came into being in 1973. Women's Aid, to help victims of domestic violence, was set up in 1974, and the Dublin Rape Crisis Centre in 1977.[162] Public attention was directed towards issues that had remained almost invisible in Irish society, including rape, incest, and family violence, and the status of single mothers. Government interest and financial support were sought. Where these were obtained, some organisations inevitably took on some of the trappings of establishment bureaucracy, a paradox that created its own problems.

Striking testimony to the developments of the decade came with the recognition by the existing political parties that there was now a women's vote that could be harnessed in support of feminist candidates. For the first time candidates with a high profile in the women's movement were selected by the main parties to stand for election to the Dáil. Graduating from the Women's Political Association, women such as Nuala Fennell, Gemma Hussey and Monica Barnes were elected in 1982 as Fine Gael TDs. Hussey was appointed Minister for Education, and Fennell Minister of State for Women's Affairs in the coalition Fine Gael-Labour government of 1982–7. The rising profile of women in public life was to be signalled dramatically in 1990 with the election of Mary Robinson, a distinguished lawyer and well-known feminist, as the first woman president of the Republic.

However, by the 1980s economic recession, rising unemployment and emigration, cutbacks in government spending, and an accompanying moral fundamentalism had created something of a backlash. This was particularly apparent in the area of sexuality, where the 1980s saw referenda in the Republic on abortion and divorce. Abortion had been a taboo subject generally in Irish society. Under the 1861 Offences Against the Person Act[163] abortion was illegal in Ireland, and the fact that some thousands of women travelled each year to Britain for abortions was quietly ignored. There had been little discussion of or support for abortion in the Irish women's movement when a small 'Women's right to choose' group emerged in 1979, aiming to decriminalise abortion and provide pregnancy-counselling services that would include information on abortion. Few Irish feminists supported abortion at all, and fewer still did so publicly. Nevertheless, a pre-emptive anti-abortion campaign was mounted by a number of conservative and religious groups and individuals. The Pro-Life Amendment

Campaign was set up in Dublin in 1981 to amend the constitution so as to render any future legalisation of abortion in Ireland unconstitutional.[164] The campaign secured the support of the leaders of the two largest political parties, Garret FitzGerald of Fine Gael and Charles Haughey of Fianna Fáil. Subsequently, in a referendum held in September 1983, the amendment, stating that the state

> acknowledges the right to life of the unborn and, with due regard to the equal right to life of the mother, guarantees in its laws to respect, and, as far as practicable, by its laws to defend and vindicate that right

was carried by a majority of 2 to 1. It thus became Article 40.3.3 of the constitution. This did not finally settle the matter; the right to disseminate literature about abortion clinics in Britain, and the right to travel outside the state to make use of abortion services were both subsequently challenged in the courts. However, a further referendum in 1992 confirmed these limited rights,[165] although an amendment providing for abortion to be carried out in Ireland where 'the life, as distinct from the health' of a pregnant woman was at risk was defeated. While there is still no universally agreed position on abortion among Irish feminists, the experience of these years has moved the focus of attention to the decision of the woman involved and away from that of religious and medical 'experts'.

In 1986 a referendum to change the constitution to permit divorce was introduced and supported by the government, by the civil libertarians and by the women's movement in general. Despite the indications of opinion polls, the proposed amendment was defeated. The reasons for defeat have been much debated. One key issue, particularly important to farming families, was family property. Moreover, separation procedures were not yet fully in place and wives remained economically vulnerable in the event of marriage breakdown. Like the 1983 abortion referendum, the 1986 divorce referendum was seen at the time as a setback for the women's movement. However, it too was to be followed by another referendum in 1995 which narrowly accepted divorce. On both abortion and divorce it is clear that Irish public opinion is becoming more complex.

The 1980s also saw further expansion and diversification in the women's movement. There was no longer any central organisation, but instead a diverse and widely spread movement. One development was the emergence of Women's Studies, which began to produce a growing body of analysis and research within and across the established disciplines. Feminist publishing houses played an important part, with Arlen House emerging first in 1975, followed in 1978 by Irish Feminist Information, which became Attic Press in 1984. From this period on, Women's Studies was to develop in a plethora of forms and locations, from community or locally based women's educational projects, to university courses at different levels.

The development of Women's Studies interacted with the emergence of working-class women's groups, the successors to the largely middle-class women's consciousness-raising groups of the 1970s and early 1980s. The new working-class groups were locally based, and have generally been described as community groups. This development was one that many believed to have the potential to bring about effective change in society. For the first time Irish working-class women in substantial numbers became active feminists and began to speak and write for themselves, some challenging the established feminist agenda on the grounds that for the most part it benefited only middle-class women. This was one facet of the new leadership role being taken by women in community activity generally, and particularly in the poorer housing estates.

The 1980s also witnessed 'an unprecedented blossoming of cultural expression by women'.[166] One sign of this was seen when the Third International Interdisciplinary Congress on Women (held in Dublin in 1987) included, side by side with the usual programme of academic papers, a major festival of art and music. These developments have sparked off more debate as to the meaning, validity and value of concepts such as 'women's art' and 'women's writing'.

Nor were the churches immune from the effects of feminism. In the Catholic Church the consciousness-raising of the new wave of feminism met the new 'release of spiritual energies among priests, laity, and religious women and men' sparked off by the second Vatican council in the 1960s.[167] Sexist language in the liturgy, the absence of women from decision-making roles in the church, and traditional stereotypes of female conduct all came in for scrutiny. In a departure from their traditional role, nuns have been very much to the fore in these challenges. Prominent also have been a small but growing number of lay female theologians. In the Protestant Churches, where the role of the laity of both sexes was afforded greater recognition from the Reformation onwards, the feminist challenge was not quite so searching, but in the Church of Ireland women's ordination became an important issue, and was adopted in 1990, some years ahead of the Church of England. Women's ordination also began to be debated in some Catholic circles.

In Northern Ireland the position of women differed in some ways from that of women in the Republic, although it was not necessarily the same as that in Great

Britain. Marriage bars in the civil service, teaching, and the banks, though removed in the late 1960s (some years earlier than in the south), contributed to the difference between the 29 per cent of married women 'economically active' in Northern Ireland (1971 figures) compared with 42 per cent in Great Britain, and only 8 per cent in the Republic (1970 figures). Family planning and contraceptives were free, as in Britain, but not easily accessible for rural and working-class women; and for some women ecclesiastical opposition was a problem. The average number of children per family has been 2.2 since 1983, and Catholic families remain larger than Protestant families, although these differences are declining.[168] Not all UK legislation was extended to Northern Ireland. Exceptions included abortion, and Northern Ireland women, as well as their counterparts in the south, travelled to Britain for abortions.

In Northern Ireland the new wave of the women's movement emerged against the background of the civil rights movement of the 1960s, and developed during the years of conflict that followed. Divided loyalties and pressure not to be seen to criticise the men on one's own side made feminist assertion particularly difficult. The main churches and political parties in Northern Ireland all tended to be conservative and patriarchal in their attitudes to women, although the Unionist Party of Northern Ireland was the first party in Ireland to elect a woman, Anne Dickson, as its leader, in September 1976. Participation in the political developments of the 1960s and early 1970s, first in housing allocation campaigns and then in the civil rights movement, brought many women to feminist awareness.[169] In both these movements women played a more central role than has generally been acknowledged:

the combination of the civil rights movement, the street politics, and the more local community development campaigns all helped to develop the political acumen so necessary for these early feminist groups.[170]

Inevitably, most, though by no means all, of the early activists were drawn from the Catholic community; in general Protestant women did not have the same incentives to challenge the status quo.

The early 1970s saw scattered individual groups emerge, followed after 1975 by more vigorous growth, debate, and argument, and more contact between groups in Northern Ireland and those in the Republic. The Northern Ireland Women's Rights Movement (NIWRM) was founded in 1975 to ensure that new UK sex discrimination legislation[171] was extended to Northern Ireland. This objective was achieved in 1976. The NIWRM drew up a charter of women's demands, and aimed to coordinate a wide range of organisations. Perhaps because of its conventional structure (unlike the women's collectives, it had a constitution and a committee) it survived despite internal tensions. From it several groups broke away, including the Socialist Women's Group (SWG) and the Women's Aid groups. The former flourished in the late 1970s and was committed to a socialist republic as a prerequisite for the success of feminism, and to putting feminism on the agenda of the left. Women's Aid groups had developed in Belfast, Coleraine, and Derry in the 1970s, and elsewhere, including Newry, North Down, and Omagh in the 1980s. A Northern Ireland Women's Aid Federation was set up in 1977. Such groups drew attention to the incidence of domestic violence against women. This problem cut across political allegiances and was exacerbated in Northern Ireland by the number of weapons held, legitimately or illegitimately, by men. In 1976 a Women's Law and Research Group was established from a number of existing groups to research and campaign on legislation affecting women. Also during the 1970s lesbian groups became better organised; a lesbian helpline was established in 1978.[172]

Within the nationalist tradition there were other problems and divisions. The old question of the primacy of the national struggle or the rights of women re-emerged. The Belfast Women's Collective (1977–80) registered its opposition to imperialism but stopped short of supporting the republican movement, while Women Against Imperialism (1978–81) put the republican programme at the top of its agenda. For some nationalist women the treatment of republican women prisoners in Armagh Prison, and particularly strip-searching, was primarily a feminist issue; for other feminists it was essentially a republican issue.

A women-led initiative to end political conflict, known as the 'Peace Women', later the 'Peace People', emerged in 1976 and attracted huge support across the religious and political divide, leading at the end of the year to the award in Oslo of the 'people's peace prize' to its leaders, Mairead Corrigan, Betty Williams, and Ciarán McKeown. Women's groups were initially enthusiastic, but later became more critical. The movement subsequently declined in numbers and influence, amid internal and external disagreements over its definition of violence and understanding of precisely what constituted 'peace'.

During the 1980s efforts continued to turn the spotlight on issues of primary concern to women. The Northern Ireland Abortion Campaign (NIAC) was set up in 1980, and the issue was taken over by the Northern Ireland Association for Law Reform on Abortion (NIALRA) from 1984. The Belfast Rape Crisis Centre was set up in 1982, followed by the Northern

Ireland Rape Crisis Association. And 1984 saw the appearance of the *Women's News*, a newspaper designed for women.[173]

The 1980s also saw what has been described as 'feminist activism as an agent of change'. This involved campaigning to include gender inequality and women's concerns in all discussions of solutions to the problems of Northern Ireland, and continuing efforts to build a feminist movement that crossed political, religious, and class divides. This has been particularly apparent in the participation of working-class women, a strong element in the Northern Ireland women's movement from the start. The early prominence of women in tenant and community organisations led to a vigorous growth of locally based women's groups, and active participation in such organisations and networks as the Women's Information Group (1980) and the Women's Resource and Development Agency (1983).[174] The greater involvement of Protestant women has been a feature in recent years, and increasingly community women's groups from both sides of the political divide have been meeting each other with the aim of understanding and coming to terms with difference. From the 1980s on there have also been renewed efforts to bring feminists, north and south, together. There appears now to be greater recognition of the fact that diversity of interests and identities are realities that have to be faced; and that there is a common interest in insisting that feminist perspectives and concerns are present when future political, social, and economic directions in both parts of Ireland are under discussion.

The dramatic changes that have taken place in the status and role of women in Ireland since the mid nineteenth century are clearly part of an international movement that has in some respects carried women far beyond the aims of most early campaigners for women's emancipation – even if some visions have yet to be realised. As this survey has shown, Irish women played a full part in promoting reform in Ireland, at times contributed to reform in the United Kingdom, and took part in international organisations. Future objectives and strategies have to be devised in the context of contemporary political, social, and economic structures: generations of women are growing up who have little acquaintance with the struggles of the past. As feminists in Ireland, both north and south, face into the twenty-first century, there is a growing perception of the need for a forum for debate about the nature, the meaning, and the future directions of feminism itself.

from J.R. Hill (ed.), *Ireland, 1921–84: A New History of Ireland, Vol VII* (Oxford, 2003), pp 826–91.

NOTES

1   Jane Rendall, *The Origins of Modern Feminism: women in Britain, France and the United States, 1780–1860* (London, 1985), p. 4.

2   William Thompson, *Appeal of One-Half of the Human Race, Women, against the Pretensions of the Other Half, Men, to Retain them in Political, and thence in Civil and Domestic Slavery* (London, 1983, first published 1825). In the 'Introductory Letter' to Anna Wheeler, Thompson regrets that she, the source of its ideas, did not write the book herself, and adds that a 'few only words therefore of the following pages are the exclusive product of your mind and pen, and written with your own hand. The reminder are our joint property, I being your interpreter and the scribe of your sentiments'. (p. xxiii).

3   Friedrich Engels, *The Origin of the Family, Private Property and the State* (Harmondsworth, 1985), ch. 2.

4   See Maria Luddy, *Women and Philanthropy in Nineteenth-Century Ireland* (Cambridge, 1995), for a comprehensive coverage.

5   The American Quaker feminist, Lucretia Mott, travelled to Ireland immediately after attending the London convention and visited Quaker communities in Dublin and Belfast.

6   In English, the term 'feminism', meaning support for the emancipation of women, first came into use, following French usage, in the 1890s; see *O.E.D.*, and Karen Offen, 'Defining Feminism; a comparative historical approach', in *Signs: Journal of Women in Culture and Society*, xiv, no. 1 (1988), pp 119–57: 126.

7   See David Hempton and Myrtle Hill, 'Women and Protestant minorities in eighteenth-century Ireland', in Margaret Mac Curtain and Mary O'Dowd (eds), *Women in Early Modern Ireland* (Dublin, 1991), pp 197–211.

8   Tony Fahey, 'Nuns in the Catholic Church in Ireland in the nineteenth century' in Mary Cullen (ed.) *Girls Don't Do Honours: Irish Women in Education in the Nineteenth and Twentieth Centuries* (Dublin, 1987), pp 7–30. The term 'nun' strictly applies to members of religious orders with solemn vows. Many Irish women religious belonged to congregations with simple vows.

9   Jacinta Prunty, *Margaret Alyward 1810–1889, Lady of Charity, Sister of Faith* (Dublin, 1996).

10 See Mary Peckham, 'Catholic Female Congregations and Religious Change in Ireland, 1770–1870' (Ph.D thesis, University of Wisconsin-Madison, 1993); Maria Luddy, 'Prostitution and Rescue Work in nineteenth-century Ireland', in Maria Luddy and Cliona Murphy (eds), *Women Surviving: Studies in Irish Women's History in the 19th and 20th centuries* (Dublin, 1989), pp 51–84.

11 See Caitriona Clear, *Nuns in Nineteenth-Century Ireland* (Dublin, 1987), 'Walls Within Walls: nuns in nineteenth-century Ireland' in Chris Curtin, Pauline Jackson and Barbara O'Connor (eds), *Gender in Irish Society* (Galway, 1987), pp 135–71; 'The Limits of Female Autonomy; nuns in nineteenth-century Ireland' in Luddy and Murphy, *Women Surviving*, pp 15–50; Tony Fahey, 'Female Asceticism in the Catholic Church: a case study of nuns in nineteenth-century Ireland' (Ph.D thesis, University of Illinois, 1981): 'Nuns in the Catholic Church'.

12 Margaret Anna Cusack (Sr M. Francis Clare), *Women's Work in Modern Society* (Kenmare, 1874), p. 11 and Appendix.

13 Pekham, 'Catholic Female Congregations'; Séamus Enright, unpublished research. See also Fahey, 'Nuns in the Catholic Church', pp 21–2.

14 Mary Cullen, 'Anna Maria Haslam', in Mary Cullen and Maria Luddy (eds), *Women, Power and Consciousness in Nineteenth-Century Ireland: Eight Biographical Studies* (Dublin, 1995), pp 161–96.

15 Maria Luddy, 'Isabella M.S. Tod', *ibid*, pp 197–230.

16 *Special Report from the Select Committee on the Married Women's Property Bill* [4417], H.C. 1867–8, cccxxxix, 74–5.

17 Lee Holcombe, *Wives and Property: Reform of the Married Women's Property Law in Nineteenth-Century England* (Oxford, 1983), p. 242.

18 33 & 34 Vict., c. 93 (9 Aug. 1870); 37 & 38 Vict., c. 50 (30 July 1874); 45 & 46 Vict., c. 75 (18 Aug. 1882); 7 Edw. Vll, c. 18 (21 Aug. 1907).

19 See Luddy, 'Prostitution and Rescue Work', p. 69; 'Women and the Contagious Diseases Acts, 1864–1886' in *History Ireland*, 1, no 1 (Spring 1991), pp 32–4.

20 Evidence of Josephine Butler, *Report of the Royal Commission upon the Administration and Operation of the Contagious Diseases Acts*, vol. II, Minutes of Evidence, p. 440, H.C. 1871 (408–1), xix).

21 Interview with Francis Sheehy Skeffington in *Irish Citizen*, 21 Mar. 1914, p. 347.

22 *Census Ireland, 1871*, pt. iii, General Report, p. 176 [C 1377], H.C. 1876, lxxxi.

23 See Éibhlín Breathnach, 'Women and Higher Education in Ireland (1870–1914) in *Crane Bag*, iv, no. 1 (1980), pp 47–54; 'Charting New Waters: women's experience in higher education, 1879–1908', in Cullen, *Girls Don't Do Honours*, pp 55–78; Anne V. O'Connor, 'The Revolution in Girls' Secondary Education in Ireland 1860–1910', *ibid*, pp 31–54; 'Anne Jellicoe' in Cullen and Luddy, *Women, Power and Consciousness*, pp 125–60; Anne V. O'Connor and Susan M. Parkes, *Gladly Learn and Gladly Teach: Alexandra College and School 1866–1966* (Tallaght, 1984).

24 Jellicoe's first aim had been to improve the employment of poorer women, but it appears that her colleagues, who saw the education of middle-class women as the first priority, carried the day.

25 O'Connor and Parkes, *Gladly Learn*, p. 7.

26 O'Connor, 'The Revolution in Girls' Secondary Education', p. 35.

27 41 & 42 Vict., c. 66 (16 Aug. 1878); 42 & 43 Vict., c. 65 (Aug. 1879).

28 O'Connor, 'The Revolution in Girls' Secondary Education', pp 42–4, 48.

29 Breathnach, 'Charting New Waters', pp 58–62.

30 *Ibid*, pp 68–9.

31 *New History of Ireland*, vi, 565–6.

32 Breathnach, 'Charting New Waters', p. 71. See Susan M. Parkes, 'Higher Education, 1793–1908', in W.E. Vaughan (ed.), *A New History of Ireland* vi (OUP 1996), pp 565–6.

33 8 Edw. V11, c. 38 (1 Aug. 1908).

34 21 & 22 Vict., c. 90 (2 Aug. 1858); 39 & 40 Vict., c. 41 (11 Aug. 1876).

35 'The Close of a Long Struggle', *Englishwoman's Review*, viii (15 Apr. 1877), pp 150–51; J.D.H. Widdess, *A History of the Royal College of Physicians of Ireland 1654–1963* (Edinburgh and London, 1963), pp 210–11.

36 See p. 325.

37 For the suffrage movement see Rosemary Cullen Owens, *Smashing Times: A History of the Irish Women's Suffrage Movement 1889–1922* (Dublin, 1984); Cliona Murphy, *The Women's Suffrage Movement and Irish Society in the Early Twentieth Century* (New York, 1989).

38 2 & 3 Will. IV, c. 88 (7 Aug. 1832).

39 30 & 31 Vict. c. 102 (15 Aug. 1867).

40 Anna Haslam, 'Irishwomen and the Local Government Act' in *Englishwoman's Review*, xxix, 15 Oct. 1898, p. 224; Cullen Owens, *Smashing Times*, p. 25.

41 48 Vict., c. 3 (6 Dec. 1884).

42 For the Ladies' Land League see Anna Parnell, *The Tale of a Great Sham*, edited with an introduction by Dana Hearne (Dublin, 1986). The author made unsuccessful efforts to have this account (written in 1907) published in her lifetime. *The Tale* is a scathing criticism of the Land League leaders and Land League policy. See also T.W. Moody, 'Anna Parnell and the Land League' in *Hermathena*, cxvii (1974), pp 5–17: Margaret Ward, *Unmanageable Revolutionaries: Women and Irish Nationalism* (Dingle and London, 1983); Jane McL. Côté, *Fanny*

and Anna Parnell: Ireland's Patriot Sisters (Dublin, 1991), Dana Hearne and Jane McL. Côté, 'Anna Parnell', in Cullen and Luddy, *Women, Power and Consciousness*, pp 263–288.

43 Patrick Buckland, *Irish Unionism: One. The Anglo-Irish and the New Ireland 1885–1922* (Dublin and New York, 1972), p. 150: Maria Luddy, 'Women and Politics in Nineteenth-Century Ireland' in Maryann G. Valiulis and Mary O'Dowd (eds), *Women and Irish History* (Dublin, 1997), pp 104–5.

44 Janet K. TeBrake, 'Irish Peasant Women in Revolt: the Land League years' in *Irish Historical Studies*, xxviii, no. 109 (May 1992), pp 63–80.

45 Parnell, *Tale of a Great Sham*, pp 16, 155.

46 T.W. Moody, *Davitt and the Irish Revolution 1846–82* (Oxford, 1981), pp 532, 545; Hearne and McL. Côté, 'Anna Parnell', pp 283–4.

47 Côté, Fanny and Anna Parnell', pp 169–70.

48 Haslam, 'Irishwomen and the Local Government Act', p. 221.

49 59 Vict., c. 5 (Mar. 1896).

50 Local Government (Ireland) Act, 61 & 62 Vict., c. 37 (12 Aug. 1898); Haslam, 'Irishwomen and the Local Government Act', pp 223–5.

51 David Fitzpatrick, '"A Share of the Honeycomb": education, emigration, and Irishwomen' in Mary Daly and David Dickson (eds), *The Origins of Popular Literacy in Ireland: Language Change and Educational Development 1700–1920* (Dublin, 1990), pp 167–87: 169.

52 For the history of nursing see Pauline Scanlon, *The Irish Nurse: A Study of Nursing in Ireland: History and Education 1718–1981* (Manorhamilton, 1991).

53 For Inghinidhe na hÉireann see Ward, *Unmanageable Revolutionaries*, pp 40–87.

54 Maud Gonne (1866–1953), daughter of an English army officer, became a convert to Irish nationalism. She had the self-confidence to seek entry to organisations such as the Irish National League, and on finding women excluded, she and others established their own.

55 Ward, *Unmanageable Revolutionaries*, p. 51.

56 Its editor Helena Molony, quoted in Cullen Owens, *Smashing Times*, pp 45–6.

57 The name 'Sinn Féin' was devised by a woman, Máire Butler, in 1905.

58   Muriel Gahan, 'Bantracht na Tuaithe 1910–1970' in *Irish Countrywomen: The Journal of Bantracht na Tuaithe* (Dec. 1970, p. 24; Sarah McNamara, *Those Intrepid United Irishwomen: Pioneers of the Irish Countrywomen's Association* (Limerick 1995).

59   Ellice Pilkington, 'The United Irishwomen – their work' in Horace Plunkett, Ellice Pilkington and George Russell, *The United Irishwomen: Their Place, Work and Ideals* (Dublin, 1911), pp 19–31: 33.

60   Hanna Sheehy Skeffington (1877–1946) came from a Dublin Catholic nationalist family. Her father, David Sheehy, was nationalist MP for Galway South (1885–1900) and Meath South (1902–18). An MA of the Royal University and founder of the Irish Association of Women Graduates (1902), she had argued for co-educational colleges in the new university system. She and husband, Francis Skeffington, both socialists, feminists and pacifists, adopted the joint name Sheehy Skeffington. See Leah Levenson and Jerry Natterstad, *Hanna Sheehy Skeffington: Irish Feminist* (Syracuse, 1986); Maria Luddy, *Hanna Sheehy Skeffington* (Dublin, 1995); Margaret Ward, *Hanna Sheehy Skeffington: A Life* (Cork, 1997).

61   Margaret Gillespie (1878–1954) came from a Protestant unionist family in Roscommon, but both she and her husband, James Cousins of Belfast, were nationalists. They both converted to theosophy and emigrated to India in 1915, where Margaret Cousins became a pioneer in the Indian women's movement. See J.H. Cousins and M.E. Cousins, *We Two Together* (Madras, 1950).

62   *Ibid*, p. 164.

63   Dana Hearne, 'The Development of Irish Feminist Thought: a critical analysis of *The Irish Citizen* 1912–1920' (Ph.D. Thesis, York University, Ontario, 1992).

64   *Irish Citizen*, 25 May 1912, p. 7.

65   Cullen Owens, *Smashing Times*, p. 43.

66   Margaret Ward, 'Conflicting Interests: the British and Irish suffrage movements', in *Feminist Review*, 1 (Summer 1995), p. 132.

67   *Bean na hÉireann*, 1, no. 13 (Nov. 1910), p. 6.

68   Diane Urquhart, '"The Female of the Species is Deadlier than the Male"? The Ulster Women's Unionist Council, 1911–1940' in Janice Holmes and Diane Urquhart (eds), *Coming Into The*

Light: The Work, Politics and Religion of Women in Ulster 1840–1940 (Belfast, 1994), pp 93–123: 97, 102.

69   Hanna Sheehy Skeffington, 'Reminiscences of an Irish suffragette' (1941) in Andreé Sheehy Skeffington and Rosemary Owens (eds), *Votes for Women: Irish Women's Struggle for the Vote* (Dublin, 1975), p. 13.

70   Cullen Owens, *Smashing Times*, p. 53.

71   Murphy, *Women's Suffrage Movement*, ch. 5: Sheehy Skeffington, 'Reminiscences', pp 20–21.

72   Cullen Owens, *Smashing Times*, pp 70–71.

73   Richard J. Evans, *The Feminists: Women's Emancipation Movements in Europe, America and Australasia, 1840–1920* (London and New York, 1977), p. 160.

74   Peter Berresford Ellis, *A History of the Irish Working Class* (London, 1972), p. 173; Levenson and Natterstad, *Hanna Sheehy Skeffington*, pp 51–2.

75   See Theresa Moriarty, *Work in Progress: Episodes from the history of Irish women's trade unionism* (Dublin and Belfast, 1994).

76   Mary Jones, *These Obstreperous Lassies: A History of the Irish Women Workers' Union* (Dublin, 1988), p. 3.

77   Helena Molony (1885–1967), nationalist, feminist and Abbey Theatre actress, devoted most of her life to the union. Sent to prison in 1911 for throwing a stone at a shop window during protests at the state visit of George V, she was imprisoned again for her part in the 1916 rising, and from prison persuaded her friend Louie Bennett to take over the leadership of the IWWU.

78   Louie Bennett (1870–1956) came from a Protestant, unionist, middle-class Dublin family. She became a feminist, pacifist, and a campaigner for social and economic justice, with a commitment to Irish nationalist objectives, though opposing the use of physical force. She founded the Irish Women's Reform League (IWRL) in 1911 and was involved in setting up the Irish Women's Suffrage Federation (IWSF). Like Molony, she devoted her life to the IWWU. In 1931 she became the first woman president of the Irish Congress of Trade Unions.

79   Cullen Owens, *Smashing Times*, p. 92.

80   Urquhart, '"The Female of the Species"', pp 100, 102: Luddy, 'Women and Politics in nineteenth-century Ireland', p. 105.

81   Ward, *Unmanageable Revolutionaries*, p. 93.

82 John C. Gordon and Ishbel M. Gordon, *'We Twa': Reminiscences of Lord and Lady Aberdeen* (2 vols, London, 1925) ii, 230.

83 Arnold Whittick, *Woman Into Citizen* (London, 1979), pp 22–32, 51.

84 Rosemary Cullen Owens, 'Women and Pacifism in Ireland, 1915–1932', in Valiulis and O'Dowd, *Women and Irish History*, pp 220–1.

85 Jill Liddington, *The Long Road to Greenham: Feminism and Antimilitarism in Britain since 1820* (London, 1989), p. 106.

86 Cullen Owens, 'Women and Pacifism in Ireland', pp 224, 227.

87 R.M. Fox, *Rebel Irishwomen* (Dublin, 1967: first published 1935), p. 75.

88 Kathleen Clarke, *Revolutionary Woman: Kathleen Clarke 1878–1972, an autobiography* (Dublin, 1991), p. 69.

89 Fox, *Rebel Irishwomen*, p. 76.

90 Ward, *Unmanageable Revolutionaries*, pp 108–14; Ruth Taillon, *When History Was Made: The Women of 1916* (Belfast, 1996).

91 Beth McKillen, 'Irish Feminism and Nationalist Separatism, 1914–1923' in *Éire-Ireland*, xvii (1982), no. 3, pp 61–7: no. 4, pp 72–7.

92 5 Geo. V, c. 8 (27 Nov. 1914).

93 7 & 8 Geo. V, c. 64 (6 Feb. 1918).

94 8 & 9 Geo. V, c. 47 (21 Nov. 1918).

95 Meeting, 12 November 1918, *Reports of the Irish Women's Suffrage and Local Government Association 1896–1918* (Dublin, 1919), pp 8–9.

96 *Irish Citizen* (April 1919), p. 656.

97 Urquhart, '"The Female of the Species"', pp 104–7.

98 Clarke, *Revolutionary Woman*, pp 170, 176.

99 Marie O'Neill, *From Parnell to de Valera: A Biography of Jennie Wyse Power 1858–1941* (Dublin, 1991), p. 119.

100 Tom Barry, quoted in Ward, *Unmanageable Revolutionaries*, p. 144.

101 *Irish Citizen* (September-December 1920), p.2.

102 Ward, *Hanna Sheehy Skeffington*, p. 238.

103 9 & 10 Geo. V, c. 71 (23 Dec. 1919).

104 See Liam O'Dowd, 'Church, State and Women: the aftermath of partition', in Curtin, Jackson and O'Connor, *Gender in Irish Society*, pp 3–36.

105 Mary E. Daly, 'Women in the Irish Workforce from Pre-industrial to Modern Times', in *Saothar*, vii (1981), pp 72–82: 77.

106 O'Dowd, 'Church, State and Women', p. 22.

107 Frances Gardiner, 'Political Interest and Participation of Irish Women 1922–1992: the unfinished revolution', in *Canadian Journal of Irish Studies*, xviii, no. 1 (July 1992), p. 18.

108 See Clarke, *Revolutionary Woman*; O'Neill, *From Parnell to de Valera: Jennie Wyse Power*.

109 Maurice Manning, 'Women in Irish national and local politics 1922–77', in Margaret Mac Curtain and Donncha Ó Corráin, (eds), *Women in Irish Society: the Historical Dimension* (Dublin, 1978), pp 92–102: 96. Manning noted that most male TDs also kept to the party line.

110 Mary Clancy, 'Aspects of women's contribution to the oireachtas debate in the Irish Free State, 1922–1937' in Luddy and Murphy, *Women Surviving*, pp 206–32: 209–10.

111 Ward, *Unmanageable Revolutionaries*, pp 171–200.

112 Cullen Owens, 'Women and Pacifism', pp 231–7.

113 Maryann G. Valiulis, 'Engendering Citizenship: women's relationship to the state in Ireland and the United States in the post-suffrage period' in Valiulis and O'Dowd (eds), *Women and Irish History*, pp 159–72: 160; Caitriona Beaumont, 'Women and the Politics of Equality: the Irish women's movement, 1930–1943', *ibid.*, pp 173–88: 175–6.

114 It is not clear precisely when these associations became affiliates, but they were listed as such in the National Council's submission to the Commission on Vocational Organisation in 1940.

115 See Clancy, 'Aspects of women's contribution'; Caitriona Beaumont, 'Irish women and the politics of equality in the 1930s' in *Pheobe*, iii, no. 1 (Spring 1991), pp 26–31: 'Women and the politics of equality': Maryann G. Valiulis, 'Defining their role in the new state: Irishwomen's protest against the juries act of 1927' in *Canadian Journal of Irish Studies*, xviii, no. 1 (July 1992), pp 43–60: 'Power, gender and identity in the Irish Free State', in *Journal of Women's History*, vi, no.4/vii, no. 1 (Winter/Spring 1995), pp 117–36; Gardiner, 'Political interest and participation of Irish women'.

116 Valiulis, 'Defining their role', p.43.

117 Quoted in Clancy, 'Aspects of women's contribution', p. 221.

118 1924/18 (23 May 1924).

119 Quoted in Valiulis, 'Defining their role', p. 45.

120 1927/23 (26 May 1927).

121 1926/41 (22 Sept. 1926).

122 1924/5 (21 Mar, 1924).

123 Speech of 17 December 1925, quoted in Clancy, 'Aspects of women's contribution', p. 218.

124 20 & 21 Vict., c. 85 (28 Aug. 1857).

125 Daisy Lawrenson Swanton, *Emerging from the Shadow: The Lives of Sarah Anne Lawrenson and Lucy Olive Kingston Based on Personal Diaries, 1883–1969* (Dublin, 1994), p. 97.

126 1929/21 (16 July 1929).

127 Clancy, 'Aspects of women's contribution', p. 212 and n. 25; Swanton, *Emerging from the Shadow*, pp 107–13. Kingston noted that at WILPF meetings there was 'almost unanimity in resolution to take part in future conferences and appoint commission on subject' (ibid., p. 109).

128 T.J. O'Connell, *History of the Irish National Teachers' Organisation 1868–1968* (Dublin, 1968), p. 281.

129 1935/6 (28 Feb. 1935).

130 Clancy, 'Aspects of women's contribution', pp 212–15: *Seanad Éireann deb.*, xix, 793–8, 1247 (12 Dec. 1934, 6 Feb. 1935).

131 Clancy, 'Aspects of women's contribution', p. 216. See also Hilda Tweedy, *A Link in the Chain: The Story of the Irish Housewives Association 1942–1992* (Dublin, 1992).

132 Michael G, Broderick, 'Women and Bunreacht na hÉireann: Aspects of the Debate in May and June 1937' (M.Phil thesis, TCD, 1994), app A, P. 82.

133 Swanton, *Emerging from the Shadow*, pp 124–5.

134 Clancy, 'Aspects of women's contribution', pp 220–21.

135 Jones, *These Obstreperous Lassies*, pp 127–30.

136 1936/2 (14 Feb. 1936).

137 For discussion of some of these issues see Mary E. Daly, 'Women, Work and Trade Unionism in Ireland', in Mac Curtain and Ó Corráin (eds), *Women in Irish Society*, pp, 71–81; Ellen Hazelkorn, 'The Social and Political Views of Louie Bennett 1870–1956' in *Saothar*, xiii (1988), pp 32–44; Jones, *These Obstreperous Lassies*.

138 *Bunreacht na hÉireann* (dréacht) (Dublin 1937).

139 For the feminist response to the draft constitution see Broderick, 'Women and Bunreacht na hÉireann', ch. 5; Beaumont, 'Women and the politics of equality'.

140 *Irish Independent*, 11 May 1937, quoted in Broderick, 'Women and Bunreacht na hÉireann', p. 28.

141 *Ibid.*, pp 32, 36–7.

142 *Ibid.*, ch. 7; Jones, *These Obstreperous Lassies*, p. 142; Clancy, 'Aspects of women's contribution', p. 224.

143 Beaumont, 'Irish Women and the politics of equality', pp 27–9.

144 O'Connell, *History of the Irish National Teachers Organisation*, pp 284–5.

145 *Minutes of Evidence to the Commission on Vocational Organisation*, 12 Dec. 1940 (NLI MS 930, xi, 3065–80). See also Caitriona Clear, '"The women cannot be blamed": the Commission on Vocational Organisation, feminism and "home-makers" in independent Ireland in the 1930s and 1940s' in Mary O'Dowd and Sabine Wichert (eds), *Chattel, Servant or Citizen: Women's Status in Church, State and Society* (Belfast, 1995), pp 179–86.

146 Gahan, 'Bantracht na Tuaithe', pp 21–8

147 *Ibid.*

148 See Tweedy, *A Link in the Chain*, p. 18.

149 1956/45 (19 Dec. 1956)

150 Tom Inglis, *Moral Monopoly: The Catholic Church in Modern Irish Society* (Dublin, 1987), p. 225: J.H. Whyte, *Church and State in Modern Ireland 1923–1979* (Dublin, 1980), p. 357.

151 Whittick, *Woman into Citizen*, p. 167.

152 Tweedy, *A Link in the Chain*, pp 35–47. Thekla Beere was the first woman secretary of an Irish government department.

153 *Commission on the Status of Women, Report* (Prl 2760) (Dublin, 1973).

154 Eunice McCarthy, 'Women and work in Ireland: the present, and preparing for the future', In Mac Curtain and Ó Corráin, *Women in Irish Society*, pp 103–171: 107–8.

155 June Levine, *Sisters: the Personal Story of an Irish Feminist* (Swords, 1982), p.139.

156 Linda Connolly, 'The women's movement in Ireland 1970–1995: a social movements analysis' in *Irish Journal of Feminist Studies*, i., no. 1 (Mar. 1996) pp 43–77. For a contemporary assessment see Catherine Rose, *The Female Experience: the Story of the Woman Movement in Ireland* (Galway, 1975).

157 Levine, *Sisters*, p. 143.

158 Office of the Minister of State for Women's Affairs, *Irishwomen into Focus 1: the Road to Equal Opportunity: a Narrative History* (Dublin [1987]), p. 11.

159 Connolly, 'The women's movement in Ireland', pp 53–62.

160 Second Commission on the Status of Women, *Report to Government*, January 1993 (Pl 9557) (Dublin, 1993), pp 363–90: 1973/17 (31 July 1973); 1976/4 (2 Mar. 1976); 1974/15 (1 July 1974); 1977/16 (11 June 1977); 1977/10 (6 Apr. 1977), sect. 6: 2 (f); 1981/2 (26 Mar. 1981); 1979/20 (23 July 1979).

161 1976/11 (6 Apr. 1976); 1976/27 (12 July 1976); 1973/10 (27 June 1973); 1974/12 (12 June 1974); 1974/14 (27 June 1974).

162 Office of the Minister of State for Women's Affairs, *Irishwomen into Focus 1*, pp 17–21.

163 24 & 25 Vict., c.100 (6 Aug. 1861), sects. 58–9.

164 See Emily O'Reilly, *Masterminds of the Right* (Dublin, 1992).

165 Eighth Amendment of the Constitution Act (7 Oct. 1983); Thirteenth Amendment (23 Dec. 1992); Fourteenth Amendment (23 Dec. 1992).

166 Ailbhe Smyth, 'The women's movement in the Republic of Ireland 1970–1990' in Ailbhe Smyth (ed.), *Irish Women's Studies Reader* (Dublin, 1993), pp 245–69: 250.

167 See Margaret Mac Curtain, 'Moving statues and Irish women' in Smyth, *Irish Women Studies Reader*, pp 203–13.

168 J.J. Sexton, 'Emigration and immigration in the twentieth century: an overview', in J.R. Hill (ed.), *A New History of Ireland: VII, Ireland 1921–1984* (Oxford, 2003), pp 796–825: 806–7.

169 Eilish Rooney, 'Political divisions, practical alliance: problems for women in conflict' in *Journal of Women's History*, vi, no. 4 (Winter/Spring 1995), pp 40–48: 41–2. For a personal story of one woman's experience see Margaret Ward, 'From civil rights to women's rights' in Michael Farrell (ed.), *Twenty Years On* (Dingle, 1988), pp 122–33.

170 See Catherine B. Shannon, 'Women in Northern Ireland' in O'Dowd and Wichert, *Chattel, Servant or Citizen*, pp 238–47; Monica McWilliams, 'Struggling for peace and justice: reflections on women's activism in Northern Ireland' in *Journal of Women's History*, vi, no. 4 (Winter/Spring 1995), p. 25.

171 Sex Discrimination Act (UK), 1975 (12 Nov. 1975, c. 65)

172 Eileen Evason, *Against the Grain: The Contemporary Women's Movement in Northern Ireland* (Dublin, 1991), pp 16–36.

173 *Ibid*, pp 36–35.

174 McWilliams, 'Struggling for peace and justice', pp 29–30.

FEMINISM, CITIZENSHIP AND SUFFRAGE:
A LONG DIALOGUE

As the volume of publication in women's history in Ireland expanded rapidly, Louise Ryan and Margaret Ward brought together two collections on women's activism in Ireland, the first in relation to nationalism and the second to suffrage. I was increasingly interested in the relationship of feminism and political thought and found the work of the political scientist Iseult Honohan on the long tradition of civic republicanism enlightening. Basic elements of the republican concept of citizenship could be clearly identified in the aims and arguments of Irish women's emancipation activists of the second half of the nineteenth century. These women were unionist in political sympathy and belonged to different Protestant denominations. None spoke of republicanism or of herself as a republican. Leaders like Anna Haslam and Isabella Tod were committed Liberals. Yet the idea of citizens, individually self-determining and free from domination, responsible for their own lives and committed to working with other citizens to achieve the common good, permeated their work and thinking. This demonstrated the patterns of continuity and change in the development of political thought. Also, it became clear that feminists did not just draw on existing ideologies and political languages. Like others, they selected from the current stock of ideas those elements relevant to the questions they asked in their specific historical location, used and modified these and themselves added new ideas to the common stock. This essay was published in Irish Women and the Vote: Becoming Citizens *in 2007.*

Introduction

Organised action by Irish feminists to gain the parliamentary franchise developed from the 1860s and achieved final success when the 1922 Constitution of the Irish Free State gave full political rights to both sexes. During the nineteenth century the franchise came to be seen as the hallmark of citizenship and essential for participation in political decision-making. Yet throughout, suffragists saw the vote as one part of a far-reaching concept of citizenship. More specifically, it appears to me that Irish suffragists' understanding of citizenship consistently incorporated basic components of civic republicanism. This essay aims to discuss this.

Normative 'Languages'

In every generation and place individuals grow up absorbing an inherited body of ideas, values and traditions, or political 'languages'. Depending on the issues seen as most pressing, participants draw on various components, emphasise some, ignore or challenge others, alter original meanings, add new ideas and values as the process of development in the whole continues. Modern feminism emerged in the interaction between economic, social and political developments and the political languages current in the eighteenth century.

The republican tradition was one of these languages. More than just a form of government, it combined political and social ideals and values. The American historian Gordon Wood sees republican values 'spread everywhere in the culture of the Western world' in the eighteenth century and essentially 'the ideology of the Enlightenment'.[1] Republican origins go back to ancient Greece and Rome, to the idea of the *res publica*, the 'public thing' belonging to and created by the individually free citizens of an independent city state. For classical theorists the organisation of the city state or *polis* aimed at 'the common good of its members and enabled them to cooperate in the pursuit of ideals that were fundamental to humanity'.[2] Freedom and interdependence went hand in hand. Citizens remained free as individuals and as a group only if they put the common good before private interests when necessary. Citizenship demanded civic virtue, including public spirit, justice, courage, prudence and moderation, to protect the state from outside aggression and internal corruption. In turn, participation contributed to the development of citizens as human persons.[3]

Republicanism ceased to be a central focus in political debate for centuries after the fall of the Roman Republic until the emergence of the city states of Renaissance Italy. Its reworking then and during the revolutionary period in seventeenth-century England produced what is called 'classical republicanism'. The growth of large territorially-defined states with large populations made representative systems appear more feasible than direct citizen participation in government, while the interests of the growing commercial classes prioritised the protection of individual property rights in emerging theories of natural rights. In her study of civic republicanism, Iseult Honohan identifies two diverging strands of thought on republican freedom in the eighteenth century. One saw it as 'security of life, liberty and property, protected by a form of representative government in which interests and power were: separated and balanced'. For the other, citizens' freedom depended on 'their being active, united and virtuous participants in their own self-government'.[4] An interacting set of values came from Enlightenment, or Age of Reason, emphasis on the equality of all human persons on the basis of shared rational nature and its critical analysis of accepted ideas and institutions. These broadened ideas of eligibility for citizenship, and added an optimism that reason and education could improve human nature and, emulating advances in scientific knowledge of the natural world, discover the laws governing human societies.

Yet another long-standing normative language, seldom seriously addressed by historians and political scientists, pervaded all the others. This was the language of masculine superiority. It saw women as dependants, subject to male authority, inferior to men in various ways, including capacity for rational judgement, and ineligible for citizenship. It co-existed with, and justified, the exclusion of women from many civil and political rights. Republican citizenship, from its origins, had been confined to a minority of men and excluded all women. Now, in the late eighteenth century, pioneering women used the democratic implications of Enlightenment thinking to claim recognition as full human beings and citizens possessing the right and duty to direct their own lives, make rational moral decisions, share responsibility for the organisation of society and develop as human persons, all basic republican values.

The Feminist Challenge: Mary Wollstonecraft

One of the most influential pioneers was the radical English writer Mary Wollstonecraft (1759–97). *A Vindication of the Rights of Woman* (1792) was an assertion of the full humanity of women. It challenged restrictions on women's freedom, stereotypes of women's 'nature' as irrational and emotional, and books by men 'of genius' that treated women as 'a kind of subordinate beings, and not as part of the human species ...' Women were rational human beings as men were, and the same standards of freedom, virtue and responsibility applied.

Rousseau had argued, in *Émile* (1762), that because their duty was to serve men's needs, women should be educated to submission and away from independent judgement. Wollstonecraft responded that it was a farce 'to call any being virtuous whose virtues do not result from the exercise of its own reason. This was Rousseau's opinion respecting men; I extend it to women ...'[5]

She did not defend women's actual behaviour. Restrictions on autonomy and conformity to stereotypes corrupted women and damaged the common good. Women who used feminine deceits instead of reasoned argument exercised a harmful influence on family, household and society. Yet, the main culprit was the 'tyranny of men', compounded by the 'plausible epithets men use to soften their insults ... [such] as fair defects, amiable weaknesses, etc'. It was 'time to restore to [women] their lost dignity – and make them, as a part of the human species, labour by reforming themselves to reform the world'.[6]

Reciprocal relationships between freedom, citizenship, the common good, civic virtue and personal development permeate the book. It recognised no boundary between public and private life. Women and men might have different duties, but they were all 'human duties' pertaining to citizenship. '[M]ake women rational creatures, and free citizens, and they will quickly become good wives, and mothers; that is – if men do not neglect the duties of husbands and fathers'. But it was not as mothers but as human beings that women claimed civil and political rights. Women's 'first duty is to themselves as rational creatures, and the next, in point of importance as citizens, is that, which includes so many, of a mother'. Economic independence was vital, since women could not be virtuous until 'in some degree, independent of men'. She opened the question of political participation, arguing that women should have their own representatives and not be 'arbitrarily governed without having any direct share allowed them in the deliberations of government'.[7]

United Irish Women: Martha McTier and Mary Ann McCracken

In eighteenth-century Ireland, as elsewhere, republicanism was one of the main political languages in use.[8] So far there has been little research on the political thought of Irish women. However, the letters of two contemporaries of Wollstonecraft, Martha McTier (1742–1837) and Mary Ann McCracken (1777–1866), both members of middle-class Presbyterian and United Irish circles in Belfast, are permeated by the language and values of republican citizenship.

For over forty years, Martha McTier and her brother, William Drennan, a founding member of the United Irishmen, maintained a correspondence where political information, ideas and advice intermingled with family matters, gossip, career, courtship and marriage.[9] Martha read the political writers of the day, sometimes before William did, and offered her opinions. Throughout, both maintained a commitment to liberty, the common good, justice and courage. Despite the personal danger to William, developing a medical practice in Dublin while engaged in anti-establishment politics, Martha gave support, encouragement, advice and sometimes exhortation. Prudence should temper action, but to a limited extent. Justice and principle could not be subordinated to personal concerns, whether William's trial for sedition, the alienation of his patients, or Martha's own safety as an open supporter of the United Irishmen. She used republican language: 'I can never believe that good policy in a state and justice and common honesty must be set at variance ... they are really one ...' Reminding William of the reasons he entered politics, she exhorted him: '... so virtue and honour regulate the conduct of those I love, with the prudence *they* allow of, I feel equal to every other trial ...' In December 1797 she lamented that

> if there is any public virtue here she dwells with the young ... She must first be got acquainted with in Greece and Rome, yet later writers have given I believe a more enlarged view of her.

She had read Wollstonecraft and spoke of her a number of times, without declaring her own position on feminist claims. That she agreed with them is suggested by her insightful yet sympathetic comment on the discrepancy between Wollstonecraft's love affairs and her advocacy of reason-controlled emotions. '[N]obly did she assert her sex's independence – yet what a miserable slave *she* was. Virtue and prudence must ever be absolutely necessary to independence'.[10]

Mary Ann McCracken was close to her older brother, Henry, who led the United Irishmen at the Battle of Antrim in May 1798. While he was in hiding after defeat, she helped him, organised an escape plan that nearly succeeded, and finally attended his trial and walked hand-in-hand with him to the place of execution. While the affection in her letters is obvious, Nancy Curtin[11] notes that she appears better read than he in the classic republican and radical texts and to have been comfortable lecturing him on politics, while John Gray remarks on her 'apparent leadership' in their relationship.[12] She had read Wollstonecraft and put the case for women's emancipation in Enlightenment and republican language in a letter to Henry in Kilmainham Jail in Dublin in 1797. Speaking of the United Irish auxiliary women's societies in Belfast, she criticised the men for having separate female societies 'as there can be no other reason for having them separate but keeping the women in the dark' and making 'tools of them ...' Women should have 'rational ideas of liberty and equality for themselves' and reject their 'present abject and dependent situation, degraded by custom and education ...' It was time to 'throw off the fetters with which they have been so long mentally bound ...' They needed a 'genuine love of Liberty and just sense of her value ... as without Liberty we can neither possess virtue or happiness ...':

> [T]here can be no argument produced in favour of the slavery of women that has not been used in favour of general slavery and which have been successfully combatted by many able writers.[13]

Early Socialism and Feminism: Anna Wheeler[14] and William Thompson

Just over a quarter of a century later, the joint work of an Irish man and an Irish woman 'offered perhaps the most comprehensive treatise on sexual equality and social and economic reform provided in the nineteenth century ...'[15] From the eighteenth-century ferment of ideas the political languages of liberalism and socialism were emerging. Both developed the republican values of individual liberty and the common good plus the democratic thrust of Enlightenment thinking, in the context of the economic and social upheaval created by the industrial revolution. Liberalism, which was adopted as its ideology by capitalist interests, defined individual liberty and equality as essentially freedom from all imposed restrictions including government interference. Socialism saw unfettered capitalist pursuit of individual profit as inimical to equality and the common good, and argued that the economy must be consciously managed in the interests of the whole community. Many early socialists aimed to achieve this by harmonious co-operation between social classes and the initiatives of middle and upper-class philanthropists.

Anna Wheeler (1785–c1850), born Anna Doyle, the daughter of a Church of Ireland clergyman, left an abusive marriage and became active in early socialist circles, both those of Henri Saint-Simon and Charles Fourier in France and of Robert Owen in England, where she met William Thompson. Thompson, a Protestant landowner from Cork, was one of the most radical and egalitarian thinkers of the Owenite co-operative movement, and he and Wheeler collaborated in the *Appeal of One Half of the Human Race, Women, Against the Pretensions of the other Half, Men, to Retain them in Political, and Thence in Civil and Domestic, Slavery.*[16] Its immediate genesis was the assertion by the Utilitarian philosopher James Mill that women could be excluded from political rights because the interests of 'almost all' women were included in those of their fathers or husbands. Like Mill, Thompson and Wheeler based their argument on Jeremy Bentham's thesis that laws and government policies should promote the greatest happiness of the greatest number of individuals. The *Appeal* developed a detailed analysis of the logical flaws in Mill's claim that women's happiness was safe in male hands while at the same he asserted that men needed political rights to protect their civil rights 'of property and person' against their propensity to exploit each other. It pointed to the evidence of men's actual behaviour towards women, giving particular emphasis to the marriage laws. It argued that in reality the happiness of the greatest number of both women and men would be increased if both sexes had equal rights in civil and criminal law. A further increment would result from equal political rights as their exercise would develop women's intellectual powers and expand their sympathies beyond the immediate family, thereby increasing their own capacity for pleasure and their contribution to the general happiness. Women were exhorted that, to be free they had 'only to desire it, to perceive their real interest, always harmonising with the interest of the whole race, and fearlessly to advocate it'. Finally, the *Appeal* asserted that only a socialist organisation of society could deliver the fullest possible happiness of the greatest number. All previous systems, from slavery to republicanism, had subjected women to men. Only under a new system of 'Association, or of Labour by Mutual Co-operation' could 'perfect equality and entire reciprocity of happiness between women and men' be achieved, by

> [l]arge numbers of men and women co-operating together for mutual happiness, all their possessions and means of enjoyment being the equal property of all – individual property and competition for ever excluded ...[17]

Towards Feminist Organisation: The Role of Philanthropy

By the 1860s, organised action for women's emancipation was emerging in Ireland. The new middle classes were growing in wealth, numbers and influence with the expansion of commerce, manufacture, banking and the professions, all increasingly male-dominated, while the separation of workplace and home grew, and with it the ideology of public-private division and 'separate spheres'. The Westminster parliament was recognised as the location of political decision-making in the United Kingdom of Great Britain and Ireland. The middle classes were wresting political power from the aristocracy. Middle-class men won the parliamentary vote in 1832 and male heads of households in 1867. The parliamentary franchise was increasingly seen as the hallmark of citizenship and the gateway to political participation.

Republicanism was no longer as prominent among political languages though, as already noted, both liberalism and socialism continued some of its values, while developing nationalism emphasised the idea of the republic as a self-determining nation where the people replaced the monarch as ruler.[18] The language of masculine superiority still flourished, described by one prominent feminist as a

> tone of depreciation of women ... [in the 1860s] frightfully common, both in society and the press – whether it was an attitude of groundless or misplaced compliment, or of patronage, or of mockery or contempt.[19]

In Ireland, no large-scale organised socialist movement had emerged and the ideas of Wheeler and Thompson do not appear to have had a conscious formative influence on the early women's emancipation campaigns. Liberalism was the generally dominant language; while the logic of its rejection of restrictions on individual freedom of choice implied support for civil and political rights for women, in practice liberal men as a group failed to actively advocate these.

The immediate route to feminist organisation for most of the pioneering Irish activists was through the interaction between republican values, Enlightenment emphasis on the individual plus its optimism that action and education could improve human nature and society, and the challenge the Christian churches faced in responding to changing social and economic conditions. From this emerged evangelical religion, or revivalism, and it influenced all denominations. It preached a dynamic Christianity, based on the individual life of self-denial, humility, submission and obedience, virtues particularly associated with women, leading to action to regenerate a sinful world. Seeing women as naturally closer to its ideals, it authorised them to uphold moral standards inside and outside the home, and associate together in charitable organisations.[20] In the process it provided a new normative language of a limited female superiority in the area of morals.

Starting in the late eighteenth century and continuing throughout the nineteenth, Western societies saw a huge expansion of middle- and upper-class female voluntary charitable work. Irish women philanthropists developed a wide range of services aimed at improving the moral and physical condition of the poor, particularly women and children.[21] They moved outside the home into more meaningful, challenging and personally-fulfilling work than was previously open to women, work for the most part initiated and organised by themselves. This gave them experience of management, finance, dealing with the male-run 'public' world and, not least, the opportunity to judge that women could manage many things as well or better. It could develop awareness of gender inequality and the limits this imposed on their work. For the few who joined anti-slavery associations, attention was directly focused on discrimination in civil and political rights, while these and temperance organisations gave experience of campaigning with male colleagues to change the laws. A minority of philanthropists moved further to openly challenge restrictions on women's autonomy and freedom of action, while a larger number were ready to move into new areas of activity opened by the feminists. Shared commitment to the common good, to being 'useful' to society, maintained on-going interaction between philanthropy and feminism.

Overall, women's response to evangelicalism indicates how widespread dissatisfaction was with the limited scope for action and development of potential sanctioned by conventions and normative languages. Its scale suggests that more than purely religious motivation was involved, powerful as this undoubtedly was. Motivations are often complex and, like all human thinking, can accommodate apparently contradictory elements. Historically, challenges to the status quo have often been represented as returns to an earlier situation or as mandated by accepted normative languages. Historians of religious congregations regularly have to decode the language of self-effacement in which women religious attributed their own initiatives to male ecclesiastics. A religious mandate was less challenging to many women – not to mention their families and communities – than open defiance of the accepted norms of female behaviour.

The Nineteenth-Century Campaigns for Civil and Political Rights

The first generation of pioneering feminists in Ireland came from Protestant denominations, with Quakers especially prominent. While Catholic women were equally involved in philanthropy, at an early stage Catholic lay pioneers translated their societies into religious congregations in a move seen as a trade-off with the hierarchy whereby they gained long-term security and support for their work at the cost of some autonomy – and perhaps the incidental side-tracking of potential feminists.[22]

Discrimination against women in civil and political rights made the contrast between their position and that of men, particularly of the developing middle classes, wider than ever. Under the common law, married women 'had no civil existence: they owned no personal property, they could neither sue nor be sued, they could not divorce their husbands, or claim any rights over their children'.[23] Women could not vote in parliamentary elections or hold public political office. They were excluded from the universities and entry to the higher professions, while the education of girls at second level aimed more at accomplishments and preparations for marriage than intellectual formation and employment. In theory, middle and upper-class women were supported by their menfolk. Failing this, the only 'respectable' employments were poorly paid governessing, teaching or needlework. The law made women the punishable party in sex-related offences such as prostitution, illegitimate births and adultery.

Campaigns developed around all these areas in Ireland from the 1860s.[24] Taken together, their combined objectives could be seen as a programme for republican citizenship. Married women's control of their own inherited or earned property was a prerequisite for their own personal autonomy, and the issue affected all women, single or married, and all social classes. Raising standards of female education so that it aimed at intellectual development was central to development of human potential and ability to reform society, as well for employment, economic independence and autonomy. Opposition to government regulation of prostitution in the Contagious Diseases Acts upheld the common good in the moral improvement of society, and challenged double sexual standards that punished prostitutes while leaving male clients untouched. The parliamentary vote was linked to recognition as full human persons, to freedom and self-determination and was increasingly seen as essential to empower women to influence legislation that would benefit society as a whole. Campaigners used two different but complementary lines of argument; firstly, the Enlightenment case that women and men were equally human persons with the same rights and responsibilities to themselves and to society; and secondly, that each sex had a different contribution to make, both important and both needed for the proper management of society. The latter drew on the language of women's moral superiority, seen as needed to control male lust, protect the family and raise moral standards generally.

These ideas were constantly articulated by the leaders. Anne Jellicoe (1823–80), a Quaker and a major figure in the reform of women's education, wrote in 1873:

> By education is not merely meant instruction, but the cultivation of all those faculties – intelligence, affection, will, conscience – such training, in short, as will enable each individual to guide herself right through the circumstances of life – to know her duty, and to do it – an education which, if so considered, is as important to women as to men, to poor as to rich.[25]

Anna Haslam (1829–1922), a Quaker in Dublin, and Isabella Tod (1836–96), a Presbyterian in Belfast, were to the forefront in all the campaigns. Thomas Haslam, Anna's husband and co-feminist, published three issues of the *Woman's Advocate* in 1874. It argued the case for women's suffrage as 'the moral right of properly qualified women to some share in the enactment of the laws which they are required to obey'. Women demanded political and educational rights and to be 'treated as reasonable beings, who are personally responsible for the talents which have been confided to their care'. In 1875, Isabella Tod wrote that women were

> ... citizens of the state, inheritors with men of all the history which ennobles a nation, guardians with men of all the best life of the nation; bound as much as men are bound to consider the good of the whole; and justified as much as men are justified in sharing the good of the whole.

Experience showed that women 'felt a deeper responsibility resting upon them, and ... attempted to carry their religious principles into the common things of life to a greater extent than men did'. Men were often drawn to politics from selfish motives while women did not campaign 'only for themselves. They fight for others; and it is because we have so much work to do that we fight as hard as we do ...'[26] For Tod, suffrage was 'not merely a claim of abstract right, but of necessary means for performing duties'.[27] It was 'the only practical means of redressing wrongs'.[28]

When women gained eligibility for election as Poor Law Guardians in 1896, Anna Haslam rejoiced that women voters crossed sectarian lines to vote for a candidate whom they knew could be 'absolutely trusted to do her duty by [the poor]'. Conscious of the links between philanthropy and feminism, she explained that many women had not become active suffragists because success seemed so impossible that they threw their energy into 'charitable work ... the results of which would be visible within their own life-time'.[29] In 1906, Thomas asserted that women

> have been brought into the world, like men, to cultivate their whole nature, physical, intellectual, moral, spiritual, political and so on, in the way most conducive to their happiness, and the well-being of the world at large.[30]

The Irish Citizen Newspaper, 1912–1920

By the early twentieth century, educational standards had been substantially raised and entry to the universities achieved, though not yet to all the higher professions. Married women had gained considerable, though not complete, control of their property. The Contagious Diseases Acts had been repealed. The vote and eligibility for women had been won in local government. The major campaigning issue was now the parliamentary vote. The numbers of active suffragists expanded rapidly around the western world. In Ireland, women from Catholic and nationalist backgrounds were joining in significant numbers, though Protestants and unionists still formed the majority.

Nationalist-unionist differences reached a climax during the lifetime of the *Irish Citizen*. Some form of Home Rule became inevitable after 1911 when the House of Lords lost its indefinite veto on legislation. An armed force, the Ulster Volunteers, was organised in 1913 to resist the imposition of Home Rule on Ulster, followed in the south by a corresponding force, the Irish Volunteers. World War I, the 1916 rising, the establishment of Dáil Éireann and the War of Independence followed. Irish feminists took varying attitudes to these developments. However, for this discussion I want to consider their thinking on citizenship as it emerges in the pages of the *Irish Citizen*, the newspaper published in association with the Irish Women's Franchise League, the most prominent of the new suffrage societies, between 1912 and 1920. It is a unique source that provided a forum for a wide range of opinion and argument.[31]

The political languages drawn on included socialism (now more developed in Ireland and interacting with the labour movement), nationalism and pacifism, as well as women's moral superiority and mission to regenerate society. Themes prominent in the earlier emancipation campaigns were discussed and new issues raised. The motto on the paper's masthead made an immediate statement: 'For men and women equally the rights of citizenship: From men and women equally the duties of citizenship'. The first editorial stated that the paper stood for the 'fullest development of a complete humanity ...' and against limits on 'human freedom and human character'.[32] Another spoke of 'adjustment between the needs of the individual and the needs of the community'.[33] An unsigned contribution argued for co-operation between men and women in a 'voluntary bond' to create a 'social organisation ... capable of giving the maximum opportunity of personal freedom to the maximum number of persons'.[34] E.A. Browning, press secretary of the Irish Women's Reform League, wrote that 'we have become sensitive to the common needs and satisfactions ... the joy of one is a gain to all, and the suffering of one an injury to all'. Women might be denied the hallmark of citizenship, but 'should this not make us anxious to prove ourselves citizens in all but name?'[35]

There was considerable agreement that women were morally superior to men in some ways, and had a different set of values; they were sexually more chaste, more concerned with the common good, with 'true life-values' – both the preservation and quality of life – and were more opposed to war and militarism. Whether these qualities were seen as biologically determined, or arising from women's experience in maternal and domestic roles, it was imperative to bring them into political decision-making. This could be done by direct participation in political decision-making or by citizen-mothers educating future citizens. For either role, education was crucial. Among others, Mary Hayden, Professor of Modern Irish History at University College Dublin, argued that girls' education must go beyond the selfish interests of the individual family, specifically include politics, economics, the place of the family in society and prepare her 'to do her duty efficiently', whether in the 'corporate life of the city or country' or as a mother.[36]

Some contributions acknowledged that women were not morally superior to men in all ways, and were held back from developing their full potential by the narrow range of opportunities open to them. Margaret Connery of the Irish Women's Franchise League saw suffrage as part of a bigger movement aiming at the 'unity of humanity ... a universal brotherhood of man'. This was not possible while half of humanity, women, were 'sunk in servitude and degradation'. Women's roles and work had become seriously impoverished and 'new forms of labour and the right to labour' were essential. If woman 'may not grow and develop, and exercise all her powers of body and mind, she, and the race through her, are threatened with ultimate extinction'.[37] Marion Duggan, a law graduate of Trinity College Dublin, argued that, while women were 'in some ways superior to men', they had 'failed to cultivate certain qualities which men have learned by experience', and wider opportunities, including the practice of law, 'may materially assist [their] moral development'.[38]

Socialist contributors, themselves mostly middle-class women, agreed that suffrage and feminism were integrally linked to the common good. In Belfast, Margaret McCoubrey, describing herself as a socialist, claimed that when women gained equality 'existing systems for maintenance of law and order, our gigantic farce called Courts of Justice' will go and there will be 'no need for charitable organisations, for prisons, or for rescue-homes'. Only with the help of women 'dare you dream of true Internationalism'.[39] However, socialists also challenged the leadership role of middle-class feminists, arguing that working-class women must achieve their own emancipation. Middle-class leadership was defended by Margaret Connery on the grounds that the poorest, most oppressed and overworked women could hardly lead the movement.[40] Marion Duggan, a regular contributor over the years, asked could 'wealthy or educated women ... be trusted to make laws for poor working women?' Should the latter be 'free and independent, or humbly receiving the legislative bounty of their better-off sisters?'[41] When demands for suffrage had first emerged only middle-class men had the vote and the demand for suffrage on the same terms as men appeared relatively unproblematic to middle-class women who saw it as their duty to improve both the physical and moral conditions of their poorer sisters. As more categories of men gained the vote, and as socialism and trade unionism developed in Ireland, such assumptions came under attack.

One editorial reported the English Fabian Society's finding that the majority of working women contributed to the support of dependants. This discredited calculations of women's wages on the needs of an individual, and only the votes of working women would change this.[42] However, most socialist contributors argued that economic reform came before the vote as a priority for working women. Economic justice was the first essential and the only basis on which international harmony and equality between men and women could be built. Working women needed to organise to improve pay and gain admission to a wider range of work. This would educate them to use and appreciate the franchise. Then they 'themselves must decide how best to get the vote, by full, frank, free discussion'.[43] Louie Bennett, later to become general secretary of the Irish Women Workers' Union, also pressed the prior need for trade unions. When women had cured sweated labour conditions they would turn to civic reforms 'which only the workers themselves will ever achieve'. She urged the *Irish Citizen* to look at 'broader aspects of feminism than purely suffrage'. Feminism and Co-operative Internationalism were 'dependent upon economic justice'. Economic justice, for workers and in international relations, was the only way to a world 'safe for democracy'.[44]

Trade unionists also recognised that the exploitation of working women in conditions, unequal pay and limited employment opportunities had to be addressed in the context of the labour movement as a whole and the co-existing exploitation of working men. Bennett went so far as to argue that the demand for equal pay and equal work for women was problematic in the present industrial system and organisation of society where 'the financial burden of keeping the home lies upon the male wage-earner, working under a system so heedless of human needs'. 'When co-operation has succeeded capitalism' the distribution of work can be 'completely readjusted'. Women workers needed to raise their whole status, pay and working conditions to have 'that self-respect as a worker which gives a note of happiness to any toil ...'[45]

On the related question of women's trade unions versus mixed unions, Bennett supported separate unions on the grounds that they gave women's voices and needs a better hearing. She was challenged by Cissie Cahalan, of the Linen Drapers' Assistants' Association and a member of the Irish Women's Franchise League, who argued that only by the sexes closing ranks, and women and men working 'shoulder to shoulder' in mixed unions could they reach the 'goal of Irish Labour – the Workers' Republic'.[46] Throughout all the debates, agreements and disagreements, the concept of free, self-determining citizens working together for the common good continued as a unifying principle and objective.

Conclusion: Feminist and Republican Values Today

Some significant points emerge from this brief overview. Firstly, the pioneering feminists identified their problem as the non-recognition of women as full human persons, in Wollstonecraft's words 'not part of the human species'.

Secondly, their chosen model incorporated the values of that strand of republican citizenship emphasising individual autonomy, active co-operation with others to create the common good, and self-development through participation. Thirdly, these values continued to inform Irish feminism throughout the late nineteenth and early twentieth centuries, when civil republicanism was no longer a political language in widespread use and to most people in Ireland republicanism meant complete independence from Britain.[47]

The demand was never simply for equality of rights with men within existing structures and value systems. Nor did feminists promote men's patterns of behaviour as the human norm to which they should aspire. Their aim was more ambitious, a transformation of society through the promotion of 'female' values. The nineteenth-century activists anticipated that women's admission to citizenship would bring new standards of morality, compassion, equality and justice into public decision-making. In the early twentieth century feminist scholars and trade unionists agreed with this but insisted that economic justice was a prerequisite for working-class women's autonomy and the common good of society.

Events since then have shown that these expectations were not fulfilled. Women's full citizenship has not transformed society in the ways envisaged by feminists. Women as a group have not supported the same political policies, but, like men, have been distributed across a wide range of often conflicting philosophies and ideologies. Universal suffrage has not delivered effective participation in political decision-making to all citizens. Nor has any consensus been reached as to whether observed differences in behaviour between women and men are the result of nature or nurture. It is more useful to look to feminist analysis of women's experience as a force for change in human society. This is not to suggest that feminist thinking has never been mistaken. Feminists have been legitimately criticised for being unduly optimistic at times, elitist, over-maternalistic or blind to class issues, and so on. Similar criticisms can and have been made of most radical ideas and, if all political thinkers or schools of thought were dismissed for these criticisms, there would be few left. Weak links in a chain of argument do not necessarily negate the values being promoted.

Today there appears be a real need for these feminist values. For most of the nineteenth and twentieth centuries, liberalism and socialism have been the dominant political languages in the West. For some people the claims of socialism were undermined by the subordination of individual freedom to a controlling elite's definition of the common good in the USSR experiment. More recently, neo-liberalism has pushed the emphasis on individual freedom to an extreme in the deregulated pursuit of corporate profit and the ideology of politics as a struggle between competing interests. Disillusionment is mounting at its failure to deliver the common good it promised. Over recent decades, political theorists have been turning again to the tradition of civic republicanism in the hope that its concept of the interdependence of individual liberty and the common good, plus the need for active, participatory citizenship to ensure both, may help to solve some of today's problems. There are many problems with no obvious solutions; not least among them how to achieve meaningful participation and how to reach agreement on what comprises the common good.

The feminist contribution to these debates can come, not by providing a blueprint for the ideal polity, but by its long commitment to a world-view that combined political and social values and saw the personal development of the individual as part of the political process, and its insistence that women be recognised as citizens and values associated with women recognised as human values essential for achieving and maintaining the common good. For this contribution to be made, the feminist tradition must be remembered, revisited and reworked for today's world. The current pervasiveness of neo-liberalism endorses a definition of feminism as aiming solely at equal participation by women and men in existing socio-political systems. Such a definition loses the potential of the historical feminist rejection of an ideology that sees some human values as appropriate in private life while a contradictory set are acceptable in public political life. This rejection opens the way to envisioning new models of human nature and behaviour and new models for the organisation of society, something a narrow definition of equal rights does not.

History has a central role here. Societies rely largely on historians for their group memory and understanding of how contemporary institutions and values have evolved. Knowing how we got to where we are is essential for potentially better and more realisable decisions as to where we go next. Most history is still written within a paradigm that sees males as the active agents in the patterns of continuity and change in human history. In the case of Irish history, most general surveys and specialist monographs devote no analysis or questioning to the political, social and economic consequences of being born a male or a female in a specific place at a specific period in history. They take for granted the centuries-long historical reality of laws, regulations and custom that combined to channel control of resources, wealth, property, access to education and political power to males and away from females. If feminism is mentioned at all, it is seen essentially as women trying to reach a stage of development already achieved by men. The result is that successive generations grow up absorbing this world-view and unaware of an important part of their historical heritage.

Gender relationships have always been a fundamental factor in human history. Until they are incorporated into 'mainstream' histories of Irish and other societies, history and group memory will continue to disseminate a distorted view of that history. Succeeding generations will have no understanding of where contemporary gender relationships came from, and no basis from which to assess their value, defects and possibilities. It is as important for boys as for girls, for men as for women, to realise that the male role in society is not *a priori* the human norm, but, like the female role, a social construct open to change over time, and equally problematic.

As the body of research in women's history grows, we move closer to the point where the paradigm of male agency, and the male role as the human norm, will no longer be sustainable and will be replaced by a more inclusive model. Incorporating the suffrage and emancipation campaigns into a general history of modern Ireland could be a good start towards a more accurate representation of the past. These campaigns show women as autonomous political actors who succeeded in changing the law to win civil and political rights for over half the total adult population and who in the process made a significant contribution to political theory. We already have a considerable body of knowledge, at present largely confined to the specialist field of women's history. Beginning to make this breakthrough may be the next stage in the development of women's history.

from Louise Ryan and Margaret Ward (eds), *Irish Women and the Vote: Becoming Citizens* (Dublin, Irish Academic Press, 2007), pp 1–20.

NOTES

1   Gordon S. Wood, *The Creation of the American Republic 1776–1787* (Chapel Hill, University of North Carolina Press, 1998), pp vii–viii.

2   John Morrow, *History of Political Thought: A Thematic Introduction* (Basingstoke and London, Palgrave, 1998), p. 19.

3   See Iseult Honohan, 'Freedom as Citizenship: The Republican Tradition in Political Theory', *The Republic*, 2 (Spring/Summer 2001), pp 7–24.

4   I. Honohan, *Civic Republicanism* (London and New York, Taylor and Francis, 2002), p. 110.

5   Mary Wollstonecraft, *A Vindication of the Rights of Woman* (Oxford, Oxford University Press, 1993), pp 7, 86–7.

6   *Ibid.*, pp 100, 113.

7   *Ibid.*, pp 119, 221, 227, 228, 265.

8   S.J. Connolly, 'Introduction: Varieties of Irish Political Thought', in S.J. Connolly (ed.), *Political Ideas in Eighteenth-Century Ireland* (Dublin, Four Courts Press, 2000), p. 18; Ian McBride, 'The Harp without the Crown: Nationalism and Republicanism in the 1790s', *ibid.*, p. 159; Stephen Small, *Political Thought in Ireland 1776–1798: Republicanism, Patriotism and Radicalism* (Oxford University Press, 2002), *passim.*

9   Jean Agnew (ed.), *The Drennan-McTier Letters* (Dublin, Women's History Project in association with the Irish Manuscripts Commission, 1999). As the general editor, Maria Luddy, points out, they are a marvellous source for social and political history. For present purposes, the letters of the 1790s provide an example of republican citizenship in action.

10   *Ibid.*, Vol. 1, 14; Vol. II, 255, 255, 387. William Godwin's *Memoir* of Wollstonecraft and her *Posthumous Works*, published early in 1798, discussed her love affairs and printed some of her love letters. The resulting scandal provided many with an excuse to ridicule her arguments. See Claire Tomalin, *The Life and Death of Mary Wollstonecraft* (London, Penguin Books, 1974), p. 233.

11   Nancy J. Curtin, 'Women and Eighteenth-Century Irish Republicanism', in Margaret Mac Curtain and Mary O'Dowd

(eds), *Women in Early Modern Ireland* (Dublin, Wolfhound Press, 1991), p. 140.

12 John Gray, 'Mary Ann McCracken', in Daire Keogh and Nicholas Furlong (eds), *The Women of 1798* (Dublin, Four Courts Press, 1998), p. 55.

13 Mary McNeill, *The Life and Times of Mary Ann McCracken 1770–1866: A Belfast Panorama* (Belfast, Blackstaff Press, 1988), pp 125–6.

14 For Wheeler, see Dolores Dooley, 'Anna Doyle Wheeler', in Mary Cullen and Maria Luddy (eds), *Women, Power and Consciousness in 19th Century Ireland* (Dublin, Attic Press, 1995), pp 19–53, and *Equality in Community: Sexual Equality in the Writings of William Thompson and Anna Doyle Wheeler* (Cork, Cork University Press, 1996).

15 Dooley, 'Anna Doyle Wheeler', p. 31.

16 The *Appeal* was first published in London in 1825 under Thompson's name. In the 'Introductory Letter to Mrs Wheeler', Thompson explicitly stated that his purpose was to put Wheeler's ideas on paper as her 'interpreter and the scribe of your sentiments', and regretted that only a few of the pages were actually 'written with your own hand'. William Thompson, *Appeal of One Half of the Human Race, Women, Against the Pretensions of the Other Half, Men, to Retain them in Political, and Thence in Civil and Domestic, Slavery* (London, Virago, 1983), p. 27

17 Thompson, *Appeal,* pp 121, 122–3, 195, 199.

18 Honohan, *Civic Republicanism,* pp 113–19.

19 Isabella Tod, cited in Helen Blackburn's obituary of Tod, *Englishwoman's Review,* 15 October 1898, p. 59. The similarity to Wollstonecraft's description seventy years earlier is striking.

20 Jane Rendall, *The Origins of Modern Feminism: Women in Britain, France and the United States, 1780–1860* (Basingstoke, Macmillan, 1985), pp 73–6.

21 See Maria Luddy, *Women and Philanthropy in Nineteenth-Century Ireland* (Cambridge, Cambridge University Press, 1995); Rosemary Raughter, 'A Natural Tenderness: The Ideal and Reality of Eighteenth-Century Female Philanthropy', in Maryann Valiulis and Mary O'Dowd (eds), *Women and Irish History* (Dublin, Wolfhound Press, 1997), pp 71–88.

22 For these developments and discussion of the issues, see Tony Fahey, 'Nuns in the Catholic Church in Ireland in the Nineteenth Century', in Mary Cullen (ed.), *Girls Don't Do Honours: Irish Women in Education in the 19th and 20th Centuries* (Dublin, WEB/Arlen House, 1987), pp 7–30; Caitríona Clear, *Nuns in Nineteenth-Century Ireland* (Dublin, Gill and Macmillan, 1987) and 'The Limits of Female Autonomy: Nuns in Nineteenth-Century Ireland' in Maria Luddy and Cliona Murphy (eds), *Women Surviving: Studies in Irish Women's History in the 19th and 20th Centuries* (Dublin, Poolbeg Press, 1989), pp 15–50; Maria Luddy, *Women and Philanthropy in Nineteenth-Century Ireland*; Rosemary Raughter, 'A Natural Tenderness', and (ed.), *Religious Women and Their History: Breaking the Silence* (Dublin, Irish Academic Press, 2005).

23 Rendall, *Origins of Modern Feminism*, p. 4. The United Kingdom divorce law of 1857 gave women the right to sue for divorce, though on more stringent conditions than applied to men, and it was not extended to Ireland.

24 Since changes in the law for all parts of the United Kingdom were made at Westminster, there was considerable co-operation between the British and Irish campaigners and, in the cases of married women's property and the Contagious Diseases Acts, Irish activism was part of an England-based campaign.

25 Cited in Anne V. O'Connor, 'Anne Jellicoe', in Cullen and Luddy (eds), *Women, Power and Consciousness*, p. 152.

26 Cited in Maria Luddy, 'Isabella M. Tod', *ibid.*, pp 217–18

27 Cited in Helen Blackburn's obituary of Tod, *Englishwoman's Review*, 15 January 1897, p. 60.

28 Cited by the Mayoress of Belfast at the unveiling of a memorial to Tod, *Englishwoman's Review*, 15 January 1898, p. 53.

29 *Englishwoman's Review*, 15 October 1898, pp 222, 224. For more on the close relationship between philanthropy and feminism see Carmel Quinlan's essay on the Haslams in Ryan and Ward, *Irish Women and the Vote*, pp 21–44.

30 Thomas Haslam, *Women's Suffrage from a Masculine Viewpoint* (Dublin, 1906), p. 15.

31 For this section I have found both Dana Hearne, 'The Development of Irish Feminist Thought: A Critical Historical

Analysis of *The Irish Citizen* 1912–1920' (PhD thesis, Ontario, 1992) and Louise Ryan, *Irish Feminism and the Vote: An Anthology of the Irish Citizen Newspaper 1912–1920* (Dublin, Folens, 1996) very useful.

32 *Irish Citizen,* 25 May 1912.
33 *Ibid.,* 17 May 1913.
34 *Ibid.,* 13 July 1912.
35 *Ibid.,* 2 August 1913.
36 *Ibid.,* 6 and 13 July 1912.
37 *Ibid.,* 29 December 1912, 4 January 1913.
38 *Ibid.,* 24 April 1915.
39 *Ibid.,* 27 February 1915.
40 *Ibid.,* 3 January 1913.
41 *Ibid.,* 8 August 1914.
42 *Ibid.,* 19 July 1913.
43 Marion Duggan, *ibid.,* 20 February 1915.
44 *Ibid.,* January 1918.
45 *Ibid.,* November 1919.
46 *Ibid.,* December 1919.
47 Irish feminism continued to incorporate the same values up to and including the second wave of feminism of the 1970s and 1980s.

THE POTENTIAL OF GENDER HISTORY

The Women's History Association of Ireland's conference held in Trinity College in 2006 was on the theme 'Doing Gender History: Methods and Modules' and the papers presented at it, with some additional contributions, were published. In her 'Introduction', the editor, Maryann Gialanella Valiulis, explained that the conference organisers' aim was to see 'what gender history would look like ... in an Irish context'. Finding that most participants saw it as 'either women's history or the study of masculinities', they asked was 'women's history now simply renamed as gender history with masculinities and femininities added to the mix?' The conference itself ended with a lively, though inconclusive, discussion of what 'gender history' meant, and general agreement that we needed to continue the debate. It is to be hoped that the WHAI continues and develops it. My own view is that gender relations, as meaning the totality of the social relationships between the sexes in a given society at a given time in history, are crucial for a more inclusive human history that approximates more closely to the reality it aims to uncover. In the upsurge in research and writing in women's history sparked by the second wave women's movement, the first question was; what did women in the past really do or not do? As the answers accumulate it becomes increasingly clear that we also need to look at men as a social group, rather than starting from the tacit premise that the male role is the norm and that what needs to be explained, if it needs explanation, is how the female role differs from it. In writing the history of a society it is as important to include explicit analysis of the political, social and economic consequences of being born a male as it is to include those of being born a female. This essay was published in Gender and Power in Irish History *in 2009.*

What do we mean by gender history? The definition used here developed during the upsurge of interest in women's history sparked off by second wave feminism in the mid-twentieth century. It became increasingly clear that many differences in the position of women and men in diverse societies could not be explained solely by biological determinism and so 'gender' was drafted in to denote the entire range of social relations between the sexes. Gender analysis takes account of the political, social and economic consequences of being born a male or a female in a particular place at a particular time in history. It sees biological sex as one factor interacting with others, such as geographical location, race, colour, class, religion, education, wealth, age and many others in locating an individual in historical context. It follows that gender analysis cannot, explicitly or implicitly, treat the masculine role as the human norm.

However, the reality is that most history books *do* treat the masculine role as the human norm, presenting a past of male agency and leadership, and female passivity and dependency. When women as a group or feminist activity are discussed at all, it is almost invariably in terms of comparison with a taken-for-granted male norm, to which women can or, depending on the point of view, cannot hope to aspire. The books seldom, if ever, consider men as a group, or the advantaged position of males, socially, economically and politically, relative to females. And what history books tell us is central to our understanding of who we are and how we got to where we are.

This article considers one example of how gender analysis might help to develop a more inclusive and genuinely 'mainstream' history. It starts with the concept of citizenship expressed explicitly and implicitly by Irish feminist campaigners from the middle of the nineteenth century up to 1922 and the Constitution of the Irish Free

State.[1] This provides the basis for a discussion of some aspects of the potential of gender history.

Political Ideologies and the Emergence of Modern Feminism

Political thought is not static. It develops as individuals or groups respond to the issues and questions they see as most pressing in their own day. In doing this, they draw on the stock of political ideas and traditions in use in current political debate. This is inevitably a selective process as participants use or emphasise elements that appear relevant or favourable to their questions and aims, ignore or take issue with others, add new ideas and arguments, and so the stock develops and changes over time. Historians aim to locate the writings of individual thinkers and other expressions of political thought in historical context to help identify the major concerns of a period and the issues most important to different groups. They ask what were the then prevailing ideologies, how these were drawn on, to what extent protagonists tailored their objectives to what could be justified in their terms, and whether they added anything new to the body of political thought.

Republicanism was a dominant ideology in the eighteenth-century Western world.[2] Its origins (*res publica*, the 'public thing') go back to ancient Greece and Rome. Based on a holistic view of the good human life, republican thinking originally posited an independent city state and polity, the Greek *polis*, whose individually free (male) citizens shared responsibility for its survival and flourishing. Freedom and interdependence were interlocked and civic virtue required citizens to co-operate and be prepared to put the common good of all before individual interest when necessary to defend the state from both internal corruption and outside aggression. By the exercise of civic virtue citizens developed their individual human potential.[3]

Republican thinking was elitist in its origins, excluding women, slaves and foreigners from citizenship. In the city states of Renaissance Italy and during the revolutionary period in seventeenth-century England, it was drawn on and developed to answer questions of sovereignty and the respective rights and duties of citizens and rulers. This reworking has been given the somewhat confusing name of 'classical' republicanism by political theorists. In the eighteenth century it was further democratised by Enlightenment, or Age of Reason, assertions of the basic equality of all rational human beings, and ideas of who could be a citizen broadened. In many countries, including Ireland, republicanism was a powerful contributor to arguments for reform of political systems, elimination of corruption and patronage in government and extension of political participation, as well as to the rebellion of the British colonies in North America in the 1770s, the French Revolution starting in 1789 and the 1798 rebellion in Ireland.

While few male thinkers applied their definitions of human rationality and equality to females, some radical women drew on the same body of ideas to challenge existing gender relations. Enlightenment egalitarianism could support their claims that women be recognised as full human persons. These claims defined full humanity in republican terminology and its concept of citizens as free individuals directing their own lives and sharing responsibility for the common good. One of the most influential expressions of Enlightenment and republican ideas applied to gender relationships was *A Vindication of the Rights of Woman* (1792) by the English radical thinker, Mary Wollstonecraft. Her basic argument was that denial of personal autonomy, of responsibility and of education aimed at developing rational judgement stunted women's development as human persons and corrupted their influence on family and society. 'Make women rational creatures and free citizens and they will quickly become good wives and mothers'.[4]

The Irish Emancipation Campaigns

By the mid-nineteenth century when organised action for women's rights emerged in Ireland, republicanism was not as prominent among the ideologies in contemporary usage and campaigners did not employ its terminology. In response to political, social and economic change, liberalism, socialism and nationalism were coming to the fore, each emphasising and developing different elements from the republican tradition. Liberalism prioritised individual freedom, making its protection from interference the primary role of government, and argued that this would in practice achieve the common good. It provided a tailor-made ideology for the rising commercial, business and financial interests. Socialism responded that unfettered pursuit of individual interest threatened the common good, and that real freedom and equality required control of the economy in the interests of the whole community. Meanwhile nationalism developed the republican emphasis on freedom from outside aggression or control.

Liberalism, dominant in mid-nineteenth century Ireland, had ambiguous messages for middle-class feminists. Its advocacy of individual liberty favoured claims for equality, though in practice liberal men gave them partial and ambiguous support. It also tended to support the ideology of separate private and public spheres, where women ruled in the home while men ran affairs in the public world. This justified the contraction of middle-class women's actual range of activity that resulted from the increasing separation of home and workplace. As commerce, bureaucracy and the professions expanded, the middle class grew in numbers and wealth and middle-class men moved into political office and exercised political power. Some historians see the widening divide between the opportunities open to middle-class males and females as the driving force behind the women's movement.[5] While this argument obviously has some merit, feminist aims, as will be seen, went well beyond equality with men within existing political, economic and social structures.

Mid-nineteenth-century women's rights advocates could draw on a new ideology of a (limited) female superiority in the area of morals. This developed from the same matrix of eighteenth-century thinking. Enlightenment ideas of equality and its optimism that human reason could reform and improve human nature and society, and republican commitment to the common good, interacted with the challenges facing Christianity in a changing world to produce Evangelical religion, or revivalism. Emerging in the late eighteenth century within Protestantism, its influence spread across all denominations. It preached an individual life of active Christianity based on humility and self-sacrifice allied to a mission to regenerate a sinful world. The virtues advocated were those seen as particularly 'female'. As a result Evangelicalism endorsed an enhanced role for women as guardians and promoters of moral standards within family and community, sanctioned their organised activity outside the home and provided an ideology and normative language of female moral superiority.[6] Evangelicalism is seen as a major impetus behind the huge growth of philanthropy among middle- and upper-class Irish women from the late eighteenth century through the nineteenth. They developed an impressively wide range of services aimed at improving the moral and physical condition of the disadvantaged in society.[7]

The leading women's rights activists in mid-nineteenth century Ireland appear to have come from middle-class backgrounds in Protestant denominations and in philanthropy.[8] A radical minority emerged to openly challenge restrictions on women's autonomy and self-direction as well as their exclusion from political decision-making. Four main campaigns developed from the mid-century:

1) for married women's control of their own inherited or earned property.

2) for improved standards in female education, access to the universities and better employment opportunities.

3) for the repeal of the Contagious Diseases Acts passed in the 1860s to protect the health of the army and navy by subjecting women suspected of being prostitutes to compulsory medical examination and, if necessary, treatment for venereal disease.

4) for the parliamentary vote on the same terms as men.[9]

As Ireland was part of the United Kingdom of Great Britain and Ireland, campaigns to change the law were aimed at the Westminster parliament. Action in Ireland was influenced by English developments and, in the cases of married women's property and the Contagious Diseases Acts, was essentially part of English-led campaigns.

Campaigners drew on Enlightenment egalitarianism, liberalism's stress on individual freedom, and Evangelical endorsement of women's moral mission, and argued that the good of society required moral standards in public life and political decision-making, standards which could only be achieved by women's participation. Also, however, and significantly for the discussion here, despite the fact that by this period republicanism was no longer prominent among the ideologies drawn on in general political debate, the campaign objectives, separately and together, incorporated many basic elements of republican citizenship. Married women's control of their own property was essential for personal autonomy and freedom from domination, and it affected all women, single or married, and all social classes. Education for intellectual development was central to development of human potential and ability to reform society, as well as for employment, economic independence and autonomy. Repeal of the Contagious Diseases Acts challenged sexual double standards and aimed at the moral improvement of society. The parliamentary vote involved recognition as full human persons, free and self-determining, plus power to influence legislation.

Isabella Tod, a Presbyterian in Belfast, and a leading figure in all the Irish campaigns, was one of the most prominent and articulate advocates of the feminist agenda. In 1875, in what could be seen an overall summary, she wrote that women were

> citizens of the state, inheritors with men of all the history which ennobles a nation, guardians with men of all the best life of the nation; bound as much as men are bound to consider the good of the whole; and justified as much as men are justified in sharing the good of the whole.[10]

Her speeches and writings constantly demonstrated how the different campaigns interacted. A 'wise and wide course of education ... enlarges and strengthens the mind ... to prepare it for all the contingencies of life'. If women had the vote they 'would be in all respects the better ... and ... the influence of women would be good at promoting all sorts of wise reforms, social and moral'. It would develop their individual potential and ability to contribute to the improvement of society. With it they could exercise 'moral responsibility and freedom of action'. The 'addition of women to the electorate would mean a far greater proportionate addition to the ranks of good'. The condition of women of 'the lower classes' might be greatly improved if 'not merely a few, but most of those in the classes above them have not only the will, but the power and the knowledge to help them'.[11]

For Tod, suffrage was 'not merely a claim of abstract right, but of necessary means for performing duties'.[12] It was 'the only practical means of redressing wrongs'.[13] This in turn was linked to women's particular contribution, which, she wrote, could be 'in the details of management of a workhouse (which needs an experience in house keeping) ... in the care of the sick, of the old, of the children, and the training of girls to earn their bread ... in the discrimination between honest poverty and imposture ... work that must be shared by women if it is to be done efficiently'.[14] It could also result from a greater commitment to the common good. Experience showed that women 'felt a deeper responsibility resting upon them, and ... attempted to carry their religious principles into the common things of life to a greater extent than men did'. Men were often drawn to politics 'from selfish motives' while women did not campaign 'only for themselves. They fight for others; and it is because we have so much work to do that we fight as hard as we do'.[15]

Women themselves, Tod argued, had a duty to make this contribution. They must demand the vote

> not only for the help which women must give to women, but even more, for the discharge of their special duty to the whole state, a duty which God has entrusted to them, and which no man can do.

They must 'feel it their task to uphold truth, purity and justice to all, in the legislation and administration of the realm'.[16]

The Irish Citizen 1912–1920[17]

The same basic concepts of citizenship continued to inform Irish feminist thinking in the changing political context of the second decade of the twentieth century. The suffrage newspaper, the *Irish Citizen*, was founded in 1912 in association with the Irish Women's Franchise League (IWFL), a new suffrage association with nationalist sympathies though non-aligned politically. By this time substantial, though far from complete, advances had been achieved in most of the campaign objectives, with the parliamentary vote the major exception. Internationally, the suffrage movement had expanded dramatically. In Ireland, where the pioneering activists had been predominantly Protestant in religion and unionist in politics, now Catholics and nationalists were taking part in increasing numbers. The *Citizen* became the forum for a wide range of opinion and discussion. Contributors drew on socialism, nationalism and pacifism as well as liberalism and women's moral superiority and mission to reform society. A socialist voice emerged to challenge what it saw as middle-class feminists' maternalistic attitude towards poorer women. By this time also, for most Irish people republicanism had come to mean complete separation from Britain. Nevertheless, the concept of citizenship as the interaction of freedom, self-determination, individual development and responsibility for the common good continued to inform the debates.

The paper's masthead carried its mission statement: 'For men and women equally the rights of citizenship: From men and women equally the duties of citizenship'. Individual development and the common good were generally accepted as its aims. The first editorial stated that it advocated the 'fullest development of a complete humanity' with no limitations on 'human freedom and human character'.[18] James Cousins[19] advocated 'adjustment between the needs of the individual and the needs of the community'.[20] Another editorial urged that women and men work together for a 'social organisation ... capable of giving the maximum opportunity of personal freedom to the maximum number of persons'.[21] The Irish Women's Reform League, whose objectives combined suffrage with working women's concerns, wrote of 'common needs and satisfactions ... the joy of one is a gain to all, and the suffering of one an injury to all'.[22]

There was wide agreement that women's participation was essential to achieve a better society for all. It was argued that women's values were different to men's, that women were sexually more chaste, more concerned with the common good, with 'true life-values' – concerning both the preservation and quality of life – and were more opposed to war and militarism. Whether these qualities were seen as biologically determined, or arising from women's experience in maternal and domestic roles, it was seen as imperative to bring them into political decision-making. M. Alexander of the Irish Women's Suffrage Society, Belfast, wrote that women's value-system would 'ultimately lead to the spiritual regeneration of the race'.[23] Lucy Kingston of the IWFL believed that women would 'influence the trend of politics in favour of a respect for humanity'.[24] Louie Bennett, general secretary of the Irish Women Workers' Union, urged that to create a better society and a co-operative system the 'voice of woman's soul ... as distinct from man's', and their 'greater sense of the sacredness of life', was needed.[25] Margaret McCoubrey, a socialist, claimed that when women gained equality, 'existing systems for maintenance of law and order, our gigantic farce called Courts of Justice' will go and there will be 'no need for charitable organisations, for prisons, or for rescue-homes'.[26]

At the same time reservations were voiced about women's preparedness to contribute this potential whether by direct political participation or as citizen-mothers educating future citizens. For both, development of potential and education for citizenship were essential. Mary Hayden, Professor of Modern Irish History at University College Dublin, deplored the general lack of a sense of 'social duty' among middle-class girls and women, and their slowness to volunteer for philanthropic work. She argued that education must go beyond the selfish interests of family, must include politics, economics, the place of the family in society, preparing a girl 'to do her duty efficiently', whether in the 'corporate life of her city or her country' or as a mother.[27] In similar vein 'Frances' wrote asking, in the name of citizenship, for volunteers for clubs for working girls in Belfast.[28] An Irish National Teacher argued that if teachers were to train their pupils to put 'principle before expediency and the good of the community before personal gain – in a word to be good citizens', then teachers themselves must be 'fearless and broadminded citizens' and not prohibited from political involvement.[29]

Socialist contributors, themselves almost all middle-class women, put forward the case for working-class women, essentially that the latter would and should achieve their own emancipation. Marion Duggan asked could 'wealthy or educated women ... be trusted to make laws for poor working women?' Should the latter be 'free and independent, or humbly receiving the legislative bounty of their better-off sisters?' Working women, it was argued, needed to organise to combat bad working conditions, unequal pay and limited employment opportunities. Then they 'themselves must decide how best to get the vote, by full, frank, free discussion'.[30] Louie Bennett urged that women workers needed to raise their status, pay and working conditions to have 'that self-respect as a worker which gives a note of happiness to any toil', and then turn to civic reforms 'which only the workers themselves will ever achieve'.[31]

Middle-class women also faced obstacles to self-development. Margaret Connery of the IWFL deplored the contraction of their 'spheres of activity'. Suffrage was part of a broad movement towards the 'unity of humanity ... a universal brotherhood of man [sic]', a goal not achievable while half of humanity, women, were 'sunk in servitude and degradation'. She argued that 'new forms of labour and the right to labour' were essential, and that if woman 'may not grow and develop, and exercise all her powers of body and mind, she, and the race through her, are threatened with ultimate extinction'.[32] The growing numbers of university-educated women were frustrated by the obstacles to women entering the higher professions.[33] Law graduate Marion Duggan, urging that women lawyers were needed in the search for international peace, wrote that, while women were 'in some ways superior to men', they had 'failed to cultivate certain qualities which men have learned by experience', and wider opportunities, including the practice of law, 'may materially assist [their] moral development'.[34]

For socialist and trade-union feminists, international harmony, equality between the sexes and the common good depended on economic reform. Louie Bennett wrote that 'economic justice' was essential for feminism and a world 'safe for democracy'.[35] Tackling the exploitation of working women in conditions, unequal pay and limited employment opportunities involved tackling the co-existing exploitation of working men. As Bennett put it, 'the financial burden of keeping the home lies upon the male wage-earner, working under a system so heedless of human needs'. When 'co-operation has succeeded capitalism' the distribution of work could be 'completely readjusted'.[36] Cissie Cahalan of the Linen Drapers' Assistants' Association, while disagreeing with Bennett on the need for separate women's unions, shared her ultimate objective; men and women must work 'shoulder to shoulder' in mixed unions for the 'goal of Irish Labour – the Workers' Republic'.[37]

Regarding attitudes to war and militarism, World War l from 1914–1918, the 1916 Easter Rising, and the War of Independence from 1919–1921 raised challenging questions for Irish feminists. Opinion expressed in the *Citizen* included support for Britain as engaged in a just war, support for Irish separatist rebellion as a just cause, and pacifism ranging from a total opposition to war to a general opposition allowing exceptions in a just cause. The issues and arguments were complex and nuanced. The Sheehy Skeffingtons provide one example of the complexities. On the eve of the world war an editorial by Francis, while accepting that not all suffragists opposed war, argued that war was a social evil 'based on a theory of society one-sidedly and arrogantly male'. It expressed confidence that 'the main current of the women's movement, in all countries, is definitely hostile to war and aims at its abolition'.[38] At roughly the same time Hanna wrote that she would support an Irish separatist rising that had a prospect of success, but 'still be radically opposed to war and militarism'.[39] Overall, it seems fair to see a general opposition to militarism and glorification of war per se, and a general agreement that women's values were basically anti-war.

Gender and Political Thought

While the foregoing has been an extremely brief overview of developments that need in-depth exploration, enough has emerged to justify some tentative discussion. This will aim:

i)   to summarise the feminists' case.

ii) to discuss their use of ideologies.

iii) to assess some aspects of their contribution to political thought.

iv) to ask what would the result if historians looked seriously at what Irish feminists were saying.

i) The Feminists' Case

As has been seen, the feminists first asserted the equality of women and men as human beings. As such, women were entitled to be recognised and treated as autonomous, self-directing individuals. Restrictions imposed by marriage and property laws, exclusion from higher education, prestigious and well-paid employment, and from participation in public political life, were all inequitable and, it was believed, must be abolished. Women had both the right and the duty to be full citizens, sharing actively in the life of society, including political decision-making.

Next, feminists went beyond a claim simply for equality of rights within the existing system. They were highly critical of the results of exclusively male political decision-making. They argued that women had a contribution to make that was different to that of men, and one that was essential for the common good. This contribution was the values associated with women; purer moral standards, compassion, care for the poor and disadvantaged, aversion to war as the way to settle disputes. These values were all needed in public decision-making, and only the participation of women could ensure their inclusion. They further asserted that, to develop their potential to make that contribution, women needed education, wider opportunities and to shoulder their share of responsibility for society.

These arguments challenged *realpolitik* views that morality need not necessarily apply in political decision-making. They undermined justification of existing gender relationships by separate spheres ideology, and the stereotypes of male and female 'natures' underpinning that ideology. These stereotypes allocated some human characteristics to men and others to women in a division that posited some more-or-less mutually exclusive groups of characteristics grounded in biological sex. Feminist claims for women's values often appeared to accept that characteristics were divided to some extent into 'masculine' and 'feminine'. It is not always clear whether they saw the differences as originating in nature or nurture. However, there was broad agreement that women could and should display such 'masculine' attributes as independence, autonomy, rationality, judgement, suitability for political decision-making, while retaining 'feminine' caring, nurturing, chastity and moral virtue. At the same time 'masculine' aggression, dominance and militarism were rejected, as also 'feminine' dependence and subordination.

The new model of female 'nature' challenged the basis of the gender power allocation, and was deeply disturbing to many men. For example, Hanna Sheehy Skeffington recalled the words of the Home Rule MP, John Dillon, whom she described as a 'fine rebel on certain lines and up to a point'. In response to a feminist deputation he replied sadly:

> Women's suffrage will, I believe, be the ruin of our Western civilisation. It will destroy the home, challenging the headship of man, laid down by God. It may come in your time – I hope not in mine.[40]

ii) The Feminists' Use of Ideologies

a) Moral Superiority

In asserting women's full equality as human beings and citizens, feminists drew on Enlightenment equality and its optimism regarding the potential of education. However, its value for women was limited by the pervasive ideology of masculine superiority, which will be discussed later. For entry into public life, Evangelicalism was the only widely-accepted authoritative voice or ideology that, while not asserting complete equality, gave women a defined, if limited, area of expertise and authority that extended beyond the home, and could be used to support the need for women's values in political decision-making. The feminists exploited this to its full potential and undoubtedly far beyond the intentions of male Evangelical leaders. And not only committed feminists did this. Rosemary Raughter sees eighteenth-century Irish female philanthropists offering a 'significant, if largely covert, challenge' to establishment ideas of women's nature and role in society. For the nineteenth century, Maria Luddy makes a similar case.[41]

So, how far was belief in women's moral superiority and mission a driving force on its own merits, and how far was its use a conscious strategy to exploit a useful ideology? It is entirely plausible that both operated and for some people both may well have operated at the same time. As has been seen, appeals to moral superiority went side by side with acknowledgement that women needed education and wider experience to develop themselves and their potential for contribution.

Nor was religious motivation incompatible with a rational critique of society. As noted above, Evangelical religion itself emerged from the matrix of eighteenth-century ideas. It was, according to one historian, 'permeated by Enlightenment influences', including scientific empiricism and inductive reasoning from perceived facts, and until well into the nineteenth century 'there was no hint of a clash between Evangelical religion and science'.[42] Inductive reasoning from perceived facts could well lead to the conclusion that the values associated with women were needed in political decision-making to create a fairer, more equitable and hence more stable, organisation of society. It could lead women to conclude that confining themselves to narrow male-dictated spheres of human activity was itself irrational.

And there is evidence of women's interest in science. During the nineteenth century a number of Irish women made substantial contributions to scientific knowledge,[43] while many more women participated in the growth of popular interest in both the natural sciences and the application of scientific method to social and economic problems. Clara Cullen has shown that from early in the century women attended public lectures on scientific subjects in Dublin, Belfast and Cork. Also, between 1854 and 1867, the years when the pioneering colleges for the higher education of women were established, the Museum of Irish Industry in Dublin ran popular courses on physics, chemistry, botany, zoology and geology, as well as 'systematic classes' leading to examinations and the award of certificates and prizes. Both were open to women and men, and the records show that women were well represented among the prize-winners and 'distinguished themselves in a high degree', according to the director, Sir Robert Kane.[44]

Mary E. Daly's work on the Statistical and Social Inquiry Society shows that women, who were eligible to be associate members, presented a number of papers, including three read by two of the most prominent feminist leaders. In 1875 Isabella Tod read a paper on the treatment of habitual drunkards, and in 1878 another on the boarding-out system for pauper children. In the 1879/80 session Anna Haslam read a paper on poor-law administration in workhouses.[45] Thomas Haslam, Anna's husband and co-feminist, was a long-time member and his 1865 pamphlet *The Real Wants of the Irish People* was published under the authorship of 'A Member of the Statistical And Social Inquiry Society of Ireland'. Carmel Quinlan's study of the Haslams[46] shows that he was actively involved in contemporary scientific debate on evolution, heredity, eugenics and methods of birth control, as well as the economic and social problems of contemporary Ireland. After his death, Anna corresponded with Marie Stopes, the birth-control pioneer, about Thomas's ideas and writings and about the Haslams' own contraceptive practice. Further research on women's intellectual interests should deepen our understanding of feminist thinking in nineteenth-century Ireland.

b) The Civic Republican Model

Whether or not campaigners consciously exploited moral superiority, it is significant that they used it to advocate a holistic model of society and polity, and to claim that certain specific values were needed in public life and political decision-making. That this model and these values continued to be widely promoted by participants in debate in the *Irish Citizen*, where contributors were drawn from a wide range of backgrounds, and included Catholics, Protestants, agnostics and atheists; nationalists and unionists; middle-class liberals, socialists and trade unionists, suggests a real and widespread commitment to the model and values promoted.

As has been argued, the model and values incorporated civic republican ideas. This has particular significance in light of the relative supersedence of civic republicanism in political debate during the nineteenth century. Iseult Honohan notes that republican 'ideas of widespread public participation in politics, of freedom as political activity and the importance of civic virtue' were declining by this time.[47] So, when feminists advocated what was essentially a feminist reworking of the republican concept of the good human life, where responsibility for the organisation of society was not seen as separate from private life, where citizens co-operated to create the common good, and individual self-development was integrally related to political participation, they were not seeking endorsement from a widely-used political language and ideology calculated to win support. For the history of political thought this raises interesting lines of inquiry about the long-lasting persistence and attraction of the basic components of this concept, of their appeal for groups denied recognition, respect and participation in decision-making, as well as their potentially universal appeal to enlightened self-interest that might see such a polity as the best guarantee for the well-being of all individuals and groups in the long run.

The issue of class in women's history opens a further dimension. The voice of working class women appears largely absent from feminist debate in Ireland during the period considered here. Their case seems to have been generally argued by middle-class women. Helena Molony of the Irish Women Workers' Union, looking back in 1930, said the women's movement had 'passed over the head of the Irish working woman and left her untouched'.[48] Further research may reveal a more complex situation. Later, during the second wave of the women's movement, starting in Ireland around 1970, women's groups in working-class areas in Dublin and other urban centres developed a local politics that combined self-development programmes with campaigns for better community facilities and services. While they did not necessarily see themselves as feminists, the same combination of freedom, self-determination and active contribution to the common good informed their activities. Two recent studies of communities in nationalist West Belfast before and after the IRA ceasefire of 1994 show a similar pattern. For the earlier period Claire Hackett shows how the internment of men propelled women into new roles combining family and community survival with nationalist political activism, merging public and private spheres. Self-development programmes, growing feminist awareness and challenges to sexism, including domestic violence, within the nationalist community itself followed.[49] Callie Persic follows the transition of a women's group on a housing estate after 1994 from nationalist to community activism, pursuing better community conditions and futures for their children, but also their own self-development through education and new skills, and engaging in power struggles in the home. Here also, while many women were unwilling to call themselves feminists, domestic and political roles merged, and Persic suggests we may have to rethink the meaning of 'political'.[50]

iii) The Feminist Contribution to Political Thought

The main points of this contribution, as they arise from the foregoing discussion, can be itemised as follows: firstly, feminists asserted the full humanity and equal citizenship of women; secondly, they asserted the need for 'women's values' in political decision-making to achieve the common good; thirdly, their challenge to male authority and privilege identified and made visible the ideology of male superiority and dominance that they saw as permeating both society and political debate. This ideology saw women as ineligible for citizenship for various reasons, God-ordained male authority and innate female irrationality among others. Feminists themselves were very much aware of its pervasiveness. Isabella Tod noted a 'tone of depreciation of women ... [in the 1860s] frightfully common, both in society and the press – whether it was an attitude of groundless or misplaced compliment, or of patronage, or of mockery or contempt'.[51] Margaret Cousins, co-founder of the IWFL, growing up in the 1880s became aware that '[b]oys were wanted and expected' in preference to girls and were given 'much more freedom of action, movement and friendship [and] more money', and that 'it was counted as a kind of curse ... to be born a girl'. She found it 'a joy later to find that such inequality and injustice and limitations were the result of circumstances which could and would be changed'.[52] Lucy Kingston, who joined the IWFL in 1912, began attending suffrage meetings in Dublin in 1911 and 'got sore, wrathful and with some cause ... [at] the condescending attitude of men towards our poor feeble wits'.[53] Hanna Sheehy Skeffington found that other Irish MPs, like John Dillon,

> good Irish rebels, many of them broken in to national revolt ... at the whisper of Votes for Women ... changed to extreme Tories or time-servers who urged us women to wait till freedom for men was won. Curiously, too, these were joined by many Sinn Féiners.[54]

Mary Hayden, writing to the *Cork Examiner* in June 1937 on the draft new constitution, noted the repressive legislation passed by successive governments in the Irish Free State during the 1920s and 1930s, imposing restrictions on women's employment and in jury service,[55] and now, 'to crown all' the proposed constitution with 'its mixture of flattery and insult'.[56]

iv) What if Historians Listened Seriously to what Feminists were Saying?

If gender analysis became a standard part of the historian's tool-kit, it would undoubtedly lead to major reassessments across the board. One focus would be on the blindness of most 'mainstream' historians to the centrality of gender relationships in the history of human societies. A substantial body of feminist scholarship over several decades has documented and analysed the ideology of masculine superiority and dominance that pervades the history of Western philosophical, theological and political thought from Aristotle onwards, yet this has not been incorporated into general histories of political thought. Historians would have to face the question why this has been the case. Their own value system would become part of that history and itself subject to scrutiny and critical analysis. Discussion of these developments lies outside the scope of this article. Here I want to consider some of the possible results if the history books in general use did include feminist political thought.

If the books included this thought, historians would have to consider to what extent political, social and economic relationships between the sexes resulted from human agency. The first question would be: *cui bono*? who benefits? For the period of the Irish emancipation campaigns, this would involve analysis of the privileged position of males in mid nineteenth-century Ireland, of how law, regulation and custom channelled social, economic and political power to males and away from females. If the focus narrowed to the objectives of the campaigns, historians would examine the consequences of the legal right of a husband to use and dispose of his wife's inherited and earned property, its benefits for men of all social classes, not least the lure of marriage to an heiress, and for women the loss of autonomy on marriage with its implications for young women's life options.

They would consider the impact on each sex of the double standards in social attitude and legal response to sexual behaviour, as well as of the male monopoly of university education, degrees, entry to the 'higher' professions, and political power from the highest office to voting at elections.

Awareness of the feminist thinking of previous generations would empower societies to absorb it and build on it. New generations would be able first to *see* this thinking, to identify and analyse it, and then to locate it in the particular political, social and economic conditions, gender relationships and political ideologies within which feminists framed their questions and which in turn influenced their answers. Locating ideas in historical context is crucial. Without context it is difficult to decide which elements we believe to have had lasting value. It is equally important to be aware of our own historical context and the factors that influence our thinking as we pass judgement on the ideas of earlier generations. For example, it can be argued that critical analysis of middle-class nineteenth-century feminists' attitudes to social class contributes to our thinking today to the extent that we understand both their historical context and ours. Political, social and economic conditions change, and so do gender relationships and dominant ideologies. Trying to understand their world involves trying to understand our own.

This empowerment would encourage the envisioning of new models of human nature, both female and male. These issues are being tackled today in women's studies and masculinity studies, both still minority interests and on the periphery of 'mainstream' intellectual programmes, and so limited in their influence. Gender analysis demonstrates the centrality of gender relationships to the 'mainstream' of human thought, and hence the importance of critical analysis of dominant models of femininity and masculinity. Nor is today's generation the first to challenge the prevailing stereotypes. Earlier Irish feminists, among others, contested them, and put forward new and more inclusively human models. While they focused most attention on the female stereotype, feminists, men as well as women, also envisioned new masculine models. For example, Margaret and James Cousins were part of contemporary circles that did this, and an *Irish Citizen* editorial argued that the 'growing inter-relationship of the sexes in the affairs of life' required a new word the 'femaculine', to name 'the new sex, the community of sex in the hidden region of the soul of humanity'.[57] In this context Catherine Candy's work opens up a little-explored area of Irish feminist history where attitudes to sexuality and interest in the occult, theosophy and vegetarianism converge.[58]

Envisioning new models of human nature and 'natures' is as important for boys and men as it is for girls and women. Conventional history and conventional stereotypes combine in socialising males to conform to a model of masculinity based largely on negative images; of not appearing weak, of not losing face, of not admitting mistakes or compromising, of not appearing like a woman or 'effeminate'. A history that includes gender analysis and feminist thought empowers men as well as women to analyse the role of stereotypes and the ideology of masculine superiority and dominance in human history, to make their own assessment of the damage these have done to individuals, men and women, to the organisation of societies and to relations between societies, and opens both sexes to the possibility of developing new models.

Linked to this is the potential of the history of feminist thought to help in envisioning new models for the organisation of society. In today's world of globalisation, increasing inequality and threat to the environment, there is renewed interest in republicanism among political theorists looking for alternatives to the current dominant ideology of extreme neo-liberalism and its endorsement of a polity based on a competitive, profit-driven market economy.[59] It appears to me that gender history has much to contribute to explorations of the potential of republicanism to answer today's questions. The history of Irish feminist thought provides one case-study of how that potential was used and adapted by women to answer some of yesterday's questions. Basic concepts of republican citizenship continued to inform the political thought of the nineteenth-century middle-class feminists, that of the still largely middle-class contributors to the *Irish Citizen*, and that of the later working-class community groups, while they successively discarded its original sexism and elitism and developed more democratic and inclusive versions.

This is not to argue that feminist concepts of citizenship by themselves hold the key to a Utopia. Like all human thinking feminist arguments are open to debate and challenge. Predictions that female suffrage would fundamentally change political decision-making for the better have yet to be fulfilled. Whether women as a group and men as a group hold different value-systems, and, if so, why, is still a contested and unresolved question. Creating genuine participatory citizenship in democratic societies with large populations presents formidable challenges. Nor does either republicanism or feminism include a blueprint of policies designed to deliver the common good. Both will need to dialogue with ideologies such as socialism that do propose such policies. And there is little in human history to suggest that an ideal society will ever be achieved. However, the history of feminist concepts of citizenship suggests that efforts to put these into practice have intrinsic value for individual human development. They are also less prone to advocate rigid stereotypes, dichotomies of black versus white or male versus female, and hold out better prospects for creating societies that at least *try* to give every citizen the opportunity to develop and flourish than do the current ones. A history that incorporated gender analysis could help move today's debates away from models of perpetual adversarial struggle of opposing interests towards more inclusive, fluid and constructive dialogue, argument and debate.

from Maryann Valiulis (ed.), *Gender and Power in Irish History* (Dublin, Irish Academic Press, 2009), pp 18–38.

NOTES

1   In a recent essay, 'Feminism, Citizenship and Suffrage: A Long Dialogue', in Louise Ryan and Margaret Ward (eds), *Irish Women and the Vote: Becoming Citizens* (Dublin, Irish Academic Press, 2007), pp 1–20, I discussed some of the issues raised in this chapter. I am grateful to the editors and publisher for agreeing to my drawing on some of its content here.

2   Gordon S. Wood, in his study of the origins of the United States of America, describes republicanism as 'the ideology of the Enlightenment', *The Creation of the American Republic 1776–1787* (Chapel Hill and London, University of North Carolina Press, 1998), p. viii.

3   See Iseult Honohan, 'Freedom as Citizenship: The Republican Tradition in Political Theory', *The Republic: A Journal of Contemporary and Historical Debate,* No. 2 (Spring/Summer, 2001), pp 7–24; *Civic Republicanism* (London and New York, Routledge, 2002); John Morrow, *History of Political Thought: A Thematic Introduction* (Basingstoke and London, Macmillan, 1998), p. 19.

4   *A Vindication of the Rights of Woman* (London, Dent, 1982), p. 213. Wollstonecraft's writings were well known in Ireland. For the

republican and feminist thinking of two United Irish women, Martha McTier and Mary Ann McCracken, see Mary Cullen, '"Rational Creatures and Free Citizens": Republicanism, Feminism and the Writing of History', *The Republic*, No. 1 (June, 2000), pp 60–70.

5   For example, Richard J. Evans, *The Feminists: Women's Emancipation Movements in Europe, America and Australasia 1840– 1928* (London, Croom Helm, 1975).

6   Jane Rendall, *The Origins of Modern Feminism: Women in Britain, France, and the United States, 1780–1860* (Basingstoke and London, Macmillan, 1985), pp 73–107.

7   For these developments see Rosemary Raughter, 'A Natural Tenderness: The Ideal and the Reality of Eighteenth-Century Female Philanthropy', in Maryann G. Valiulis and Mary O'Dowd (eds), *Women and Irish History* (Dublin, Wolfhound, 1997), pp 71–88, and Maria Luddy, *Women and Philanthropy in Nineteenth-Century Ireland* (Cambridge University Press, 1995).

8   Catholic women were also active in philanthropic work, but by the mid-nineteenth century the huge growth of female religious congregations had absorbed most Catholic philanthropists and few Catholic women appear to have become women's rights activists until the end of the century. See Caitriona Clear, *Nuns in Nineteenth-century Ireland* (Dublin, Gill and Macmillan, 1987) and 'The Limits of Female Autonomy: Nuns in Nineteenth-Century Ireland', in Maria Luddy and Cliona Murphy (eds), *Women Surviving: Studies in Irish Women's History in the 19th and 20th Centuries* (Dublin, Poolbeg, 1989), pp 15–50; Mary Peckham Magray, *The Transforming Power of Nuns: Women, Religion and Cultural Change in Ireland 1750–1900* (New York, Oxford University Press, 1998).

9   For a brief overview of these campaigns see Mary Cullen, 'Women, Emancipation and Politics 1860–1984', in J.R. Hill (ed.), *A New History of Ireland*, Vol. VII (Oxford University Press, 2003), pp 826–91. The property qualification for the male franchise meant that in the 1860s the vote on the same terms as men would in practice be votes for single or widowed middle-class women. This changed over time as married women gained control of their own property and the property qualification for the male franchise was reduced by successive acts of parliament and finally abolished in 1918.

10 Cited in Maria Luddy, 'Isabella M. Tod (1836–1896)', in Mary Cullen and Maria Luddy, (eds), *Women, Power and Consciousness in Nineteenth-Century Ireland* (Dublin, Attic Press, 1995) p. 217.

11 *Ibid.*, pp 205, 217, 219, 212, 205.

12 Helen Blackburn's obituary of Tod, *Englishwoman's Review,* 15 October 1897, p. 60.

13 The Mayoress of Belfast at the unveiling of a memorial to Tod, *Englishwoman's Review,* 15 January 1898, p. 53

14 Luddy, 'Isabella Tod', p. 216

15 *Ibid.*, pp 217–18

16 *Ibid.*, pp 215, 217.

17 For this section both Dana Hearne, 'The Development of Irish Feminist Thought; A Critical Historical Analysis of The *Irish Citizen* 1912–1920' (PhD thesis, University of Ontario, 1992) and Louise Ryan, *Irish Feminism and the Vote; an Anthology of the Irish Citizen Newspaper 1912–1920* (Dublin, Folens, 1996) were very useful.

18 *Irish Citizen,* 25 May 1912, p. 1.

19 While the majority of contributors to the *Citizen* were women, James Cousins and Francis Sheehy Skeffington, husbands respectively of Margaret Cousins and Hanna Sheehy Skeffington, founders of the Irish Women's Franchise League, were joint editors until the Cousins left Ireland in 1913. The editors wrote unsigned editorial articles and notes and also individually signed articles. After Francis's death in 1916 Hanna took over the editorship, with Louie Bennett acting editor during her absence in the United States.

20 *Irish Citizen,* 17 May 1913, p. 411.

21 *Ibid.*, 13 July 1912, p. 60.

22 *Ibid.*, 2 August 1913, p. 83.

23 *Ibid.*, 29 November 1913, p. 225.

24 *Ibid.*, August 1917, p. 373. (By this time the *Citizen* was published only monthly).

25 *Ibid.*, May 1917, p. 260.

26 *Ibid.*, 27 February 1915, p. 317.

27 *Ibid.*, 6 July 1912, p. 51 and 13 July 1912, p. 59.

28 *Ibid.*, 13 July 1912, p. 59.

29 *Ibid.*, 25 May 1912, p. 19.

30 *Ibid.*, 8 August 1914, pp 93–4, 20 February 1915, p. 307.

31 *Ibid.*, November 1919, p. 44.

32 *Ibid.*, 28 December 1912, p. 251, 4 January 1913, p. 259. As noted above, the growing separation of home and work-place increasingly excluded women from their former participation in their husband's or family's occupation.

33 The reality of these obstacles was recognised by the passing of the Sex Disqualification (Removal) Act of December 1919 which made disqualification on grounds of sex or marriage for civil professions and jury service illegal.

34 *Irish Citizen*, 24 April 1915, p. 381.

35 *Ibid.*, January 1918, pp 394–5.

36 *Ibid.*, November 1919, p. 44.

37 *Ibid.*, December 1919, p. 53.

38 *Ibid.*, 22 August 1914, p. 108.

39 Cited in Margaret Ward, '"Rolling Up the Map of Suffrage": Irish Suffrage and the First World War', in Ryan and Ward, *Irish Women and the Vote*, p. 149. For further discussion of Irish feminists' definitions of pacifism and their location in the context of international feminism, see also Ward, 'Nationalism, Pacifism, Internationalism: Louie Bennett, Hanna Sheehy Skeffington and the Problems of "Defining Feminism"', in Anthony Bradley and Maryann Valiulis (eds), *Gender and Sexuality in Modern Ireland* (Amherst, University of Massachusetts Press, 1997), pp 60–84; Rosemary Cullen Owens, 'Women and Pacifism in Ireland 1915–1932', in Valiulis and O'Dowd, *Women and Irish History*, pp 220–238;

40 Hanna Sheehy Skeffington, 'Reminiscences of an Irish Suffragette' [1941] in *Votes for Women: Irish Women's Struggle for the Vote* (Dublin, Andreé Sheehy Skeffington and Rosemary Owens, 1975), p. 18.

41 Raughter, 'A Natural Tenderness', p. 72; Luddy, *Women and Philanthropy*, p. 1.

42 D.W. Bebbington, *Evangelicalism in Modern Britain: A History from the 1730s to the 1980s* (London, Unwin Hyman, 1989), p. 57.

43 See Mary Mulvihill and Patricia Deevy (eds), *Stars, Shells and Bluebells: Women Scientists and Pioneers* (Dublin, Women in Science and Technology, 1997); Susan McKenna-Lawlor, *Whatever Shines Should Be Observed: 'quicquid nitet notandum'* (Dublin, Royal Irish Academy, 2002).

44 Clara Cullen, 'Women, the Museum of Irish Industry and the Pursuit of Scientific Learning in Nineteenth-Century Dublin', in

Ciara Meehan and Emma Lyons (eds), *History Matters 11* (Dublin, School of History and Archives, UCD, 2006), pp 9–19.

45 Mary E. Daly, *The Spirit of Earnest Inquiry: The Statistical and Social Inquiry Society of Ireland 1847–1997* (Dublin, Statistical and Social Inquiry Society of Ireland, 1997), pp 73–4.

46 Carmel Quinlan, *Genteel Revolutionaries: Anna and Thomas Haslam and the Irish Women's Movement* (Cork, Cork University Press, 2002)

47 Honohan, *Civic Republicanism*, pp 113–4.

48 Cited in Rosemary Cullen Owens, *Smashing Times: A History of the Irish Women's Suffrage Movement 1889–1922* (Dublin, Attic Press, 1984), p. 92.

49 Claire Hackett, 'Narrative of Political Activism from Women in West Belfast', in Louise Ryan and Margaret Ward (eds), *Irish Women and Nationalism: Soldiers, New Women and Wicked Hags* (Dublin, Irish Academic Press, 2004) pp 145–66.

50 Callie Persic, 'The Emergence of a Gender Consciousness: Women and Community Work in West Belfast', *Ibid.*, pp 167–83.

51 Isabella Tod, cited in Helen Blackburn's obituary of Tod, *Englishwoman's Review*, 15 October 1898, p. 59.

52 J.H. Cousins and M.E. Cousins, *We Two Together* (Madras, Ganesh and Co., 1950), pp 55, 128–30.

53 Daisy Lawrenson Swanton, *Emerging from the Shadow: The Lives of Sarah Anne Lawrenson and Lucy Olive Kingston* (Dublin, Attic Press, 1994), p. 55.

54 Sheehy Skeffington, 'Reminiscences', pp 12–3.

55 For these developments see Maryann Valiulis, 'Defining their Role in the New State: Irishwomen's Protest against the Juries Act of 1927', in *Canadian Journal of Irish Studies*, Vol XVIII, No. 1 (July 1992) pp 43–60; 'Power, Gender and Identity in the Irish Free State', in *Journal of Women's History*, Vol. VI, No. 4/Vol. VII, No. 1 (Winter/Spring 1995) pp 117–36; 'Engendering Citizenship: Women's Relation to the State in Ireland and the United States in the Post-Suffrage Period', in Valiulis and O'Dowd, *Women and Irish History*, pp 159–172.

56 Cited in Joyce Padbury, 'Mary Hayden' (unpublished research).

57 *Irish Citizen*, 12 May 1912, p. 12.

58 Catherine Candy, 'Margaret Cousins (1878–1954)' in Mary Cullen and Maria Luddy (eds), *Female Activists: Irish Women and Change 1900–1960* (Dublin, Woodfield Press, 2001), pp 113–140; and '"Untouchability", Vegetarianism and the Suffragist

Ideology of Margaret Cousins', in Ryan and Ward, *Irish Women and the Vote*, pp 154–170.

59 See Honohan, *Civic Republicanism*, 'Part ll: Contemporary Debates', for a wide-ranging discussion of these developments.

MacBride, John 55
Mac Curtain, Margaret 6, 7, 14, 25, 88, 151, 152, 194, 199, 226, 227, 247, 266, 272, 368, 375, 376, 377, 378, 404, 448
MacDonagh, Thomas 80, 319
MacSwiney, Mary 325
McAuley, Catherine 279
McCoubrey, Margaret 397, 419
McCracken, Henry 233, 238, 239, 254, 384
McCracken, Mary Ann 232, 233, 235, 238, 239, 242, 246, 247, 254, 255, 266, 384, 385, 405, 436
McCracken, William 239
McGladdery, Rose 239
McKeown, Ciarán 365
McKillen, Beth 226, 374
McNeill, Mary 232, 233, 246, 247, 266, 405
McTier, Martha 232, 384, 436
Madden, Dr R.R. 239, 242, 245, 247, 248
Magan, Francis 240
Manning, Maurice 375
Manning, Susan 349
Markievicz, Constance 47, 53, 55, 80, 217, 303, 314, 319, 322, 323, 325, 328
Married Women's Property Acts 71, 89, 195, 415
Married Women's Property Committee 284

Martin, Molly 244
Marwick, Arthur 46, 51, 64
Mill, James 387
Mill, John Stuart 22, 24, 293
Millett, Kate 31
Milligan, Alice 303
Mitchell, Juliet 33
Mokyr, Joel 127
Molony, Helena 303, 314, 320, 331, 371, 373, 428
Moore, James 240
Moore, Miss 239
Mulvihill, Mary 438
Munster Women's Franchise League 182, 307, 316
Murphy, Cliona 91, 127, 151, 197, 226, 368, 370, 373, 375, 406, 436

Nagle, Nano 279
National University 74, 219, 292, 332
National University Women Graduates Association 335, 345
Natterstad, Jerry H. 372, 373
Nicholls, George 124
North of Ireland Society for Women's Suffrage 169, 176, 293
Northern Ireland Women's Coalition 199, 200, 223
Northern Ireland Women's Rights Movement 222, 364

ABOUT THE AUTHOR

Mary Cullen taught in the History Department at St. Patrick's College Maynooth, now NUI Maynooth, from 1968 until she retired in 1994 as Senior Lecturer. She is currently a Research Associate at the Centre for Gender and Women's Studies at Trinity College Dublin. A feminist as well as a historian, her main area of research and publication is in the history of the Irish women's movement and its thinking. She has edited a number of books including *Girls Don't Do Honours: Irish Women in Education in the 19th and 20th Centuries* (Women's Education Bureau/Arlen House, 1987); *1798: 200 Years of Resonance* (Irish Reporter, 1998); and, with Maria Luddy, two volumes of biographical studies, *Women, Power and Consciousness in Nineteenth-Century Ireland; Eight Biographical Studies* (Attic Press, 1995), and *Female Activists: Irish Women and Change 1900–1960* (Woodfield Press, 2001). With Margaret Mac Curtain she co-founded the Women's History Association of Ireland. In 2011 she was conferred with an Honorary Doctorate of Literature by NUI Maynooth.